BLACK PANTHER
THE LONG SHADOW

BLACK PANTHER

BLACK PANTHER

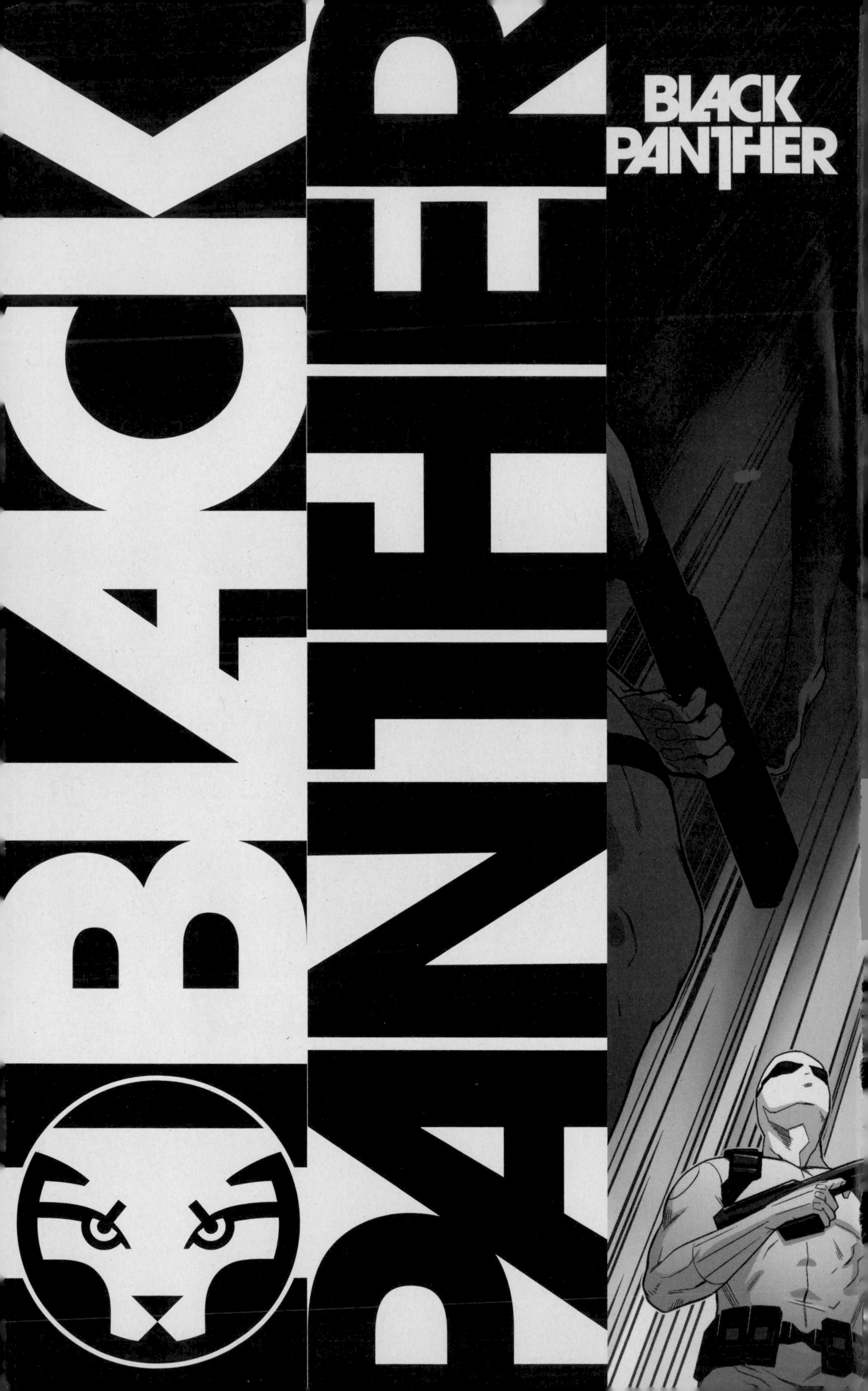

THE LONG SHADOW

Writer	**JOHN RIDLEY**
Artists	**JUANN CABAL** with **IBRAHIM MOUSTAFA** (#3-4) & **STEFANO LANDINI** (#5)
Color Artists	**FEDERICO BLEE** (#1-2) & **MATT MILLA** (#3-5)
Letterer	VC's **JOE SABINO**
Cover Art	**ALEX ROSS**
Logo	**JAY BOWEN**
Wakandan Flag	**BRIAN STELFREEZE**
Assistant Editors	**KAT GREGOROWICZ** & **KAITLYN LINDTVEDT**
Associate Editor	**ALANNA SMITH**
Editor	**WIL MOSS**

Collection Editor	**JENNIFER GRÜNWALD**
Assistant Editor	**DANIEL KIRCHHOFFER**
Assistant Managing Editor	**MAIA LOY**
Associate Manager, Talent Relations	**LISA MONTALBANO**
VP Production & Special Projects	**JEFF YOUNGQUIST**
SVP Print, Sales & Marketing	**DAVID GABRIEL**
Book Designer	**JAY BOWEN**
Editor in Chief	**C.B. CEBULSKI**

BLACK PANTHER CREATED BY **STAN LEE** & **JACK KIRBY**

BLACK PANTHER BY JOHN RIDLEY VOL. 1: THE LONG SHADOW. Contains material originally published in magazine form as BLACK PANTHER (2021) #1-5. First printing 2022. ISBN 978-1-302-92882-7. Published by MARVEL WORLDWIDE, INC., a subsidiary of MARVEL ENTERTAINMENT, LLC. OFFICE OF PUBLICATION: 1290 Avenue of the Americas, New York, NY 10104. © 2022 MARVEL No similarity between any of the names, characters, persons, and/or institutions in this book with those of any living or dead person or institution is intended, and any such similarity which may exist is purely coincidental. **Printed in Canada.** KEVIN FEIGE, Chief Creative Officer; DAN BUCKLEY, President, Marvel Entertainment; JOE QUESADA, EVP & Creative Director; DAVID BOGART, Associate Publisher & SVP of Talent Affairs; TOM BREVOORT, VP, Executive Editor; NICK LOWE, Executive Editor, VP of Content, Digital Publishing; DAVID GABRIEL, VP of Print & Digital Publishing; MARK ANNUNZIATO, VP of Planning & Forecasting; JEFF YOUNGQUIST, VP of Production & Special Projects; ALEX MORALES, Director of Publishing Operations; DAN EDINGTON, Director of Editorial Operations; RICKEY PURDIN, Director of Talent Relations; JENNIFER GRÜNWALD, Director of Production & Special Projects; SUSAN CRESPI, Production Manager; STAN LEE, Chairman Emeritus. For information regarding advertising in Marvel Comics or on Marvel.com, please contact Vit DeBellis, Custom Solutions & Integrated Advertising Manager, at vdebellis@ marvel.com. For Marvel subscription inquiries, please call 888-511-5480. **Manufactured between 3/25/2022 and 4/26/2022 by SOLISCO PRINTERS, SCOTT, QC, CANADA.**

10 9 8 7 6 5 4 3 2 1

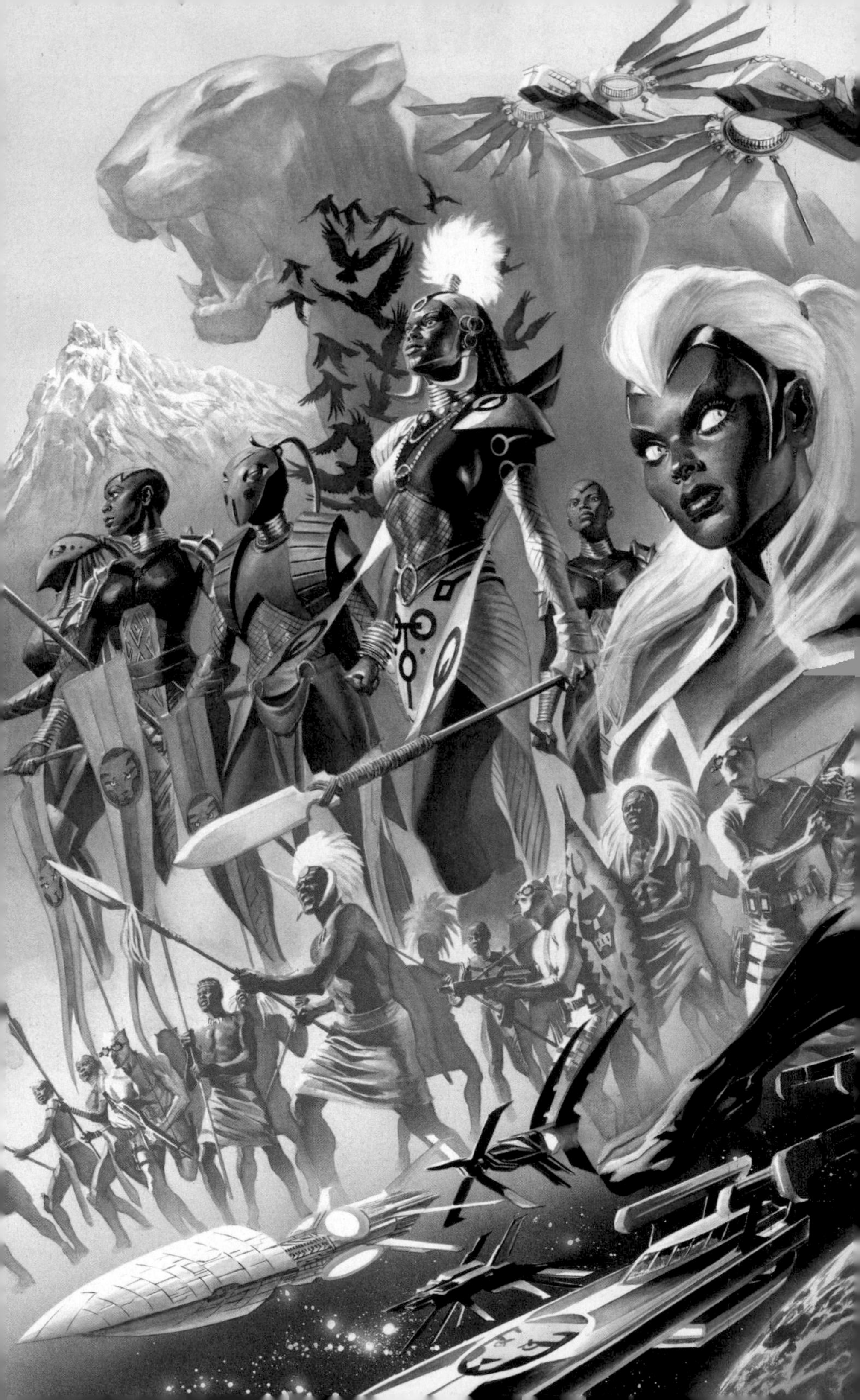

1

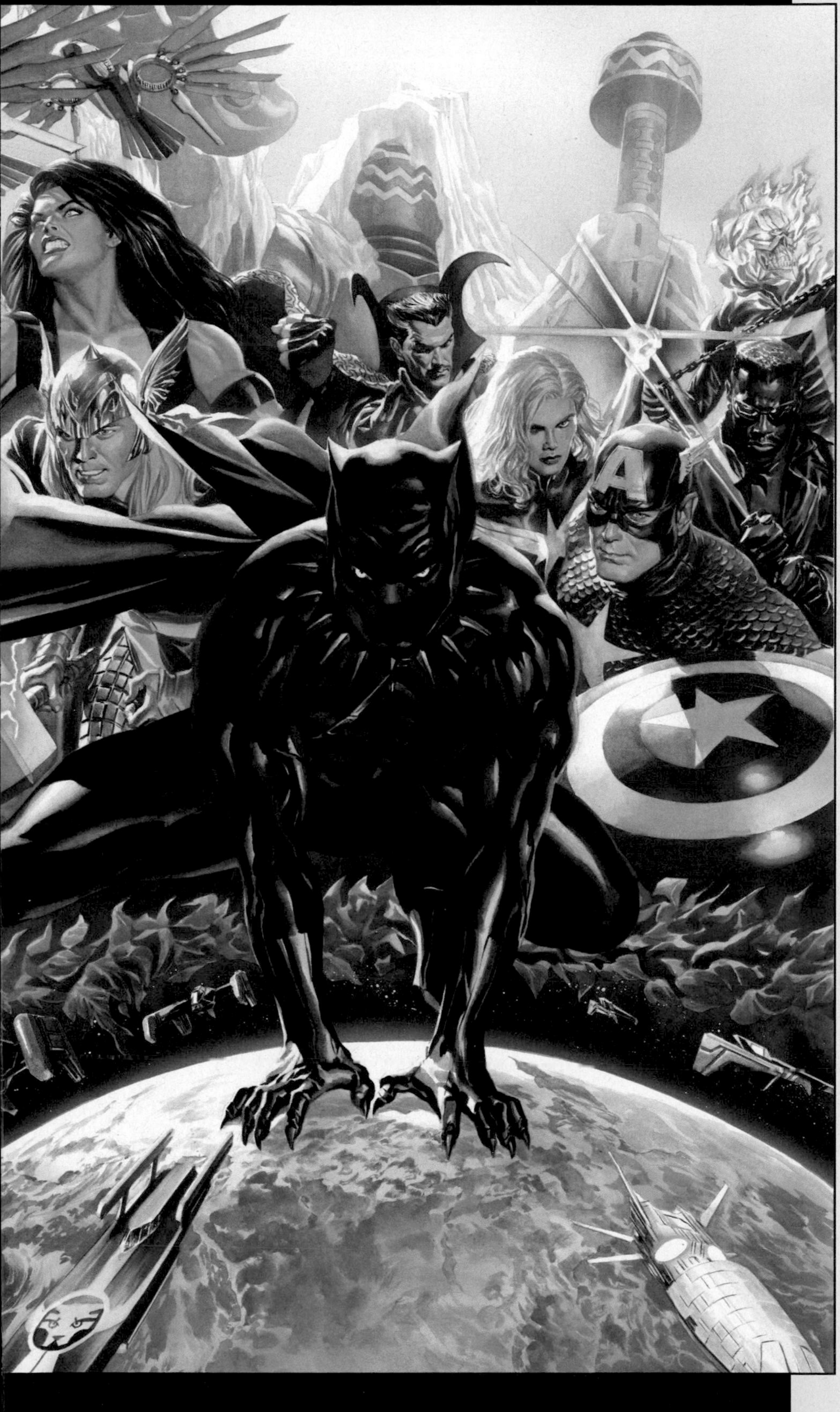

#1 Variant **SAM SPRATT**

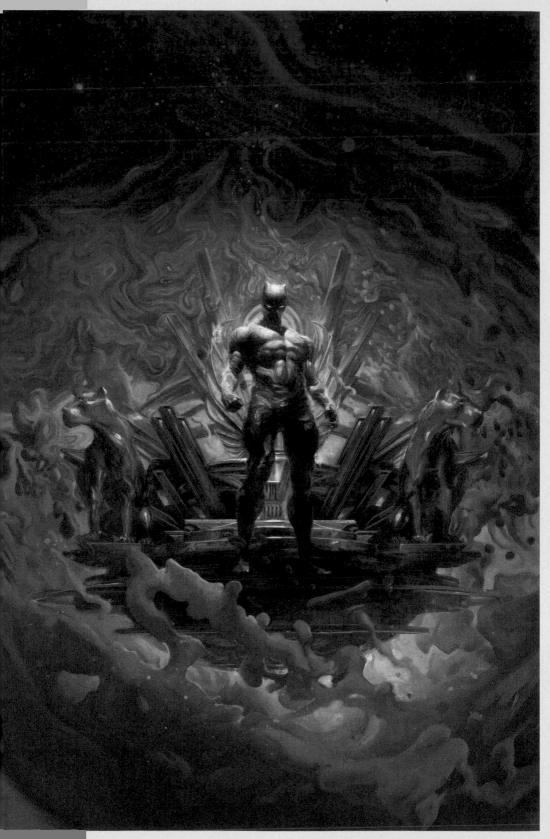

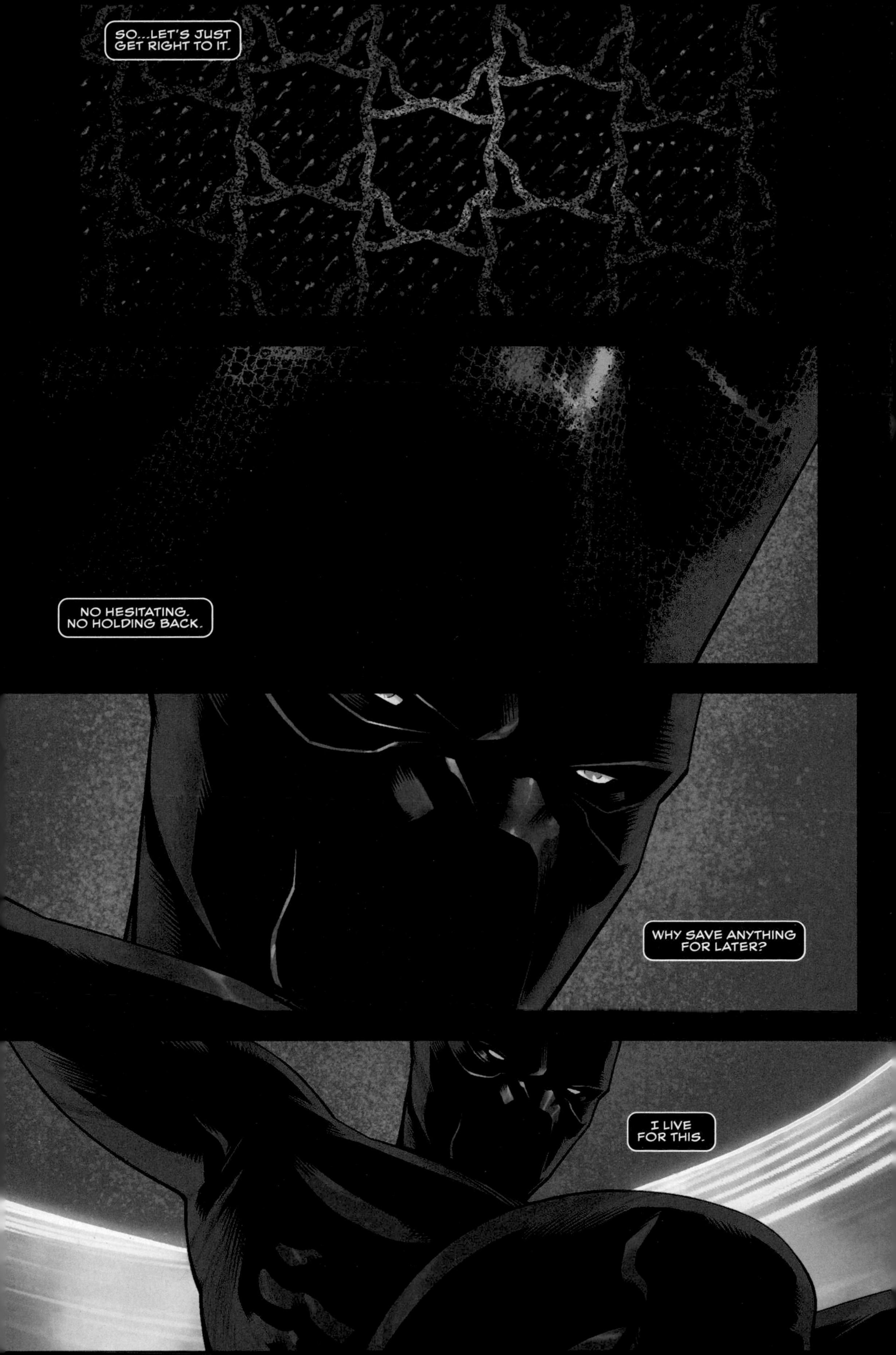
SO...LET'S JUST GET RIGHT TO IT.
NO HESITATING. NO HOLDING BACK.
WHY SAVE ANYTHING FOR LATER?
I LIVE FOR THIS.

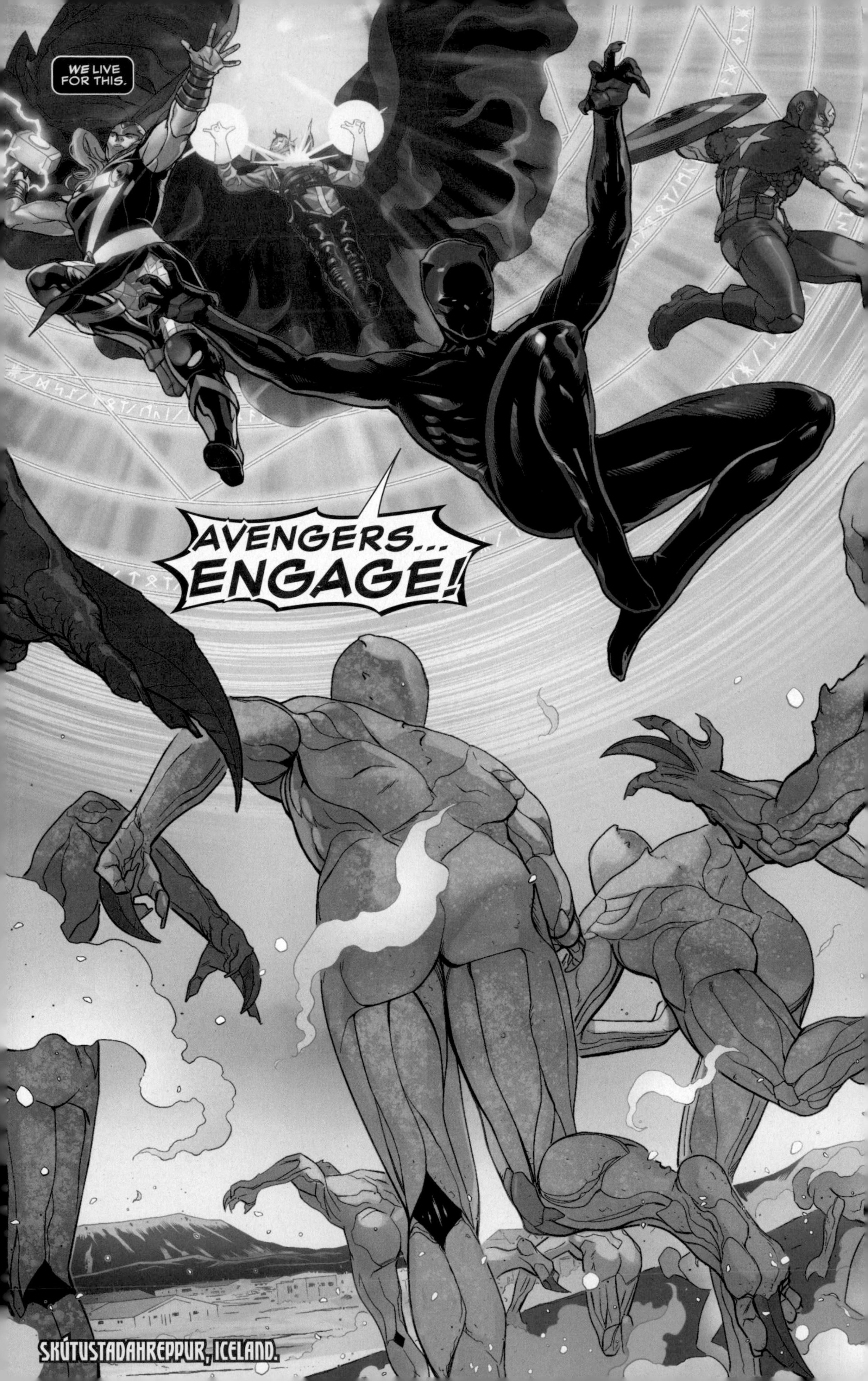
WE LIVE FOR THIS.
AVENGERS... ENGAGE!
SKÚTUSTADAHREPPUR, ICELAND.

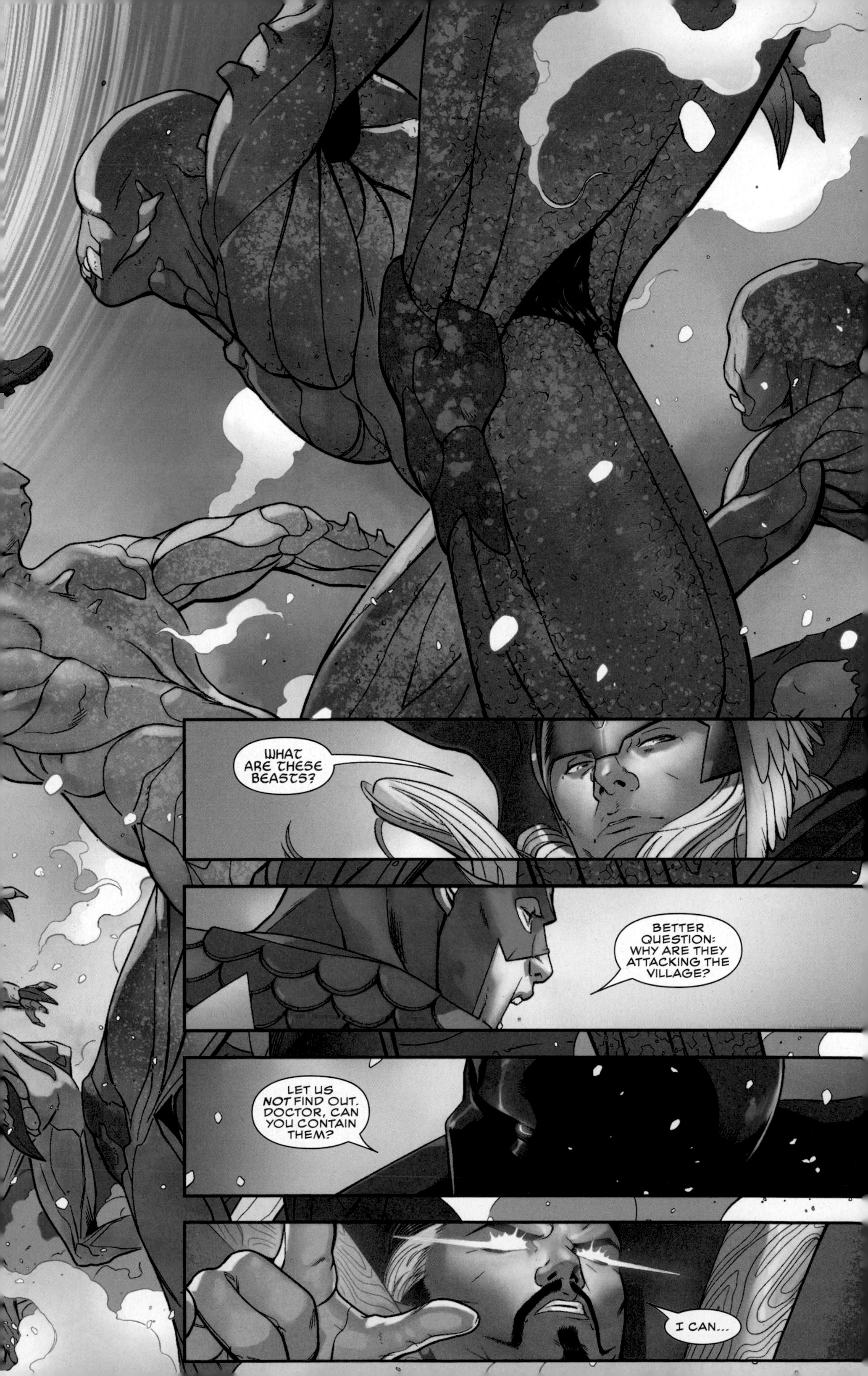
WHAT ARE THESE BEASTS?
BETTER QUESTION: WHY ARE THEY ATTACKING THE VILLAGE?
LET US **NOT** FIND OUT. DOCTOR, CAN YOU CONTAIN THEM?
I CAN...

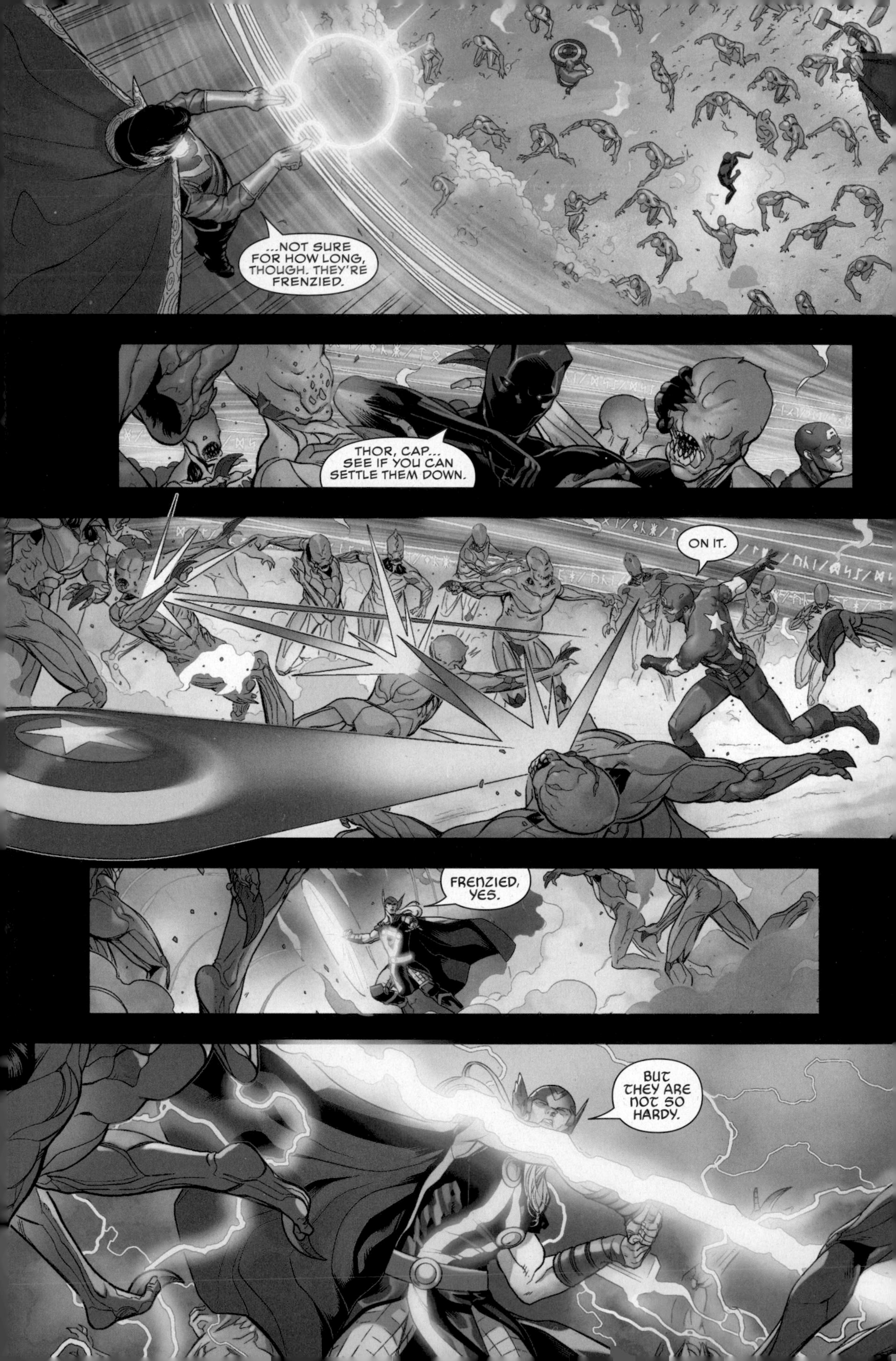
...NOT SURE FOR HOW LONG, THOUGH. THEY'RE FRENZIED.
THOR, CAP... SEE IF YOU CAN SETTLE THEM DOWN.
ON IT.
FRENZIED, YES.
BUT THEY ARE NOT SO HARDY.

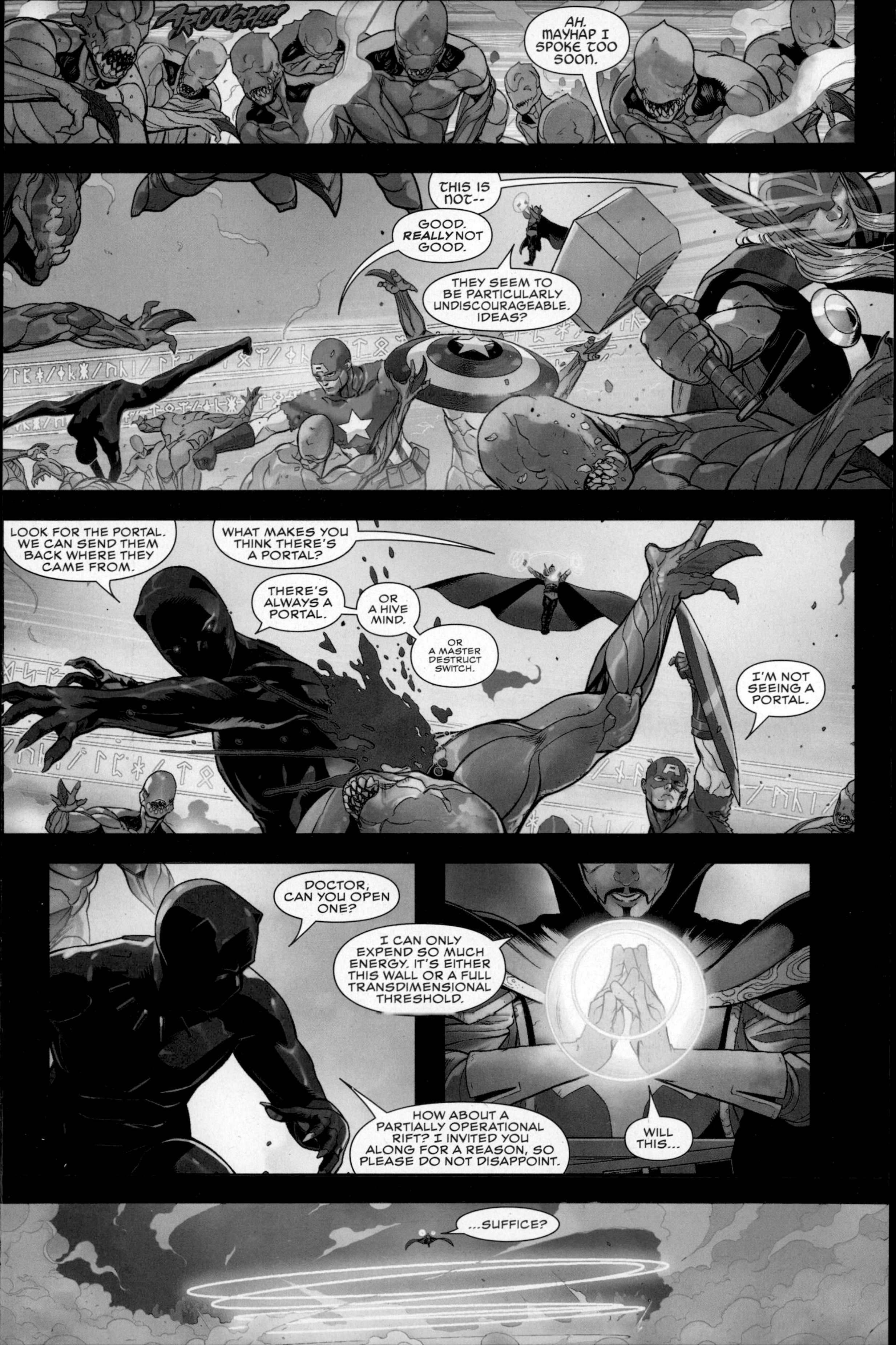
ARUGH!!!
AH. MAYHAP I SPOKE TOO SOON.
THIS IS NOT--
GOOD. REALLY NOT GOOD.
THEY SEEM TO BE PARTICULARLY UNDISCOURAGEABLE. IDEAS?
LOOK FOR THE PORTAL. WE CAN SEND THEM BACK WHERE THEY CAME FROM.
WHAT MAKES YOU THINK THERE'S A PORTAL?
THERE'S ALWAYS A PORTAL.
OR A HIVE MIND.
OR A MASTER DESTRUCT SWITCH.
I'M NOT SEEING A PORTAL.
DOCTOR, CAN YOU OPEN ONE?
I CAN ONLY EXPEND SO MUCH ENERGY. IT'S EITHER THIS WALL OR A FULL TRANSDIMENSIONAL THRESHOLD.
HOW ABOUT A PARTIALLY OPERATIONAL RIFT? I INVITED YOU ALONG FOR A REASON, SO PLEASE DO NOT DISAPPOINT.
WILL THIS...
...SUFFICE?

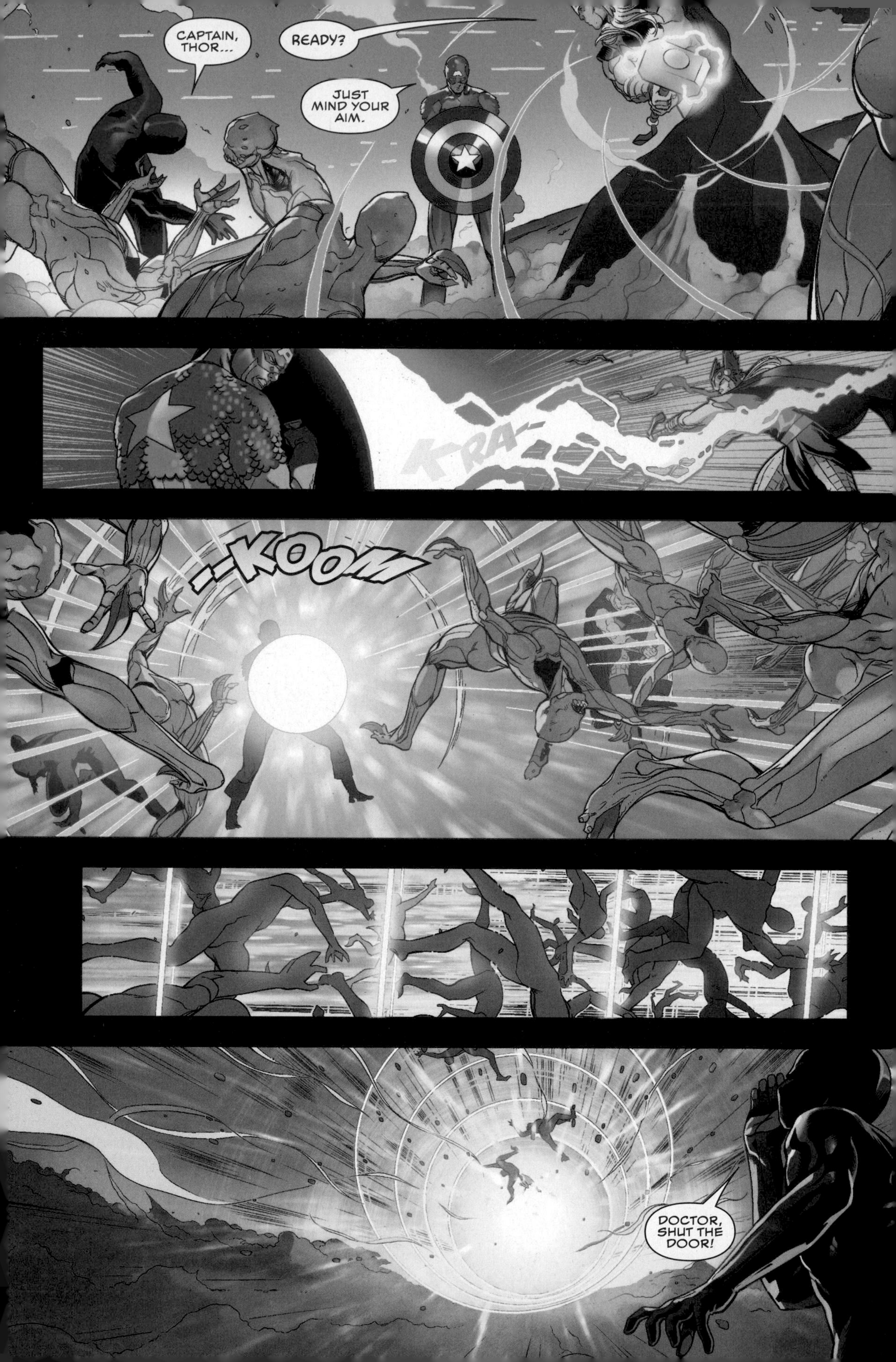
CAPTAIN, THOR...
READY?
JUST MIND YOUR AIM.
KRA--
--KOOM
DOCTOR, SHUT THE DOOR!

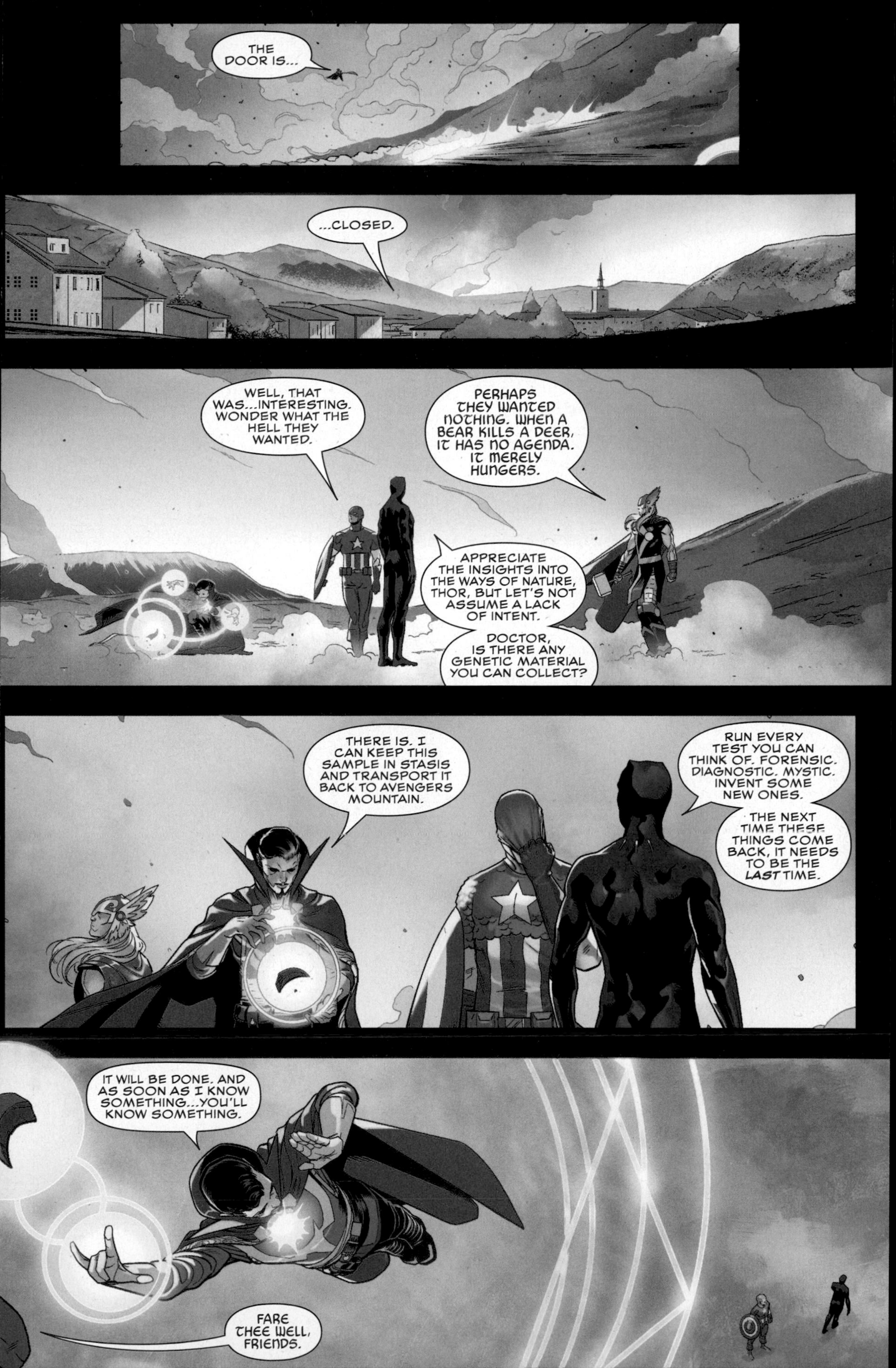
THE DOOR IS...
...CLOSED.
WELL, THAT WAS...INTERESTING. WONDER WHAT THE HELL THEY WANTED.
PERHAPS THEY WANTED NOTHING. WHEN A BEAR KILLS A DEER, IT HAS NO AGENDA. IT MERELY HUNGERS.
APPRECIATE THE INSIGHTS INTO THE WAYS OF NATURE, THOR, BUT LET'S NOT ASSUME A LACK OF INTENT.
DOCTOR, IS THERE ANY GENETIC MATERIAL YOU CAN COLLECT?
THERE IS. I CAN KEEP THIS SAMPLE IN STASIS AND TRANSPORT IT BACK TO AVENGERS MOUNTAIN.
RUN EVERY TEST YOU CAN THINK OF. FORENSIC. DIAGNOSTIC. MYSTIC. INVENT SOME NEW ONES.
THE NEXT TIME THESE THINGS COME BACK, IT NEEDS TO BE THE LAST TIME.
IT WILL BE DONE. AND AS SOON AS I KNOW SOMETHING...YOU'LL KNOW SOMETHING.
FARE THEE WELL, FRIENDS.

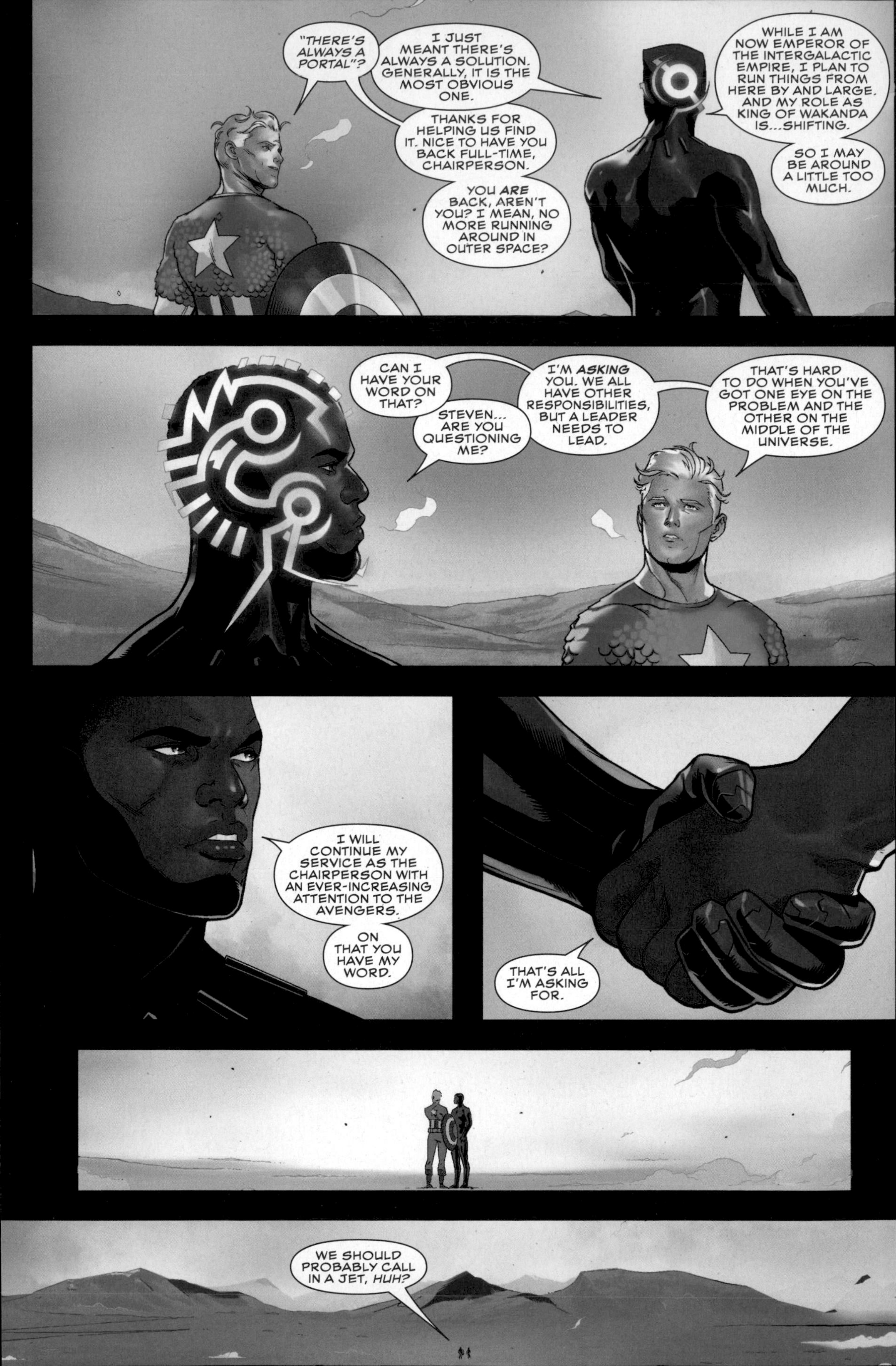
"THERE'S ALWAYS A PORTAL"?
I JUST MEANT THERE'S ALWAYS A SOLUTION. GENERALLY, IT IS THE MOST OBVIOUS ONE.
THANKS FOR HELPING US FIND IT. NICE TO HAVE YOU BACK FULL-TIME, CHAIRPERSON.
YOU *ARE* BACK, AREN'T YOU? I MEAN, NO MORE RUNNING AROUND IN OUTER SPACE?
WHILE I AM NOW EMPEROR OF THE INTERGALACTIC EMPIRE, I PLAN TO RUN THINGS FROM HERE BY AND LARGE. AND MY ROLE AS KING OF WAKANDA IS...SHIFTING.
SO I MAY BE AROUND A LITTLE TOO MUCH.
CAN I HAVE YOUR WORD ON THAT?
STEVEN... ARE YOU QUESTIONING ME?
I'M *ASKING* YOU. WE ALL HAVE OTHER RESPONSIBILITIES, BUT A LEADER NEEDS TO LEAD.
THAT'S HARD TO DO WHEN YOU'VE GOT ONE EYE ON THE PROBLEM AND THE OTHER ON THE MIDDLE OF THE UNIVERSE.
I WILL CONTINUE MY SERVICE AS THE CHAIRPERSON WITH AN EVER-INCREASING ATTENTION TO THE AVENGERS.
ON THAT YOU HAVE MY WORD.
THAT'S ALL I'M ASKING FOR.
WE SHOULD PROBABLY CALL IN A JET, *HUH?*

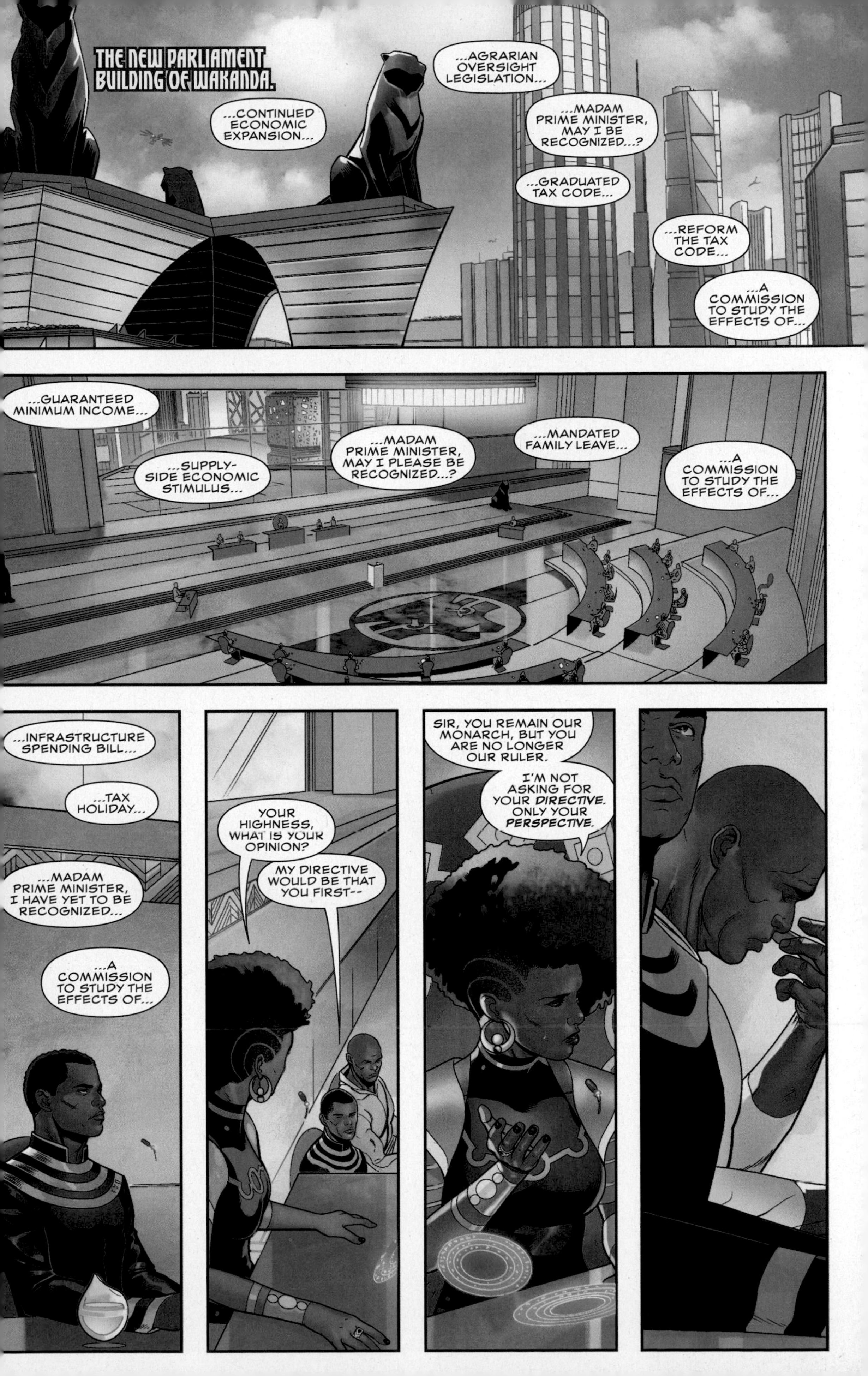
THE NEW PARLIAMENT BUILDING OF WAKANDA.
...CONTINUED ECONOMIC EXPANSION...
...AGRARIAN OVERSIGHT LEGISLATION...
...MADAM PRIME MINISTER, MAY I BE RECOGNIZED...?
...GRADUATED TAX CODE...
...REFORM THE TAX CODE...
...A COMMISSION TO STUDY THE EFFECTS OF...
...GUARANTEED MINIMUM INCOME...
...SUPPLY-SIDE ECONOMIC STIMULUS...
...MADAM PRIME MINISTER, MAY I PLEASE BE RECOGNIZED...?
...MANDATED FAMILY LEAVE...
...A COMMISSION TO STUDY THE EFFECTS OF...
...INFRASTRUCTURE SPENDING BILL...
...TAX HOLIDAY...
...MADAM PRIME MINISTER, I HAVE YET TO BE RECOGNIZED...
...A COMMISSION TO STUDY THE EFFECTS OF...
YOUR HIGHNESS, WHAT IS YOUR OPINION?
MY DIRECTIVE WOULD BE THAT YOU FIRST--
SIR, YOU REMAIN OUR MONARCH, BUT YOU ARE NO LONGER OUR RULER.
I'M NOT ASKING FOR YOUR *DIRECTIVE*. ONLY YOUR *PERSPECTIVE*.

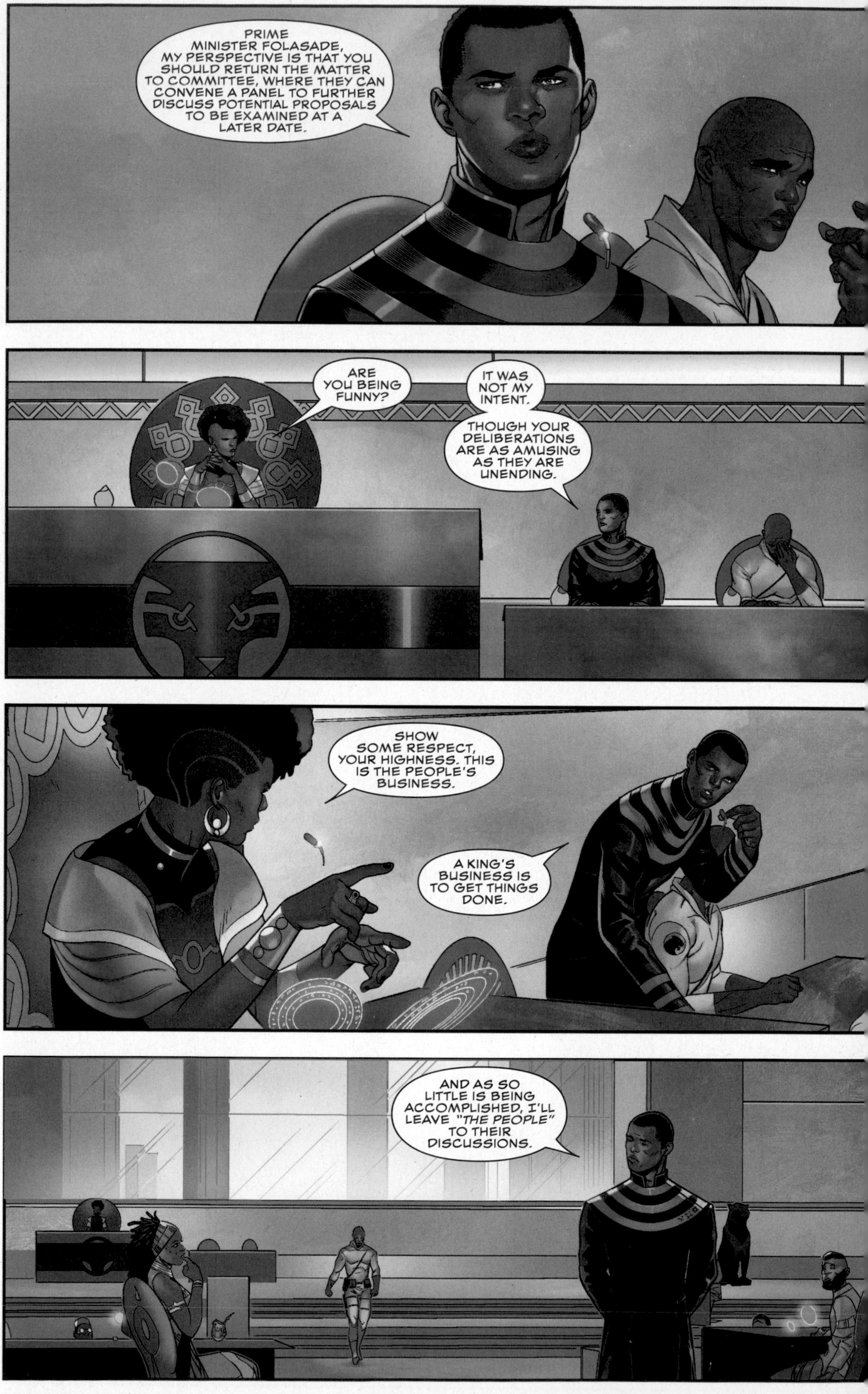
PRIME MINISTER FOLASADE, MY PERSPECTIVE IS THAT YOU SHOULD RETURN THE MATTER TO COMMITTEE, WHERE THEY CAN CONVENE A PANEL TO FURTHER DISCUSS POTENTIAL PROPOSALS TO BE EXAMINED AT A LATER DATE.
ARE YOU BEING FUNNY?
IT WAS NOT MY INTENT.
THOUGH YOUR DELIBERATIONS ARE AS AMUSING AS THEY ARE UNENDING.
SHOW SOME RESPECT, YOUR HIGHNESS. THIS IS THE PEOPLE'S BUSINESS.
A KING'S BUSINESS IS TO GET THINGS DONE.
AND AS SO LITTLE IS BEING ACCOMPLISHED, I'LL LEAVE *"THE PEOPLE"* TO THEIR DISCUSSIONS.

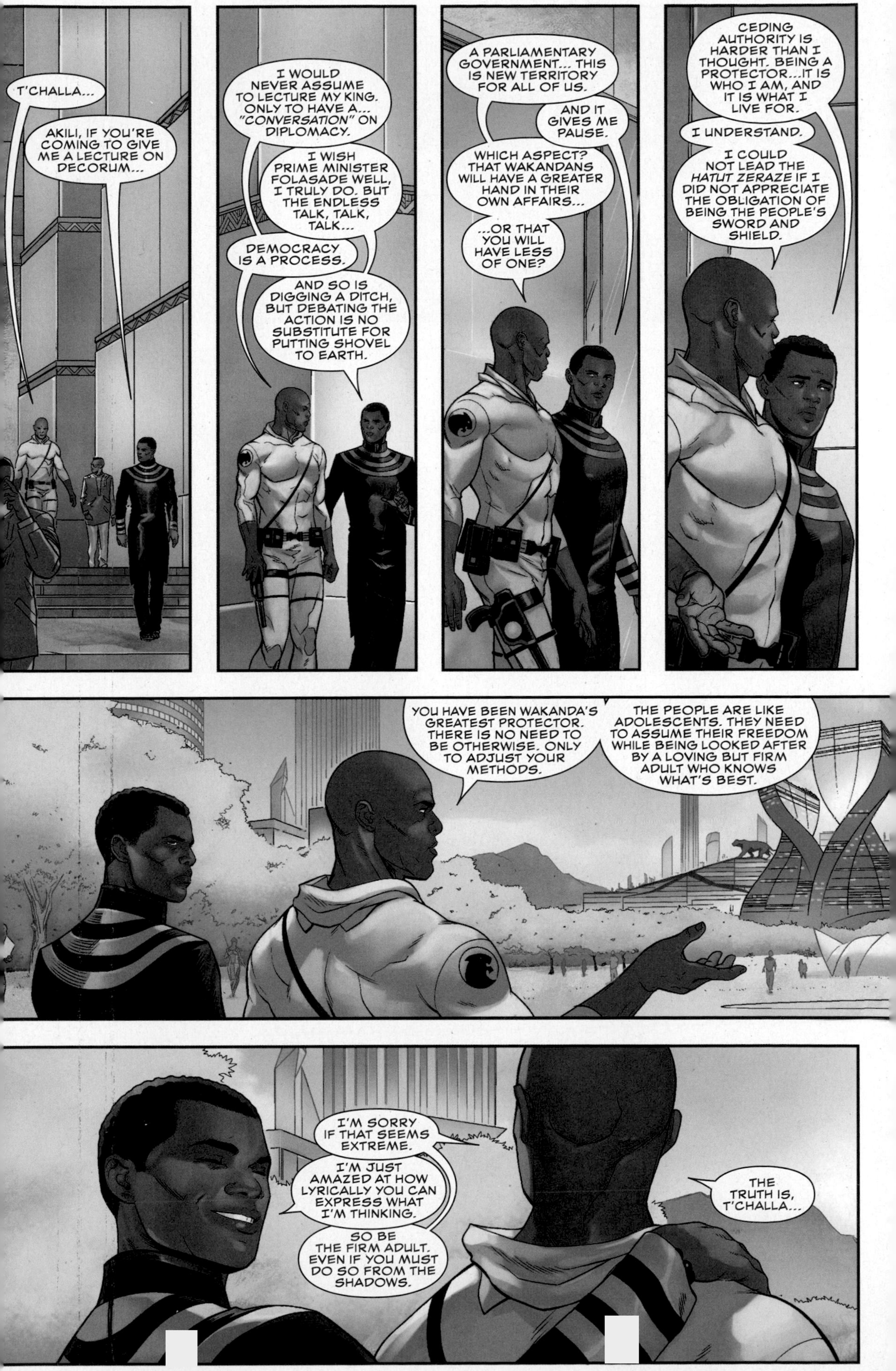
T'CHALLA...
AKILI, IF YOU'RE COMING TO GIVE ME A LECTURE ON DECORUM...
I WOULD NEVER ASSUME TO LECTURE MY KING. ONLY TO HAVE A... "CONVERSATION" ON DIPLOMACY.
I WISH PRIME MINISTER FOLASADE WELL, I TRULY DO. BUT THE ENDLESS TALK, TALK, TALK...
DEMOCRACY IS A PROCESS.
AND SO IS DIGGING A DITCH, BUT DEBATING THE ACTION IS NO SUBSTITUTE FOR PUTTING SHOVEL TO EARTH.
A PARLIAMENTARY GOVERNMENT... THIS IS NEW TERRITORY FOR ALL OF US.
AND IT GIVES ME PAUSE.
WHICH ASPECT? THAT WAKANDANS WILL HAVE A GREATER HAND IN THEIR OWN AFFAIRS...
...OR THAT YOU WILL HAVE LESS OF ONE?
CEDING AUTHORITY IS HARDER THAN I THOUGHT. BEING A PROTECTOR...IT IS WHO I AM, AND IT IS WHAT I LIVE FOR.
I UNDERSTAND.
I COULD NOT LEAD THE *HATUT ZERAZE* IF I DID NOT APPRECIATE THE OBLIGATION OF BEING THE PEOPLE'S SWORD AND SHIELD.
YOU HAVE BEEN WAKANDA'S GREATEST PROTECTOR. THERE IS NO NEED TO BE OTHERWISE. ONLY TO ADJUST YOUR METHODS.
THE PEOPLE ARE LIKE ADOLESCENTS. THEY NEED TO ASSUME THEIR FREEDOM WHILE BEING LOOKED AFTER BY A LOVING BUT FIRM ADULT WHO KNOWS WHAT'S BEST.
I'M SORRY IF THAT SEEMS EXTREME.
I'M JUST AMAZED AT HOW LYRICALLY YOU CAN EXPRESS WHAT I'M THINKING.
SO BE THE FIRM ADULT. EVEN IF YOU MUST DO SO FROM THE SHADOWS.
THE TRUTH IS, T'CHALLA...

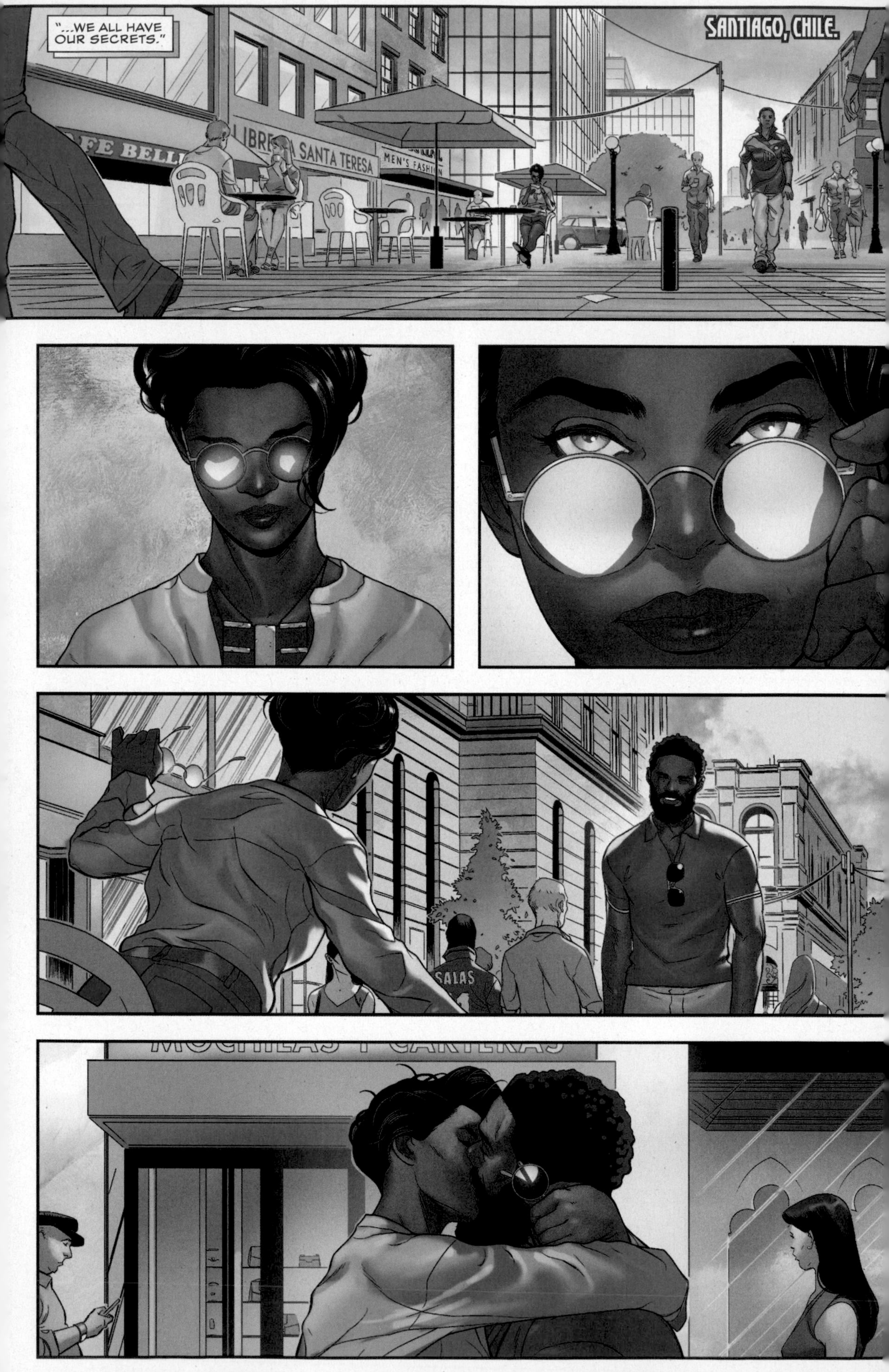
"...WE ALL HAVE OUR SECRETS."
SANTIAGO, CHILE.
LIBRERIA SANTA TERESA
MEN'S FASHION
SALAS
MOCHILAS Y CARTERAS

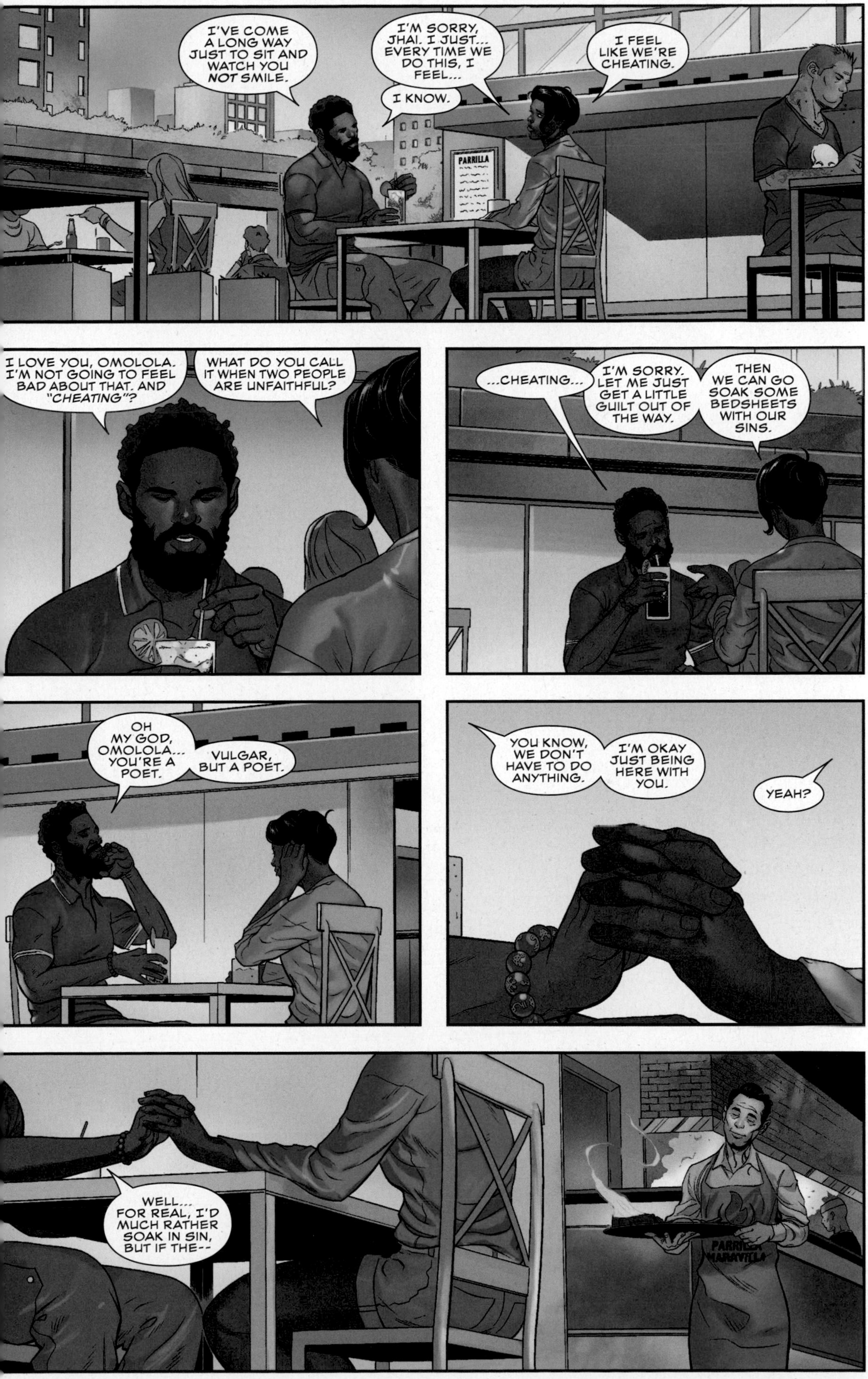
I'VE COME A LONG WAY JUST TO SIT AND WATCH YOU *NOT* SMILE.
I'M SORRY, JHAI. I JUST... EVERY TIME WE DO THIS, I FEEL...
I KNOW.
I FEEL LIKE WE'RE CHEATING.
PARRILLA
I LOVE YOU, OMOLOLA. I'M NOT GOING TO FEEL BAD ABOUT THAT. AND *"CHEATING"*?
WHAT DO YOU CALL IT WHEN TWO PEOPLE ARE UNFAITHFUL?
...CHEATING...
I'M SORRY. LET ME JUST GET A LITTLE GUILT OUT OF THE WAY.
THEN WE CAN GO SOAK SOME BEDSHEETS WITH OUR SINS.
OH MY GOD, OMOLOLA... YOU'RE A POET.
VULGAR, BUT A POET.
YOU KNOW, WE DON'T HAVE TO DO ANYTHING.
I'M OKAY JUST BEING HERE WITH YOU.
YEAH?
WELL... FOR REAL, I'D MUCH RATHER SOAK IN SIN, BUT IF THE--

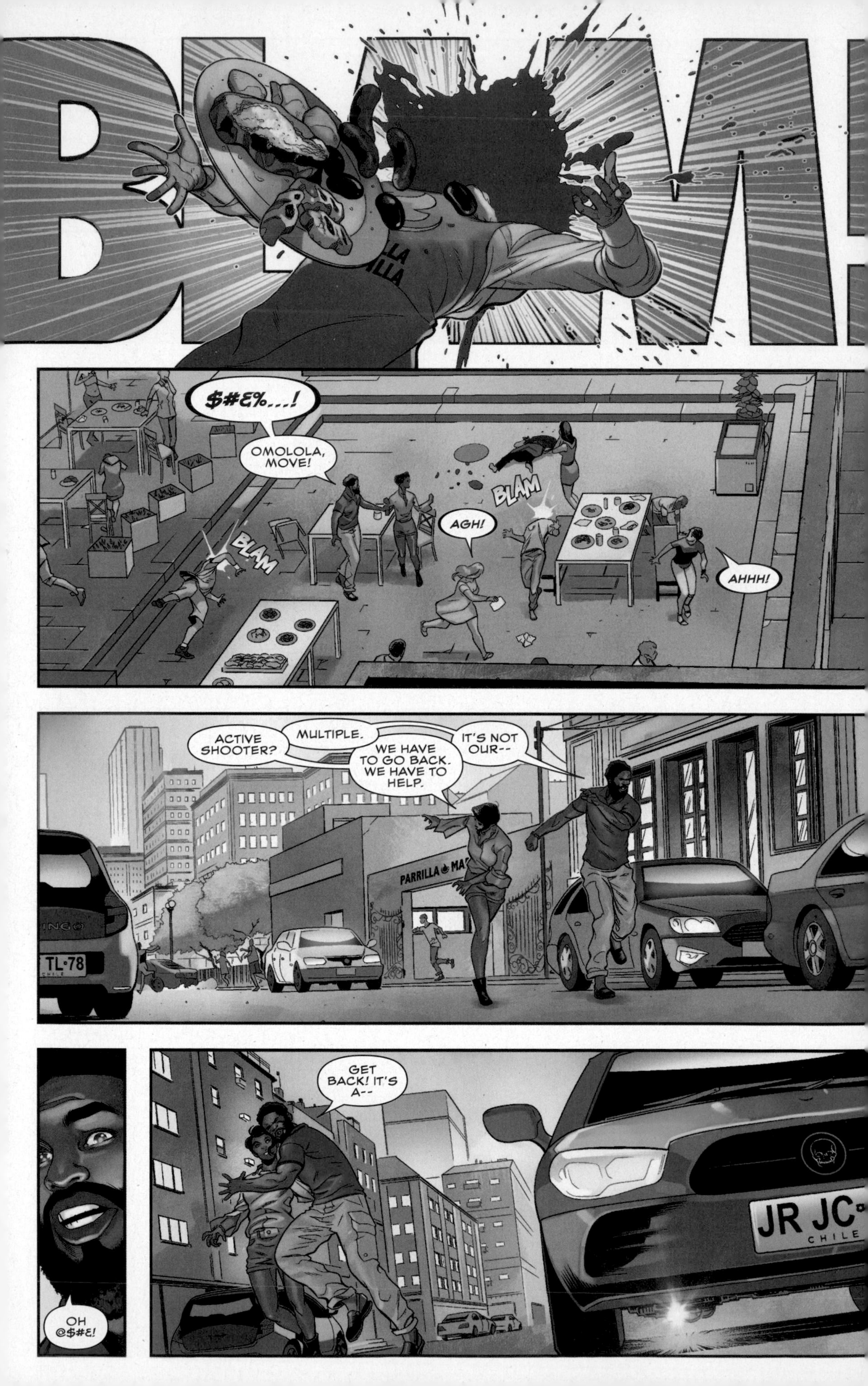
BLAM
$#Ɛ%...!
OMOLOLA, MOVE!
BLAM
AGH!
BLAM
AHHH!
ACTIVE SHOOTER?
MULTIPLE.
IT'S NOT OUR--
WE HAVE TO GO BACK. WE HAVE TO HELP.
PARRILLA MA
TL·78
OH @$#Ɛ!
GET BACK! IT'S A--
JR JC
CHILE

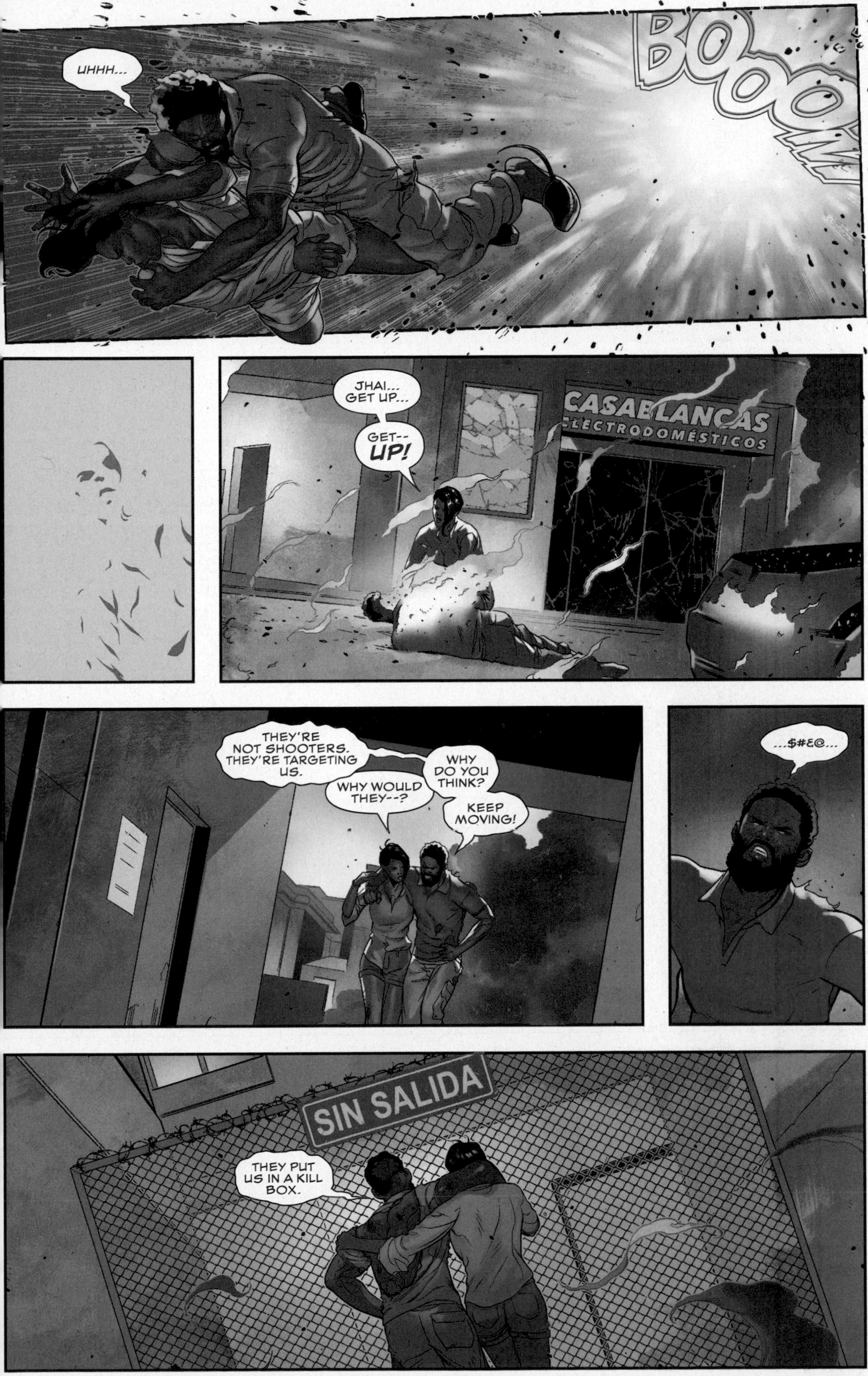
UHHH...
BOOOOM
JHAI... GET UP...
GET-- UP!
CASABLANCAS
ELECTRODOMÉSTICOS
THEY'RE NOT SHOOTERS. THEY'RE TARGETING US.
WHY WOULD THEY--?
WHY DO YOU THINK?
KEEP MOVING!
...$#Ɛ@...
SIN SALIDA
THEY PUT US IN A KILL BOX.

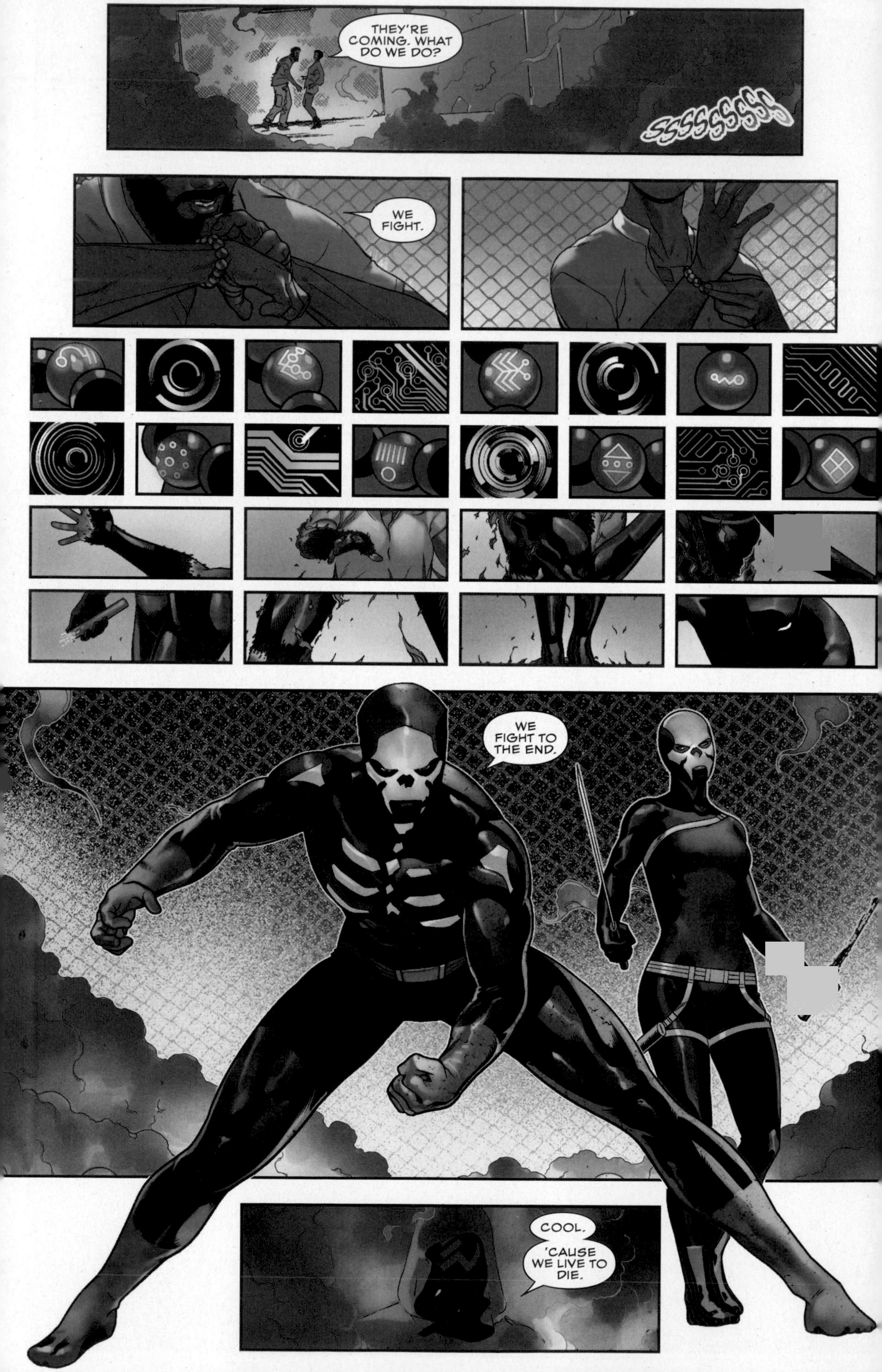
THEY'RE COMING. WHAT DO WE DO?
SSSSSSSSS
WE FIGHT.
WE FIGHT TO THE END.
COOL.
'CAUSE WE LIVE TO DIE.

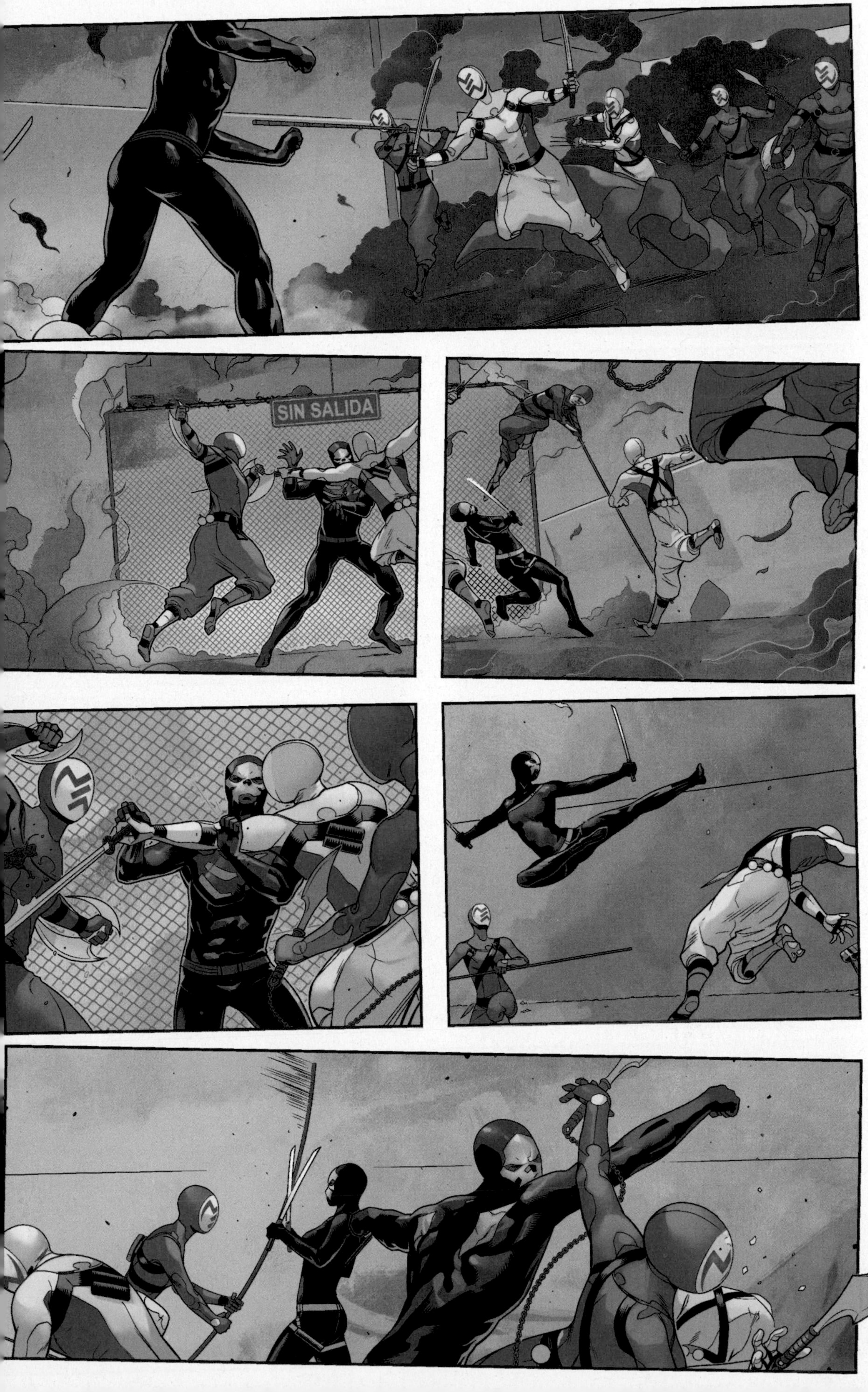
SIN SALIDA

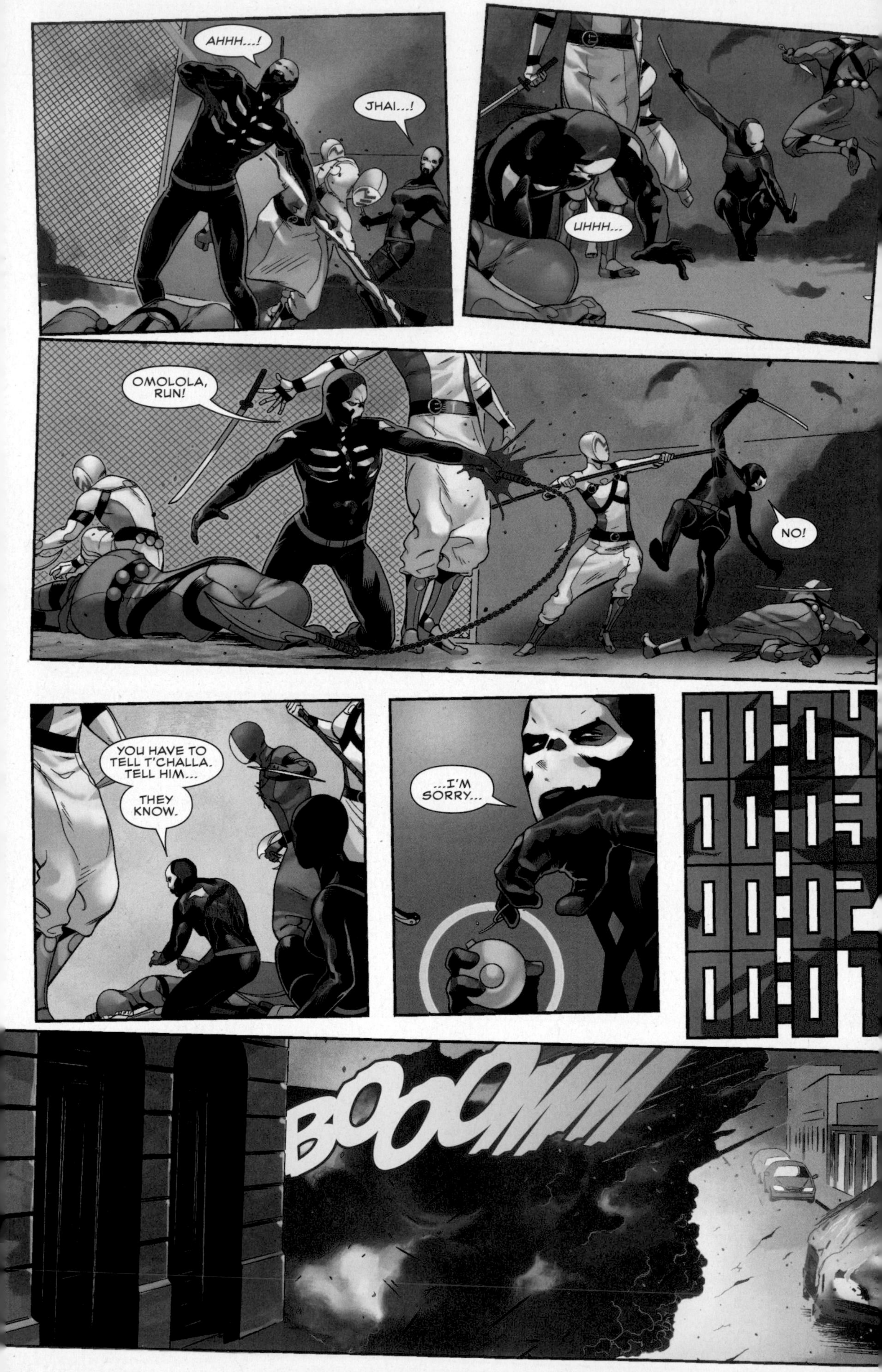
AHHH...!
JHAI...!
UHHH...
OMOLOLA, RUN!
NO!
YOU HAVE TO TELL T'CHALLA. TELL HIM...
THEY KNOW.
...I'M SORRY...
BOOOMM

T'CHALLA...IT'S OMOLOLA.

WHAT ARE YOU DOING?! UNDER NO CIRCUMSTANCES WERE YOU TO *EVER* CONTA--

LISTEN TO ME!

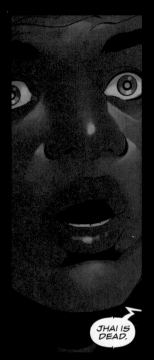

JHAI IS DEAD.

T'CHALLA...?

SEND ME YOUR LOCATION. I'LL COME TO YOU.

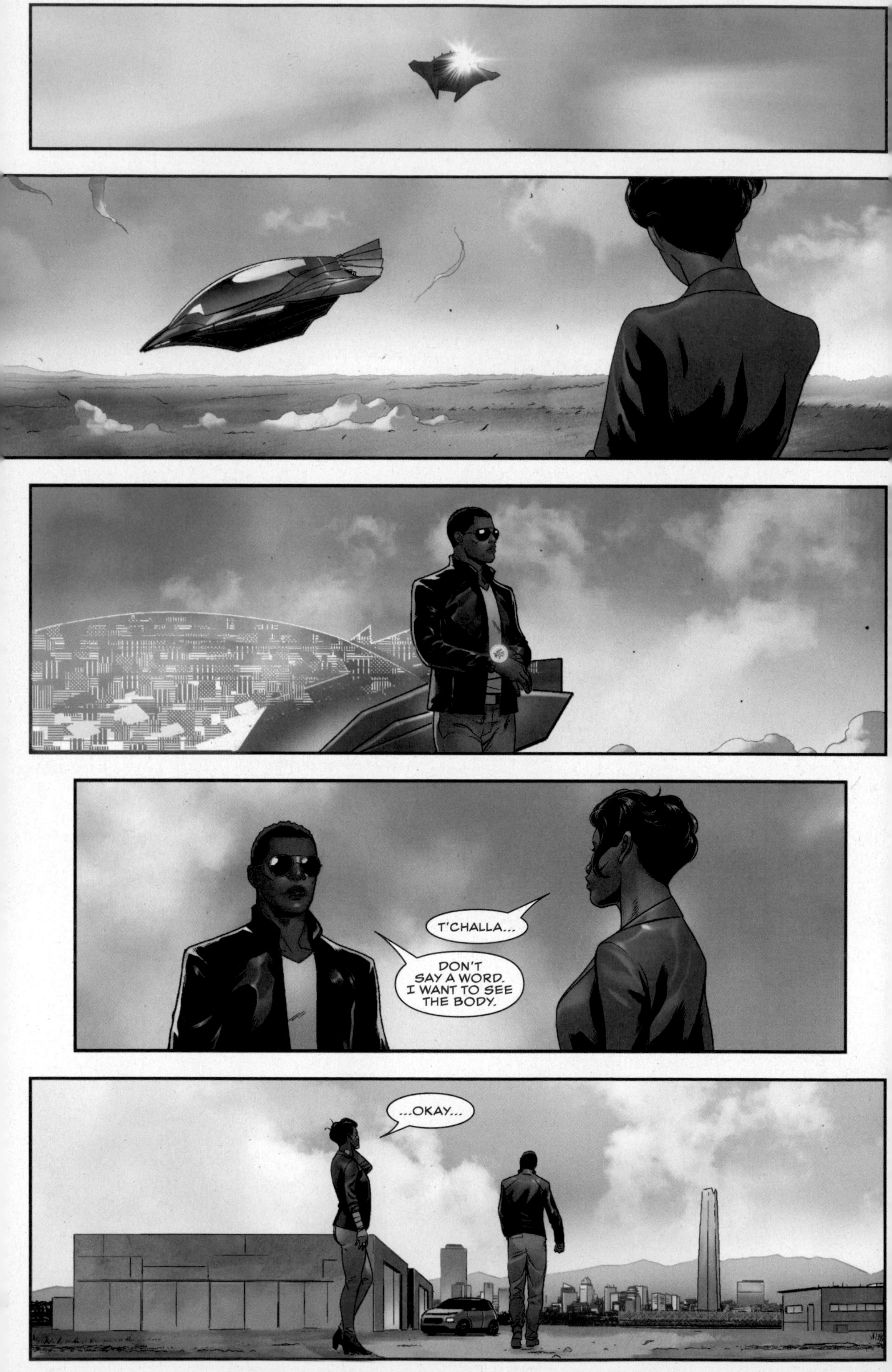
T'CHALLA...
DON'T SAY A WORD. I WANT TO SEE THE BODY.
...OKAY...

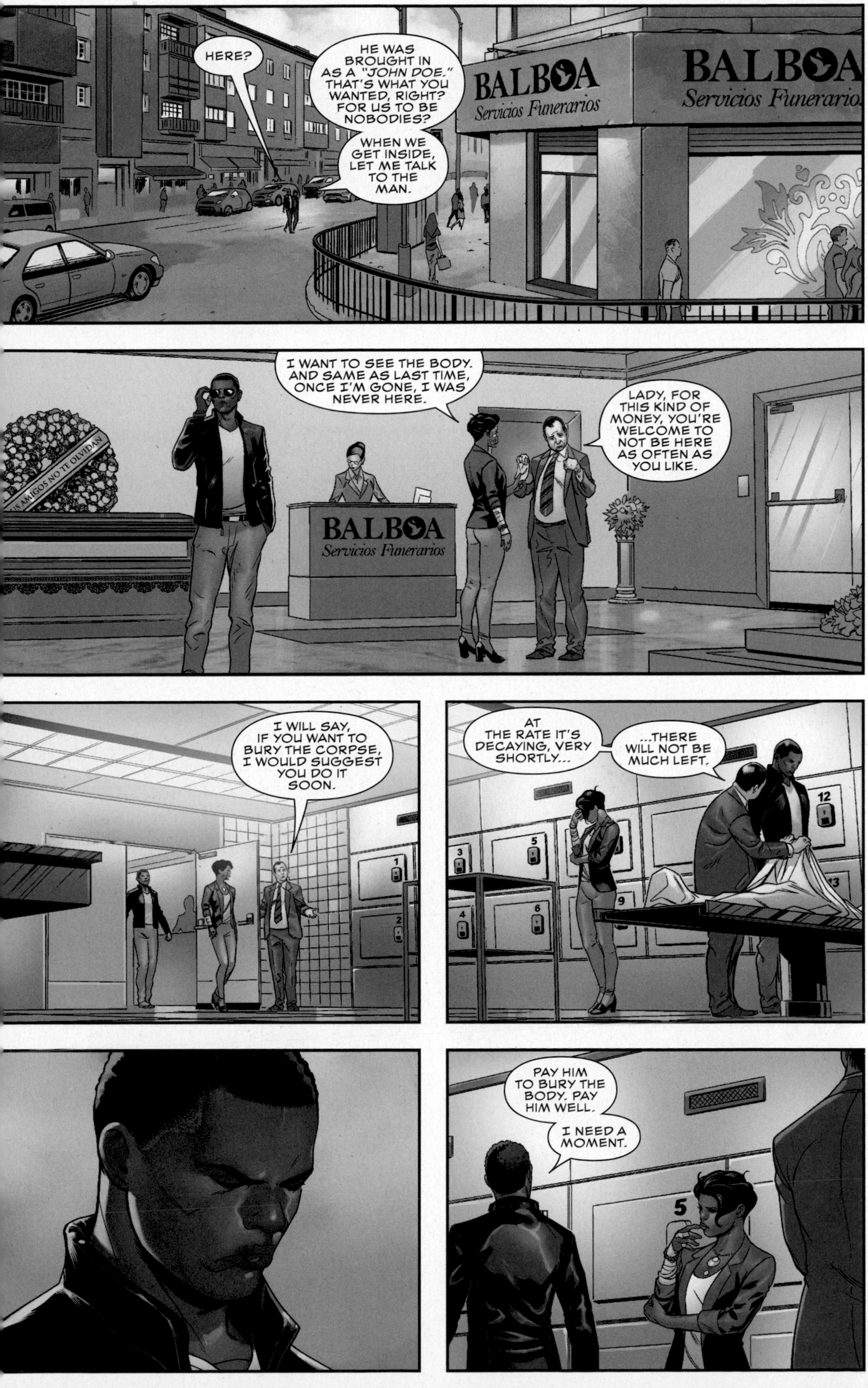
HERE?
HE WAS BROUGHT IN AS A "JOHN DOE." THAT'S WHAT YOU WANTED, RIGHT? FOR US TO BE NOBODIES?
WHEN WE GET INSIDE, LET ME TALK TO THE MAN.
BALBOA Servicios Funerarios
BALBOA Servicios Funerarios
I WANT TO SEE THE BODY. AND SAME AS LAST TIME, ONCE I'M GONE, I WAS NEVER HERE.
LADY, FOR THIS KIND OF MONEY, YOU'RE WELCOME TO NOT BE HERE AS OFTEN AS YOU LIKE.
AMIGOS NO TE OLVIDAN
BALBOA Servicios Funerarios
I WILL SAY, IF YOU WANT TO BURY THE CORPSE, I WOULD SUGGEST YOU DO IT SOON.
AT THE RATE IT'S DECAYING, VERY SHORTLY...
...THERE WILL NOT BE MUCH LEFT.
PAY HIM TO BURY THE BODY. PAY HIM WELL.
I NEED A MOMENT.

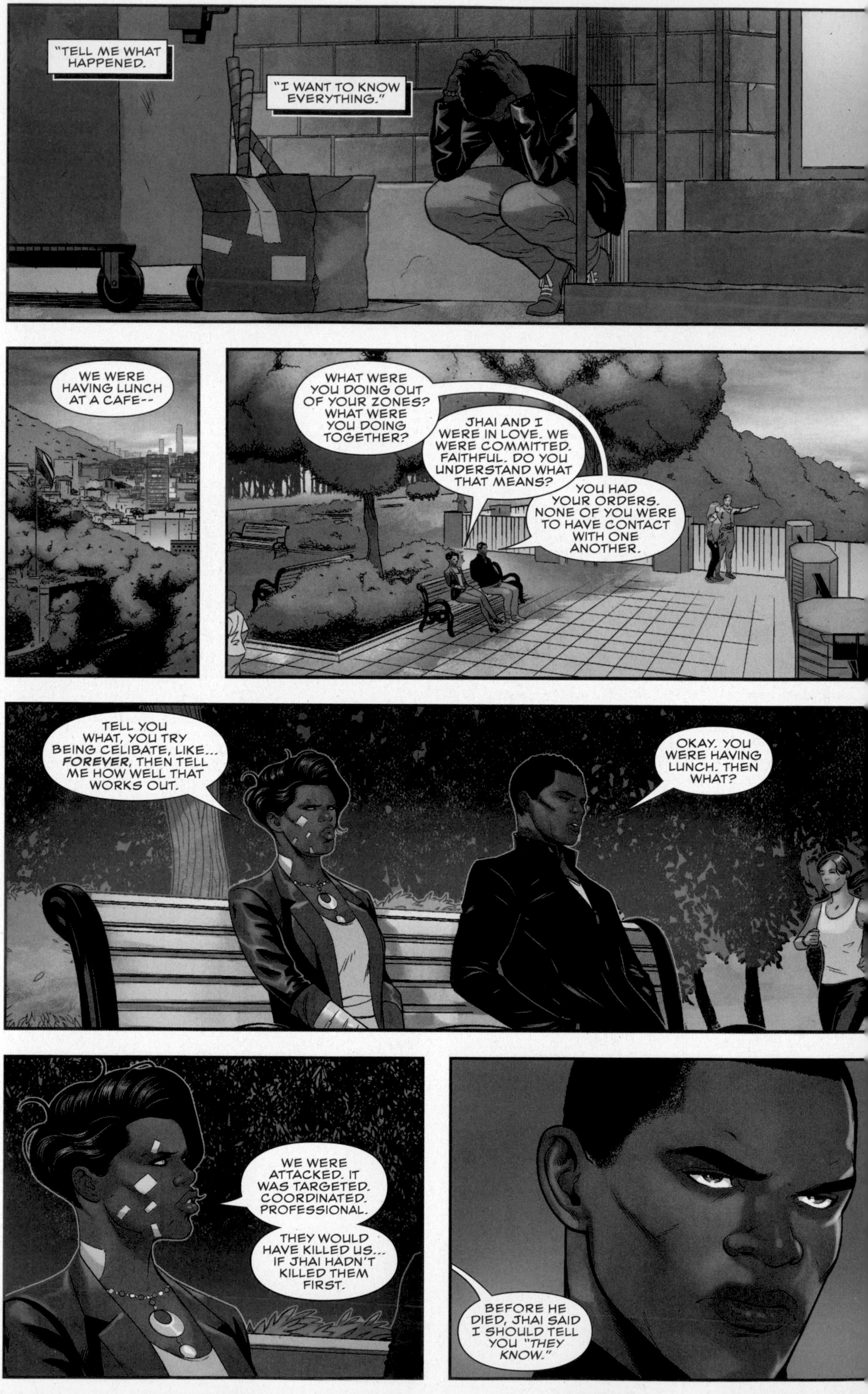

"TELL ME WHAT HAPPENED.
"I WANT TO KNOW EVERYTHING."
WE WERE HAVING LUNCH AT A CAFE--
WHAT WERE YOU DOING OUT OF YOUR ZONES? WHAT WERE YOU DOING TOGETHER?
JHAI AND I WERE IN LOVE. WE WERE COMMITTED. FAITHFUL. DO YOU UNDERSTAND WHAT THAT MEANS?
YOU HAD YOUR ORDERS. NONE OF YOU WERE TO HAVE CONTACT WITH ONE ANOTHER.
TELL YOU WHAT, YOU TRY BEING CELIBATE, LIKE... *FOREVER*, THEN TELL ME HOW WELL THAT WORKS OUT.
OKAY. YOU WERE HAVING LUNCH. THEN WHAT?
WE WERE ATTACKED. IT WAS TARGETED. COORDINATED. PROFESSIONAL.
THEY WOULD HAVE KILLED US... IF JHAI HADN'T KILLED THEM FIRST.
BEFORE HE DIED, JHAI SAID I SHOULD TELL YOU *"THEY KNOW."*

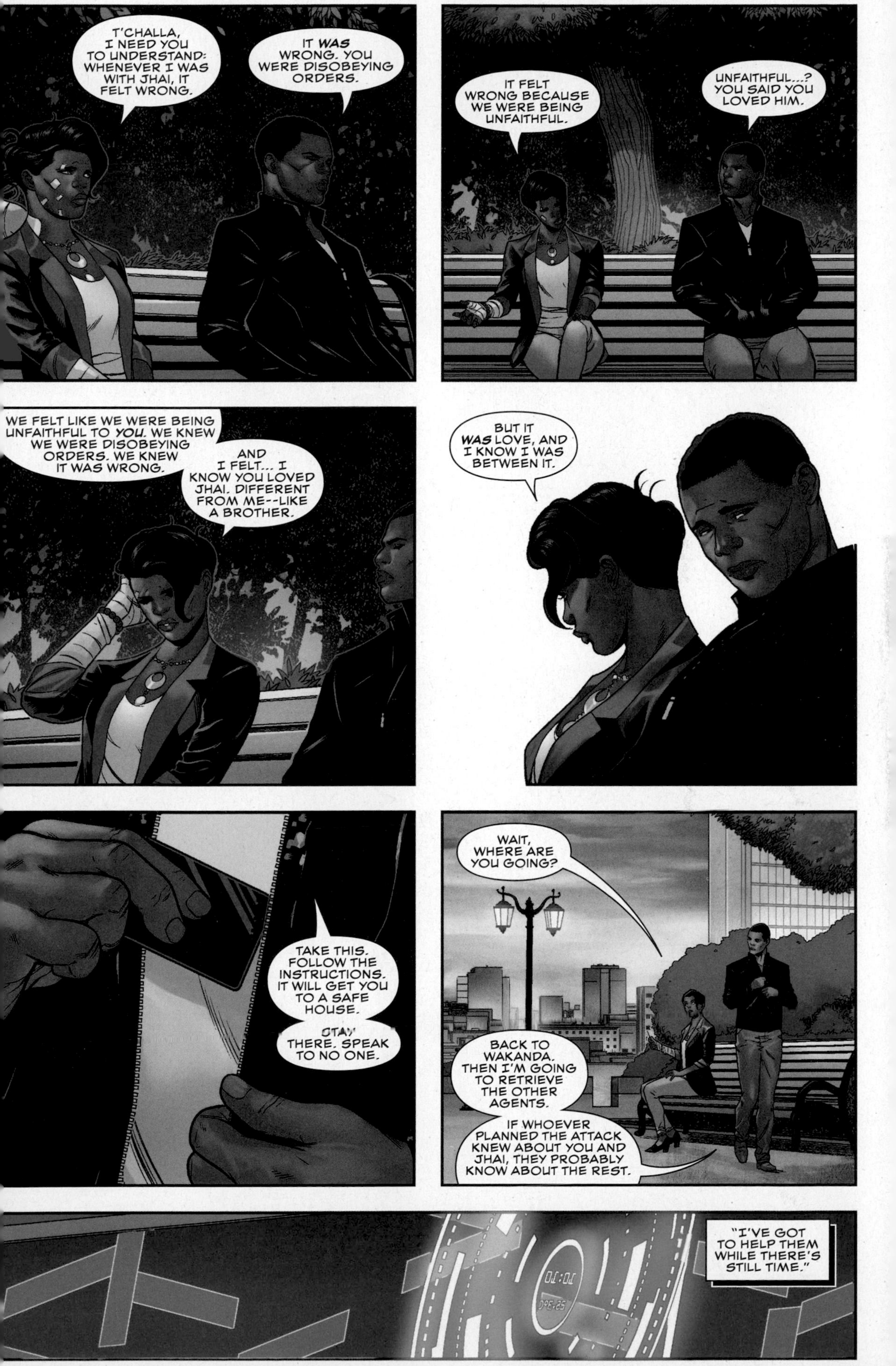
T'CHALLA, I NEED YOU TO UNDERSTAND: WHENEVER I WAS WITH JHAI, IT FELT WRONG.
IT *WAS* WRONG. YOU WERE DISOBEYING ORDERS.
IT FELT WRONG BECAUSE WE WERE BEING UNFAITHFUL.
UNFAITHFUL...? YOU SAID YOU LOVED HIM.
WE FELT LIKE WE WERE BEING UNFAITHFUL TO *YOU*. WE KNEW WE WERE DISOBEYING ORDERS. WE KNEW IT WAS WRONG.
AND I FELT... I KNOW YOU LOVED JHAI. DIFFERENT FROM ME--LIKE A BROTHER.
BUT IT *WAS* LOVE, AND I KNOW I WAS BETWEEN IT.
TAKE THIS. FOLLOW THE INSTRUCTIONS. IT WILL GET YOU TO A SAFE HOUSE.
STAY THERE. SPEAK TO NO ONE.
WAIT, WHERE ARE YOU GOING?
BACK TO WAKANDA. THEN I'M GOING TO RETRIEVE THE OTHER AGENTS.
IF WHOEVER PLANNED THE ATTACK KNEW ABOUT YOU AND JHAI, THEY PROBABLY KNOW ABOUT THE REST.
"I'VE GOT TO HELP THEM WHILE THERE'S STILL TIME."

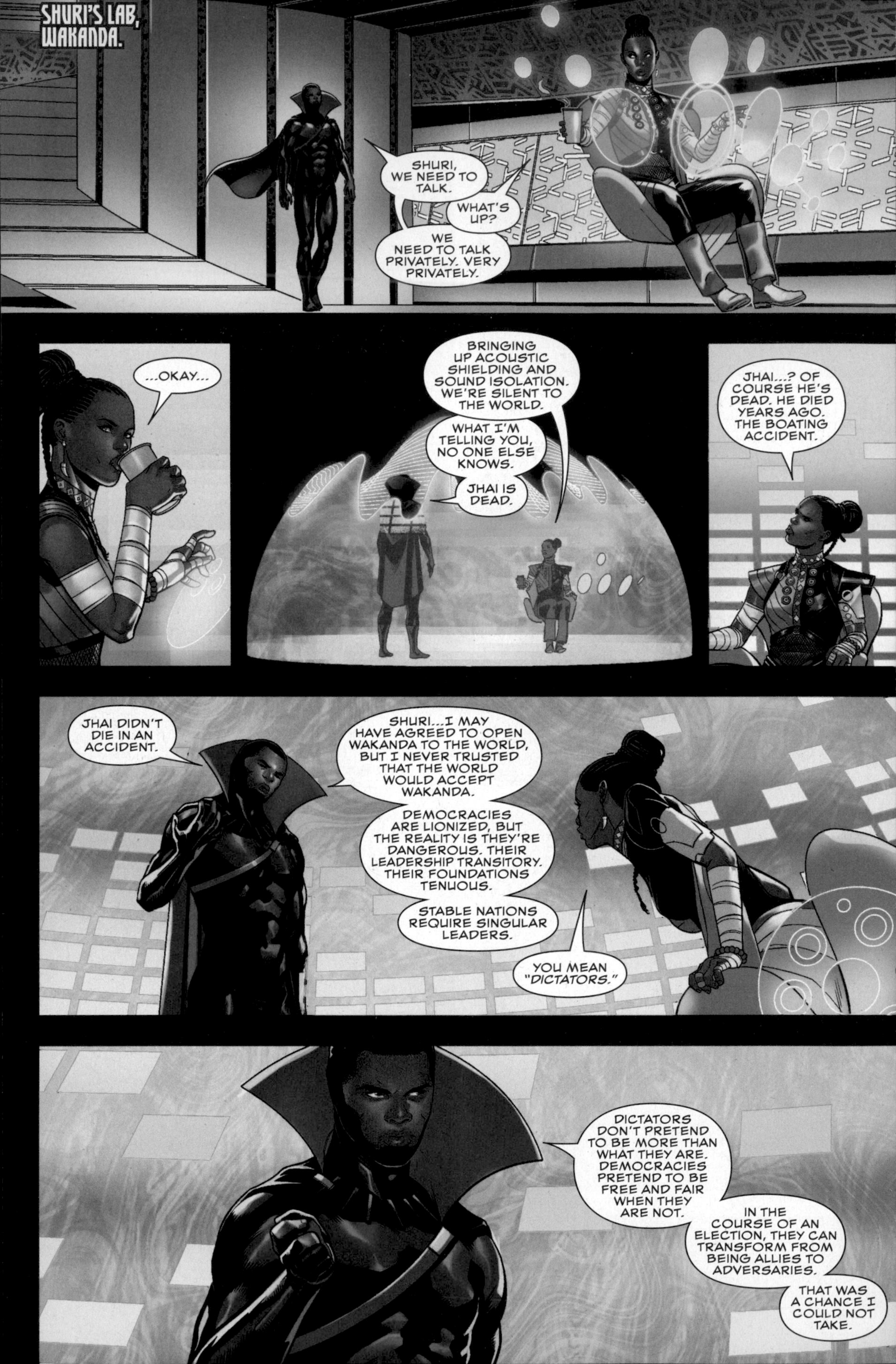
SHURI'S LAB, WAKANDA.
SHURI, WE NEED TO TALK.
WHAT'S UP?
WE NEED TO TALK PRIVATELY. VERY PRIVATELY.
...OKAY...
BRINGING UP ACOUSTIC SHIELDING AND SOUND ISOLATION. WE'RE SILENT TO THE WORLD.
WHAT I'M TELLING YOU, NO ONE ELSE KNOWS.
JHAI IS DEAD.
JHAI...? OF COURSE HE'S DEAD. HE DIED YEARS AGO. THE BOATING ACCIDENT.
JHAI DIDN'T DIE IN AN ACCIDENT.
SHURI...I MAY HAVE AGREED TO OPEN WAKANDA TO THE WORLD, BUT I NEVER TRUSTED THAT THE WORLD WOULD ACCEPT WAKANDA.
DEMOCRACIES ARE LIONIZED, BUT THE REALITY IS THEY'RE DANGEROUS. THEIR LEADERSHIP TRANSITORY. THEIR FOUNDATIONS TENUOUS.
STABLE NATIONS REQUIRE SINGULAR LEADERS.
YOU MEAN "DICTATORS."
DICTATORS DON'T PRETEND TO BE MORE THAN WHAT THEY ARE. DEMOCRACIES PRETEND TO BE FREE AND FAIR WHEN THEY ARE NOT.
IN THE COURSE OF AN ELECTION, THEY CAN TRANSFORM FROM BEING ALLIES TO ADVERSARIES.
THAT WAS A CHANCE I COULD NOT TAKE.

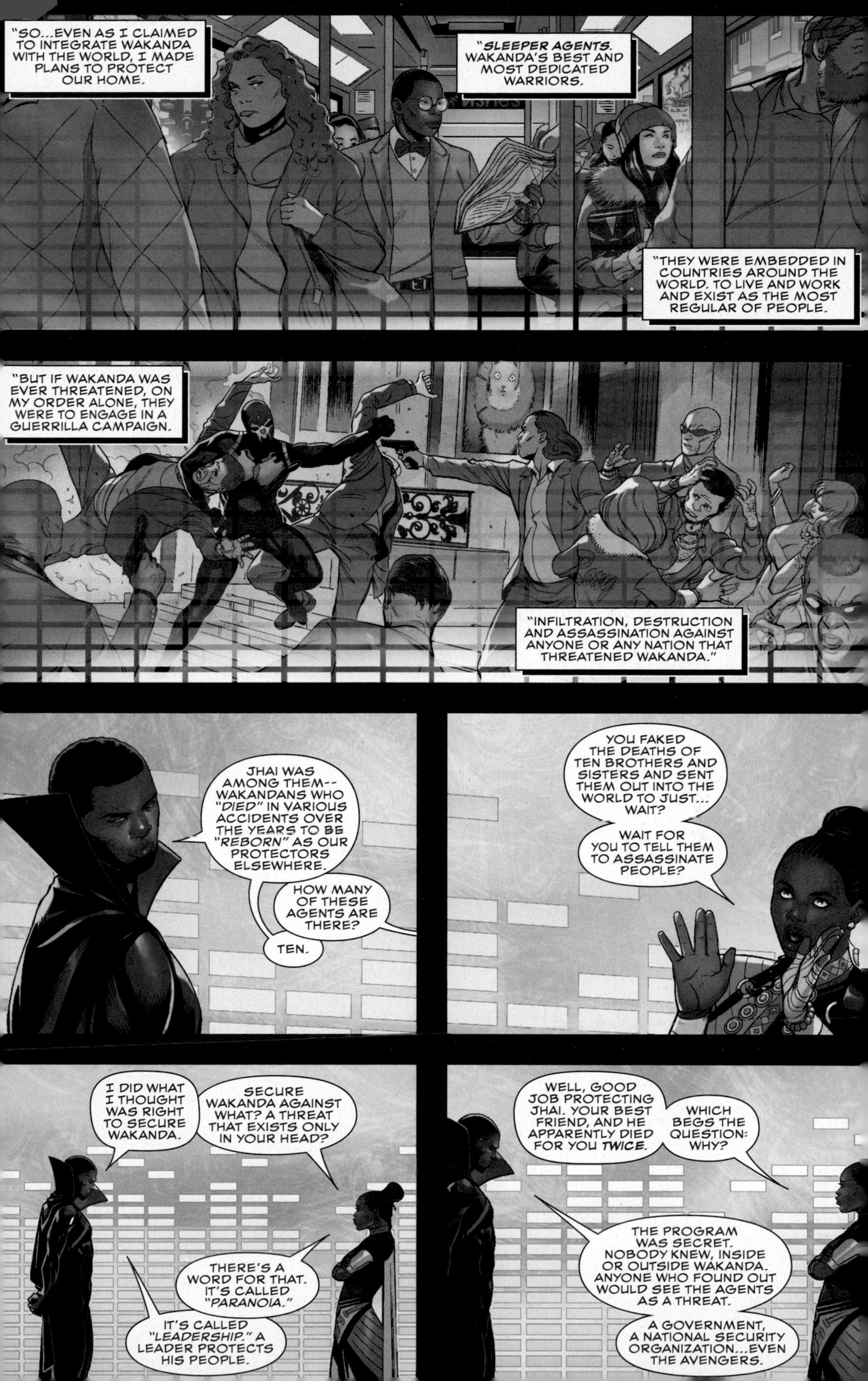
"SO...EVEN AS I CLAIMED TO INTEGRATE WAKANDA WITH THE WORLD, I MADE PLANS TO PROTECT OUR HOME.
"SLEEPER AGENTS. WAKANDA'S BEST AND MOST DEDICATED WARRIORS.
"THEY WERE EMBEDDED IN COUNTRIES AROUND THE WORLD. TO LIVE AND WORK AND EXIST AS THE MOST REGULAR OF PEOPLE.
"BUT IF WAKANDA WAS EVER THREATENED, ON MY ORDER ALONE, THEY WERE TO ENGAGE IN A GUERRILLA CAMPAIGN.
"INFILTRATION, DESTRUCTION AND ASSASSINATION AGAINST ANYONE OR ANY NATION THAT THREATENED WAKANDA."
JHAI WAS AMONG THEM--WAKANDANS WHO "DIED" IN VARIOUS ACCIDENTS OVER THE YEARS TO BE "REBORN" AS OUR PROTECTORS ELSEWHERE.
HOW MANY OF THESE AGENTS ARE THERE?
TEN.
YOU FAKED THE DEATHS OF TEN BROTHERS AND SISTERS AND SENT THEM OUT INTO THE WORLD TO JUST... WAIT?
WAIT FOR YOU TO TELL THEM TO ASSASSINATE PEOPLE?
I DID WHAT I THOUGHT WAS RIGHT TO SECURE WAKANDA.
SECURE WAKANDA AGAINST WHAT? A THREAT THAT EXISTS ONLY IN YOUR HEAD?
THERE'S A WORD FOR THAT. IT'S CALLED "PARANOIA."
IT'S CALLED "LEADERSHIP." A LEADER PROTECTS HIS PEOPLE.
WELL, GOOD JOB PROTECTING JHAI. YOUR BEST FRIEND, AND HE APPARENTLY DIED FOR YOU TWICE.
WHICH BEGS THE QUESTION: WHY?
THE PROGRAM WAS SECRET. NOBODY KNEW, INSIDE OR OUTSIDE WAKANDA. ANYONE WHO FOUND OUT WOULD SEE THE AGENTS AS A THREAT.
A GOVERNMENT, A NATIONAL SECURITY ORGANIZATION...EVEN THE AVENGERS.

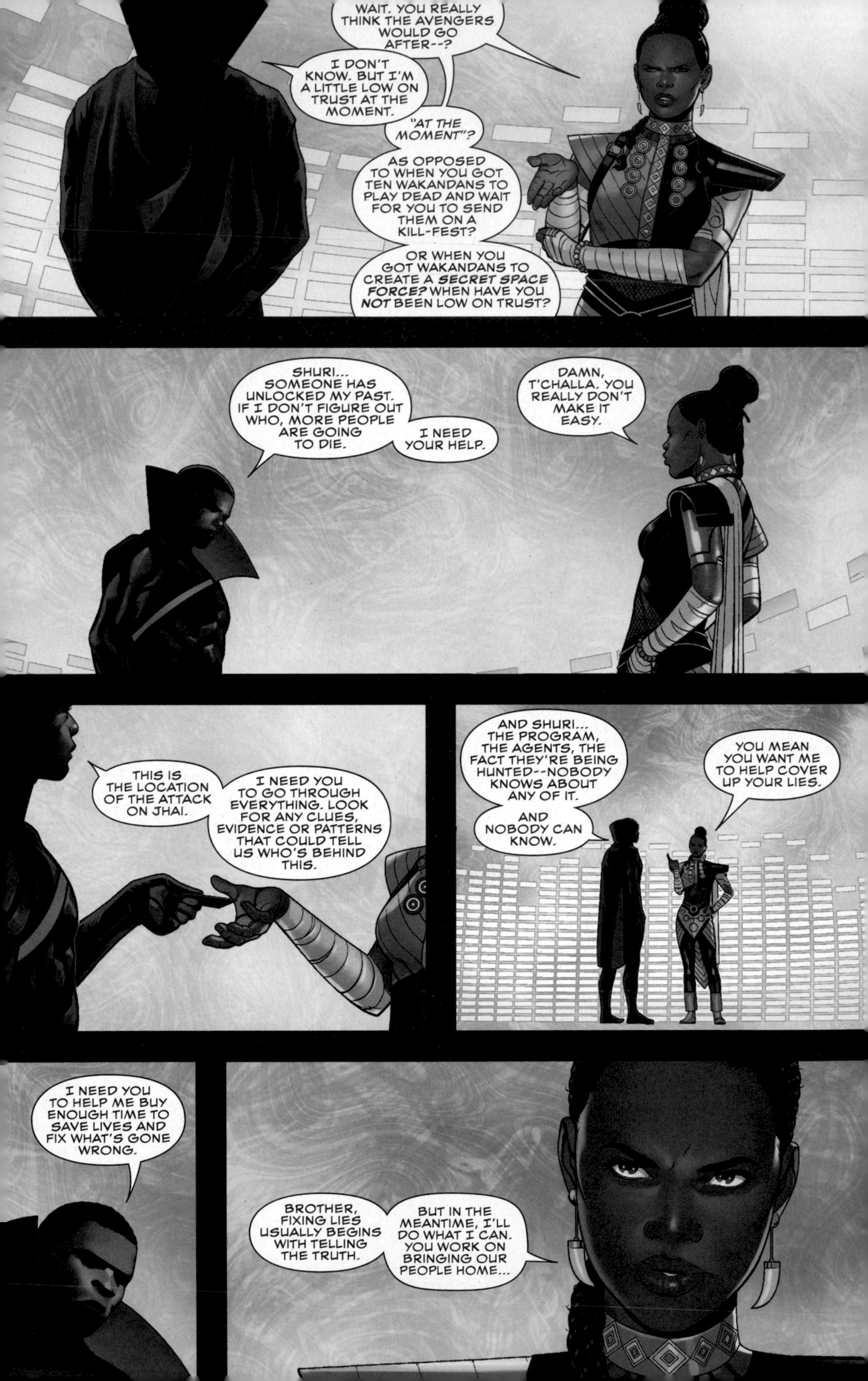
WAIT. YOU REALLY THINK THE AVENGERS WOULD GO AFTER--?
I DON'T KNOW. BUT I'M A LITTLE LOW ON TRUST AT THE MOMENT.
"AT THE MOMENT"?
AS OPPOSED TO WHEN YOU GOT TEN WAKANDANS TO PLAY DEAD AND WAIT FOR YOU TO SEND THEM ON A KILL-FEST?
OR WHEN YOU GOT WAKANDANS TO CREATE A *SECRET SPACE FORCE?* WHEN HAVE YOU *NOT* BEEN LOW ON TRUST?
SHURI... SOMEONE HAS UNLOCKED MY PAST. IF I DON'T FIGURE OUT WHO, MORE PEOPLE ARE GOING TO DIE.
I NEED YOUR HELP.
DAMN, T'CHALLA. YOU REALLY DON'T MAKE IT EASY.
THIS IS THE LOCATION OF THE ATTACK ON JHAI.
I NEED YOU TO GO THROUGH EVERYTHING. LOOK FOR ANY CLUES, EVIDENCE OR PATTERNS THAT COULD TELL US WHO'S BEHIND THIS.
AND SHURI... THE PROGRAM, THE AGENTS, THE FACT THEY'RE BEING HUNTED--NOBODY KNOWS ABOUT ANY OF IT.
AND NOBODY CAN KNOW.
YOU MEAN YOU WANT ME TO HELP COVER UP YOUR LIES.
I NEED YOU TO HELP ME BUY ENOUGH TIME TO SAVE LIVES AND FIX WHAT'S GONE WRONG.
BROTHER, FIXING LIES USUALLY BEGINS WITH TELLING THE TRUTH.
BUT IN THE MEANTIME, I'LL DO WHAT I CAN. YOU WORK ON BRINGING OUR PEOPLE HOME...

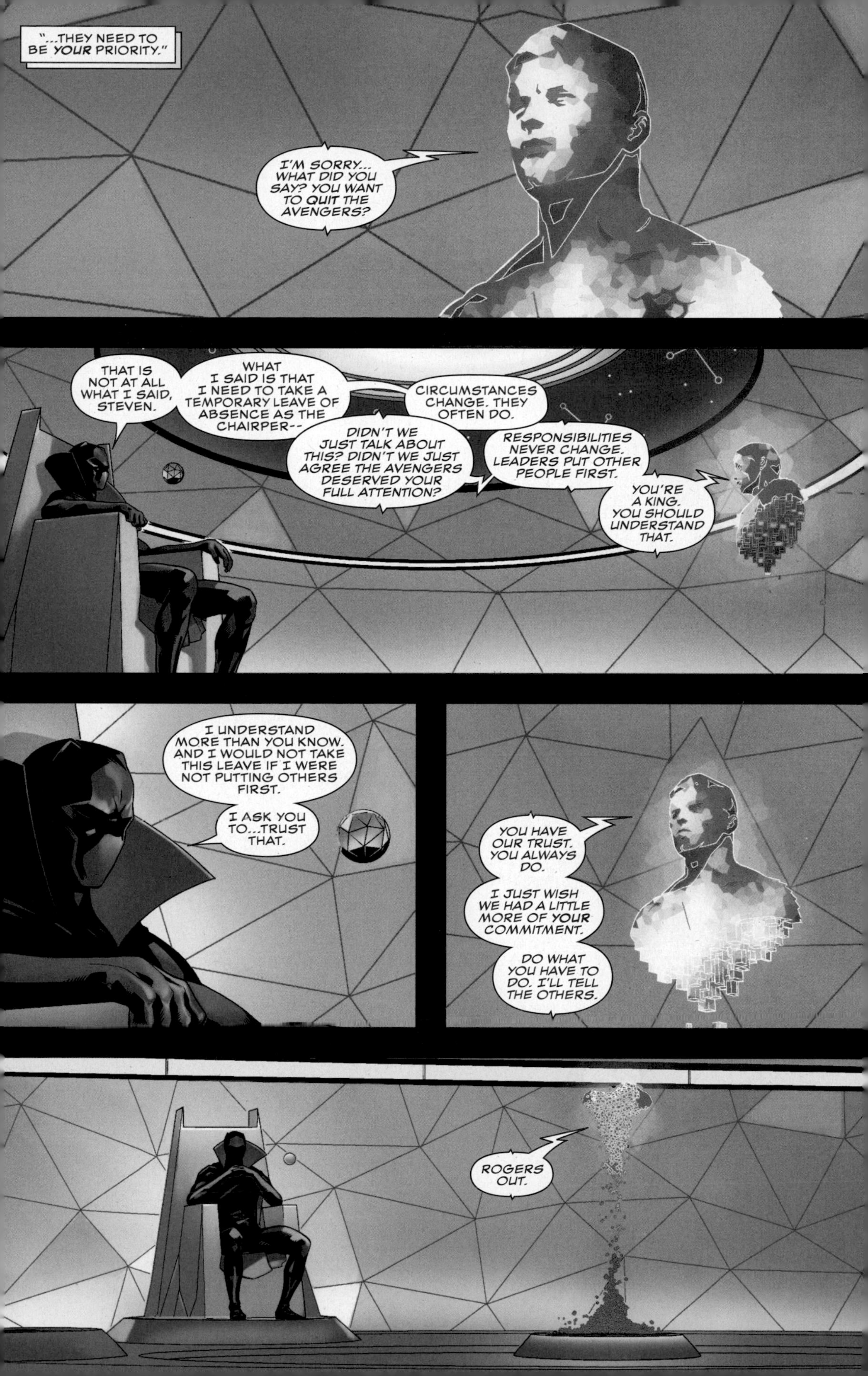
"...THEY NEED TO BE YOUR PRIORITY."
I'M SORRY... WHAT DID YOU SAY? YOU WANT TO QUIT THE AVENGERS?
THAT IS NOT AT ALL WHAT I SAID, STEVEN.
WHAT I SAID IS THAT I NEED TO TAKE A TEMPORARY LEAVE OF ABSENCE AS THE CHAIRPER--
DIDN'T WE JUST TALK ABOUT THIS? DIDN'T WE JUST AGREE THE AVENGERS DESERVED YOUR FULL ATTENTION?
CIRCUMSTANCES CHANGE. THEY OFTEN DO.
RESPONSIBILITIES NEVER CHANGE. LEADERS PUT OTHER PEOPLE FIRST.
YOU'RE A KING. YOU SHOULD UNDERSTAND THAT.
I UNDERSTAND MORE THAN YOU KNOW. AND I WOULD NOT TAKE THIS LEAVE IF I WERE NOT PUTTING OTHERS FIRST.
I ASK YOU TO...TRUST THAT.
YOU HAVE OUR TRUST. YOU ALWAYS DO.
I JUST WISH WE HAD A LITTLE MORE OF YOUR COMMITMENT.
DO WHAT YOU HAVE TO DO. I'LL TELL THE OTHERS.
ROGERS OUT.

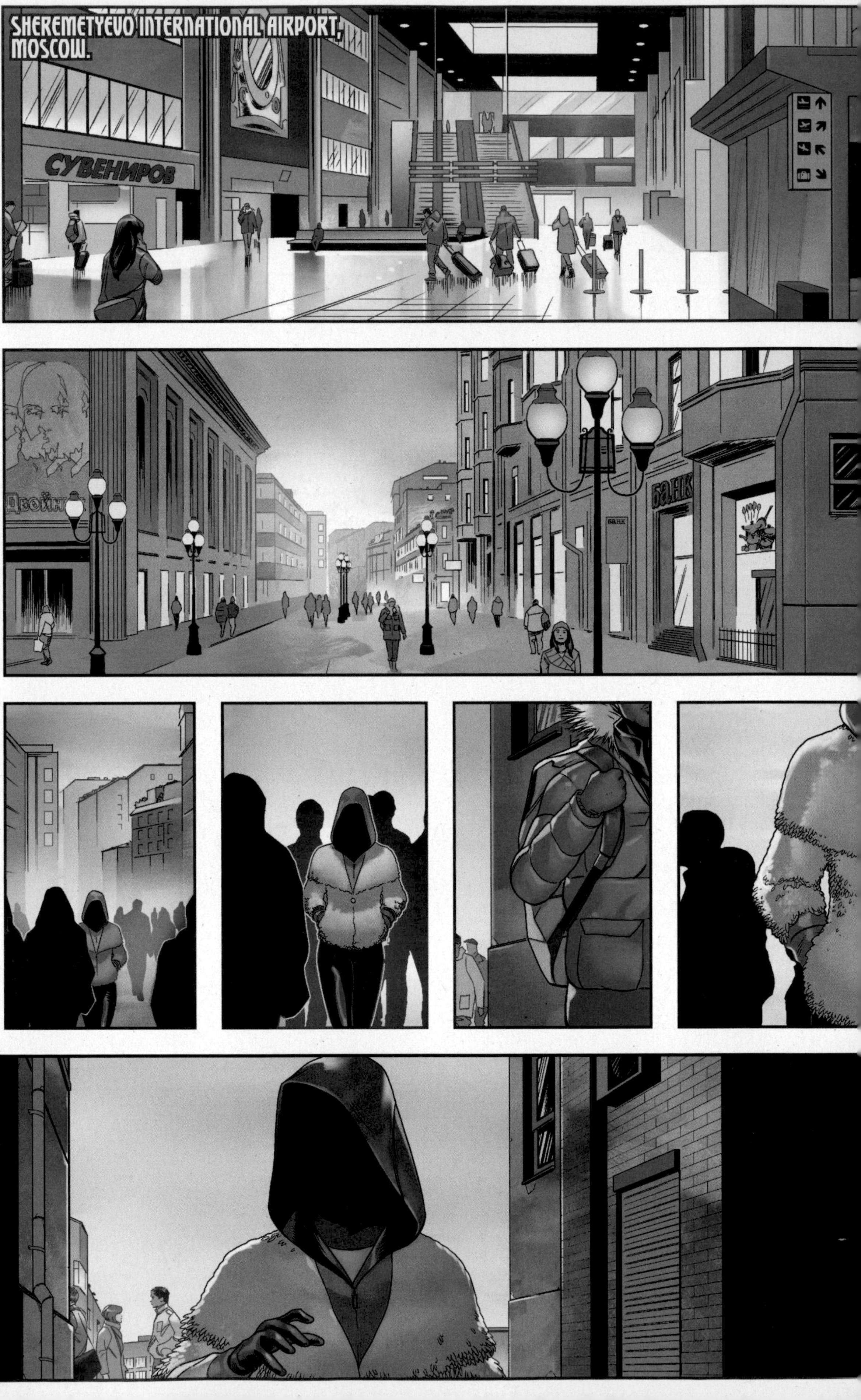
SHEREMETYEVO INTERNATIONAL AIRPORT, MOSCOW.
СУВЕНИРОВ
БАНК

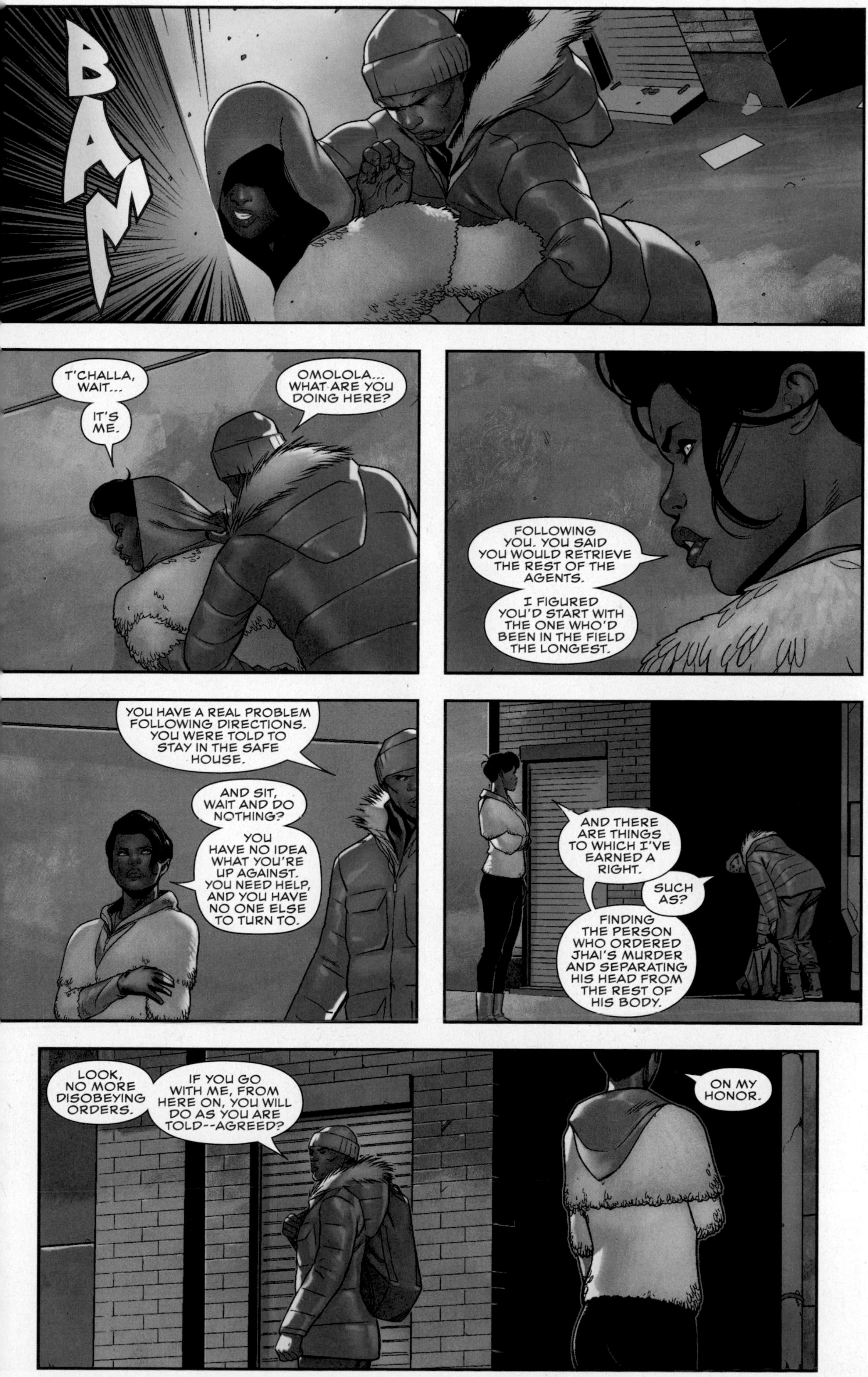
BAM
T'CHALLA, WAIT...
IT'S ME.
OMOLOLA... WHAT ARE YOU DOING HERE?
FOLLOWING YOU. YOU SAID YOU WOULD RETRIEVE THE REST OF THE AGENTS.
I FIGURED YOU'D START WITH THE ONE WHO'D BEEN IN THE FIELD THE LONGEST.
YOU HAVE A REAL PROBLEM FOLLOWING DIRECTIONS. YOU WERE TOLD TO STAY IN THE SAFE HOUSE.
AND SIT, WAIT AND DO NOTHING?
YOU HAVE NO IDEA WHAT YOU'RE UP AGAINST. YOU NEED HELP, AND YOU HAVE NO ONE ELSE TO TURN TO.
AND THERE ARE THINGS TO WHICH I'VE EARNED A RIGHT.
SUCH AS?
FINDING THE PERSON WHO ORDERED JHAI'S MURDER AND SEPARATING HIS HEAD FROM THE REST OF HIS BODY.
LOOK, NO MORE DISOBEYING ORDERS.
IF YOU GO WITH ME, FROM HERE ON, YOU WILL DO AS YOU ARE TOLD--AGREED?
ON MY HONOR.

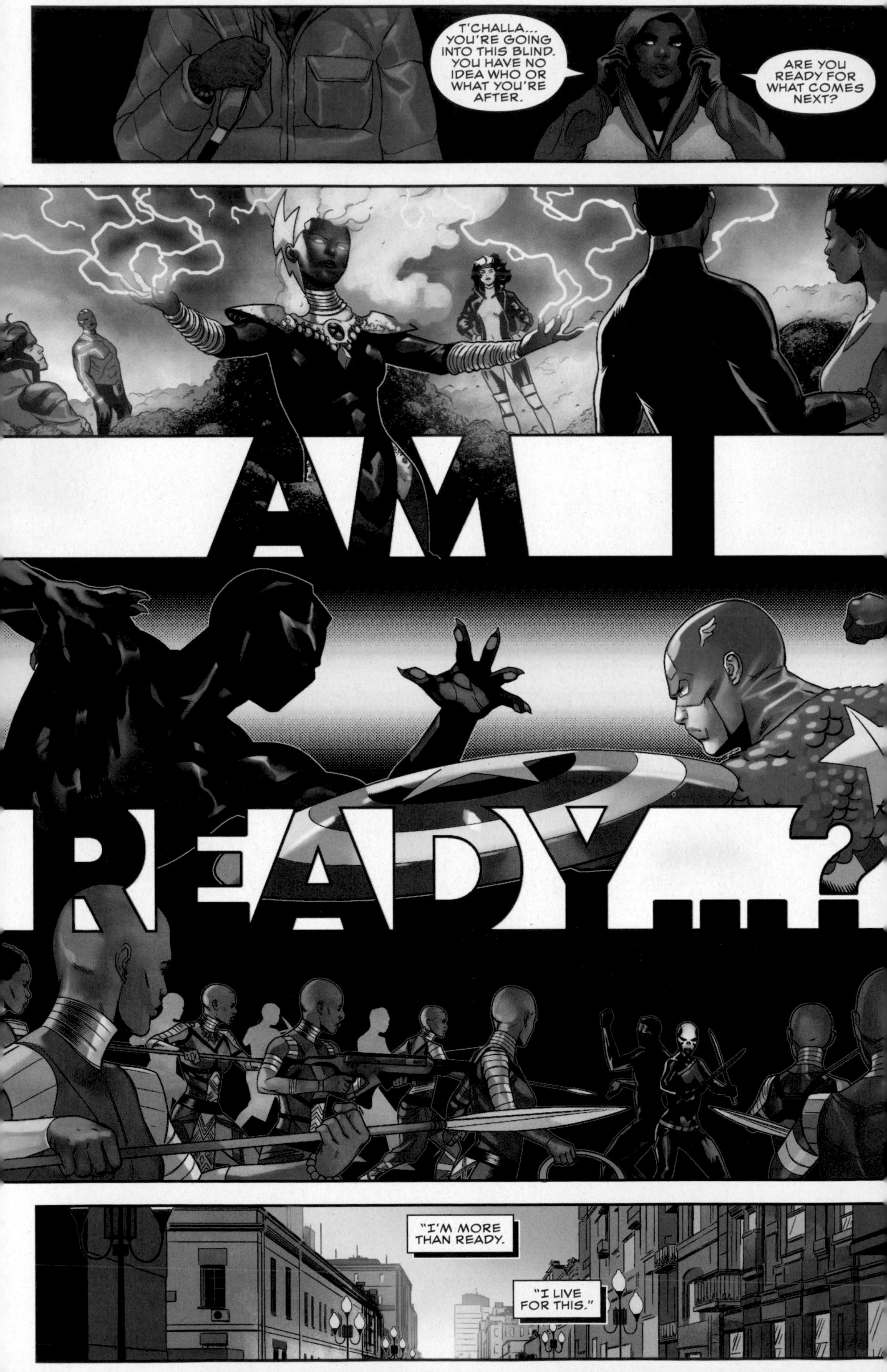
T'CHALLA... YOU'RE GOING INTO THIS BLIND. YOU HAVE NO IDEA WHO OR WHAT YOU'RE AFTER.
ARE YOU READY FOR WHAT COMES NEXT?
AM I READY...?
"I'M MORE THAN READY.
"I LIVE FOR THIS."

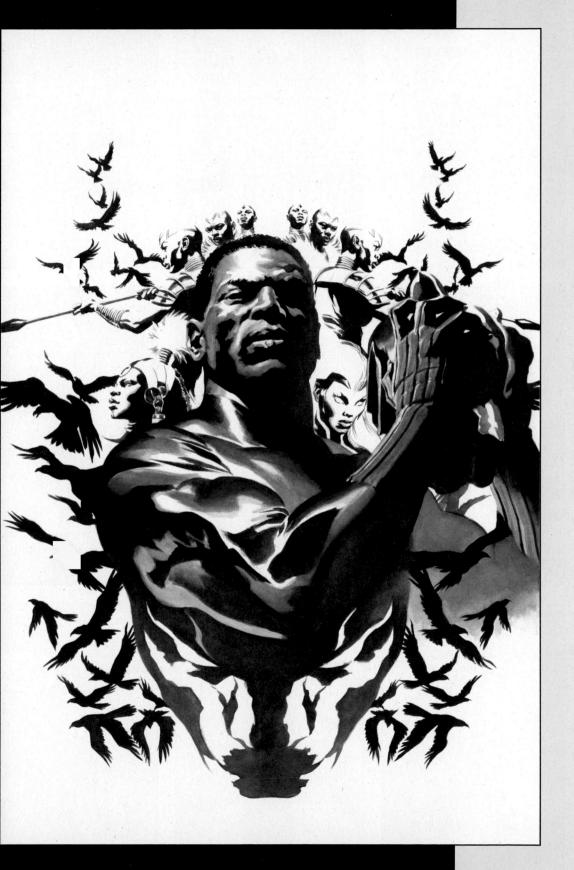

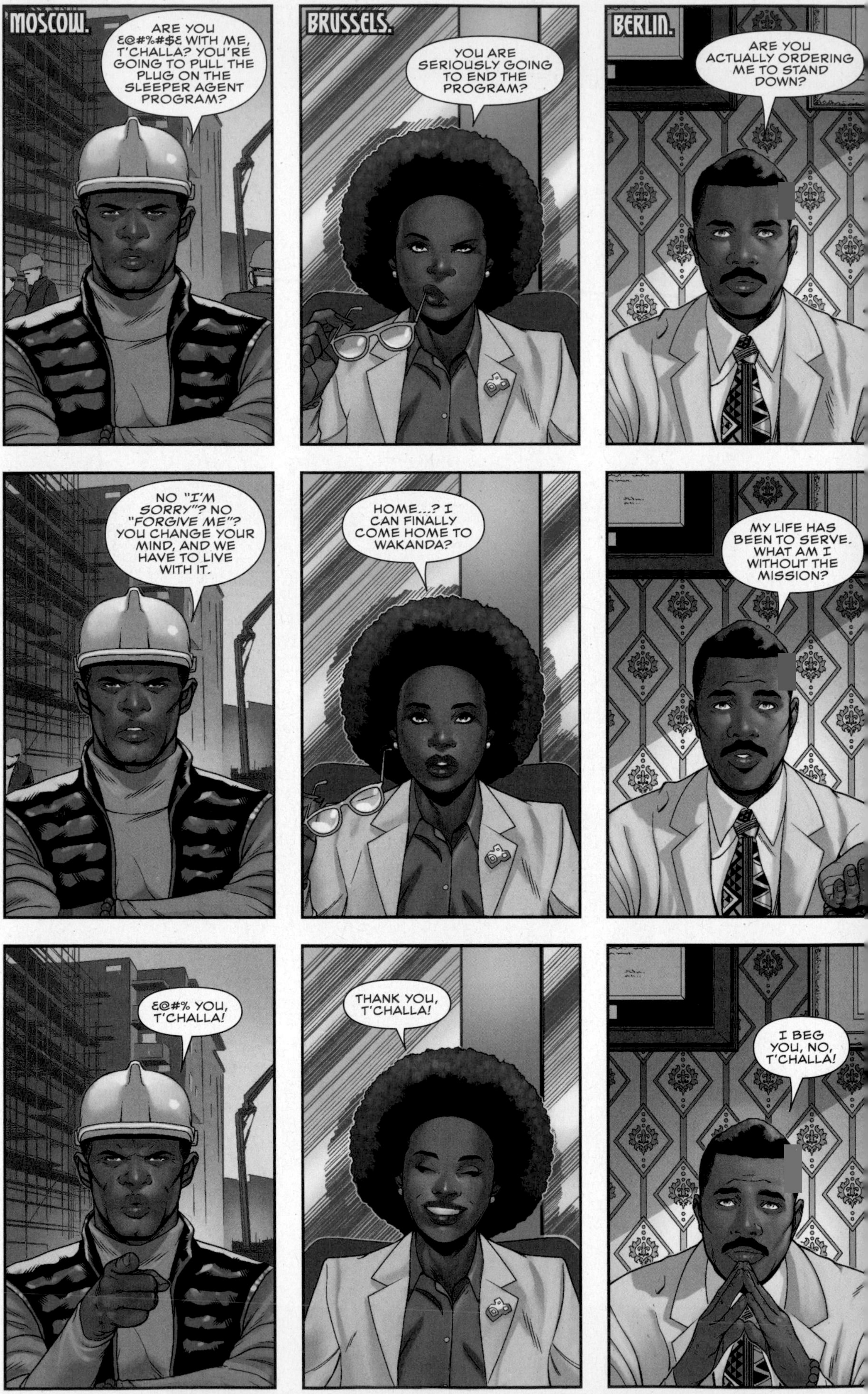
MOSCOW.
ARE YOU Ɛ@#%#$Ɛ WITH ME, T'CHALLA? YOU'RE GOING TO PULL THE PLUG ON THE SLEEPER AGENT PROGRAM?
BRUSSELS.
YOU ARE SERIOUSLY GOING TO END THE PROGRAM?
BERLIN.
ARE YOU ACTUALLY ORDERING ME TO STAND DOWN?
NO "I'M SORRY"? NO "FORGIVE ME"? YOU CHANGE YOUR MIND, AND WE HAVE TO LIVE WITH IT.
HOME...? I CAN FINALLY COME HOME TO WAKANDA?
MY LIFE HAS BEEN TO SERVE. WHAT AM I WITHOUT THE MISSION?
Ɛ@#% YOU, T'CHALLA!
THANK YOU, T'CHALLA!
I BEG YOU, NO, T'CHALLA!

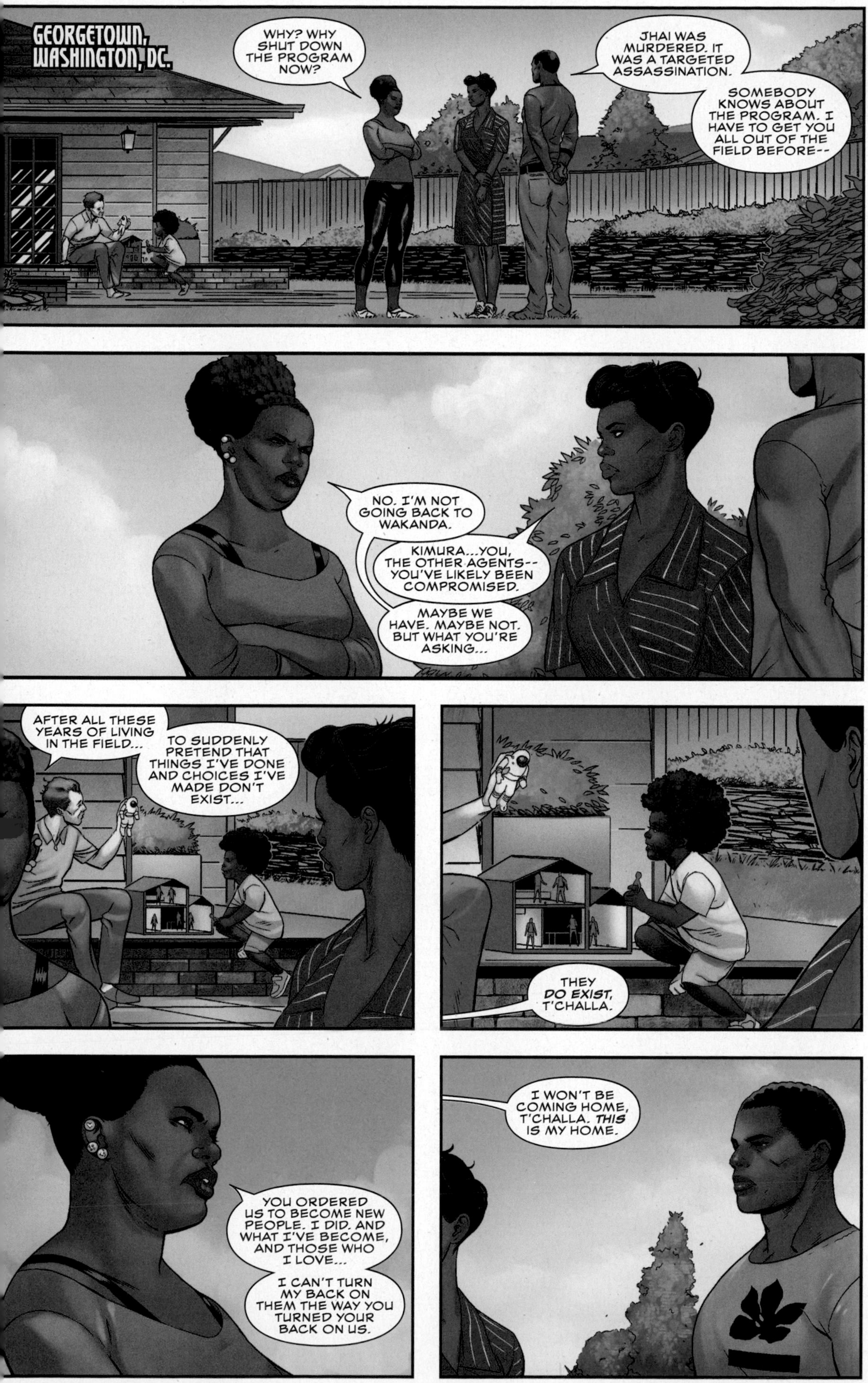
GEORGETOWN, WASHINGTON, DC.
WHY? WHY SHUT DOWN THE PROGRAM NOW?
JHAI WAS MURDERED. IT WAS A TARGETED ASSASSINATION.
SOMEBODY KNOWS ABOUT THE PROGRAM. I HAVE TO GET YOU ALL OUT OF THE FIELD BEFORE--
NO. I'M NOT GOING BACK TO WAKANDA.
KIMURA...YOU, THE OTHER AGENTS--YOU'VE LIKELY BEEN COMPROMISED.
MAYBE WE HAVE. MAYBE NOT. BUT WHAT YOU'RE ASKING...
AFTER ALL THESE YEARS OF LIVING IN THE FIELD...
TO SUDDENLY PRETEND THAT THINGS I'VE DONE AND CHOICES I'VE MADE DON'T EXIST...
THEY *DO EXIST*, T'CHALLA.
YOU ORDERED US TO BECOME NEW PEOPLE. I DID. AND WHAT I'VE BECOME, AND THOSE WHO I LOVE...
I CAN'T TURN MY BACK ON THEM THE WAY YOU TURNED YOUR BACK ON US.
I WON'T BE COMING HOME, T'CHALLA. *THIS* IS MY HOME.

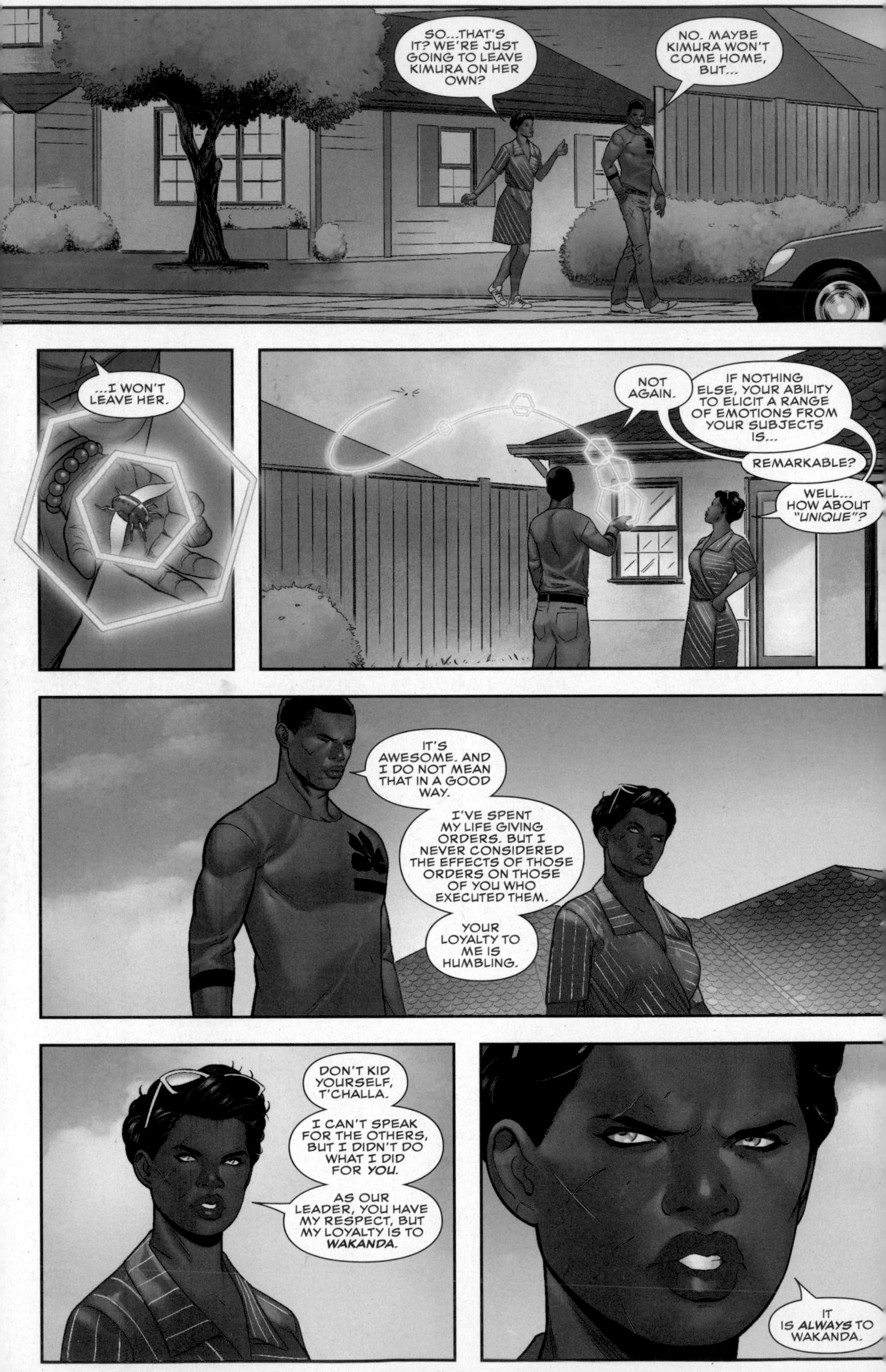
SO...THAT'S IT? WE'RE JUST GOING TO LEAVE KIMURA ON HER OWN?
NO. MAYBE KIMURA WON'T COME HOME, BUT...
...I WON'T LEAVE HER.
NOT AGAIN.
IF NOTHING ELSE, YOUR ABILITY TO ELICIT A RANGE OF EMOTIONS FROM YOUR SUBJECTS IS...
REMARKABLE?
WELL... HOW ABOUT "UNIQUE"?
IT'S AWESOME. AND I DO NOT MEAN THAT IN A GOOD WAY.
I'VE SPENT MY LIFE GIVING ORDERS. BUT I NEVER CONSIDERED THE EFFECTS OF THOSE ORDERS ON THOSE OF YOU WHO EXECUTED THEM.
YOUR LOYALTY TO ME IS HUMBLING.
DON'T KID YOURSELF, T'CHALLA.
I CAN'T SPEAK FOR THE OTHERS, BUT I DIDN'T DO WHAT I DID FOR YOU.
AS OUR LEADER, YOU HAVE MY RESPECT, BUT MY LOYALTY IS TO WAKANDA.
IT IS ALWAYS TO WAKANDA.

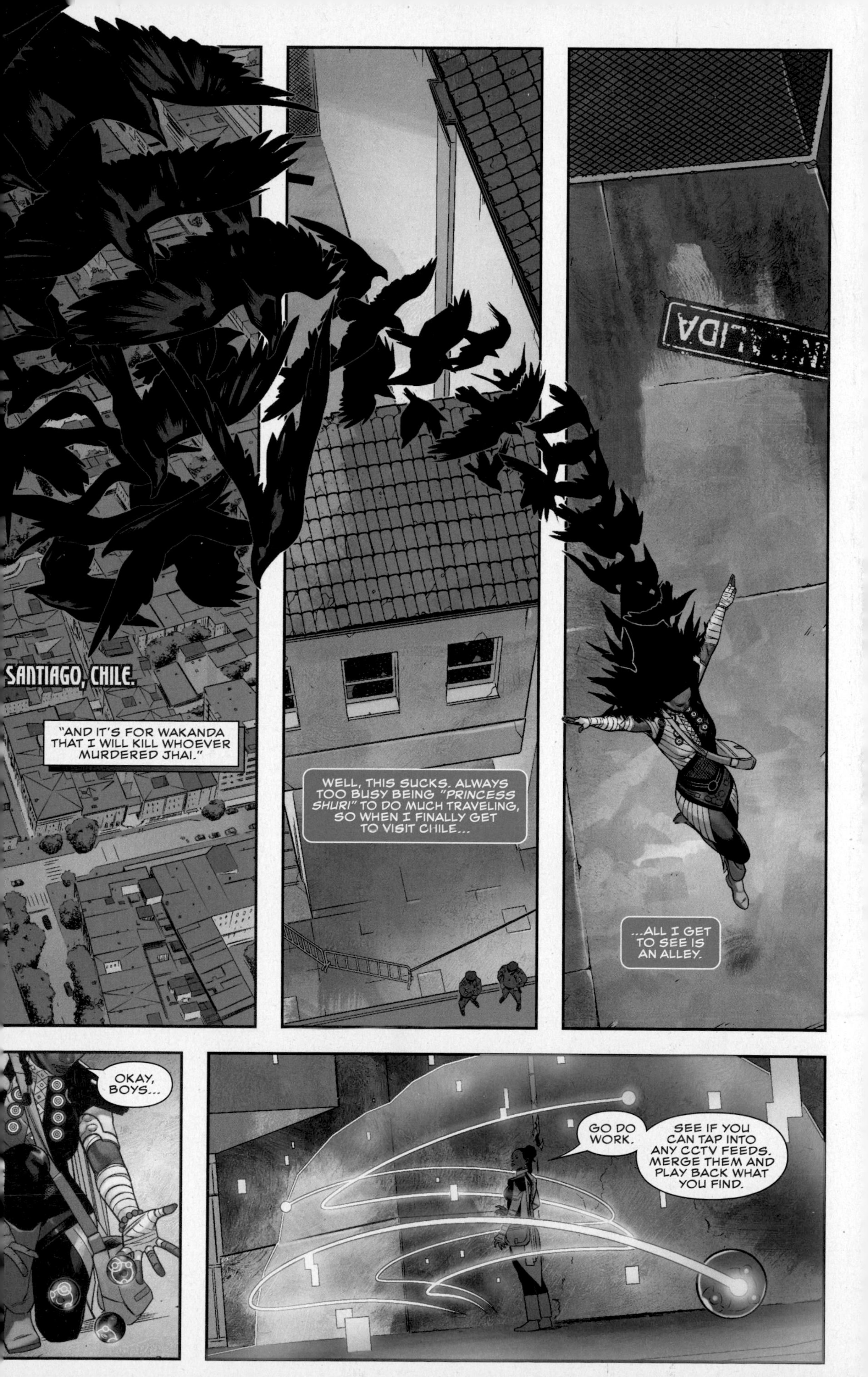
SANTIAGO, CHILE.
"AND IT'S FOR WAKANDA THAT I WILL KILL WHOEVER MURDERED JHAI."
WELL, THIS SUCKS. ALWAYS TOO BUSY BEING "PRINCESS SHURI" TO DO MUCH TRAVELING, SO WHEN I FINALLY GET TO VISIT CHILE...
...ALL I GET TO SEE IS AN ALLEY.
OKAY, BOYS...
GO DO WORK.
SEE IF YOU CAN TAP INTO ANY CCTV FEEDS. MERGE THEM AND PLAY BACK WHAT YOU FIND.

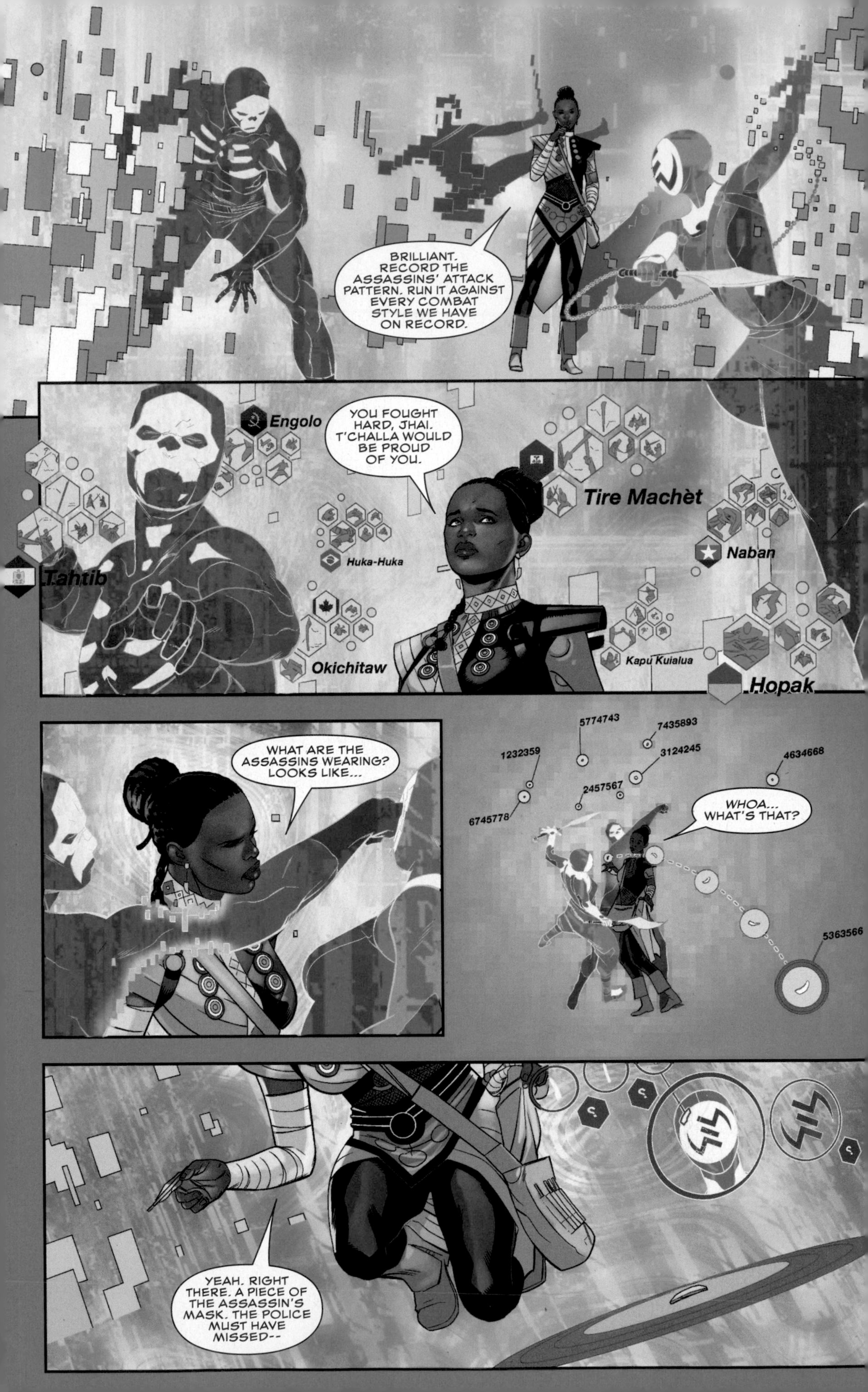
BRILLIANT. RECORD THE ASSASSINS' ATTACK PATTERN. RUN IT AGAINST EVERY COMBAT STYLE WE HAVE ON RECORD.
YOU FOUGHT HARD, JHAI. T'CHALLA WOULD BE PROUD OF YOU.
Engolo
Tahtib
Huka-Huka
Okichitaw
Tire Machèt
Naban
Kapu Kuialua
Hopak
WHAT ARE THE ASSASSINS WEARING? LOOKS LIKE...
5774743
7435893
1232359
3124245
4634668
2457567
6745778
WHOA... WHAT'S THAT?
5363566
YEAH. RIGHT THERE. A PIECE OF THE ASSASSIN'S MASK. THE POLICE MUST HAVE MISSED--

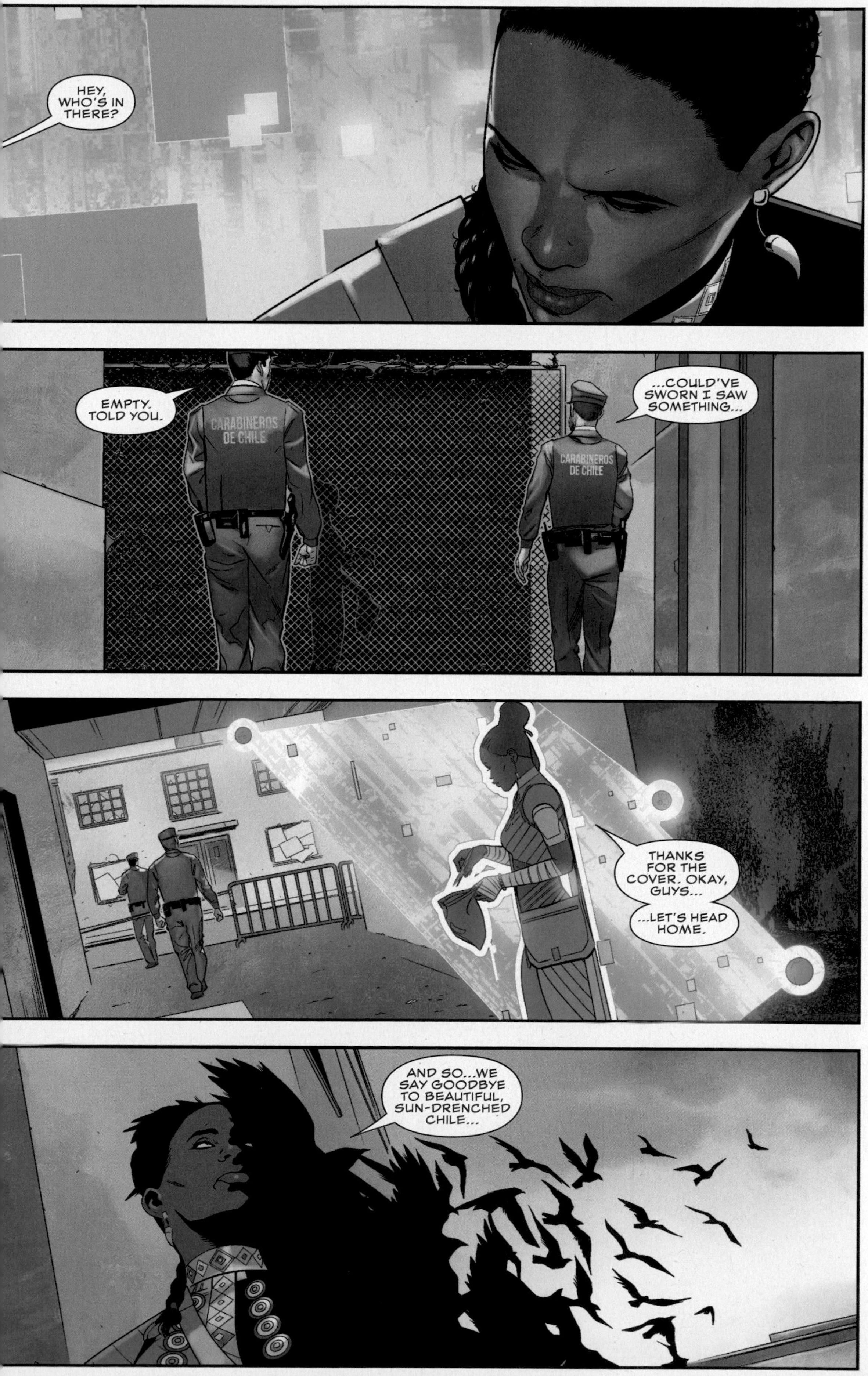
HEY, WHO'S IN THERE?
EMPTY. TOLD YOU.
...COULD'VE SWORN I SAW SOMETHING...
CARABINEROS DE CHILE
CARABINEROS DE CHILE
THANKS FOR THE COVER. OKAY, GUYS...
...LET'S HEAD HOME.
AND SO...WE SAY GOODBYE TO BEAUTIFUL, SUN-DRENCHED CHILE...

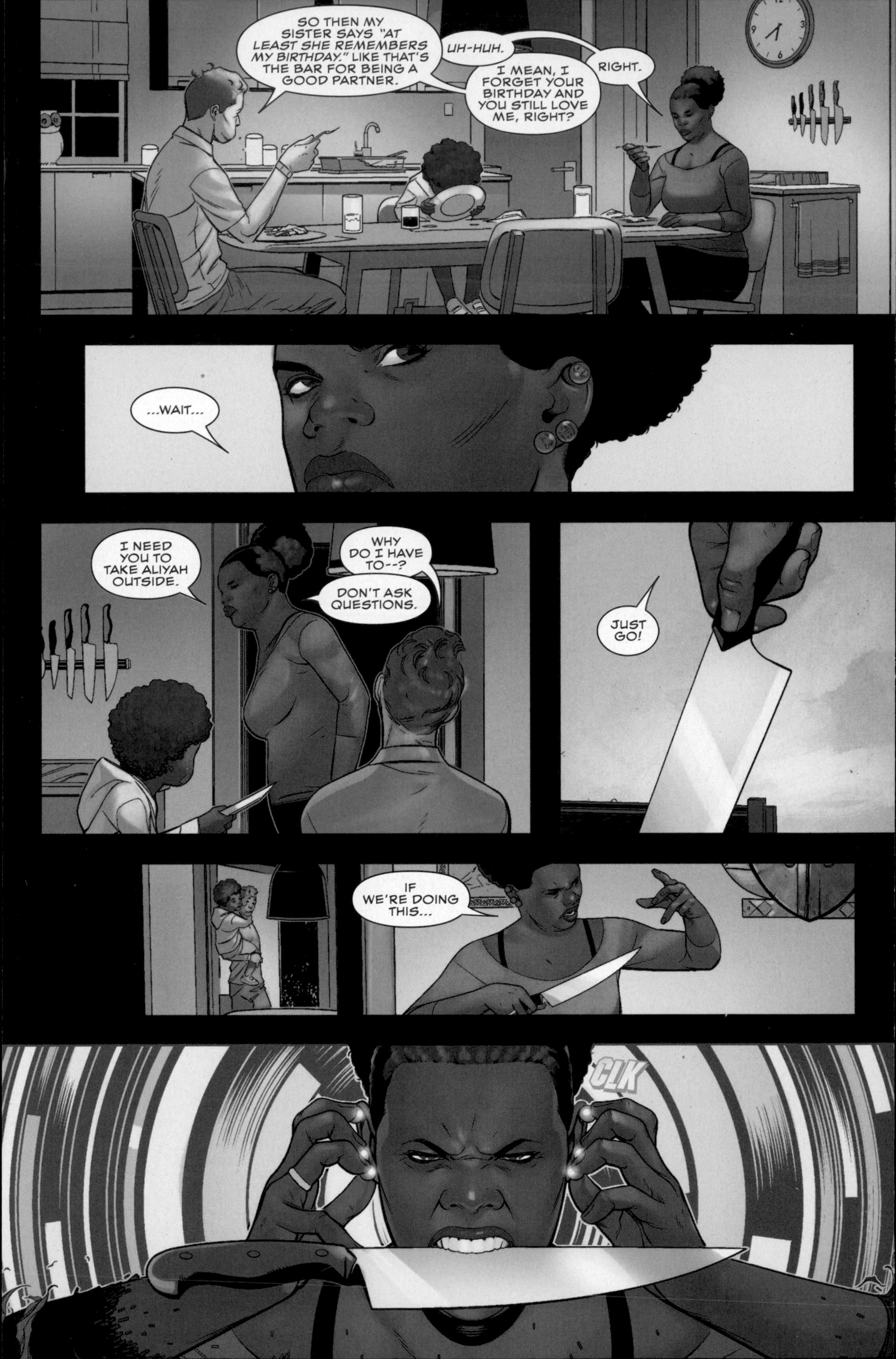
SO THEN MY SISTER SAYS "AT LEAST SHE REMEMBERS MY BIRTHDAY." LIKE THAT'S THE BAR FOR BEING A GOOD PARTNER.
UH-HUH.
RIGHT.
I MEAN, I FORGET YOUR BIRTHDAY AND YOU STILL LOVE ME, RIGHT?
...WAIT...
I NEED YOU TO TAKE ALIYAH OUTSIDE.
WHY DO I HAVE TO--?
DON'T ASK QUESTIONS.
JUST GO!
IF WE'RE DOING THIS...
CLK

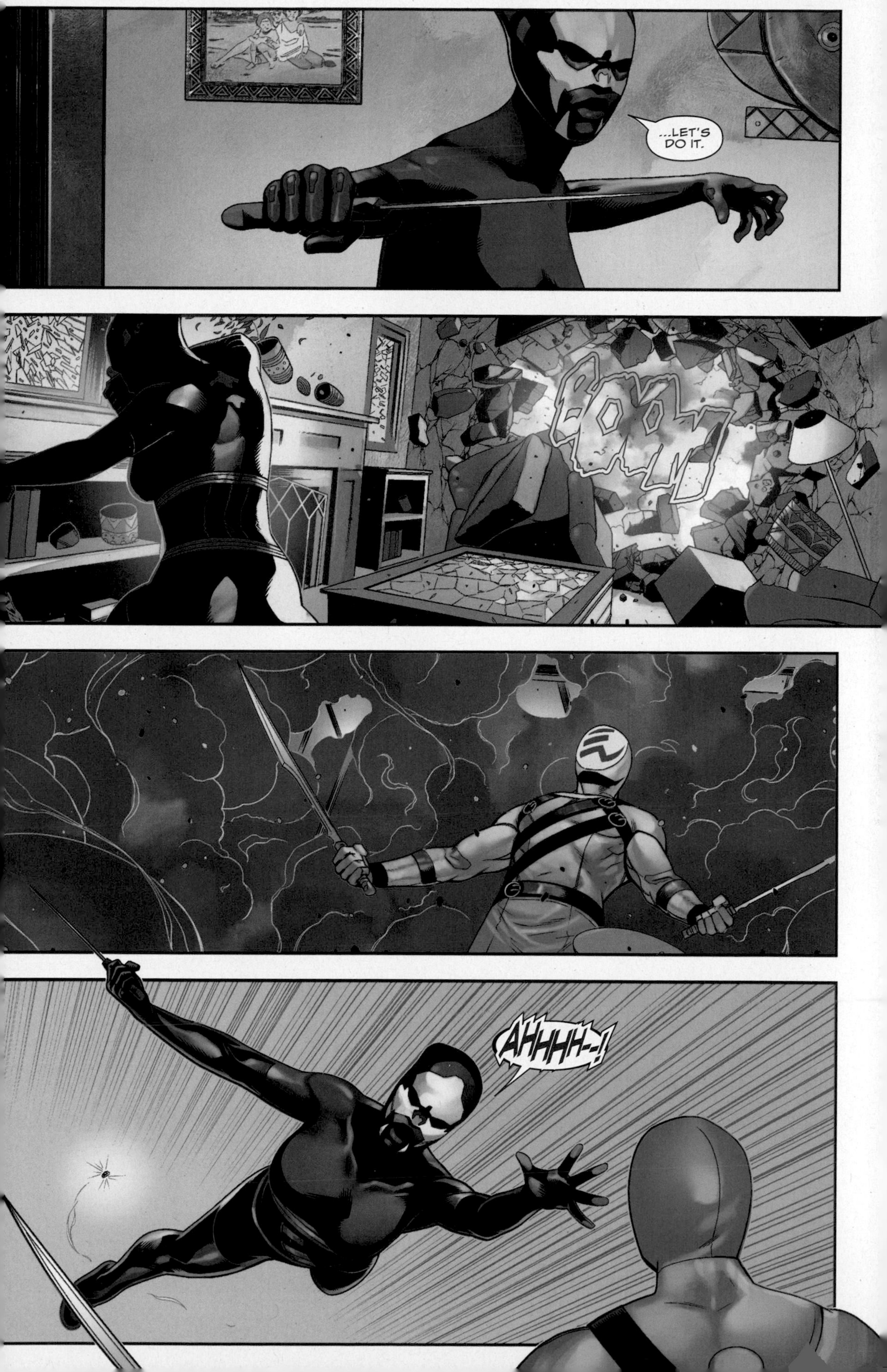
...LET'S DO IT.
BOOM
AHHHH--!

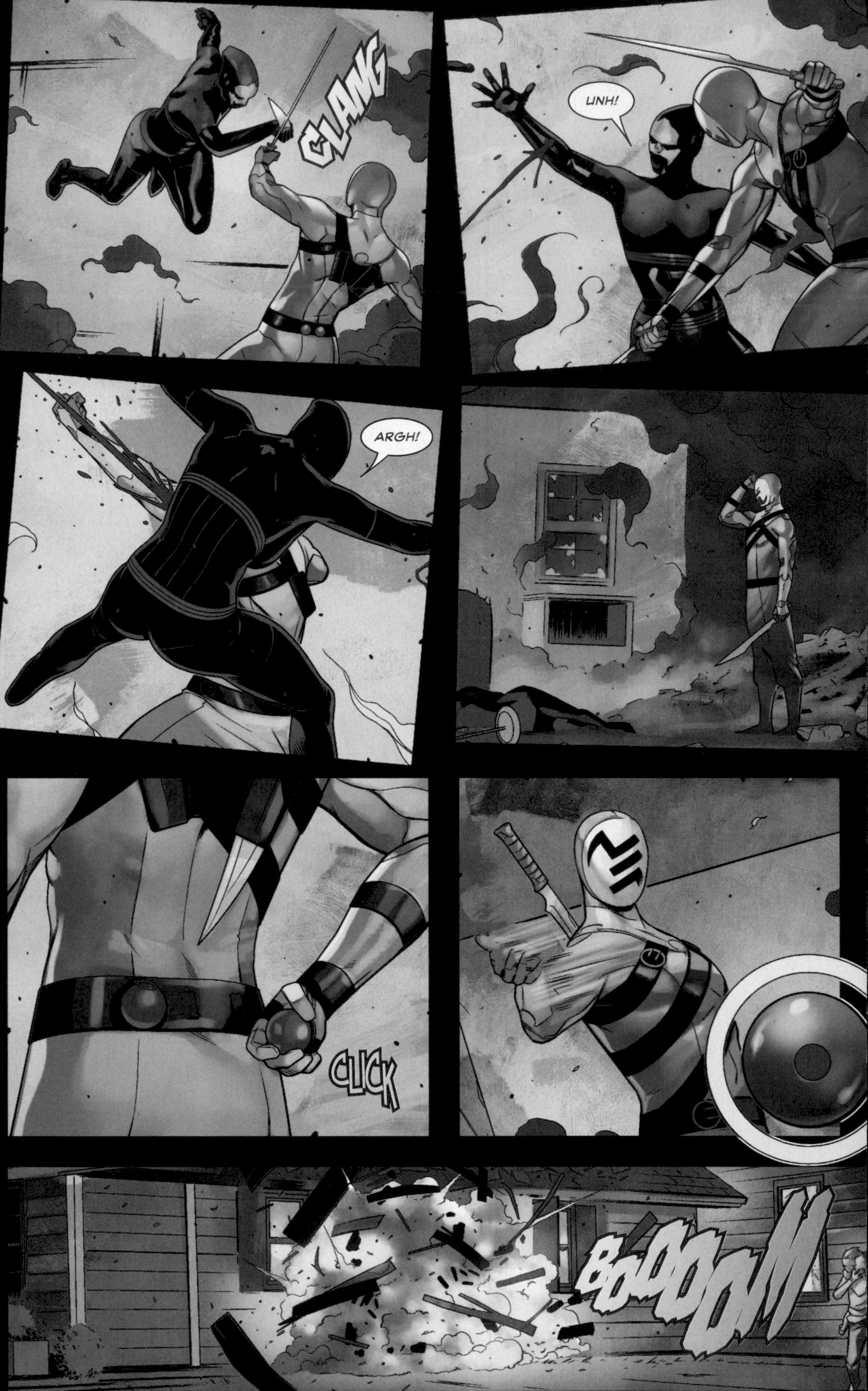
CLANG
UNH!
ARGH!
CLICK
BOOOOOM

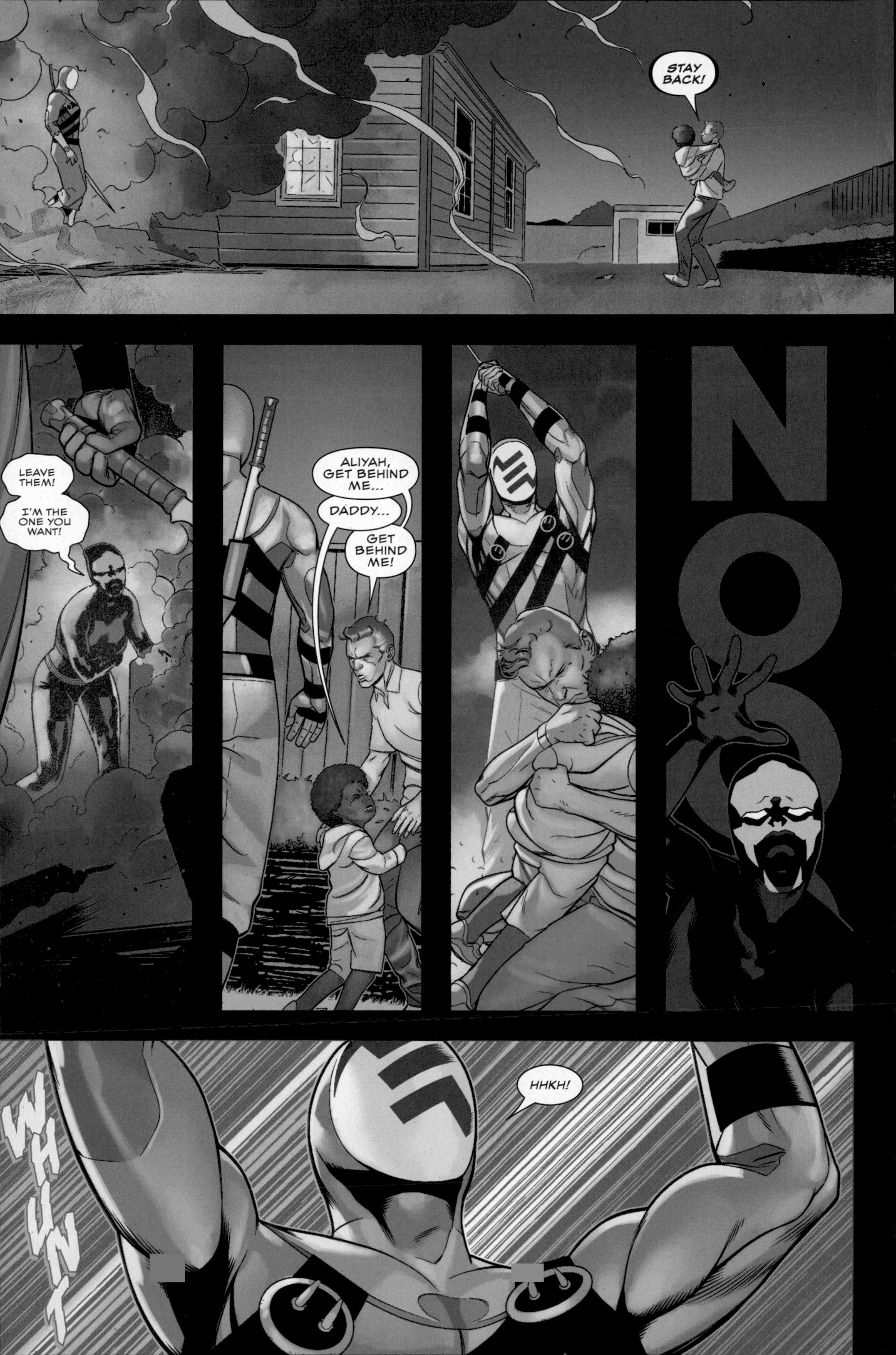
STAY BACK!
LEAVE THEM!
I'M THE ONE YOU WANT!
ALIYAH, GET BEHIND ME...
DADDY...
GET BEHIND ME!
NO
HHKH!
WHUNT

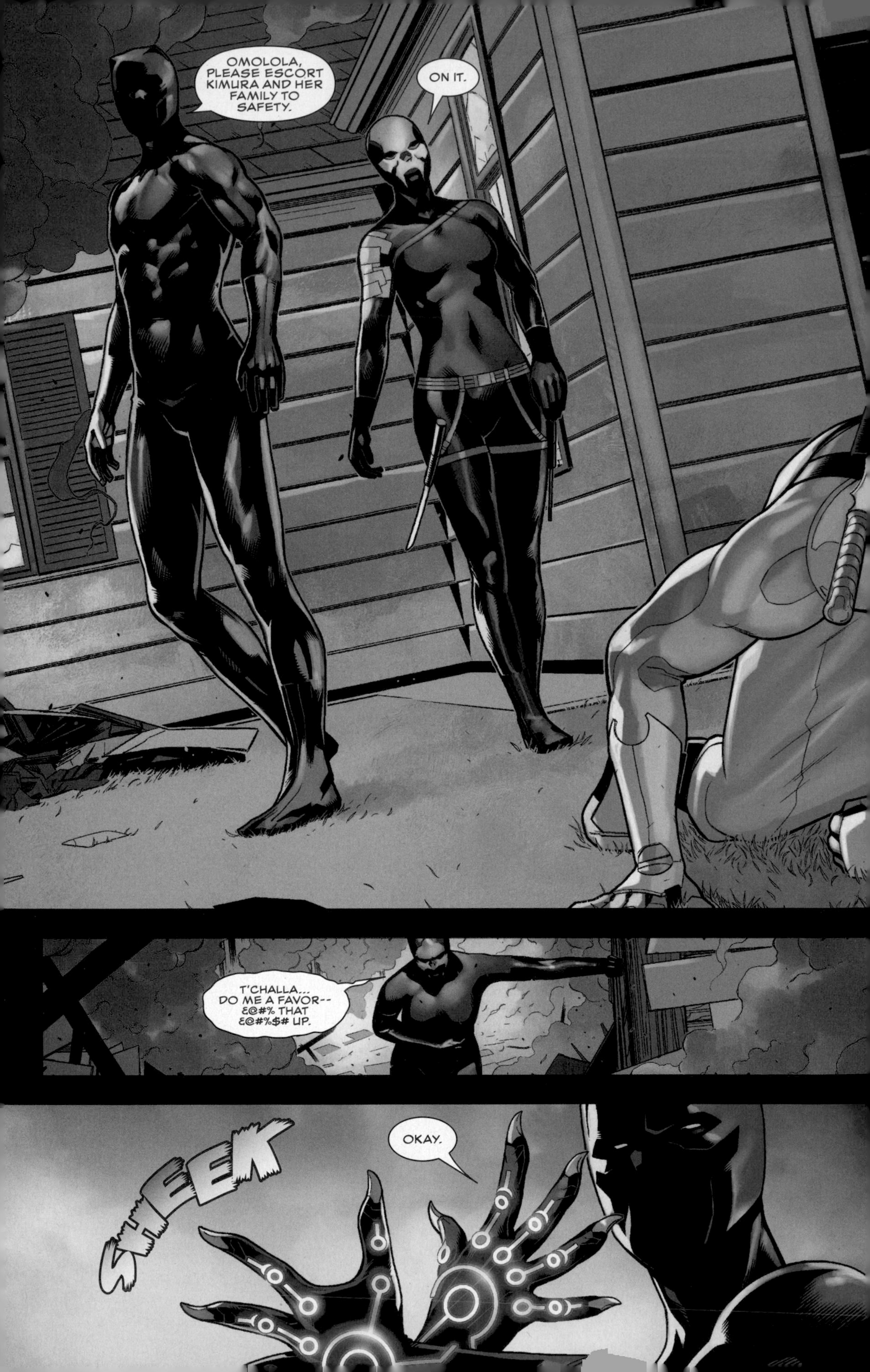
OMOLOLA, PLEASE ESCORT KIMURA AND HER FAMILY TO SAFETY.
ON IT.
T'CHALLA... DO ME A FAVOR-- &@#% THAT &@#%$# UP.
SHEEK
OKAY.

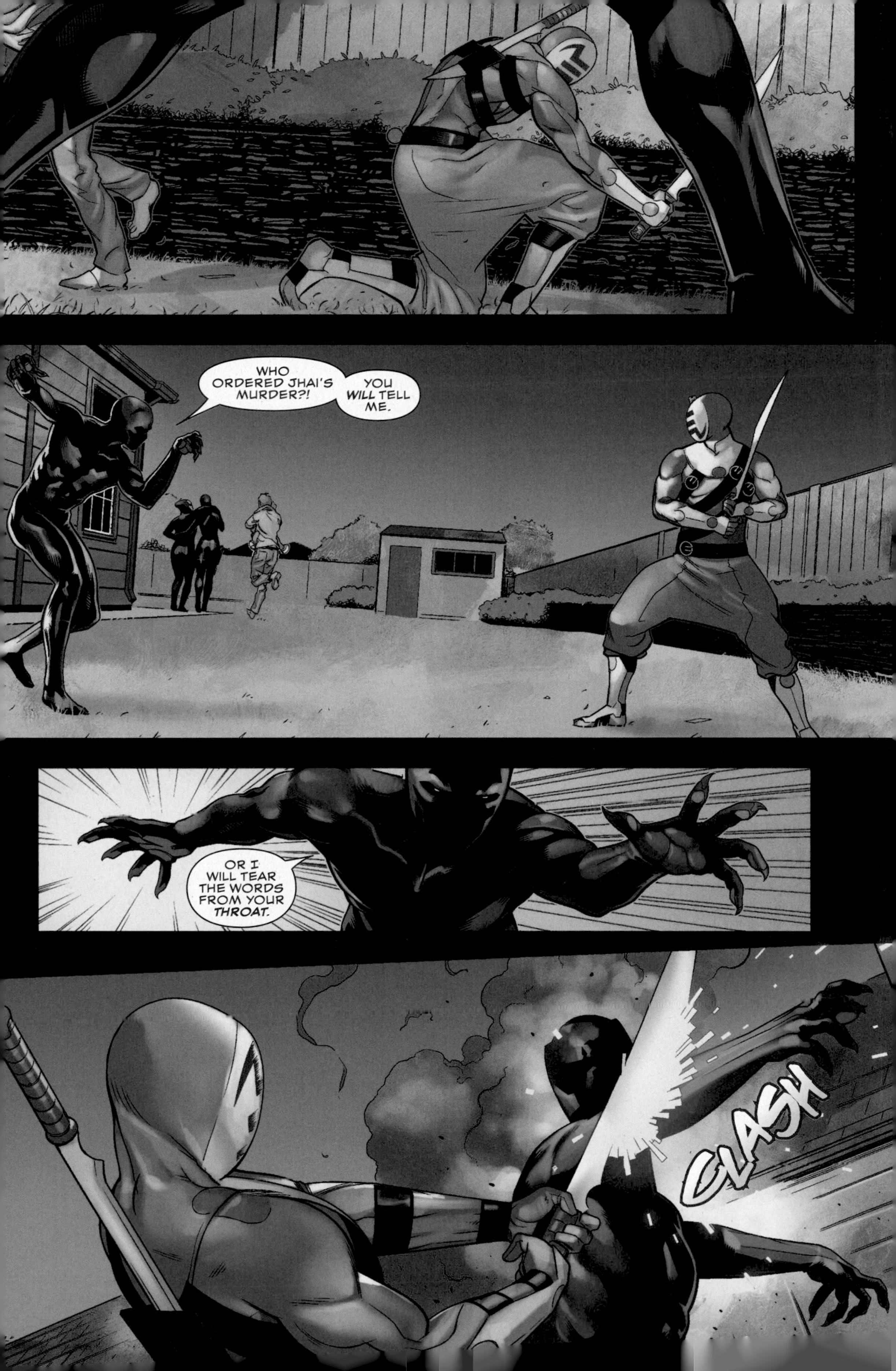
WHO ORDERED JHAI'S MURDER?!
YOU *WILL* TELL ME.
OR I WILL TEAR THE WORDS FROM YOUR *THROAT.*
CLASH

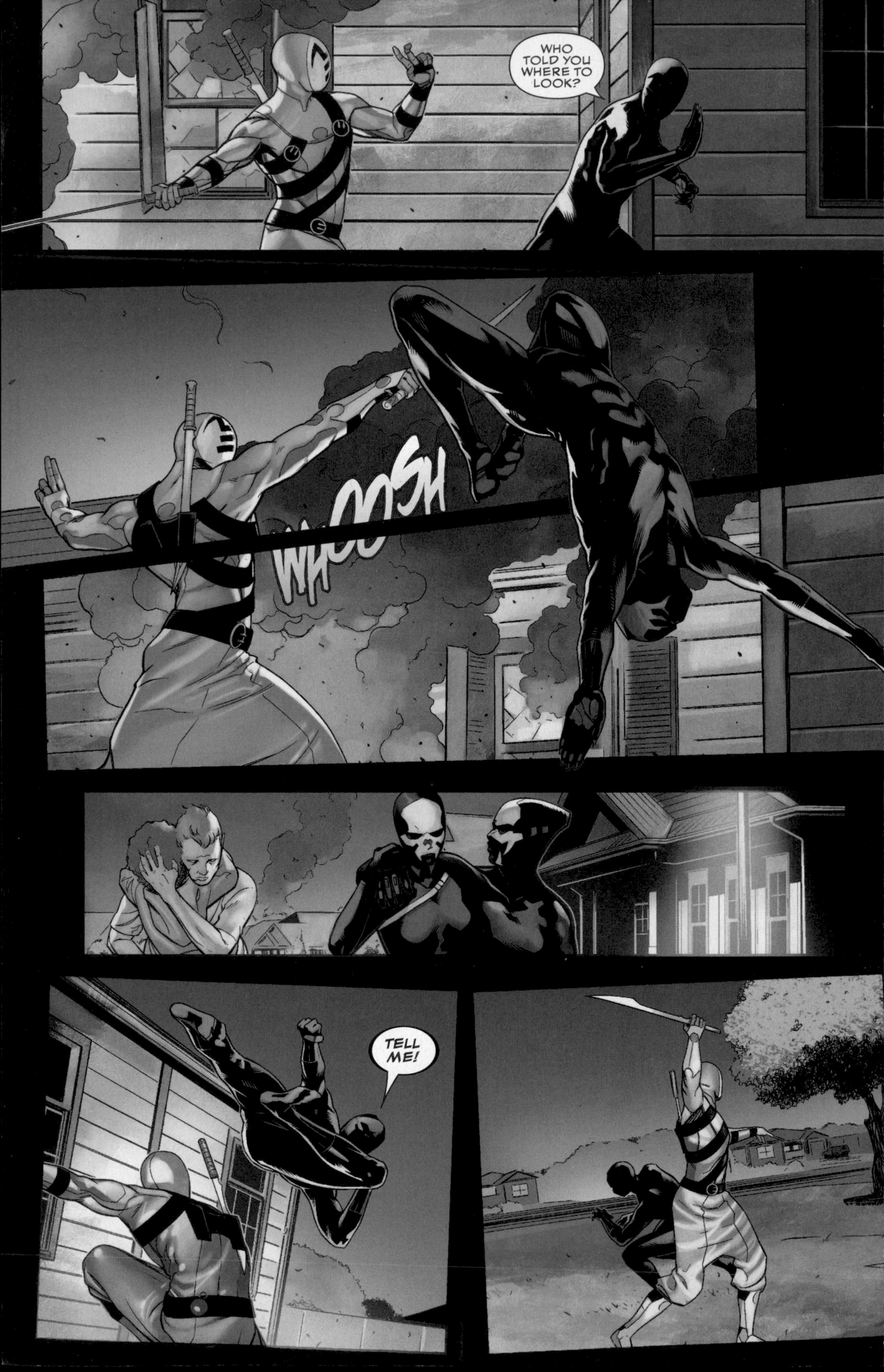
WHO TOLD YOU WHERE TO LOOK?
WHOOSH
TELL ME!

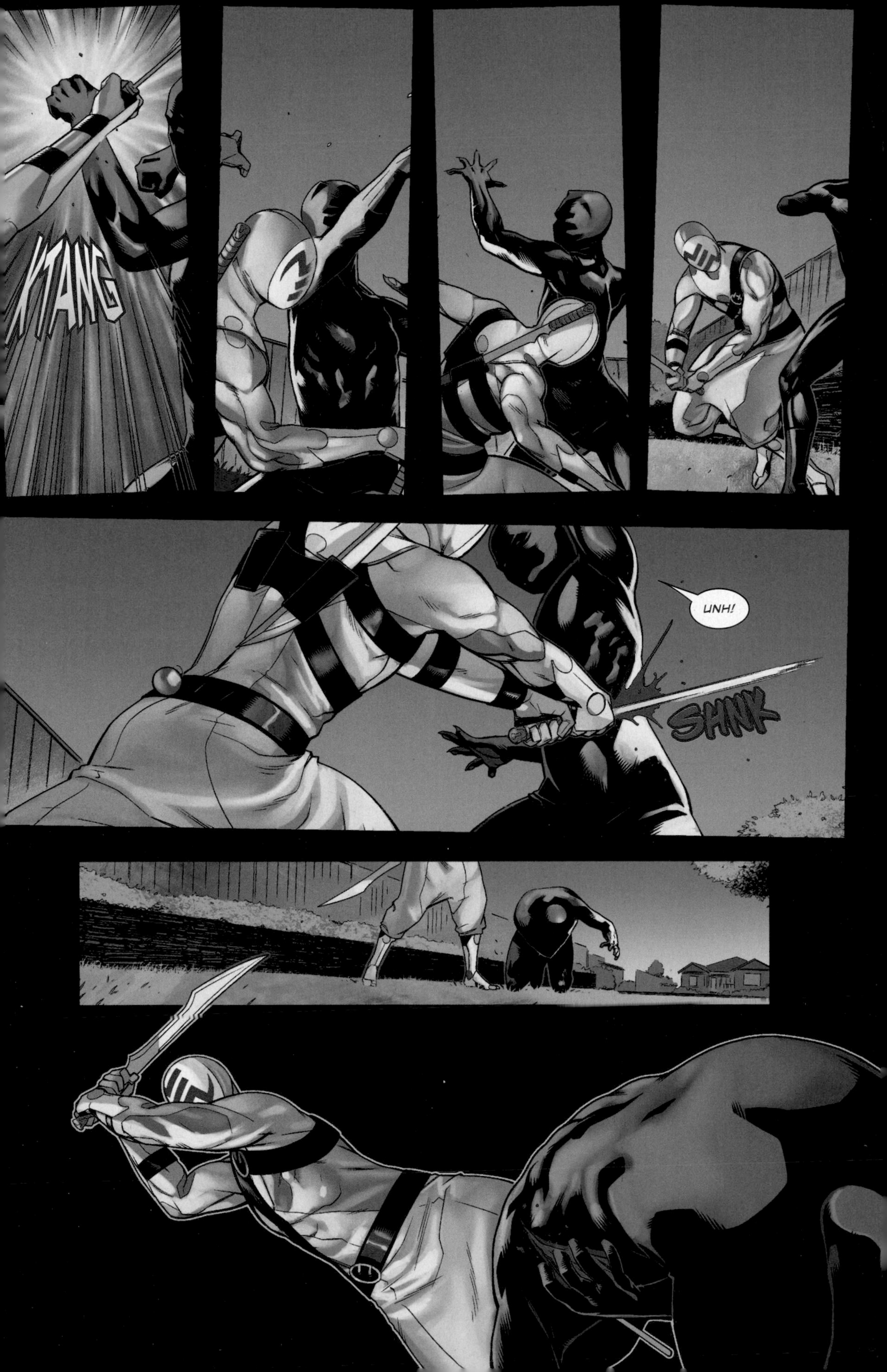
KTANG
UNH!
SHNK

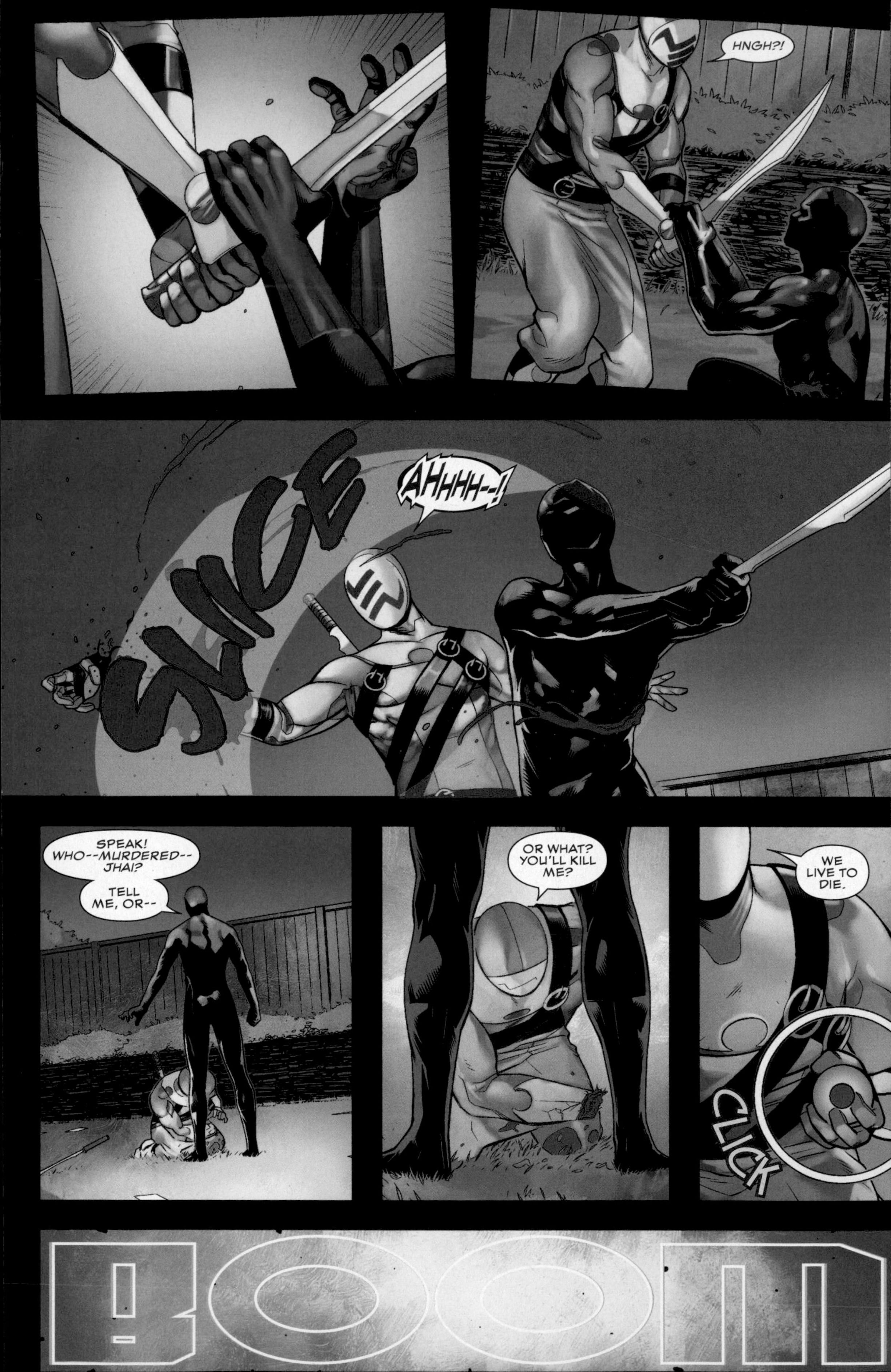
HNGH?!
SLICE
AHHHH--!
SPEAK! WHO--MURDERED--JHAI?
TELL ME, OR--
OR WHAT? YOU'LL KILL ME?
WE LIVE TO DIE.
CLICK
BOOM

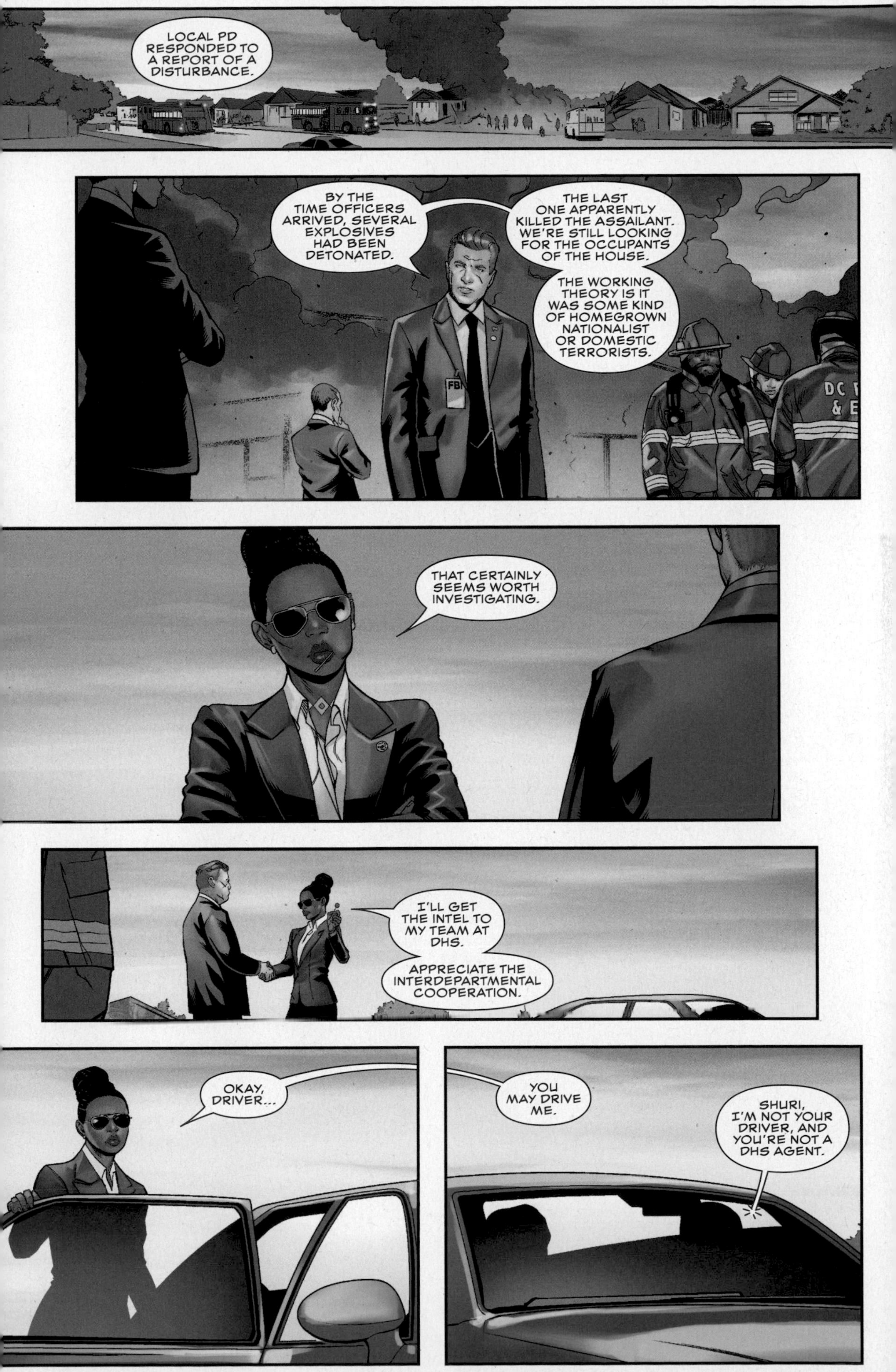
LOCAL PD RESPONDED TO A REPORT OF A DISTURBANCE.
BY THE TIME OFFICERS ARRIVED, SEVERAL EXPLOSIVES HAD BEEN DETONATED.
THE LAST ONE APPARENTLY KILLED THE ASSAILANT. WE'RE STILL LOOKING FOR THE OCCUPANTS OF THE HOUSE.
THE WORKING THEORY IS IT WAS SOME KIND OF HOMEGROWN NATIONALIST OR DOMESTIC TERRORISTS.
FBI
DC
& E
THAT CERTAINLY SEEMS WORTH INVESTIGATING.
I'LL GET THE INTEL TO MY TEAM AT DHS.
APPRECIATE THE INTERDEPARTMENTAL COOPERATION.
OKAY, DRIVER...
YOU MAY DRIVE ME.
SHURI, I'M NOT YOUR DRIVER, AND YOU'RE NOT A DHS AGENT.

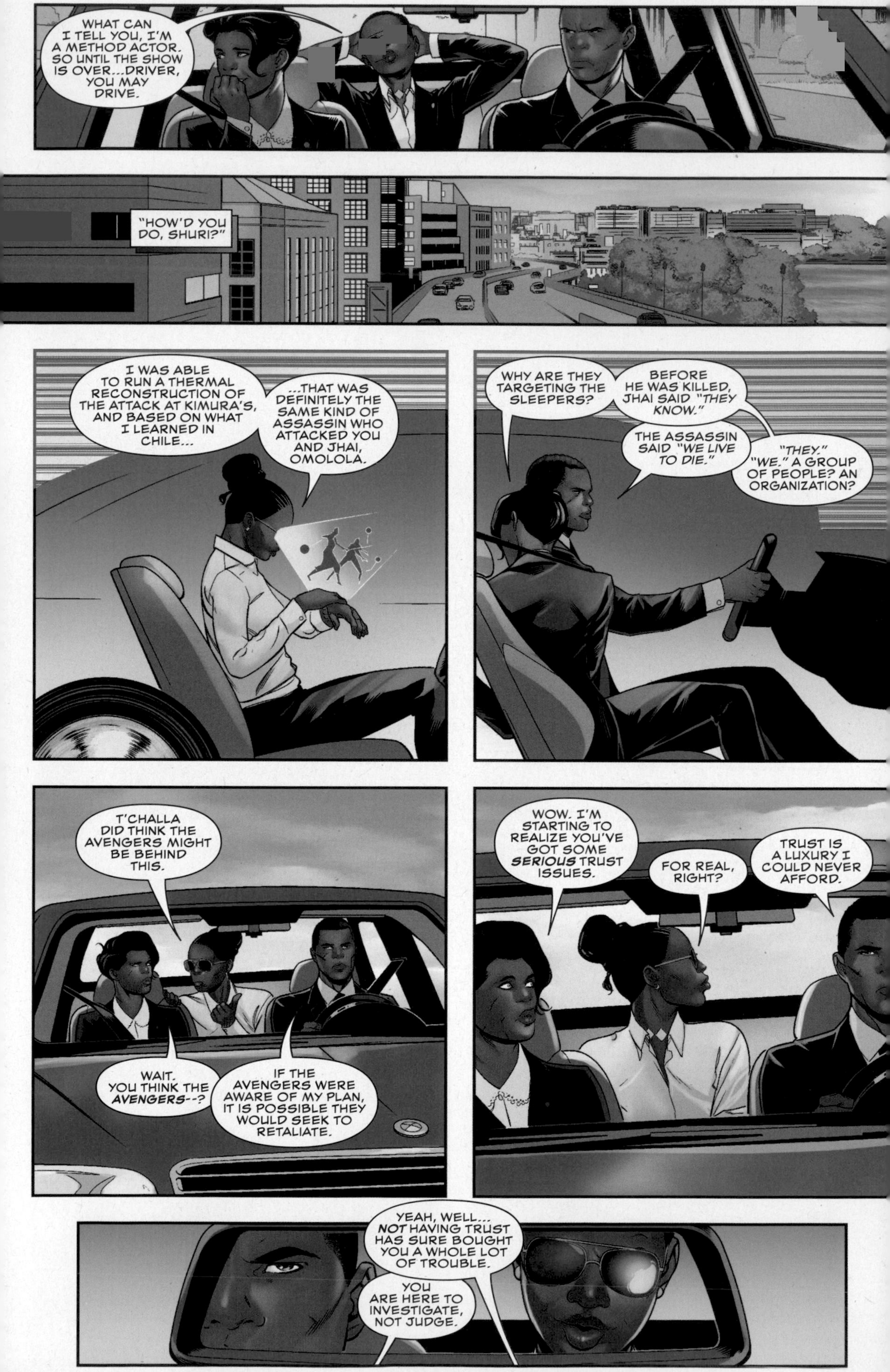
WHAT CAN I TELL YOU, I'M A METHOD ACTOR. SO UNTIL THE SHOW IS OVER...DRIVER, YOU MAY DRIVE.
"HOW'D YOU DO, SHURI?"
I WAS ABLE TO RUN A THERMAL RECONSTRUCTION OF THE ATTACK AT KIMURA'S, AND BASED ON WHAT I LEARNED IN CHILE...
...THAT WAS DEFINITELY THE SAME KIND OF ASSASSIN WHO ATTACKED YOU AND JHAI, OMOLOLA.
WHY ARE THEY TARGETING THE SLEEPERS?
BEFORE HE WAS KILLED, JHAI SAID *"THEY KNOW."*
THE ASSASSIN SAID *"WE LIVE TO DIE."*
"THEY." "WE." A GROUP OF PEOPLE? AN ORGANIZATION?
T'CHALLA DID THINK THE AVENGERS MIGHT BE BEHIND THIS.
WAIT. YOU THINK THE ***AVENGERS***--?
IF THE AVENGERS WERE AWARE OF MY PLAN, IT IS POSSIBLE THEY WOULD SEEK TO RETALIATE.
WOW. I'M STARTING TO REALIZE YOU'VE GOT SOME ***SERIOUS*** TRUST ISSUES.
FOR REAL, RIGHT?
TRUST IS A LUXURY I COULD NEVER AFFORD.
YEAH, WELL... ***NOT*** HAVING TRUST HAS SURE BOUGHT YOU A WHOLE LOT OF TROUBLE.
YOU ARE HERE TO INVESTIGATE, NOT JUDGE.

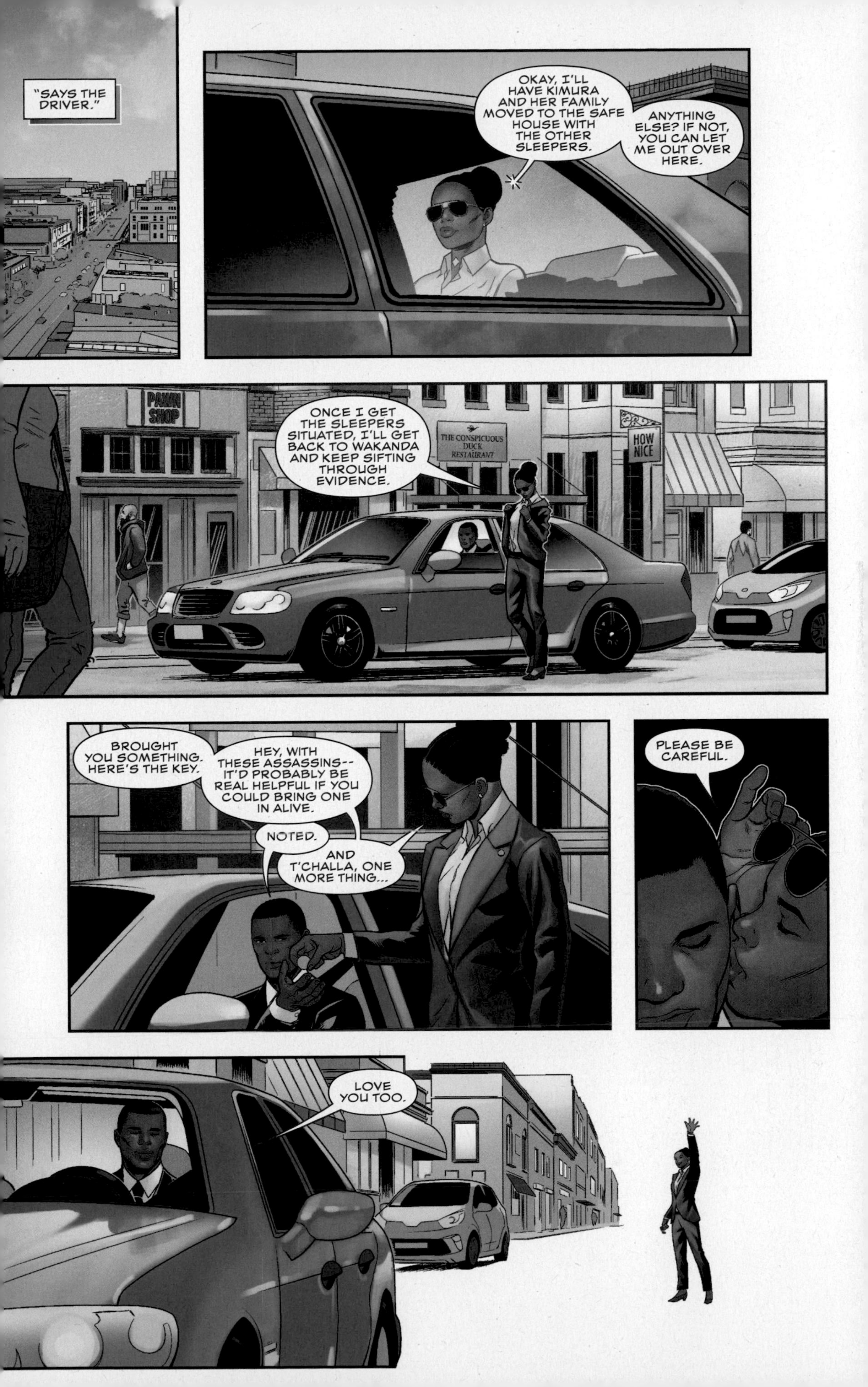
"SAYS THE DRIVER."
OKAY, I'LL HAVE KIMURA AND HER FAMILY MOVED TO THE SAFE HOUSE WITH THE OTHER SLEEPERS.
ANYTHING ELSE? IF NOT, YOU CAN LET ME OUT OVER HERE.
PAWN SHOP
THE CONSPICUOUS DUCK RESTAURANT
HOW NICE
ONCE I GET THE SLEEPERS SITUATED, I'LL GET BACK TO WAKANDA AND KEEP SIFTING THROUGH EVIDENCE.
BROUGHT YOU SOMETHING. HERE'S THE KEY.
HEY, WITH THESE ASSASSINS-- IT'D PROBABLY BE REAL HELPFUL IF YOU COULD BRING ONE IN ALIVE.
NOTED.
AND T'CHALLA, ONE MORE THING...
PLEASE BE CAREFUL.
LOVE YOU TOO.

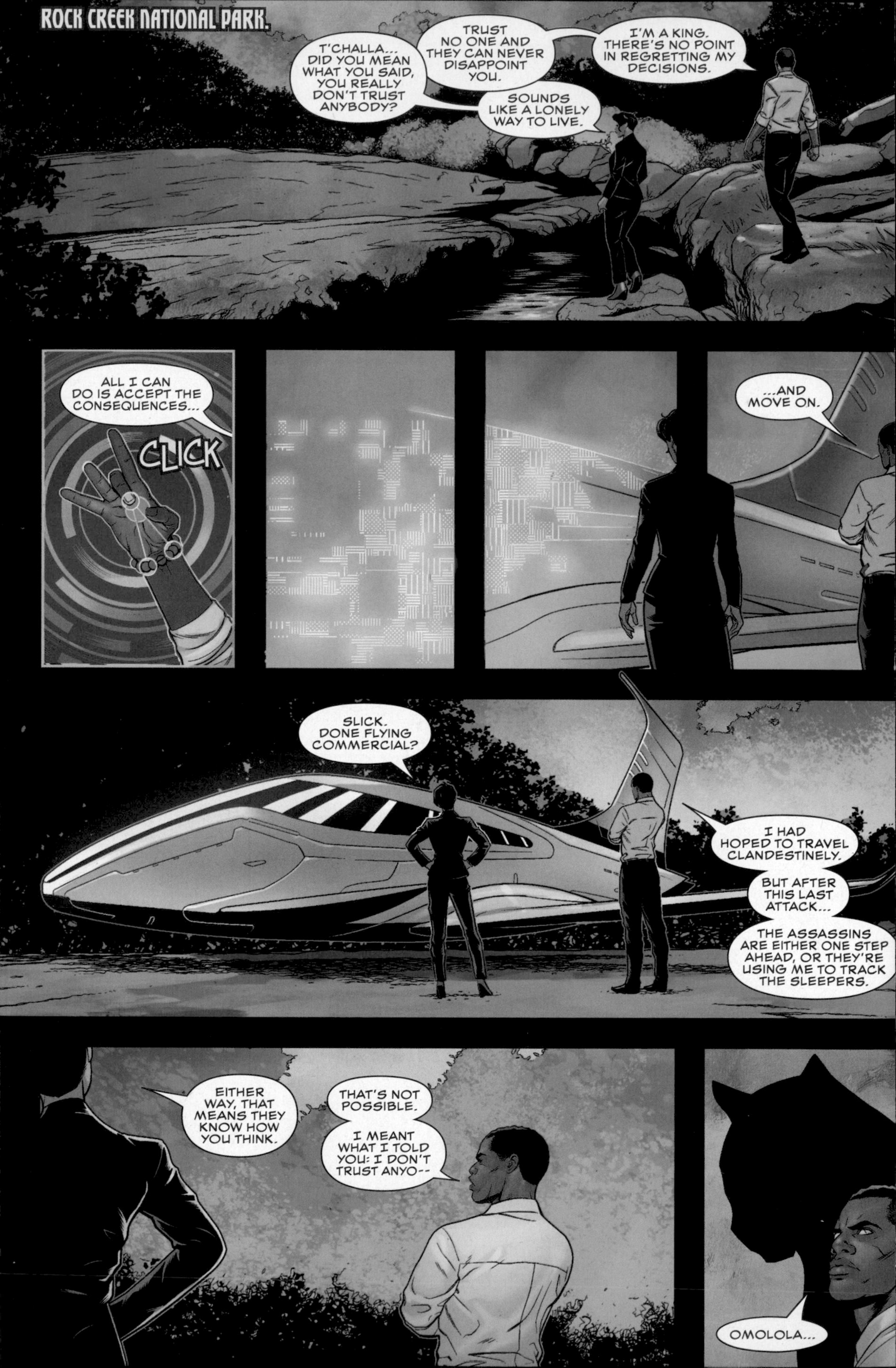
ROCK CREEK NATIONAL PARK.
T'CHALLA... DID YOU MEAN WHAT YOU SAID, YOU REALLY DON'T TRUST ANYBODY?
TRUST NO ONE AND THEY CAN NEVER DISAPPOINT YOU.
SOUNDS LIKE A LONELY WAY TO LIVE.
I'M A KING. THERE'S NO POINT IN REGRETTING MY DECISIONS.
ALL I CAN DO IS ACCEPT THE CONSEQUENCES...
CLICK
...AND MOVE ON.
SLICK. DONE FLYING COMMERCIAL?
I HAD HOPED TO TRAVEL CLANDESTINELY.
BUT AFTER THIS LAST ATTACK...
THE ASSASSINS ARE EITHER ONE STEP AHEAD, OR THEY'RE USING ME TO TRACK THE SLEEPERS.
EITHER WAY, THAT MEANS THEY KNOW HOW YOU THINK.
THAT'S NOT POSSIBLE.
I MEANT WHAT I TOLD YOU: I DON'T TRUST ANYO--
OMOLOLA...

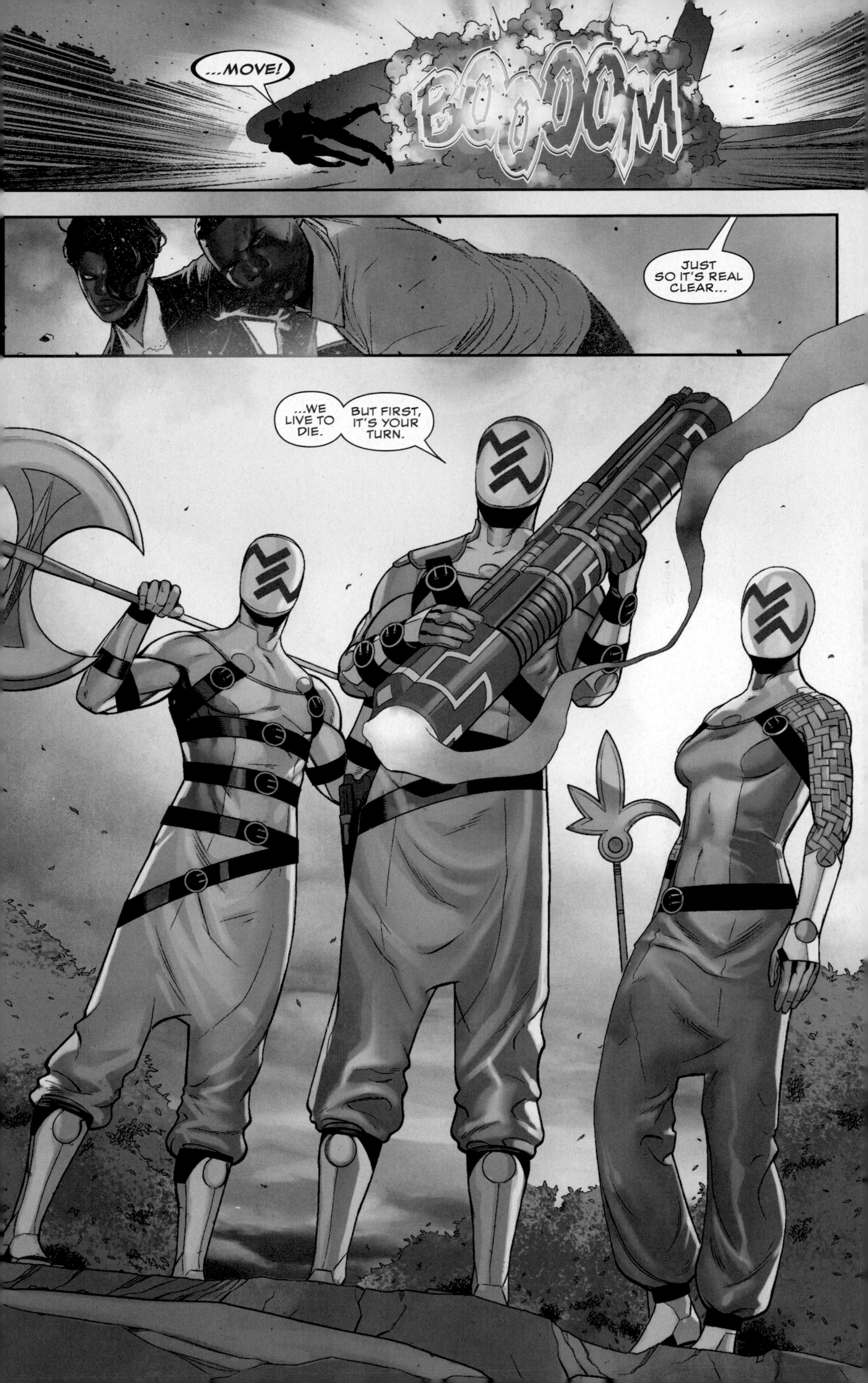
...MOVE!
BOOOOOM
JUST SO IT'S REAL CLEAR...
...WE LIVE TO DIE.
BUT FIRST, IT'S YOUR TURN.

3

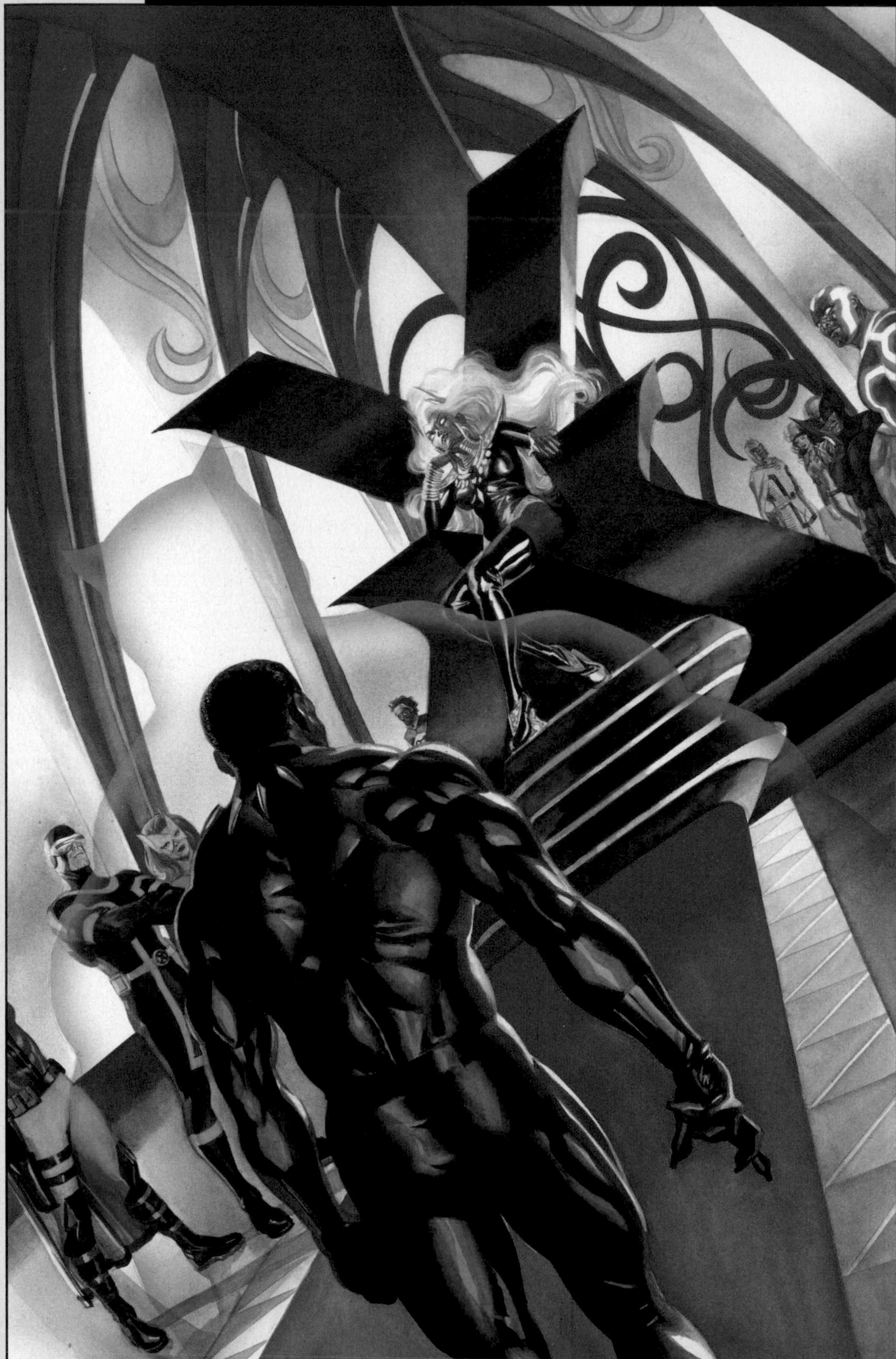

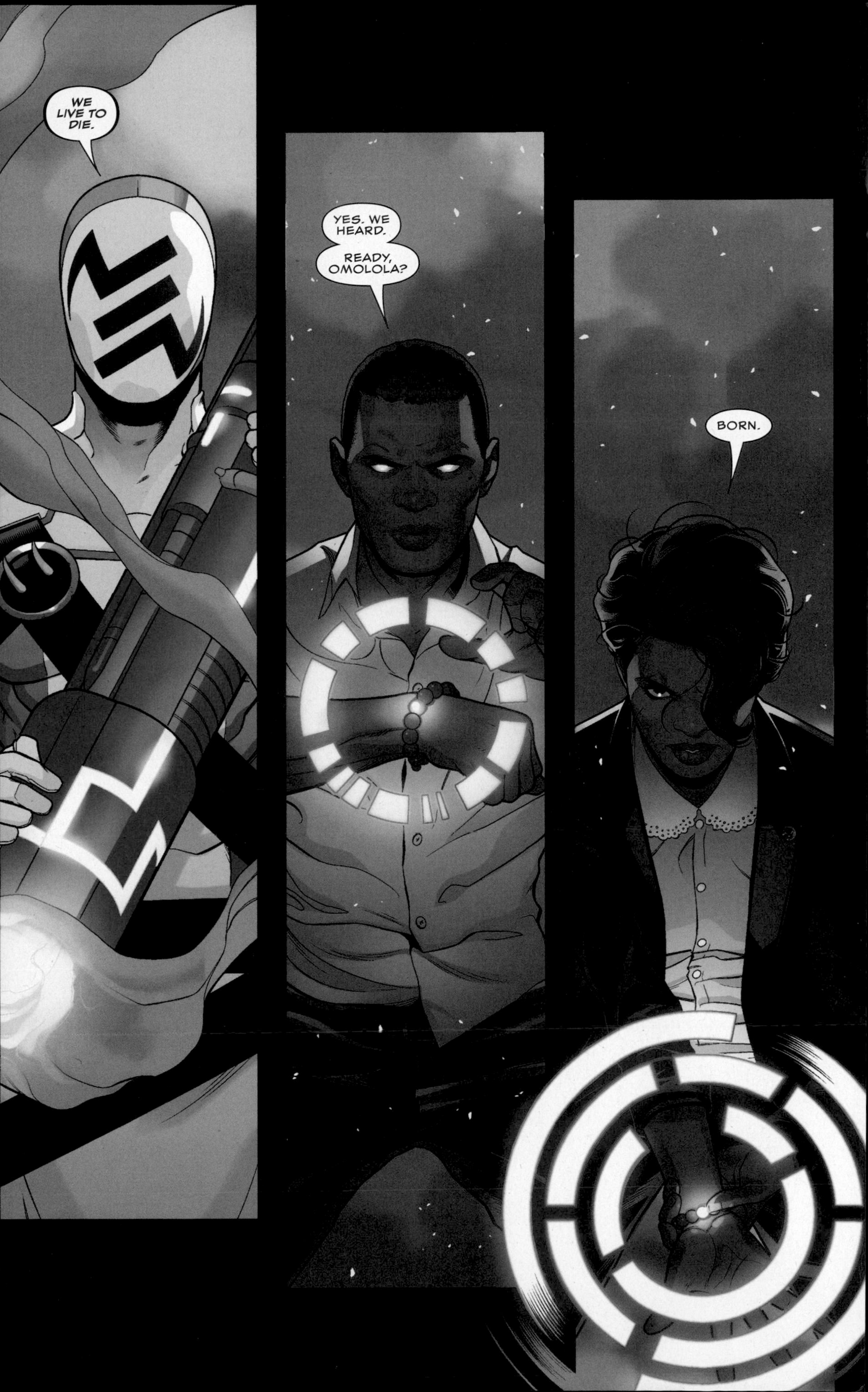
WE LIVE TO DIE.
YES. WE HEARD.
READY, OMOLOLA?
BORN.

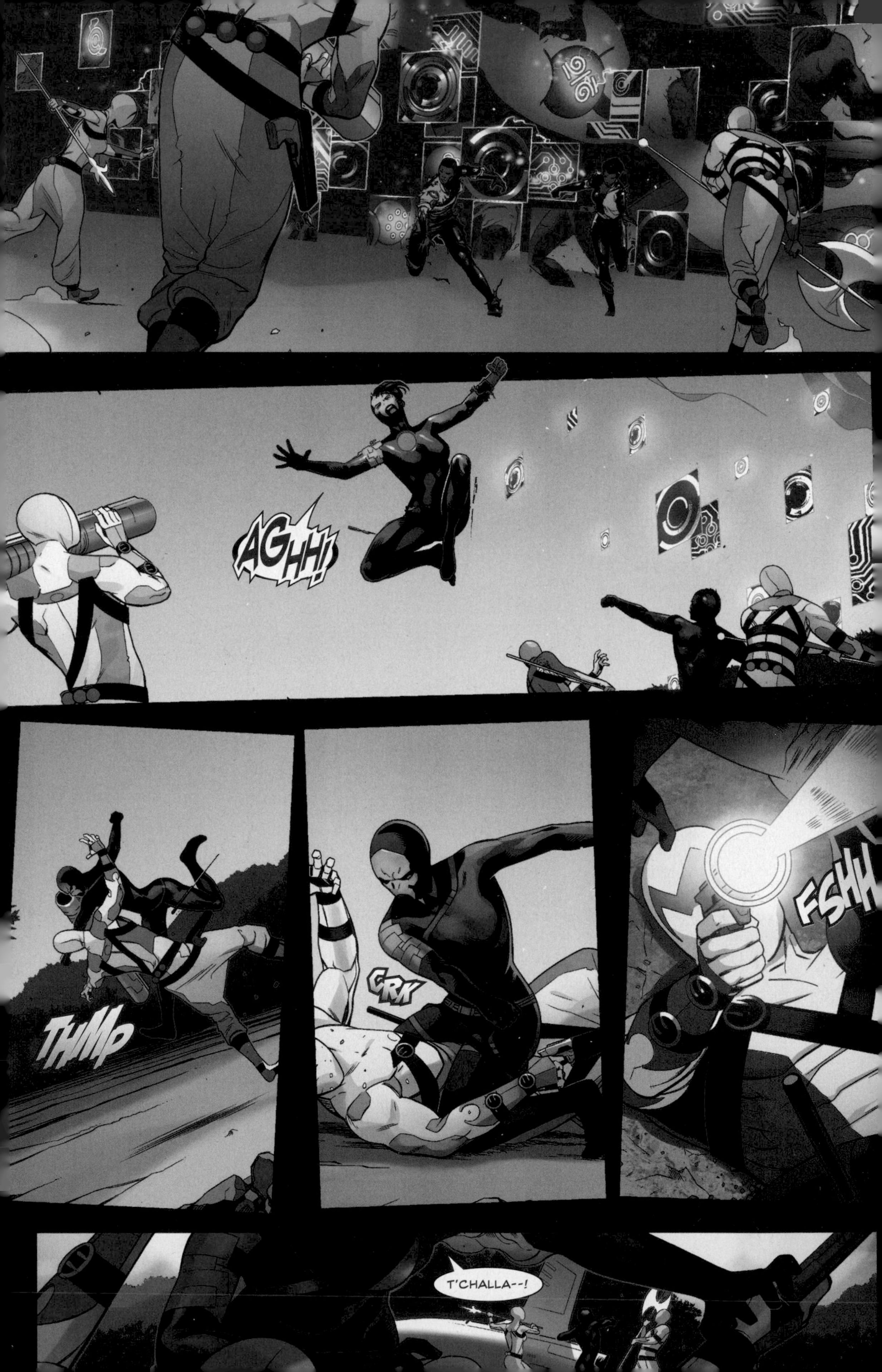
AGHH!
THMP
GRK
FSHH
T'CHALLA--!

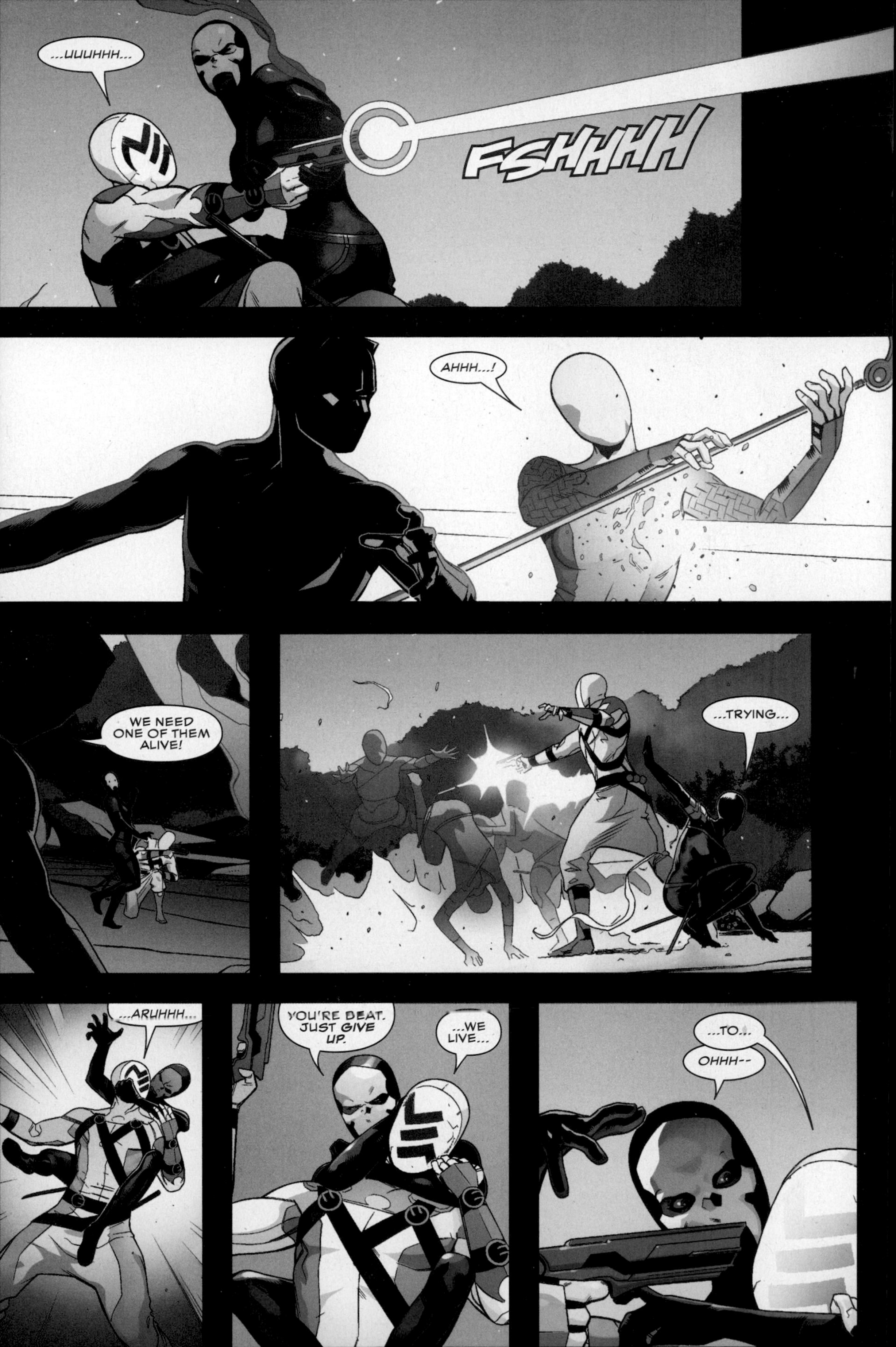
...UUUHHH...
FSHHHH
AHHH...!
WE NEED ONE OF THEM ALIVE!
...TRYING...
...ARUHHH...
YOU'RE BEAT. JUST GIVE UP.
...WE LIVE...
...TO...
OHHH--

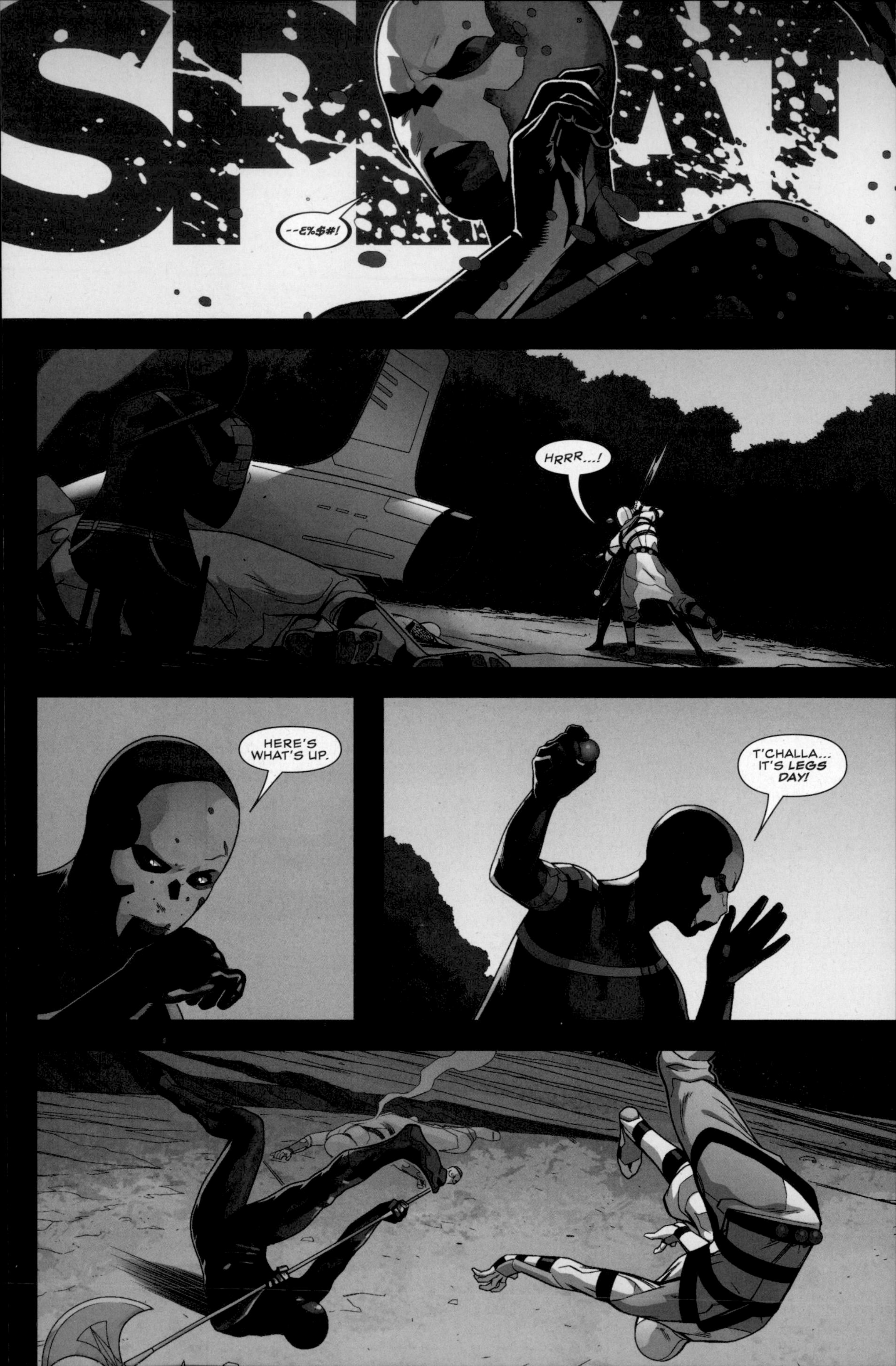
--&%$#!
HRRR...!
HERE'S WHAT'S UP.
T'CHALLA... IT'S LEGS DAY!

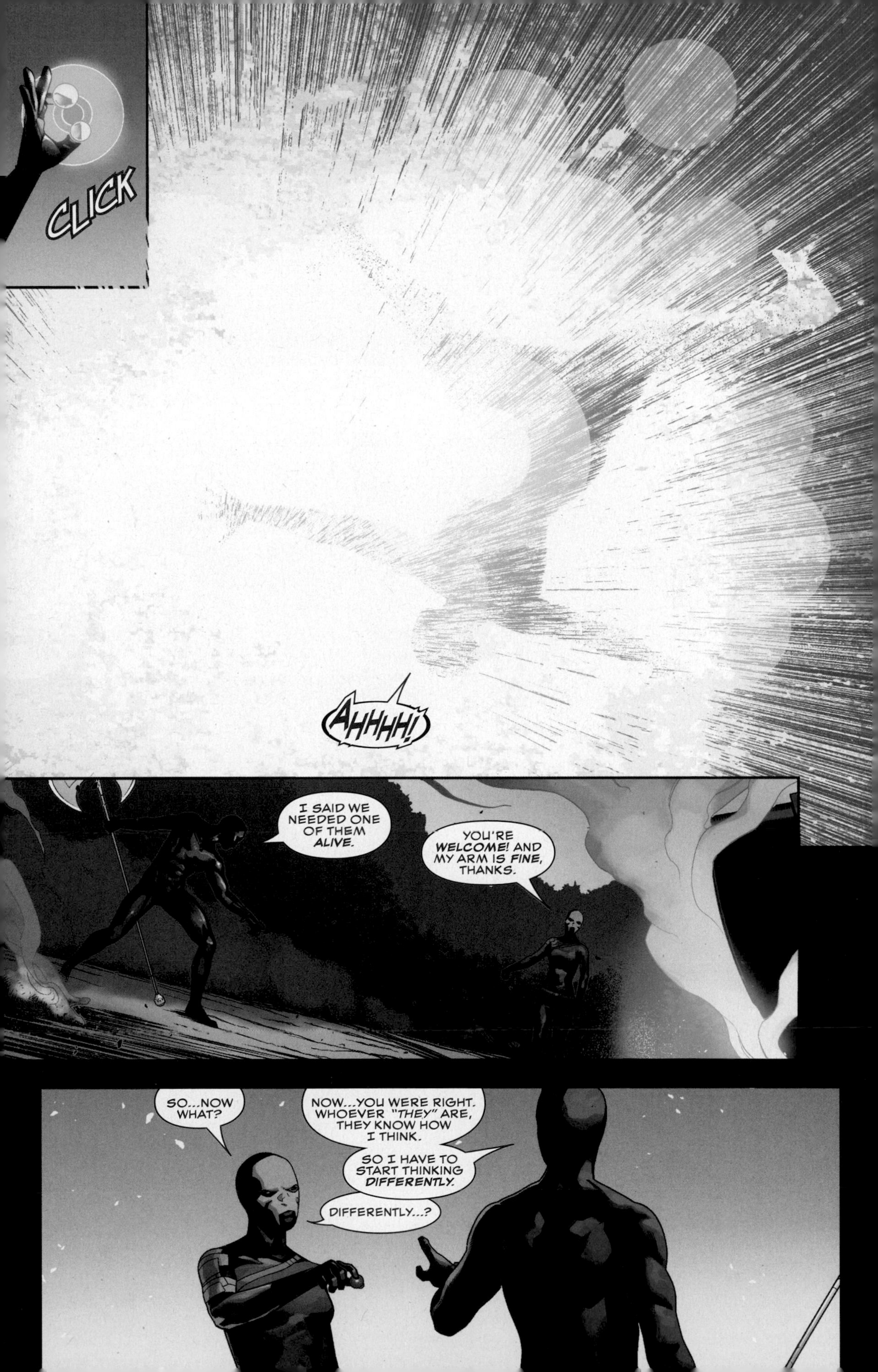
CLICK
AHHHH!
I SAID WE NEEDED ONE OF THEM ALIVE.
YOU'RE WELCOME! AND MY ARM IS FINE, THANKS.
SO...NOW WHAT?
NOW...YOU WERE RIGHT. WHOEVER "THEY" ARE, THEY KNOW HOW I THINK.
SO I HAVE TO START THINKING DIFFERENTLY.
DIFFERENTLY...?

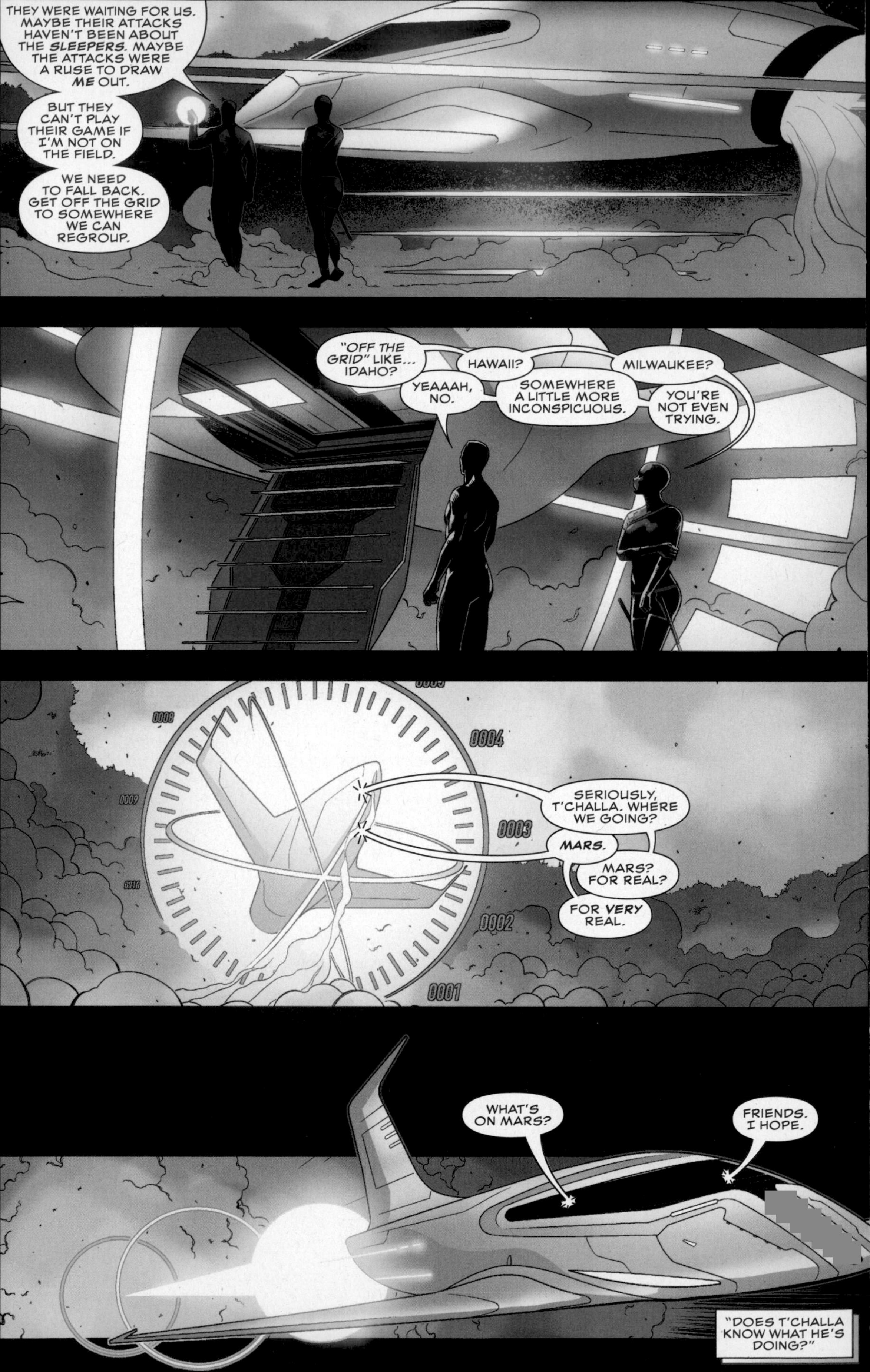

THEY WERE WAITING FOR US. MAYBE THEIR ATTACKS HAVEN'T BEEN ABOUT THE SLEEPERS. MAYBE THE ATTACKS WERE A RUSE TO DRAW ME OUT.
BUT THEY CAN'T PLAY THEIR GAME IF I'M NOT ON THE FIELD.
WE NEED TO FALL BACK. GET OFF THE GRID TO SOMEWHERE WE CAN REGROUP.
"OFF THE GRID" LIKE... IDAHO?
YEAAAH, NO.
HAWAII?
SOMEWHERE A LITTLE MORE INCONSPICUOUS.
MILWAUKEE?
YOU'RE NOT EVEN TRYING.
0008
0004
0009
0003
0010
0002
0001
SERIOUSLY, T'CHALLA. WHERE WE GOING?
MARS.
MARS? FOR REAL?
FOR VERY REAL.
WHAT'S ON MARS?
FRIENDS. I HOPE.
"DOES T'CHALLA KNOW WHAT HE'S DOING?"

WAKANDA.

"DOES T'CHALLA"...?

DOES HE *UNDERSTAND* THAT NOW IS NOT THE BEST TIME FOR HIM TO BE AWAY?

AWAY *AGAIN.*

PRINCESS SHURI, YOUR BROTHER IS NEEDED IN PARLIAMENT.

T'CHALLA'S JUST A CEREMONIAL LEADER NOW, AKILI.

IN CONCEPT, MAYBE. BUT T'CHALLA REMAINS A FIGURE OF GREAT RESPECT.

THERE ARE FACTIONS FORMING IN THE GOVERNMENT THAT AGREE ON ONLY ONE THING: T'CHALLA IS A MAN OF WISDOM.

HIS WORD, IS THE *LAST* WORD.

THAT SOUNDS A LITTLE DRAMATIC.

OUR NEW GOVERNMENT IS FRAGILE.

IRONICALLY, THE PERSON WHO CAN BEST HELP WAKANDA HOLD ONTO DEMOCRACY IS OUR FORMER KING.

SHURI, T'CHALLA NEEDS TO BE HERE. AND AS YOU'RE THE ONLY ONE WHO KNOWS WHERE HE IS...

I'LL MAKE SURE TO COMMUNICATE YOUR CONCERNS TO HIM.

IT'S APPRECIATED.

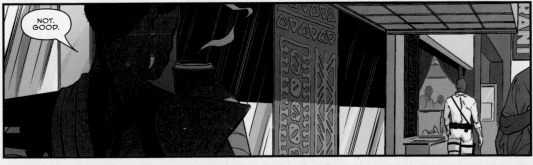

NOT. GOOD.

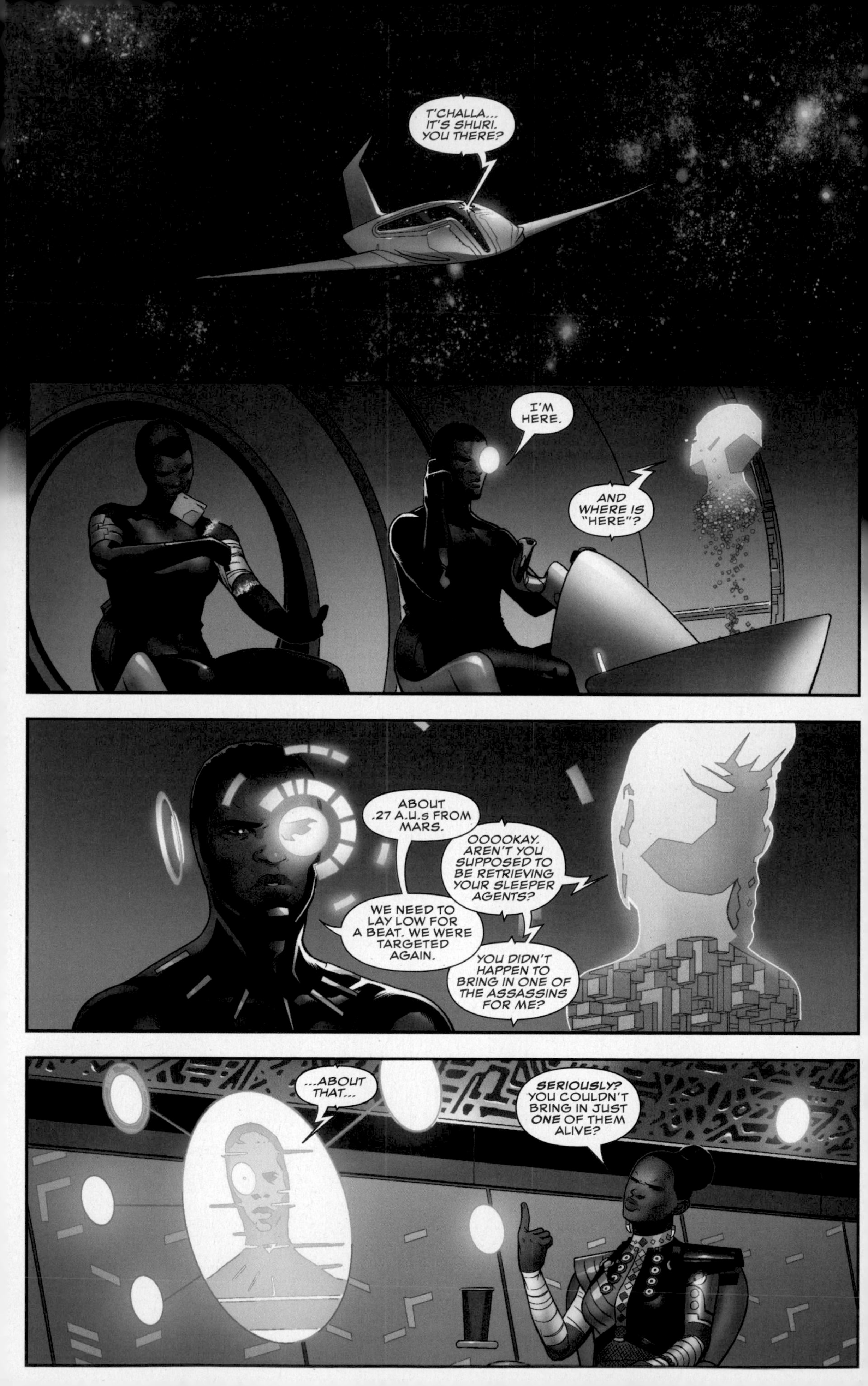
T'CHALLA... IT'S SHURI. YOU THERE?
I'M HERE.
AND WHERE IS "HERE"?
ABOUT .27 A.U.s FROM MARS.
OOOOKAY. AREN'T YOU SUPPOSED TO BE RETRIEVING YOUR SLEEPER AGENTS?
WE NEED TO LAY LOW FOR A BEAT. WE WERE TARGETED AGAIN.
YOU DIDN'T HAPPEN TO BRING IN ONE OF THE ASSASSINS FOR ME?
...ABOUT THAT...
SERIOUSLY? YOU COULDN'T BRING IN JUST ONE OF THEM ALIVE?

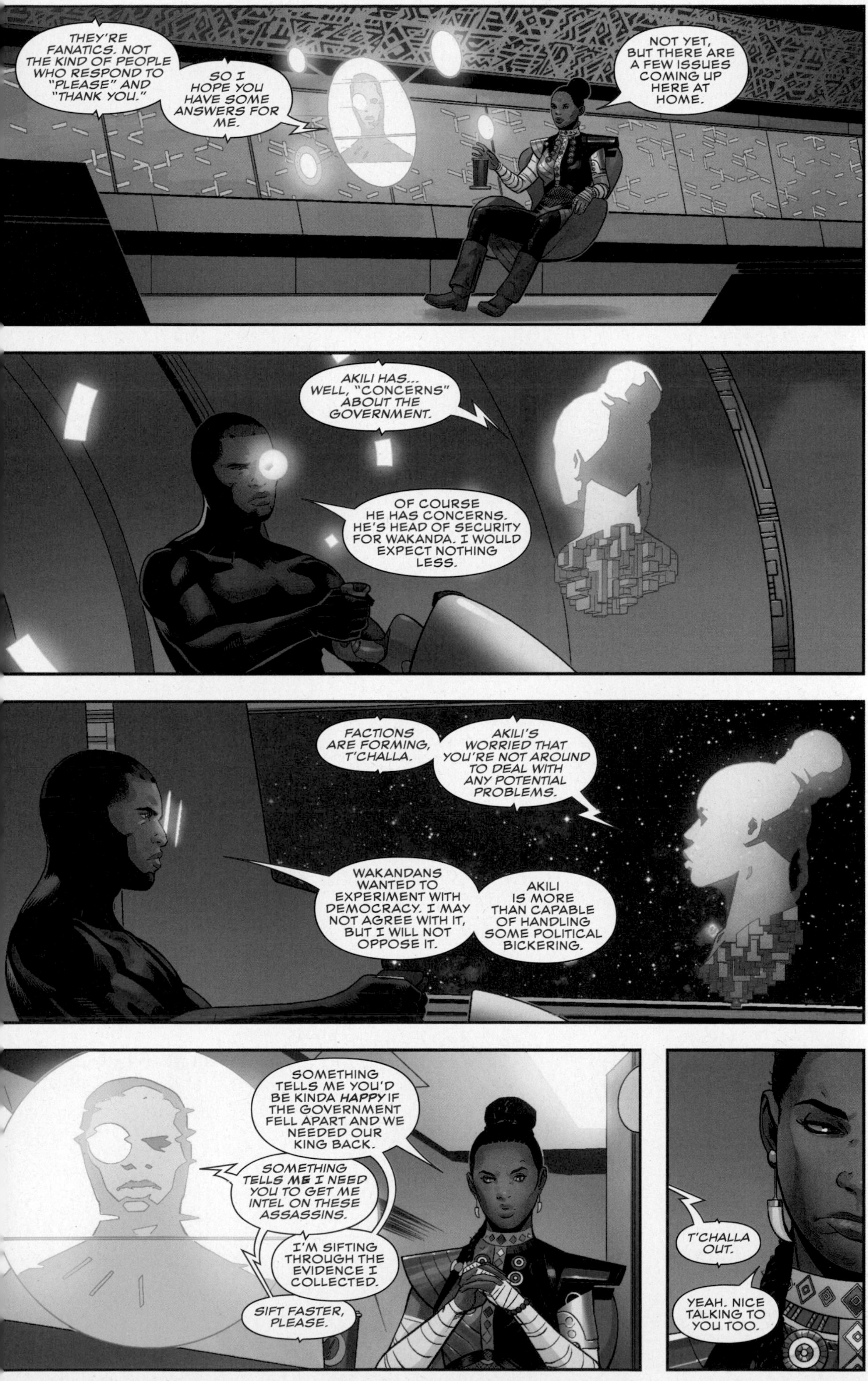

THEY'RE FANATICS. NOT THE KIND OF PEOPLE WHO RESPOND TO "PLEASE" AND "THANK YOU."
SO I HOPE YOU HAVE SOME ANSWERS FOR ME.
NOT YET, BUT THERE ARE A FEW ISSUES COMING UP HERE AT HOME.
AKILI HAS... WELL, "CONCERNS" ABOUT THE GOVERNMENT.
OF COURSE HE HAS CONCERNS. HE'S HEAD OF SECURITY FOR WAKANDA. I WOULD EXPECT NOTHING LESS.
FACTIONS ARE FORMING, T'CHALLA.
AKILI'S WORRIED THAT YOU'RE NOT AROUND TO DEAL WITH ANY POTENTIAL PROBLEMS.
WAKANDANS WANTED TO EXPERIMENT WITH DEMOCRACY. I MAY NOT AGREE WITH IT, BUT I WILL NOT OPPOSE IT.
AKILI IS MORE THAN CAPABLE OF HANDLING SOME POLITICAL BICKERING.
SOMETHING TELLS ME YOU'D BE KINDA HAPPY IF THE GOVERNMENT FELL APART AND WE NEEDED OUR KING BACK.
SOMETHING TELLS ME I NEED YOU TO GET ME INTEL ON THESE ASSASSINS.
I'M SIFTING THROUGH THE EVIDENCE I COLLECTED.
SIFT FASTER, PLEASE.
T'CHALLA OUT.
YEAH. NICE TALKING TO YOU TOO.

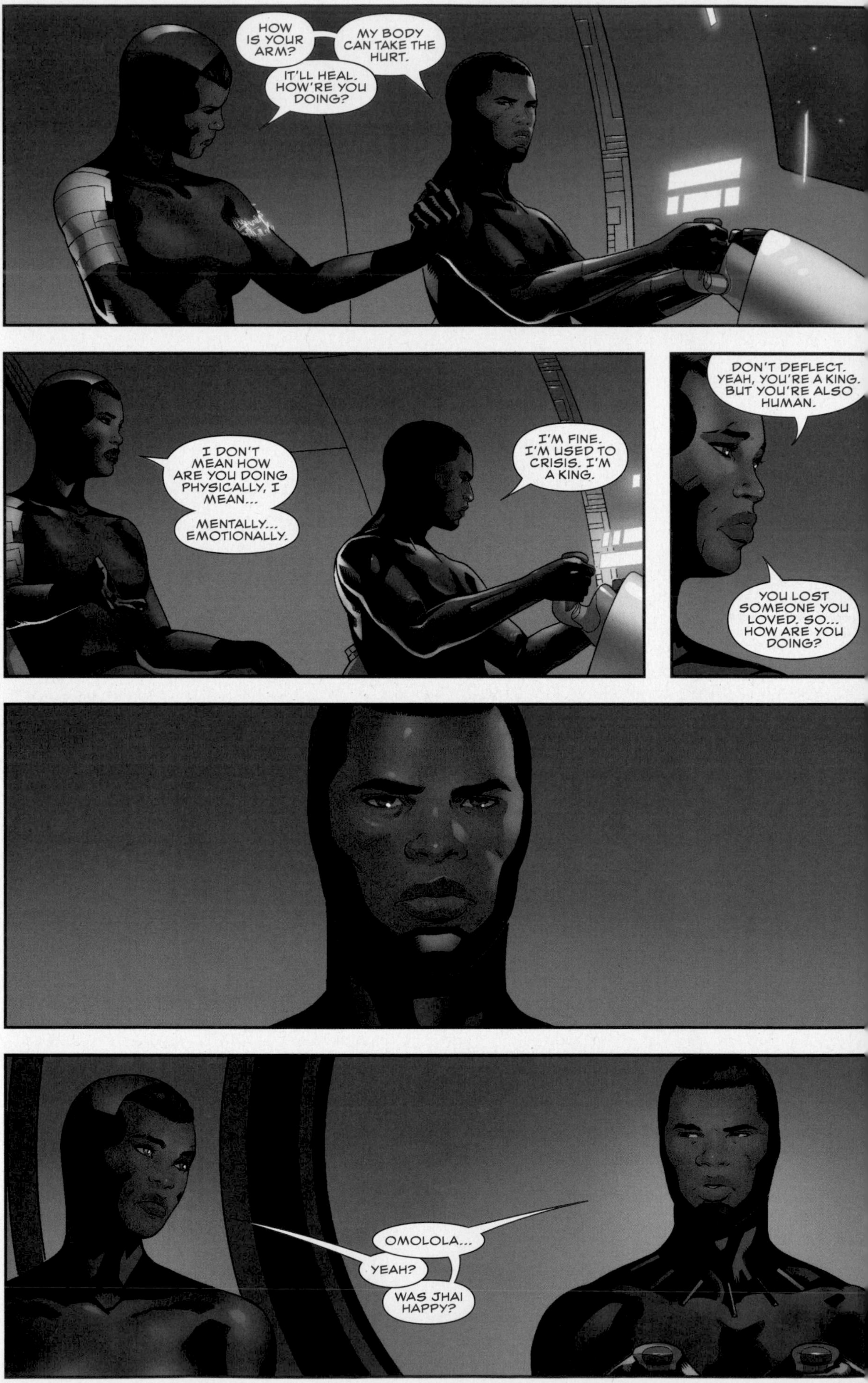
HOW IS YOUR ARM?
MY BODY CAN TAKE THE HURT.
IT'LL HEAL. HOW'RE YOU DOING?
I DON'T MEAN HOW ARE YOU DOING PHYSICALLY, I MEAN...
MENTALLY... EMOTIONALLY.
I'M FINE. I'M USED TO CRISIS. I'M A KING.
DON'T DEFLECT. YEAH, YOU'RE A KING. BUT YOU'RE ALSO HUMAN.
YOU LOST SOMEONE YOU LOVED. SO... HOW ARE YOU DOING?
OMOLOLA...
YEAH?
WAS JHAI HAPPY?

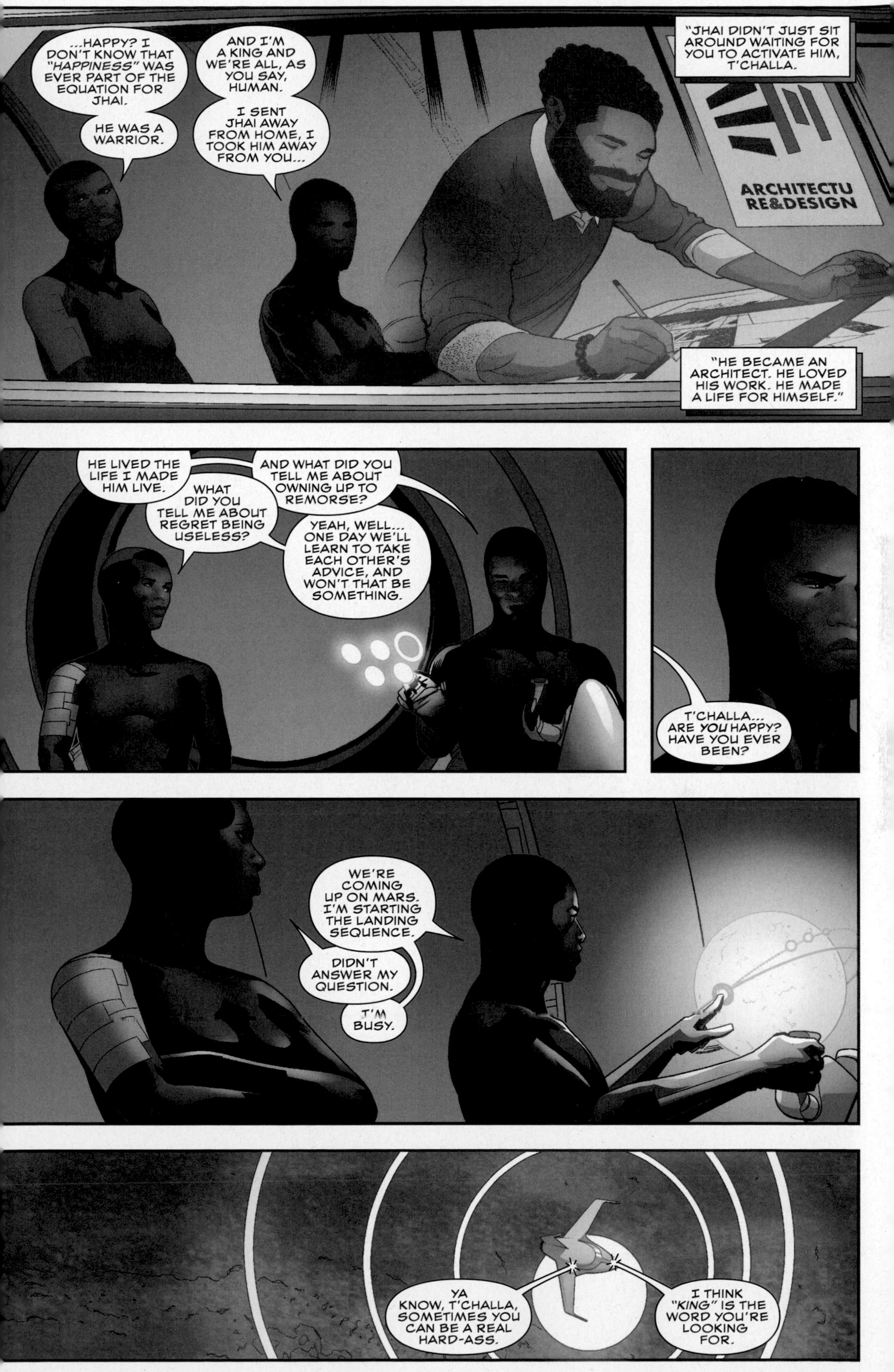
...HAPPY? I DON'T KNOW THAT "HAPPINESS" WAS EVER PART OF THE EQUATION FOR JHAI.
HE WAS A WARRIOR.
AND I'M A KING AND WE'RE ALL, AS YOU SAY, HUMAN.
I SENT JHAI AWAY FROM HOME, I TOOK HIM AWAY FROM YOU...
"JHAI DIDN'T JUST SIT AROUND WAITING FOR YOU TO ACTIVATE HIM, T'CHALLA.
ARCHITECTU RE&DESIGN
"HE BECAME AN ARCHITECT. HE LOVED HIS WORK. HE MADE A LIFE FOR HIMSELF."
HE LIVED THE LIFE I MADE HIM LIVE.
AND WHAT DID YOU TELL ME ABOUT OWNING UP TO REMORSE?
WHAT DID YOU TELL ME ABOUT REGRET BEING USELESS?
YEAH, WELL... ONE DAY WE'LL LEARN TO TAKE EACH OTHER'S ADVICE, AND WON'T THAT BE SOMETHING.
T'CHALLA... ARE YOU HAPPY? HAVE YOU EVER BEEN?
WE'RE COMING UP ON MARS. I'M STARTING THE LANDING SEQUENCE.
DIDN'T ANSWER MY QUESTION.
I'M BUSY.
YA KNOW, T'CHALLA, SOMETIMES YOU CAN BE A REAL HARD-ASS.
I THINK "KING" IS THE WORD YOU'RE LOOKING FOR.

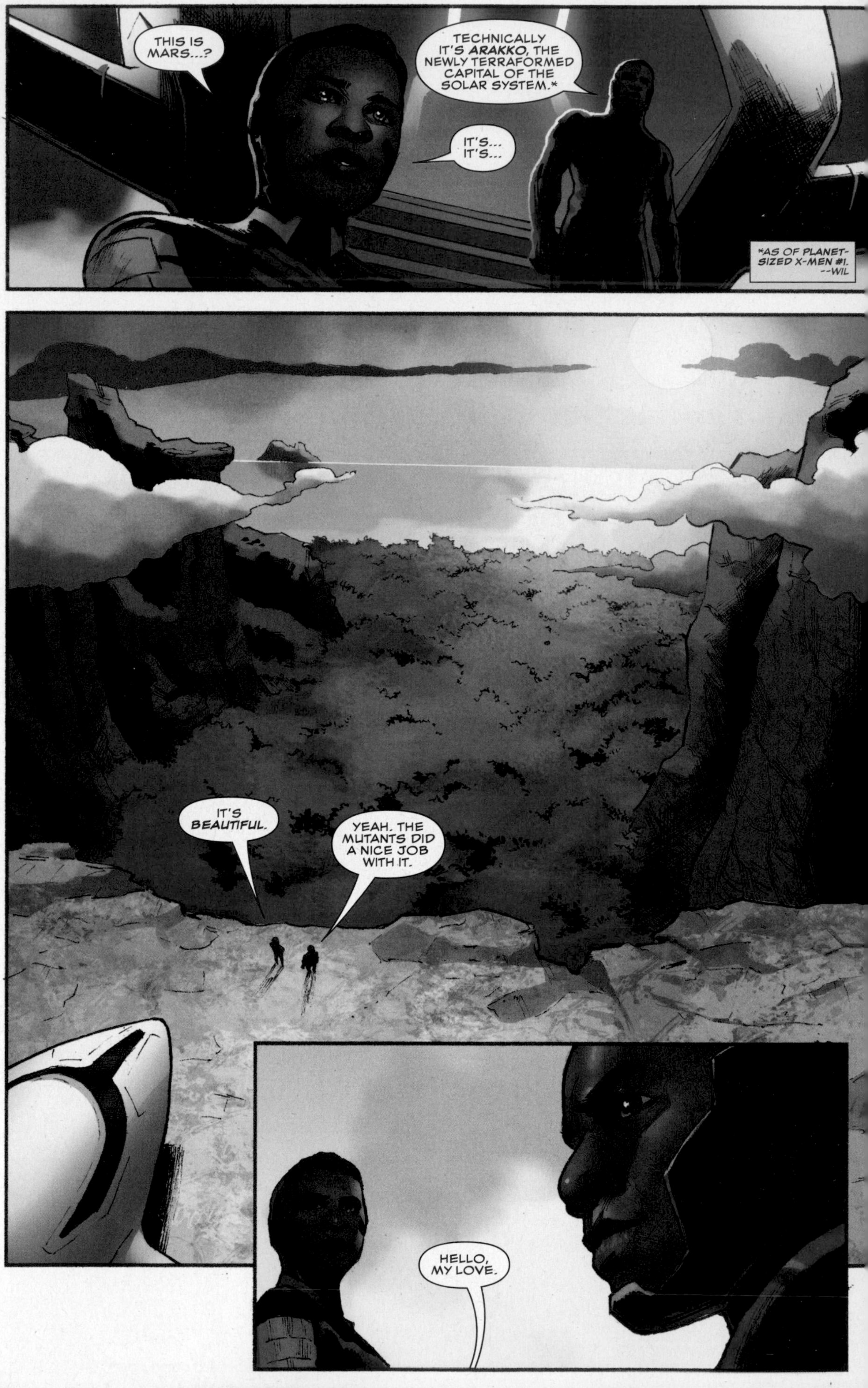
THIS IS MARS...?
TECHNICALLY IT'S ARAKKO, THE NEWLY TERRAFORMED CAPITAL OF THE SOLAR SYSTEM.*
IT'S... IT'S...
*AS OF PLANET-SIZED X-MEN #1. --WIL
IT'S BEAUTIFUL.
YEAH. THE MUTANTS DID A NICE JOB WITH IT.
HELLO, MY LOVE.

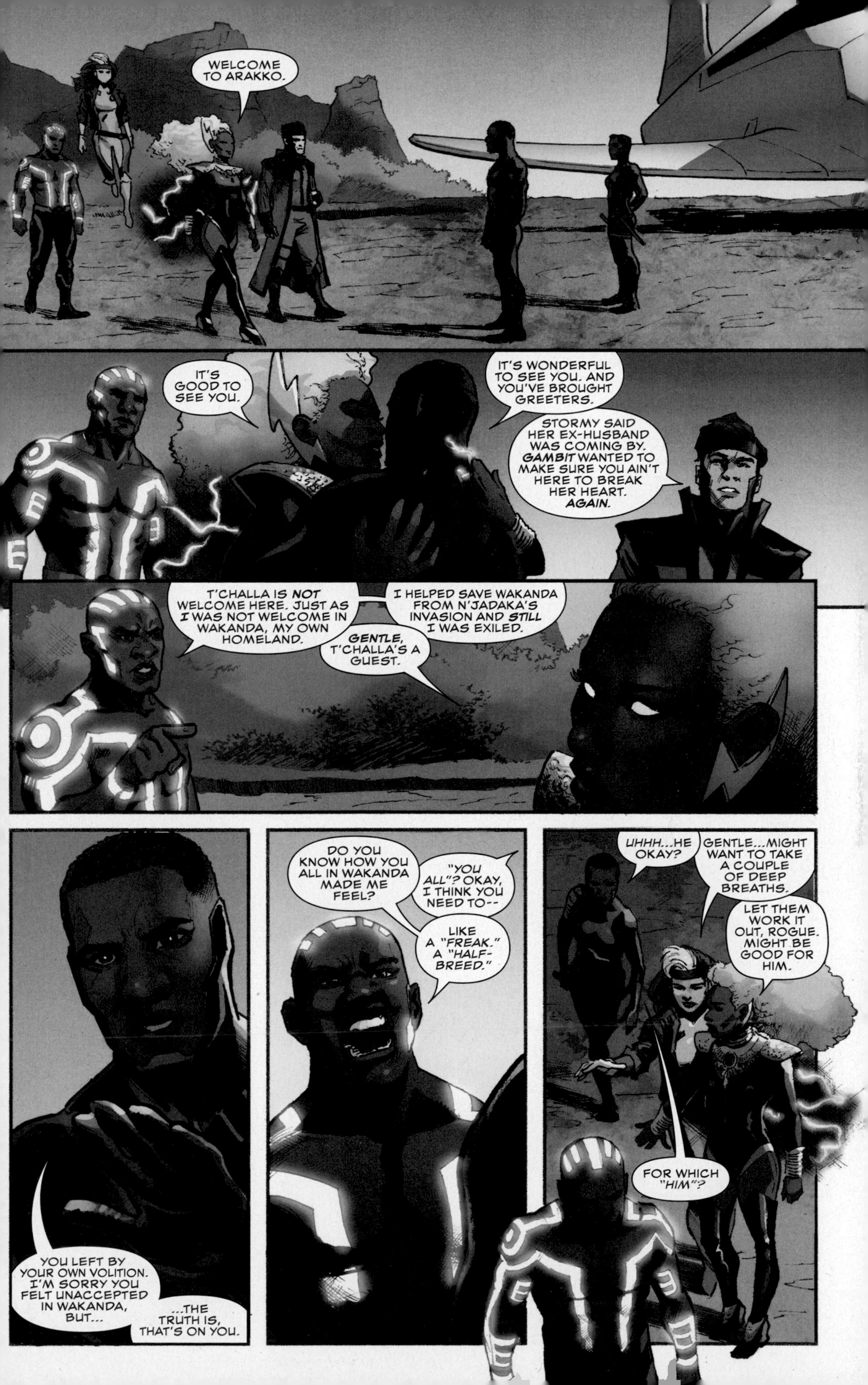
WELCOME TO ARAKKO.
IT'S GOOD TO SEE YOU.
IT'S WONDERFUL TO SEE YOU. AND YOU'VE BROUGHT GREETERS.
STORMY SAID HER EX-HUSBAND WAS COMING BY. GAMBIT WANTED TO MAKE SURE YOU AIN'T HERE TO BREAK HER HEART. AGAIN.
T'CHALLA IS NOT WELCOME HERE. JUST AS I WAS NOT WELCOME IN WAKANDA, MY OWN HOMELAND.
I HELPED SAVE WAKANDA FROM N'JADAKA'S INVASION AND STILL I WAS EXILED.
GENTLE, T'CHALLA'S A GUEST.
YOU LEFT BY YOUR OWN VOLITION. I'M SORRY YOU FELT UNACCEPTED IN WAKANDA, BUT...
...THE TRUTH IS, THAT'S ON YOU.
DO YOU KNOW HOW YOU ALL IN WAKANDA MADE ME FEEL?
"YOU ALL"? OKAY, I THINK YOU NEED TO--
LIKE A "FREAK." A "HALF-BREED."
UHHH...HE OKAY?
GENTLE...MIGHT WANT TO TAKE A COUPLE OF DEEP BREATHS.
LET THEM WORK IT OUT, ROGUE. MIGHT BE GOOD FOR HIM.
FOR WHICH "HIM"?

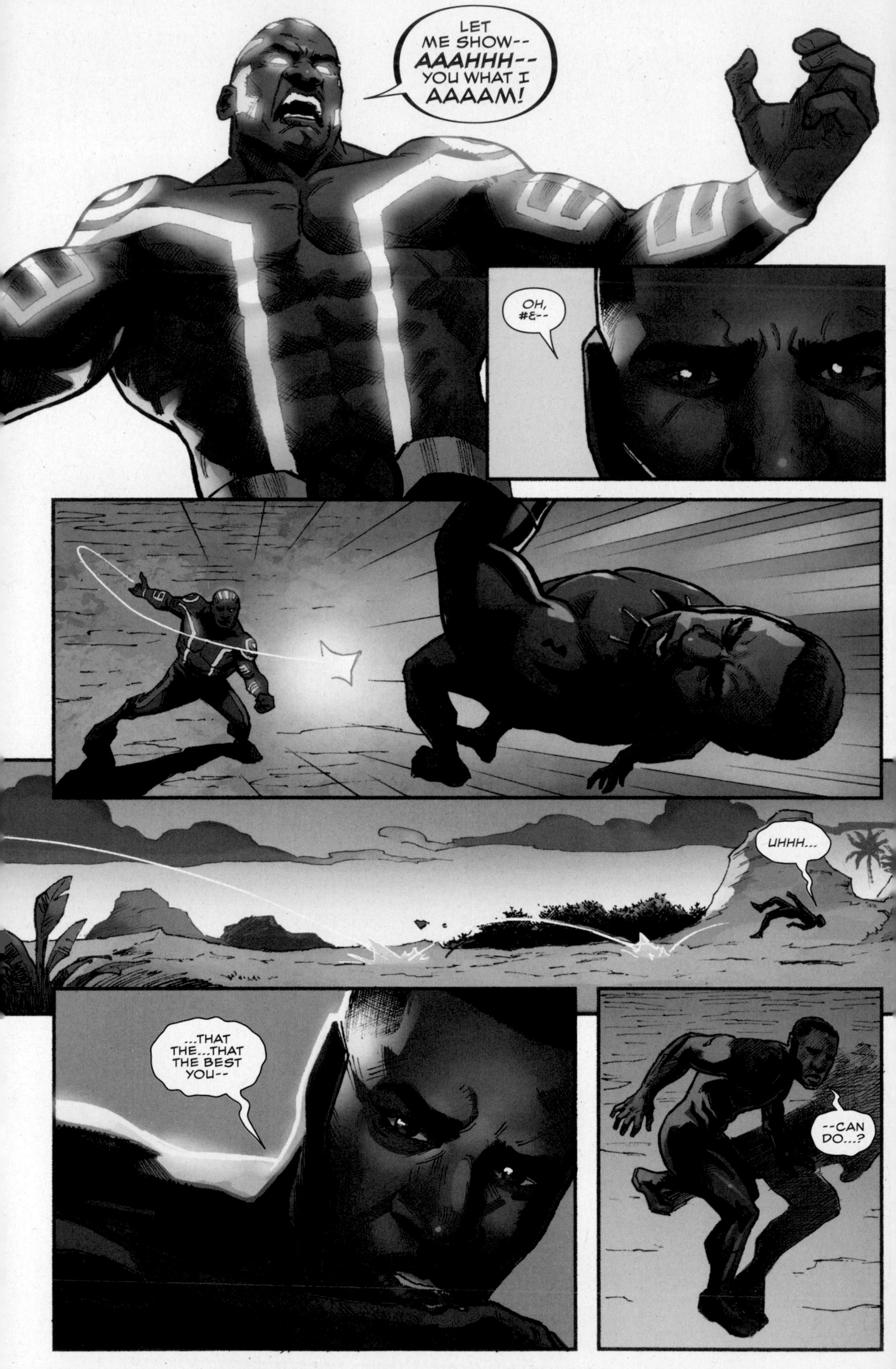
LET ME SHOW-- AAAHHH-- YOU WHAT I AAAAM!
OH, #&--
UHHH...
...THAT THE...THAT THE BEST YOU--
--CAN DO...?

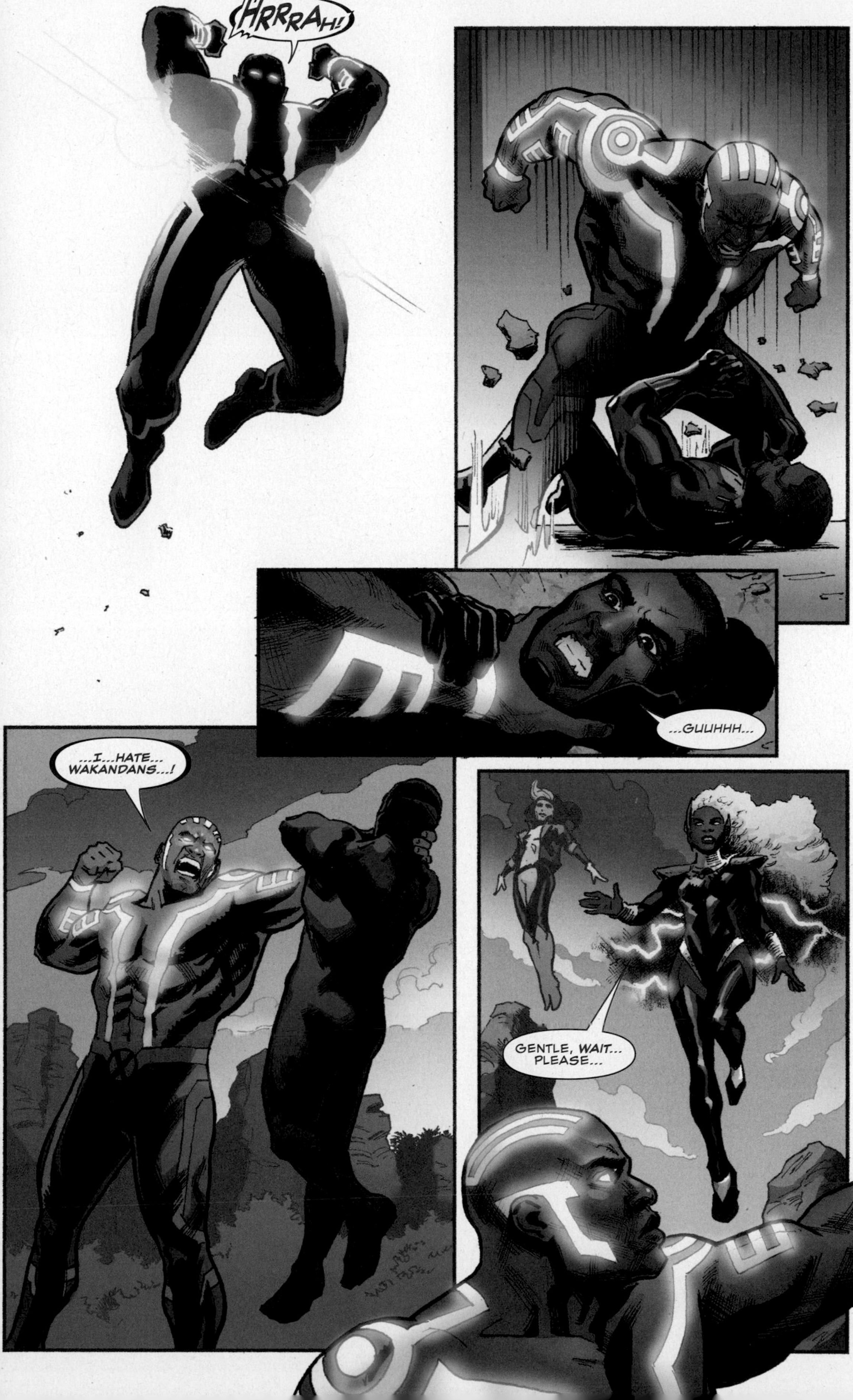
HRRRAH!
...GUUHHH...
...I...HATE... WAKANDANS...!
GENTLE, WAIT... PLEASE...

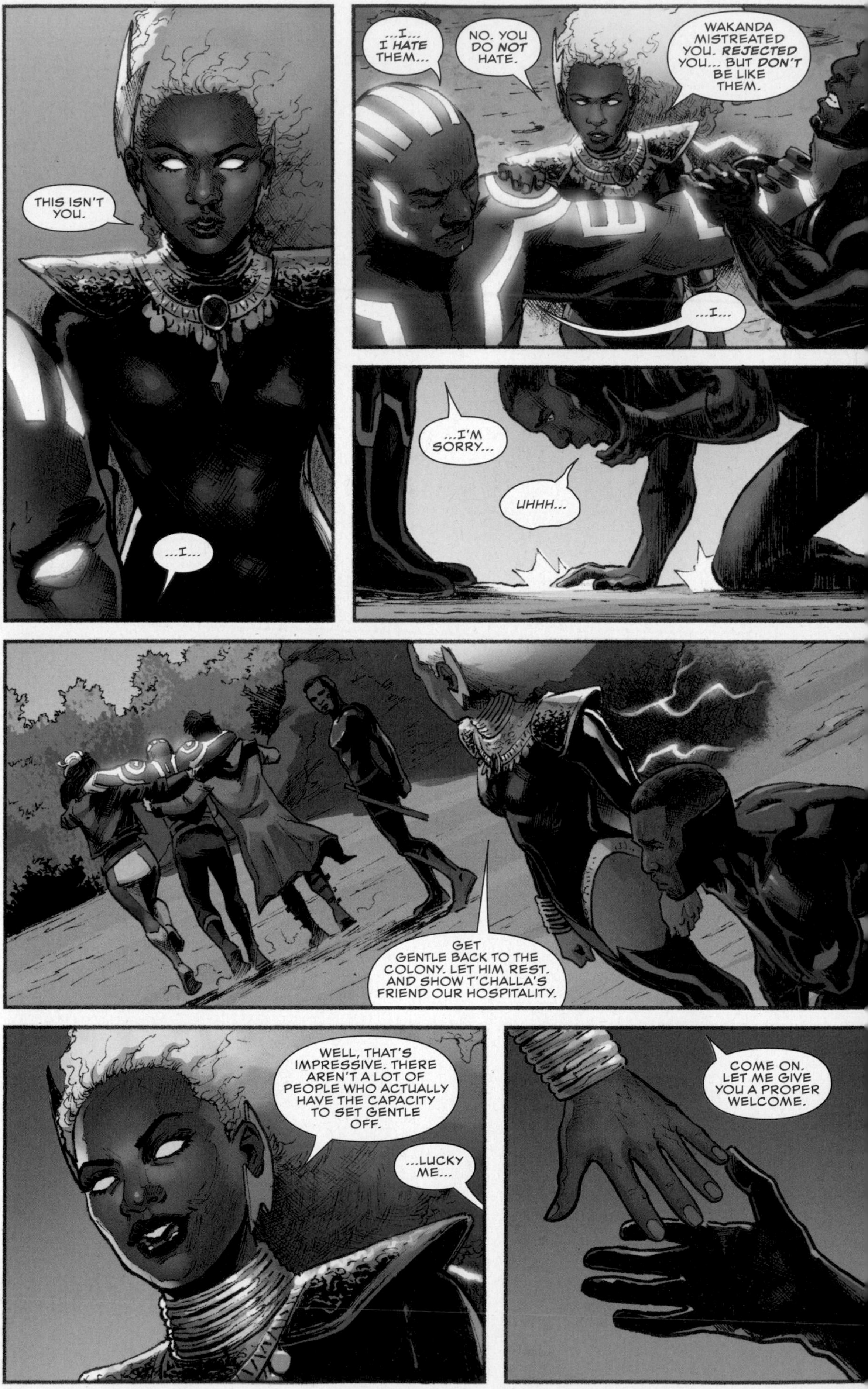
THIS ISN'T YOU.
...I...
...I... I HATE THEM...
NO. YOU DO NOT HATE.
WAKANDA MISTREATED YOU. REJECTED YOU... BUT DON'T BE LIKE THEM.
...I...
...I'M SORRY...
UHHH...
GET GENTLE BACK TO THE COLONY. LET HIM REST. AND SHOW T'CHALLA'S FRIEND OUR HOSPITALITY.
WELL, THAT'S IMPRESSIVE. THERE AREN'T A LOT OF PEOPLE WHO ACTUALLY HAVE THE CAPACITY TO SET GENTLE OFF.
...LUCKY ME...
COME ON. LET ME GIVE YOU A PROPER WELCOME.

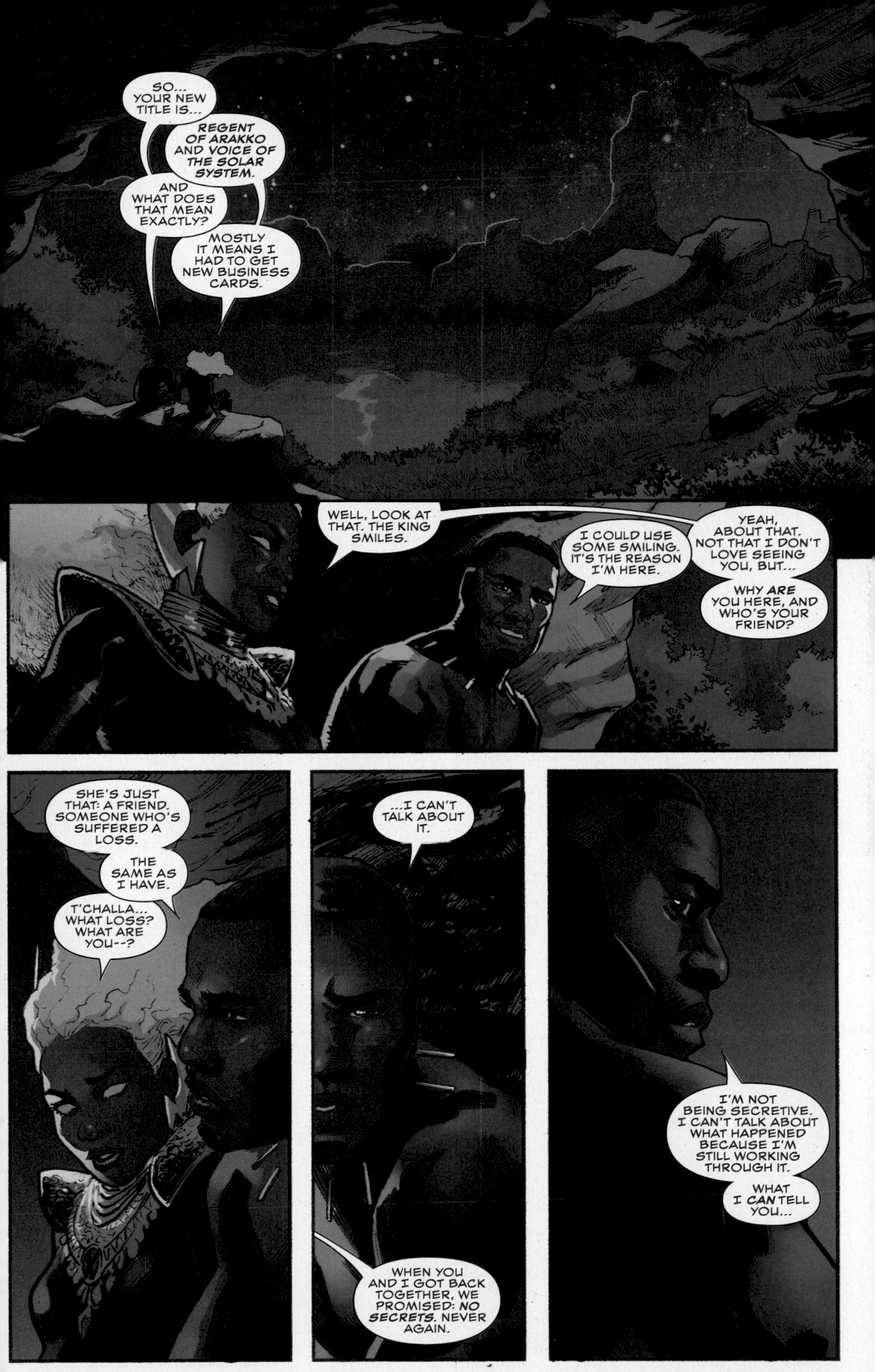
SO... YOUR NEW TITLE IS...
REGENT OF ARAKKO AND VOICE OF THE SOLAR SYSTEM.
AND WHAT DOES THAT MEAN EXACTLY?
MOSTLY IT MEANS I HAD TO GET NEW BUSINESS CARDS.
WELL, LOOK AT THAT. THE KING SMILES.
I COULD USE SOME SMILING. IT'S THE REASON I'M HERE.
YEAH, ABOUT THAT. NOT THAT I DON'T LOVE SEEING YOU, BUT...
WHY ARE YOU HERE, AND WHO'S YOUR FRIEND?
SHE'S JUST THAT: A FRIEND. SOMEONE WHO'S SUFFERED A LOSS.
THE SAME AS I HAVE.
T'CHALLA... WHAT LOSS? WHAT ARE YOU--?
...I CAN'T TALK ABOUT IT.
WHEN YOU AND I GOT BACK TOGETHER, WE PROMISED: NO SECRETS. NEVER AGAIN.
I'M NOT BEING SECRETIVE. I CAN'T TALK ABOUT WHAT HAPPENED BECAUSE I'M STILL WORKING THROUGH IT.
WHAT I CAN TELL YOU...

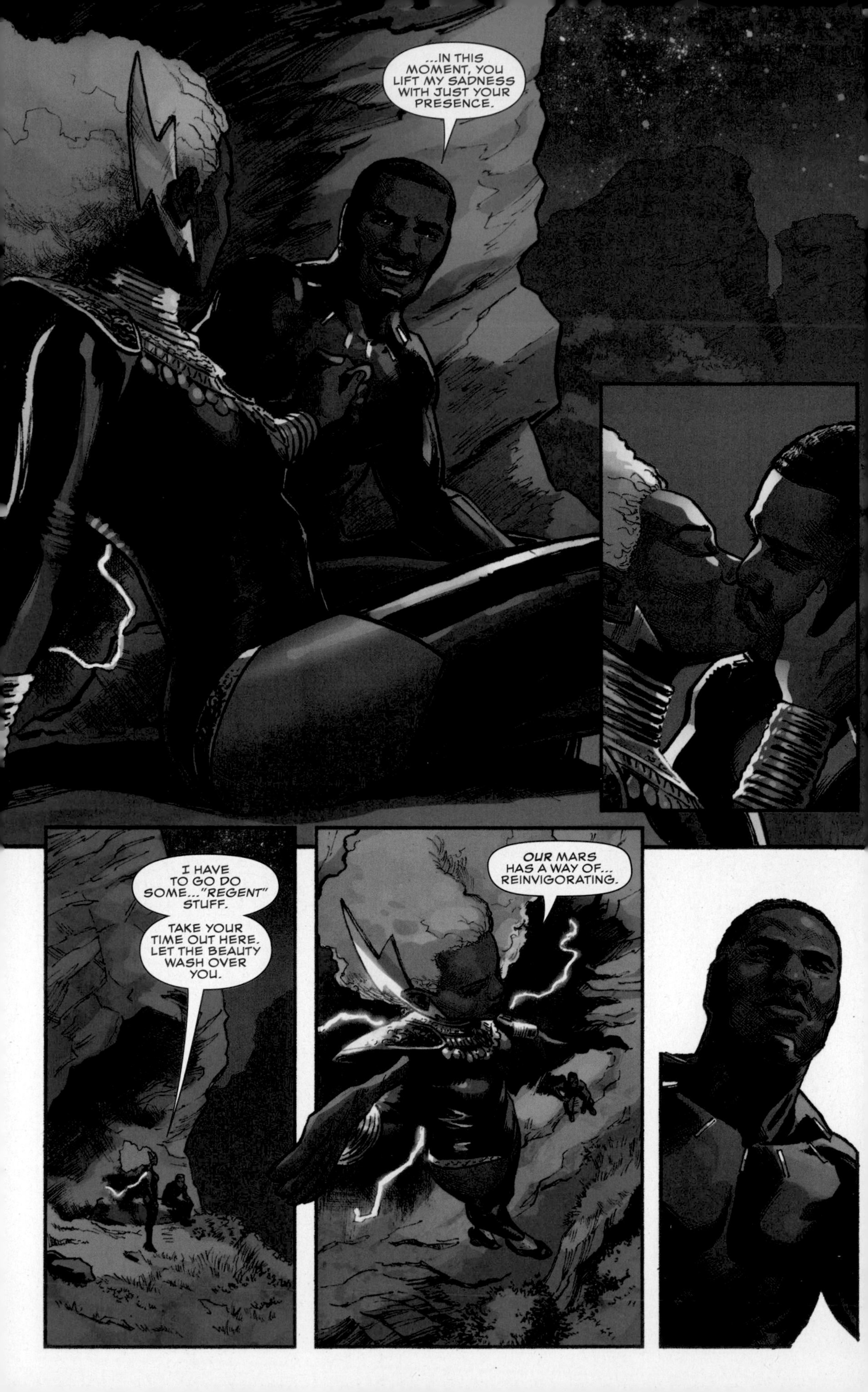
...IN THIS MOMENT, YOU LIFT MY SADNESS WITH JUST YOUR PRESENCE.
I HAVE TO GO DO SOME..."REGENT" STUFF.
TAKE YOUR TIME OUT HERE. LET THE BEAUTY WASH OVER YOU.
OUR MARS HAS A WAY OF... REINVIGORATING.

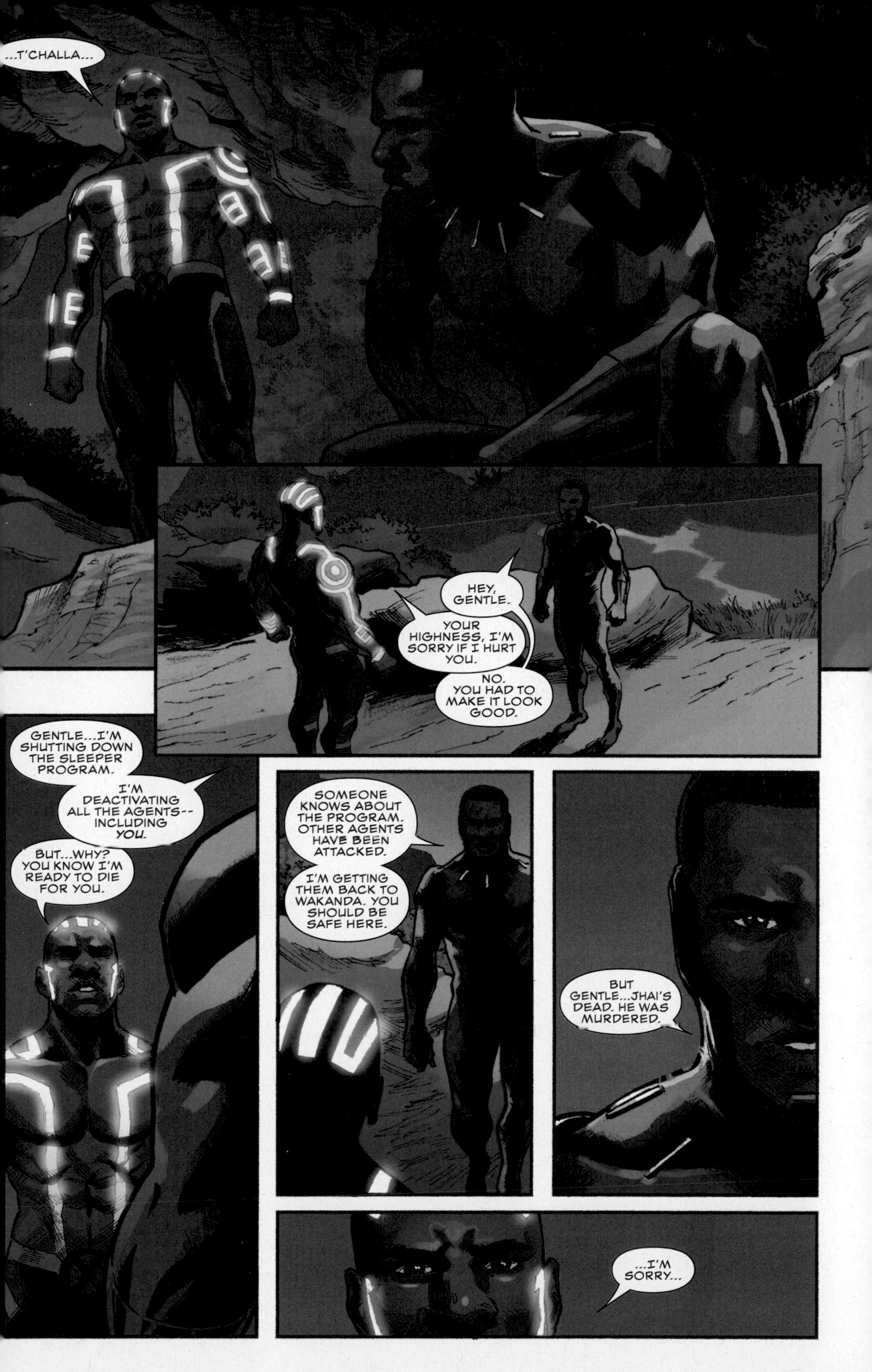
...T'CHALLA...
HEY, GENTLE.
YOUR HIGHNESS, I'M SORRY IF I HURT YOU.
NO. YOU HAD TO MAKE IT LOOK GOOD.
GENTLE...I'M SHUTTING DOWN THE SLEEPER PROGRAM.
I'M DEACTIVATING ALL THE AGENTS--INCLUDING YOU.
BUT...WHY? YOU KNOW I'M READY TO DIE FOR YOU.
SOMEONE KNOWS ABOUT THE PROGRAM. OTHER AGENTS HAVE BEEN ATTACKED.
I'M GETTING THEM BACK TO WAKANDA. YOU SHOULD BE SAFE HERE.
BUT GENTLE...JHAI'S DEAD. HE WAS MURDERED.
...I'M SORRY...

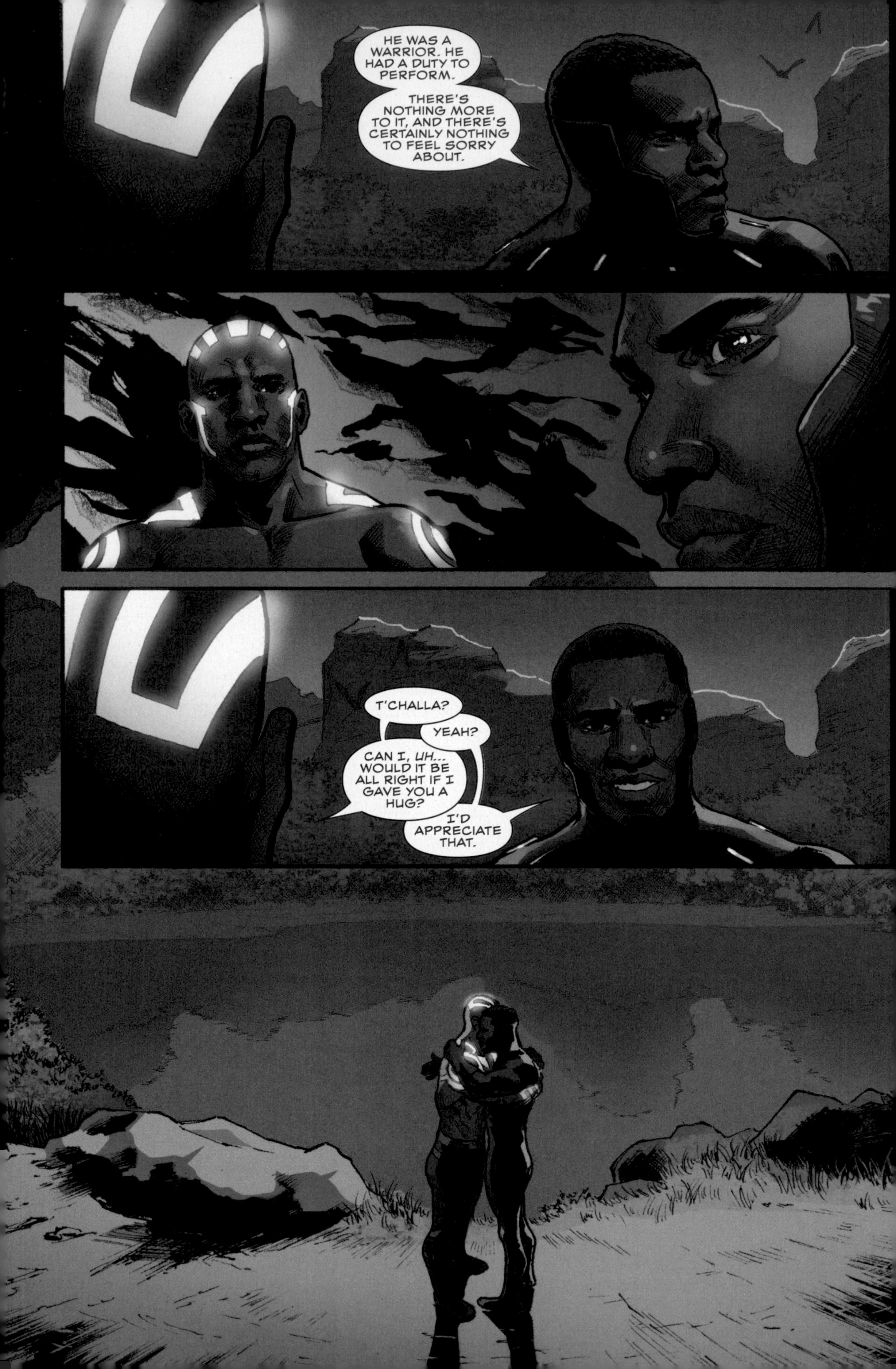
HE WAS A WARRIOR. HE HAD A DUTY TO PERFORM.
THERE'S NOTHING MORE TO IT, AND THERE'S CERTAINLY NOTHING TO FEEL SORRY ABOUT.
T'CHALLA?
YEAH?
CAN I, *UH...* WOULD IT BE ALL RIGHT IF I GAVE YOU A HUG?
I'D APPRECIATE THAT.

This is the 200TH issue of **BLACK PANTHER** since the launch of his first solo series in 1977 (which was written and drawn by his co-creator, **Jack "King" Kirby**). To celebrate this momentous milestone, we've got two additional bonus stories for you! One is a tale from early in T'Challa's reign as king of Wakanda by the amazingly talented cartoonist **Juni Ba** (check out his Image series called *Monkey Meat*!). And the other is a tale set in the very near future about a new Wakandan hero who will be playing a significant role in the series going forward.

BLACK PANTHER
MARVEL COMICS GROUP
30¢
1 JAN 02685
FIRST ISSUE! THE ALL-NEW, ALL-EXCITING
BLACK PANTHER
HE'S BACK! AS ONLY JACK KIRBY CAN DO IT!
THEY SEARCHED FOR IT! THEY FOUGHT--AND EVEN KILLED FOR IT! WHAT WAS IT?
KING SOLOMON'S FROG!

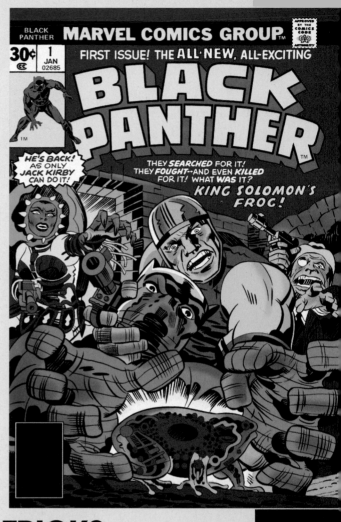

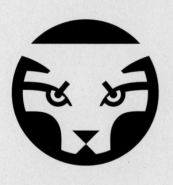

A TALL TALE OF TRICKS

Writer/Artist **JUNI BA**

Color Artist **CHRIS O'HALLORAN**

Letterer **VC's JOE SABINO**

THE WAKANDAN

Writer **JOHN RIDLEY**

Artist **GERMÁN PERALTA**

Color Artist **JESUS ABURTOV**

Letterer **VC's JOE SABINO**

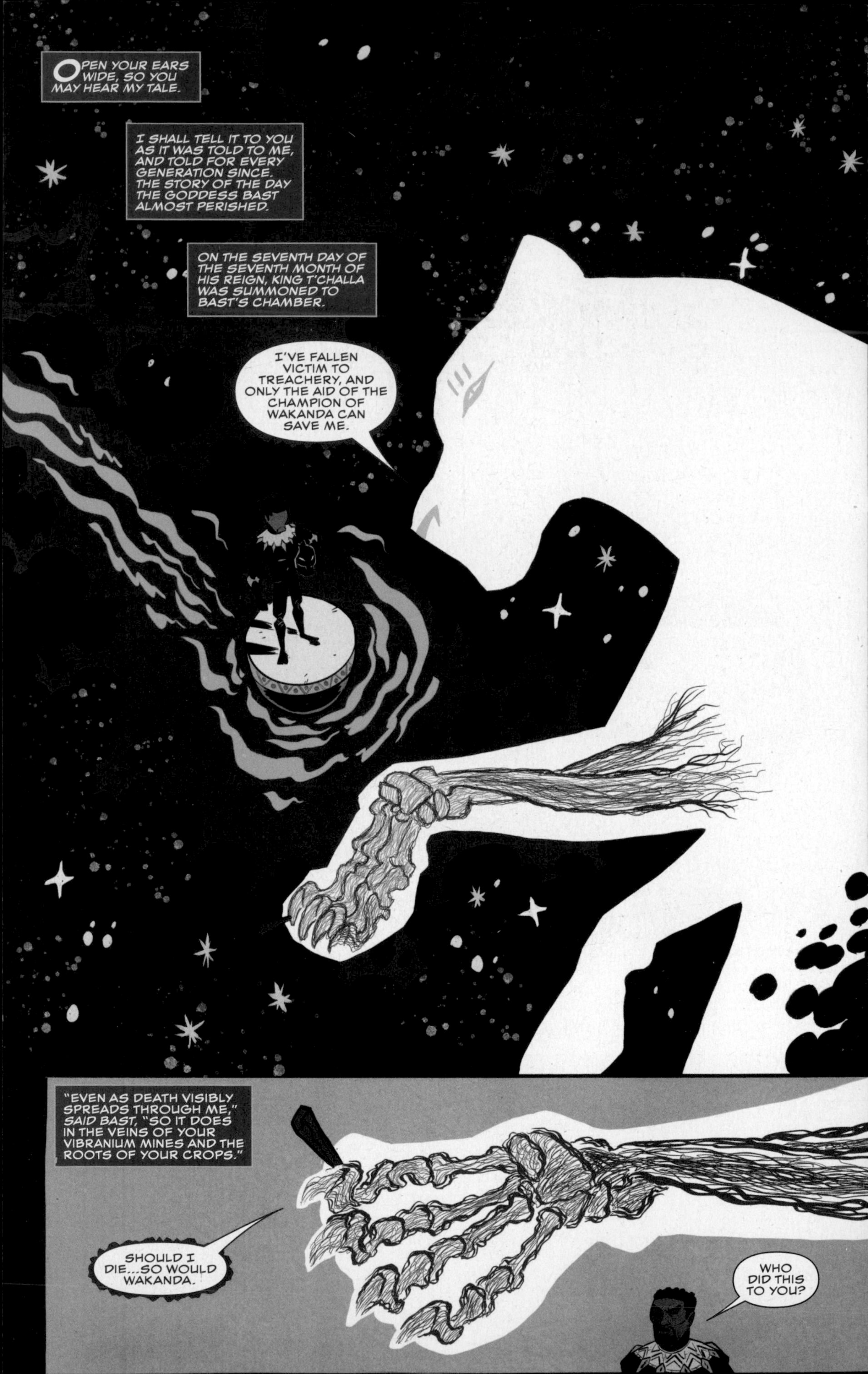
OPEN YOUR EARS WIDE, SO YOU MAY HEAR MY TALE.
I SHALL TELL IT TO YOU AS IT WAS TOLD TO ME, AND TOLD FOR EVERY GENERATION SINCE. THE STORY OF THE DAY THE GODDESS BAST ALMOST PERISHED.
ON THE SEVENTH DAY OF THE SEVENTH MONTH OF HIS REIGN, KING T'CHALLA WAS SUMMONED TO BAST'S CHAMBER.
I'VE FALLEN VICTIM TO TREACHERY, AND ONLY THE AID OF THE CHAMPION OF WAKANDA CAN SAVE ME.
"EVEN AS DEATH VISIBLY SPREADS THROUGH ME," SAID BAST, "SO IT DOES IN THE VEINS OF YOUR VIBRANIUM MINES AND THE ROOTS OF YOUR CROPS."
SHOULD I DIE...SO WOULD WAKANDA.
WHO DID THIS TO YOU?

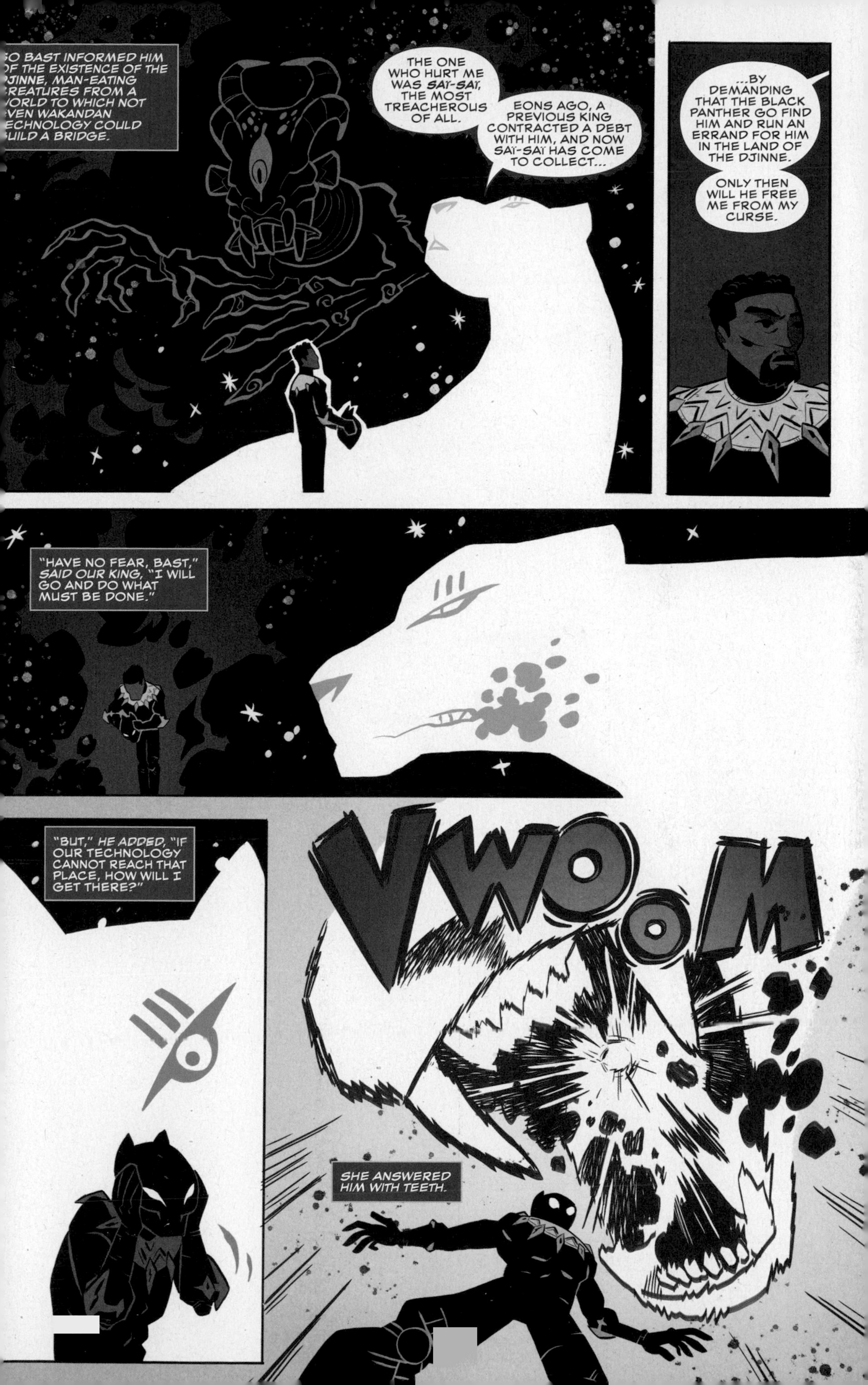

SO BAST INFORMED HIM OF THE EXISTENCE OF THE DJINNE, MAN-EATING CREATURES FROM A WORLD TO WHICH NOT EVEN WAKANDAN TECHNOLOGY COULD BUILD A BRIDGE.
THE ONE WHO HURT ME WAS SAÏ-SAÏ, THE MOST TREACHEROUS OF ALL.
EONS AGO, A PREVIOUS KING CONTRACTED A DEBT WITH HIM, AND NOW SAÏ-SAÏ HAS COME TO COLLECT...
...BY DEMANDING THAT THE BLACK PANTHER GO FIND HIM AND RUN AN ERRAND FOR HIM IN THE LAND OF THE DJINNE.
ONLY THEN WILL HE FREE ME FROM MY CURSE.
"HAVE NO FEAR, BAST," SAID OUR KING, "I WILL GO AND DO WHAT MUST BE DONE."
"BUT," HE ADDED, "IF OUR TECHNOLOGY CANNOT REACH THAT PLACE, HOW WILL I GET THERE?"
VWOOOM
SHE ANSWERED HIM WITH TEETH.

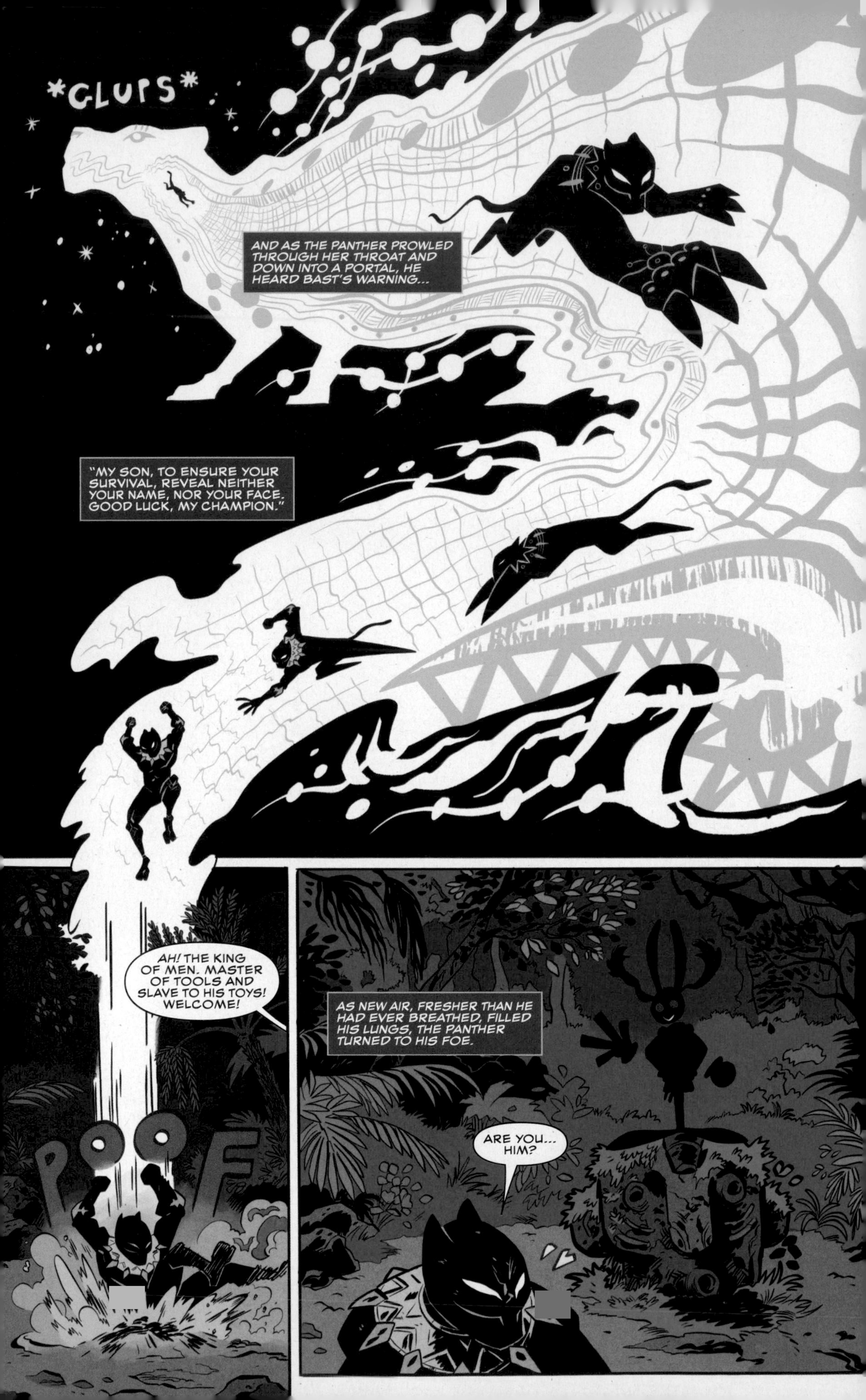
GLUPS
AND AS THE PANTHER PROWLED THROUGH HER THROAT AND DOWN INTO A PORTAL, HE HEARD BAST'S WARNING...
"MY SON, TO ENSURE YOUR SURVIVAL, REVEAL NEITHER YOUR NAME, NOR YOUR FACE. GOOD LUCK, MY CHAMPION."
AH! THE KING OF MEN. MASTER OF TOOLS AND SLAVE TO HIS TOYS! WELCOME!
POOF
AS NEW AIR, FRESHER THAN HE HAD EVER BREATHED, FILLED HIS LUNGS, THE PANTHER TURNED TO HIS FOE.
ARE YOU... HIM?

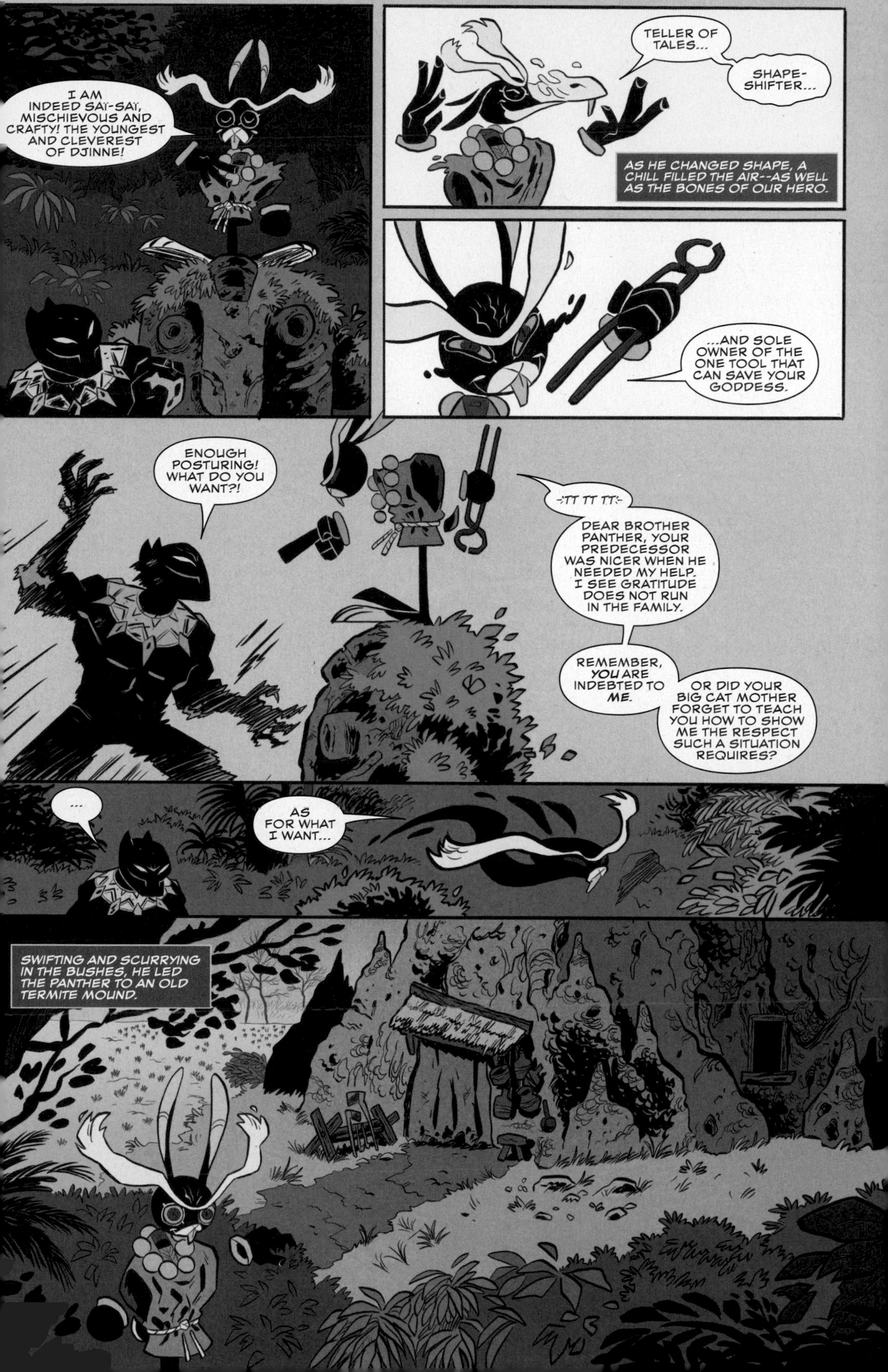
I AM INDEED SAÏ-SAÏ, MISCHIEVOUS AND CRAFTY! THE YOUNGEST AND CLEVEREST OF DJINNE!
TELLER OF TALES...
SHAPE-SHIFTER...
AS HE CHANGED SHAPE, A CHILL FILLED THE AIR--AS WELL AS THE BONES OF OUR HERO.
...AND SOLE OWNER OF THE ONE TOOL THAT CAN SAVE YOUR GODDESS.
ENOUGH POSTURING! WHAT DO YOU WANT?!
-TT TT TT-
DEAR BROTHER PANTHER, YOUR PREDECESSOR WAS NICER WHEN HE NEEDED MY HELP. I SEE GRATITUDE DOES NOT RUN IN THE FAMILY.
REMEMBER, YOU ARE INDEBTED TO ME.
OR DID YOUR BIG CAT MOTHER FORGET TO TEACH YOU HOW TO SHOW ME THE RESPECT SUCH A SITUATION REQUIRES?
...
AS FOR WHAT I WANT...
SWIFTING AND SCURRYING IN THE BUSHES, HE LED THE PANTHER TO AN OLD TERMITE MOUND.

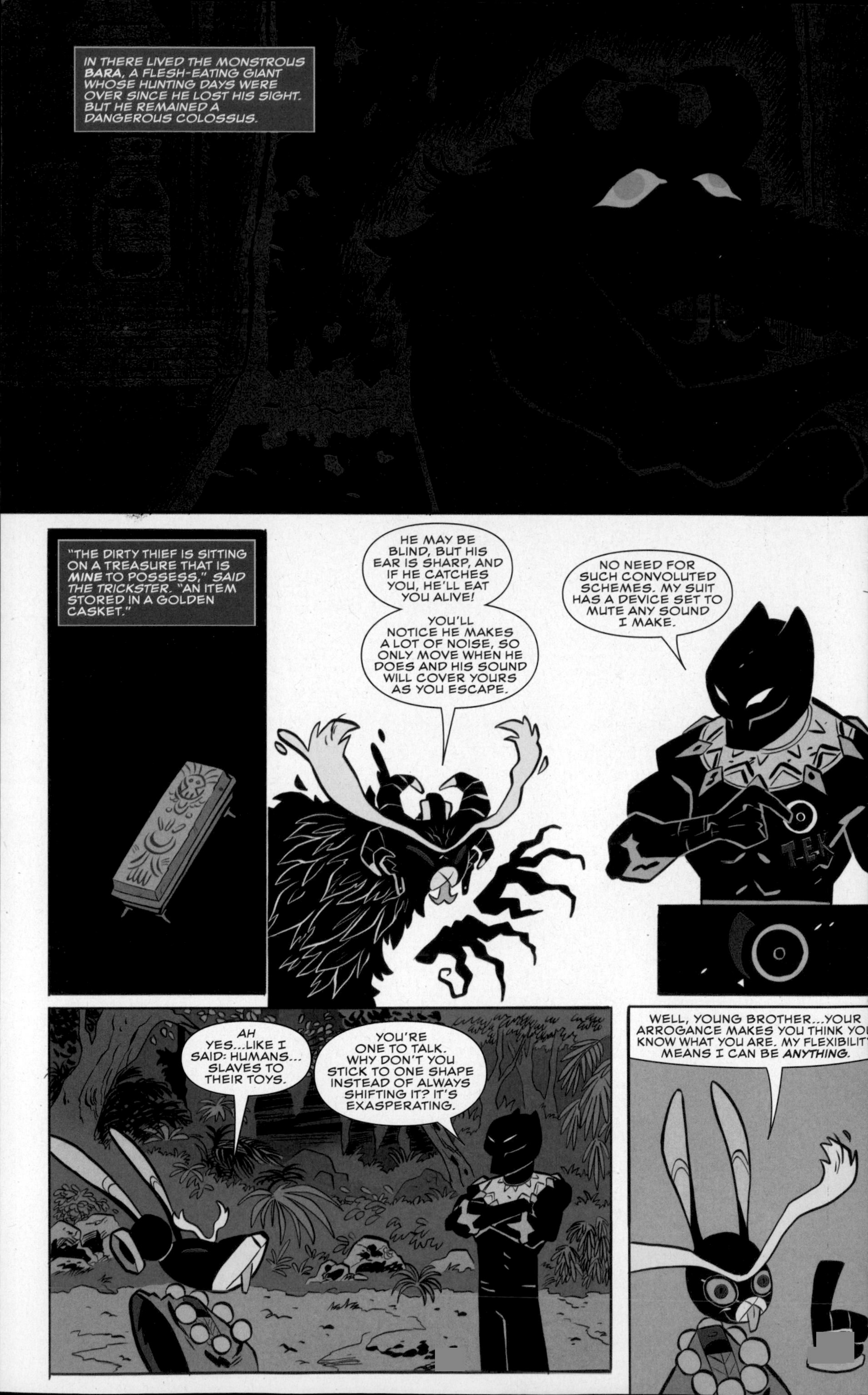
IN THERE LIVED THE MONSTROUS BARA, A FLESH-EATING GIANT WHOSE HUNTING DAYS WERE OVER SINCE HE LOST HIS SIGHT. BUT HE REMAINED A DANGEROUS COLOSSUS.
"THE DIRTY THIEF IS SITTING ON A TREASURE THAT IS MINE TO POSSESS," SAID THE TRICKSTER. "AN ITEM STORED IN A GOLDEN CASKET."
HE MAY BE BLIND, BUT HIS EAR IS SHARP, AND IF HE CATCHES YOU, HE'LL EAT YOU ALIVE!
YOU'LL NOTICE HE MAKES A LOT OF NOISE, SO ONLY MOVE WHEN HE DOES AND HIS SOUND WILL COVER YOURS AS YOU ESCAPE.
NO NEED FOR SUCH CONVOLUTED SCHEMES. MY SUIT HAS A DEVICE SET TO MUTE ANY SOUND I MAKE.
T-EK
AH YES...LIKE I SAID: HUMANS... SLAVES TO THEIR TOYS.
YOU'RE ONE TO TALK. WHY DON'T YOU STICK TO ONE SHAPE INSTEAD OF ALWAYS SHIFTING IT? IT'S EXASPERATING.
WELL, YOUNG BROTHER...YOUR ARROGANCE MAKES YOU THINK YOU KNOW WHAT YOU ARE. MY FLEXIBILITY MEANS I CAN BE ANYTHING.

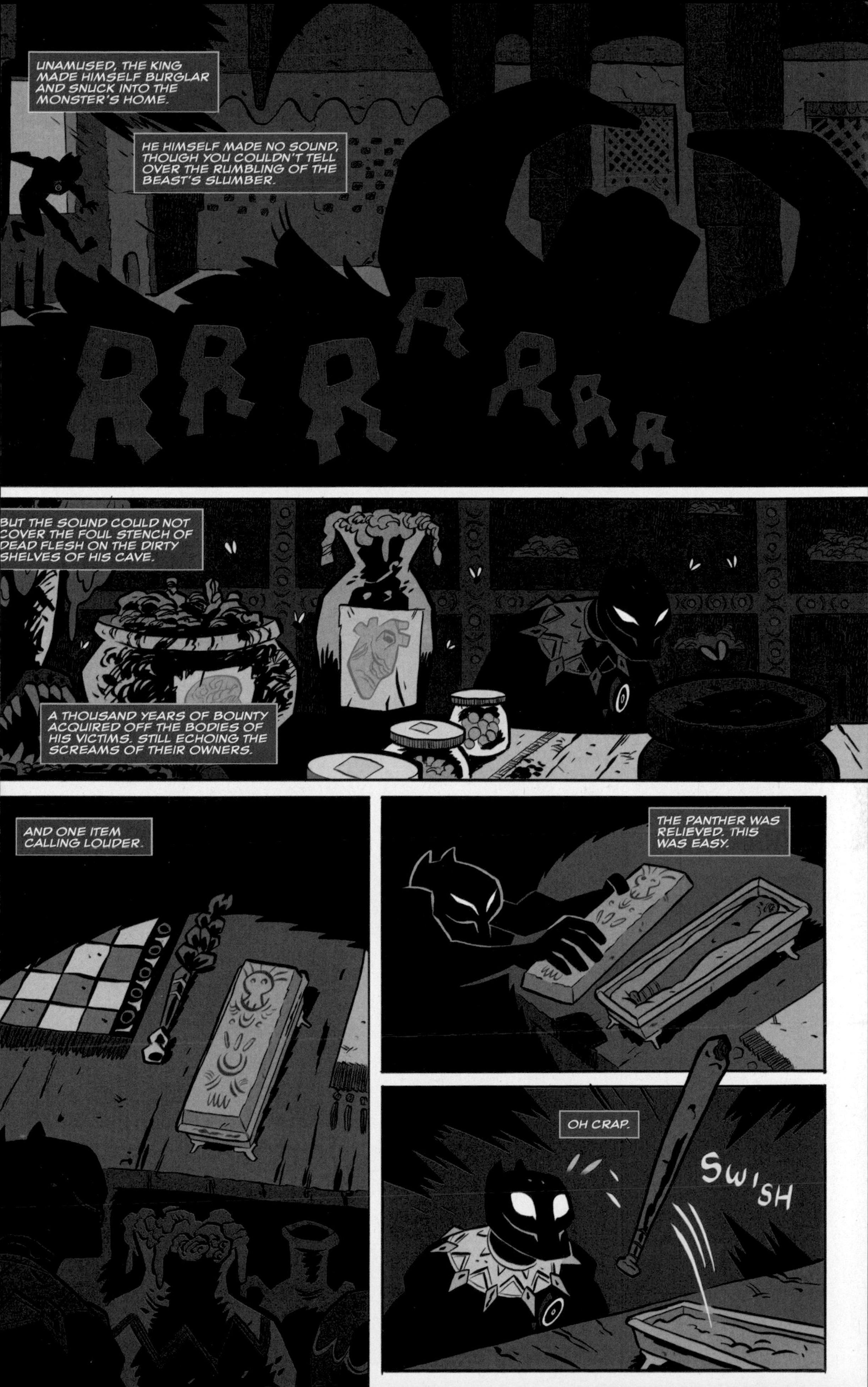
UNAMUSED, THE KING MADE HIMSELF BURGLAR AND SNUCK INTO THE MONSTER'S HOME.
HE HIMSELF MADE NO SOUND, THOUGH YOU COULDN'T TELL OVER THE RUMBLING OF THE BEAST'S SLUMBER.
RRRRRRRR
BUT THE SOUND COULD NOT COVER THE FOUL STENCH OF DEAD FLESH ON THE DIRTY SHELVES OF HIS CAVE.
A THOUSAND YEARS OF BOUNTY ACQUIRED OFF THE BODIES OF HIS VICTIMS. STILL ECHOING THE SCREAMS OF THEIR OWNERS.
AND ONE ITEM CALLING LOUDER.
THE PANTHER WAS RELIEVED. THIS WAS EASY.
OH CRAP.
SWISH

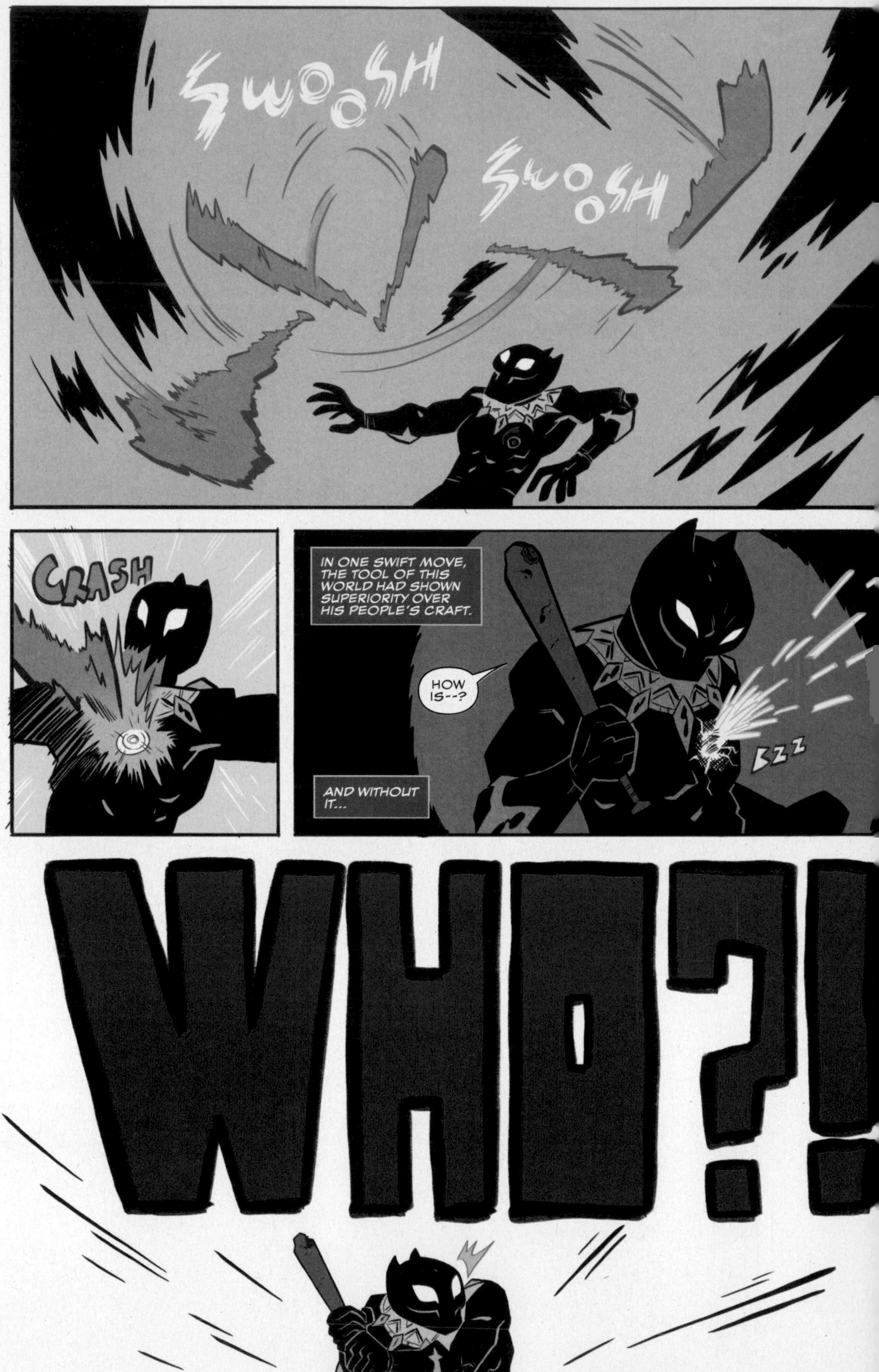
SWOOSH
SWOOSH
CRASH
IN ONE SWIFT MOVE, THE TOOL OF THIS WORLD HAD SHOWN SUPERIORITY OVER HIS PEOPLE'S CRAFT.
HOW IS--?
BZZ
AND WITHOUT IT...
WHO?!

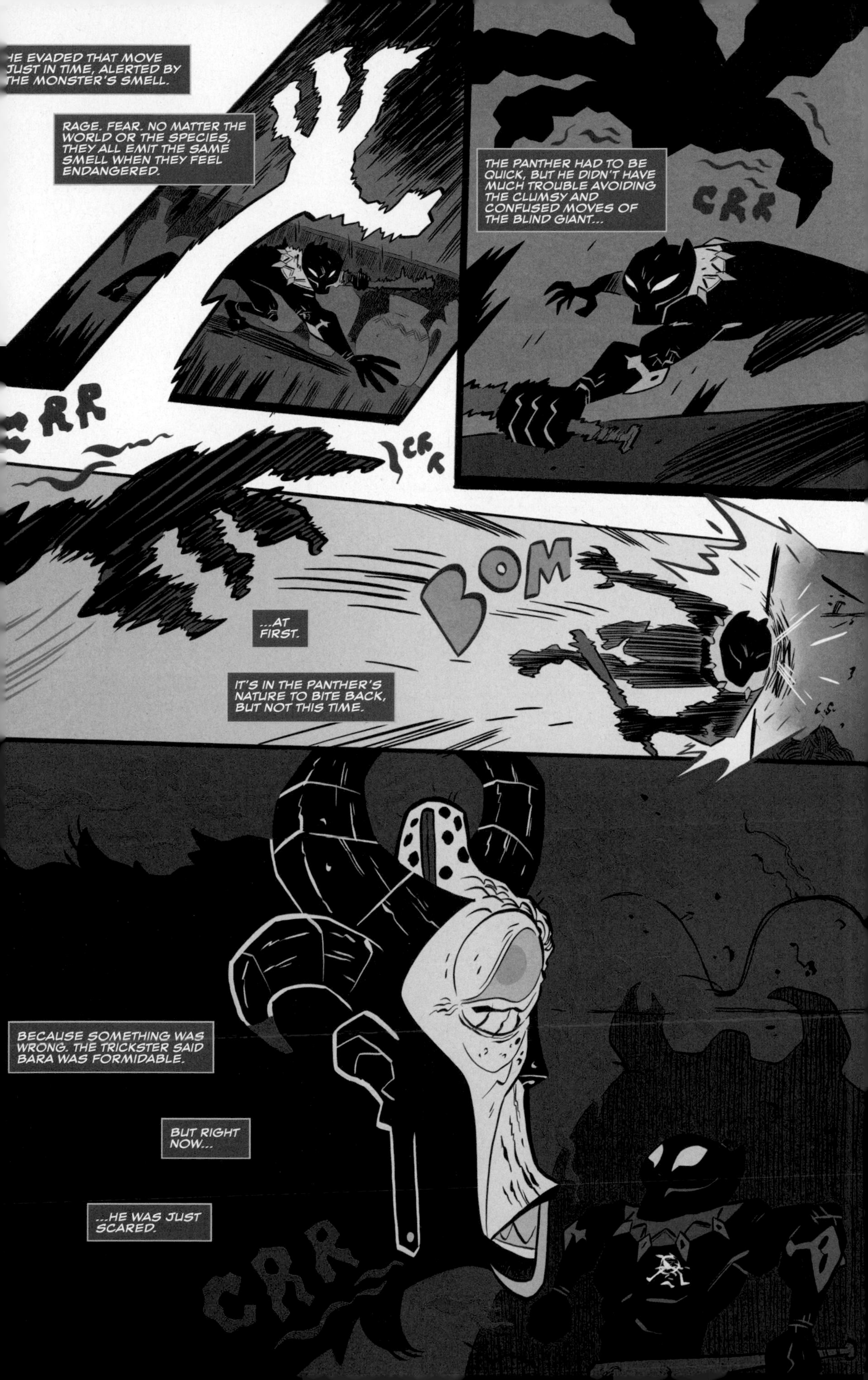
HE EVADED THAT MOVE JUST IN TIME, ALERTED BY THE MONSTER'S SMELL.
RAGE. FEAR. NO MATTER THE WORLD OR THE SPECIES, THEY ALL EMIT THE SAME SMELL WHEN THEY FEEL ENDANGERED.
THE PANTHER HAD TO BE QUICK, BUT HE DIDN'T HAVE MUCH TROUBLE AVOIDING THE CLUMSY AND CONFUSED MOVES OF THE BLIND GIANT...
CRR
CRR
CRR
BOM
...AT FIRST.
IT'S IN THE PANTHER'S NATURE TO BITE BACK, BUT NOT THIS TIME.
BECAUSE SOMETHING WAS WRONG. THE TRICKSTER SAID BARA WAS FORMIDABLE.
BUT RIGHT NOW...
...HE WAS JUST SCARED.
CRR

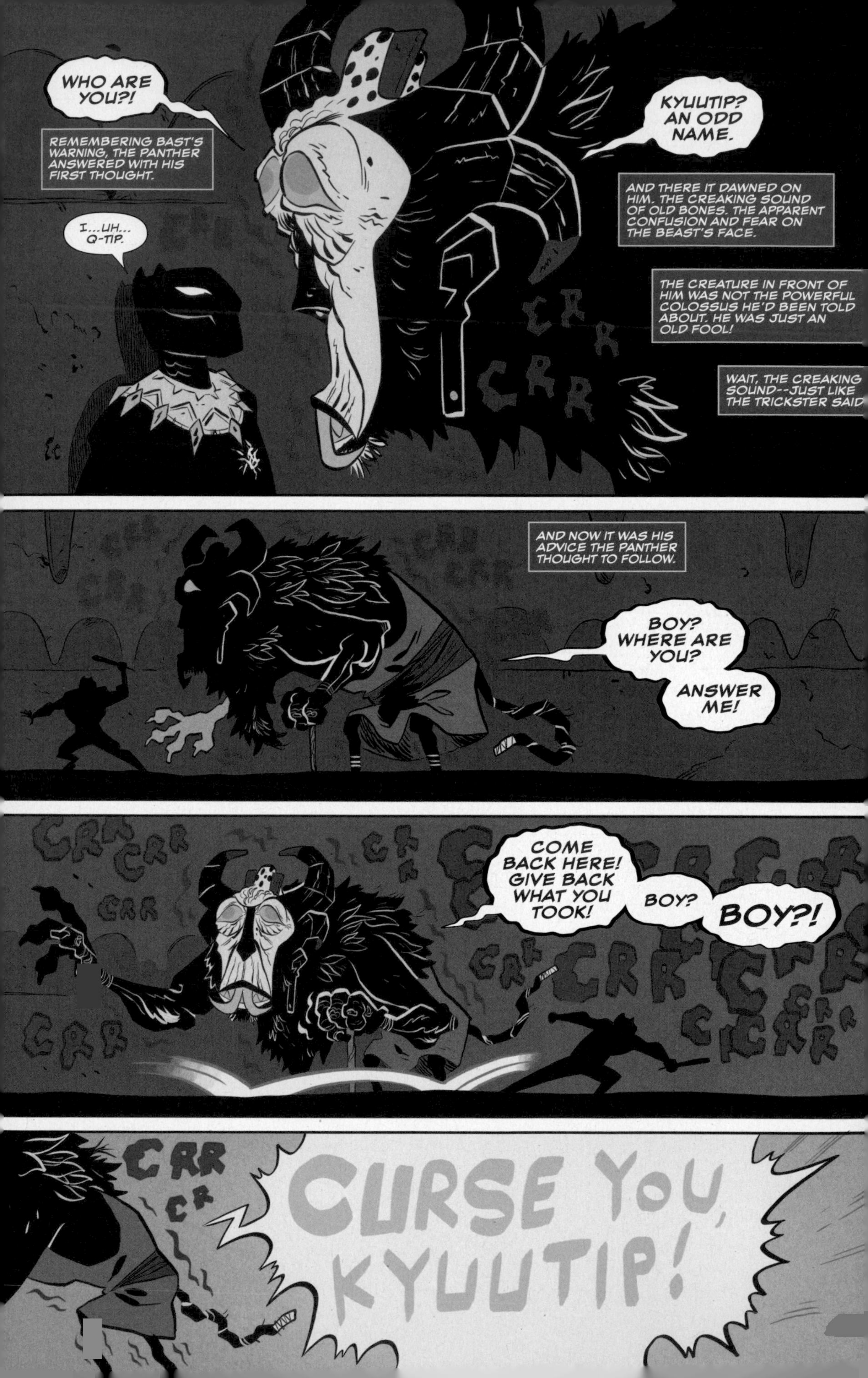
WHO ARE YOU?!
REMEMBERING BAST'S WARNING, THE PANTHER ANSWERED WITH HIS FIRST THOUGHT.
I...UH... Q-TIP.
KYUUTIP? AN ODD NAME.
AND THERE IT DAWNED ON HIM. THE CREAKING SOUND OF OLD BONES. THE APPARENT CONFUSION AND FEAR ON THE BEAST'S FACE.
THE CREATURE IN FRONT OF HIM WAS NOT THE POWERFUL COLOSSUS HE'D BEEN TOLD ABOUT. HE WAS JUST AN OLD FOOL!
CRR
CRR
WAIT, THE CREAKING SOUND--JUST LIKE THE TRICKSTER SAID
AND NOW IT WAS HIS ADVICE THE PANTHER THOUGHT TO FOLLOW.
BOY? WHERE ARE YOU?
ANSWER ME!
COME BACK HERE! GIVE BACK WHAT YOU TOOK!
BOY?
BOY?!
CRR
CRR
CURSE YOU, KYUUTIP!

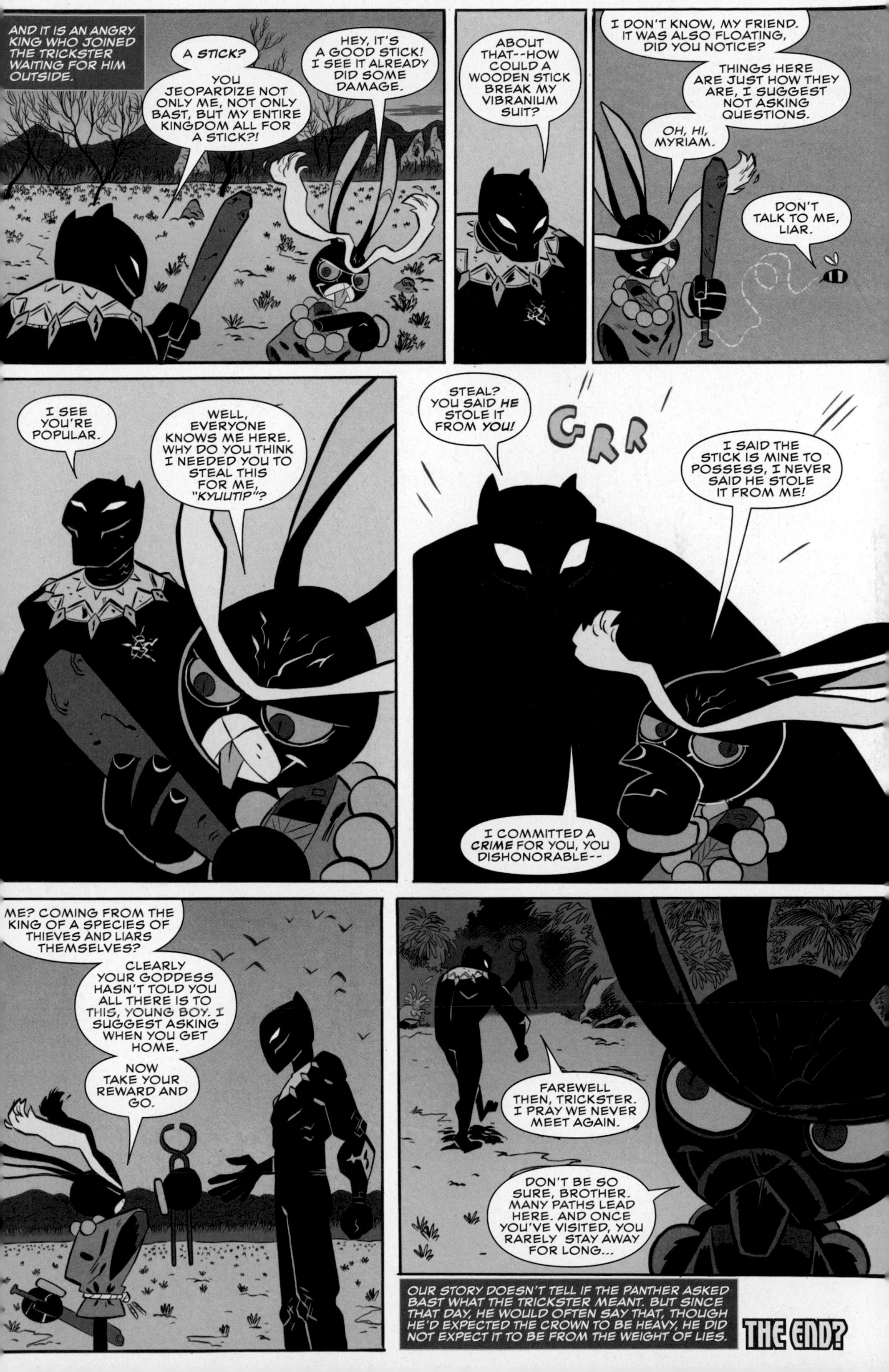

AND IT IS AN ANGRY KING WHO JOINED THE TRICKSTER WAITING FOR HIM OUTSIDE.
A STICK?
YOU JEOPARDIZE NOT ONLY ME, NOT ONLY BAST, BUT MY ENTIRE KINGDOM ALL FOR A STICK?!
HEY, IT'S A GOOD STICK! I SEE IT ALREADY DID SOME DAMAGE.
ABOUT THAT--HOW COULD A WOODEN STICK BREAK MY VIBRANIUM SUIT?
I DON'T KNOW, MY FRIEND. IT WAS ALSO FLOATING, DID YOU NOTICE?
THINGS HERE ARE JUST HOW THEY ARE, I SUGGEST NOT ASKING QUESTIONS.
OH, HI, MYRIAM.
DON'T TALK TO ME, LIAR.
I SEE YOU'RE POPULAR.
WELL, EVERYONE KNOWS ME HERE. WHY DO YOU THINK I NEEDED YOU TO STEAL THIS FOR ME, "KYUUTIP"?
STEAL? YOU SAID HE STOLE IT FROM YOU!
GRR
I SAID THE STICK IS MINE TO POSSESS, I NEVER SAID HE STOLE IT FROM ME!
I COMMITTED A CRIME FOR YOU, YOU DISHONORABLE--
ME? COMING FROM THE KING OF A SPECIES OF THIEVES AND LIARS THEMSELVES?
CLEARLY YOUR GODDESS HASN'T TOLD YOU ALL THERE IS TO THIS, YOUNG BOY. I SUGGEST ASKING WHEN YOU GET HOME.
NOW TAKE YOUR REWARD AND GO.
FAREWELL THEN, TRICKSTER. I PRAY WE NEVER MEET AGAIN.
DON'T BE SO SURE, BROTHER. MANY PATHS LEAD HERE. AND ONCE YOU'VE VISITED, YOU RARELY STAY AWAY FOR LONG...
OUR STORY DOESN'T TELL IF THE PANTHER ASKED BAST WHAT THE TRICKSTER MEANT. BUT SINCE THAT DAY, HE WOULD OFTEN SAY THAT, THOUGH HE'D EXPECTED THE CROWN TO BE HEAVY, HE DID NOT EXPECT IT TO BE FROM THE WEIGHT OF LIES.
THE END?

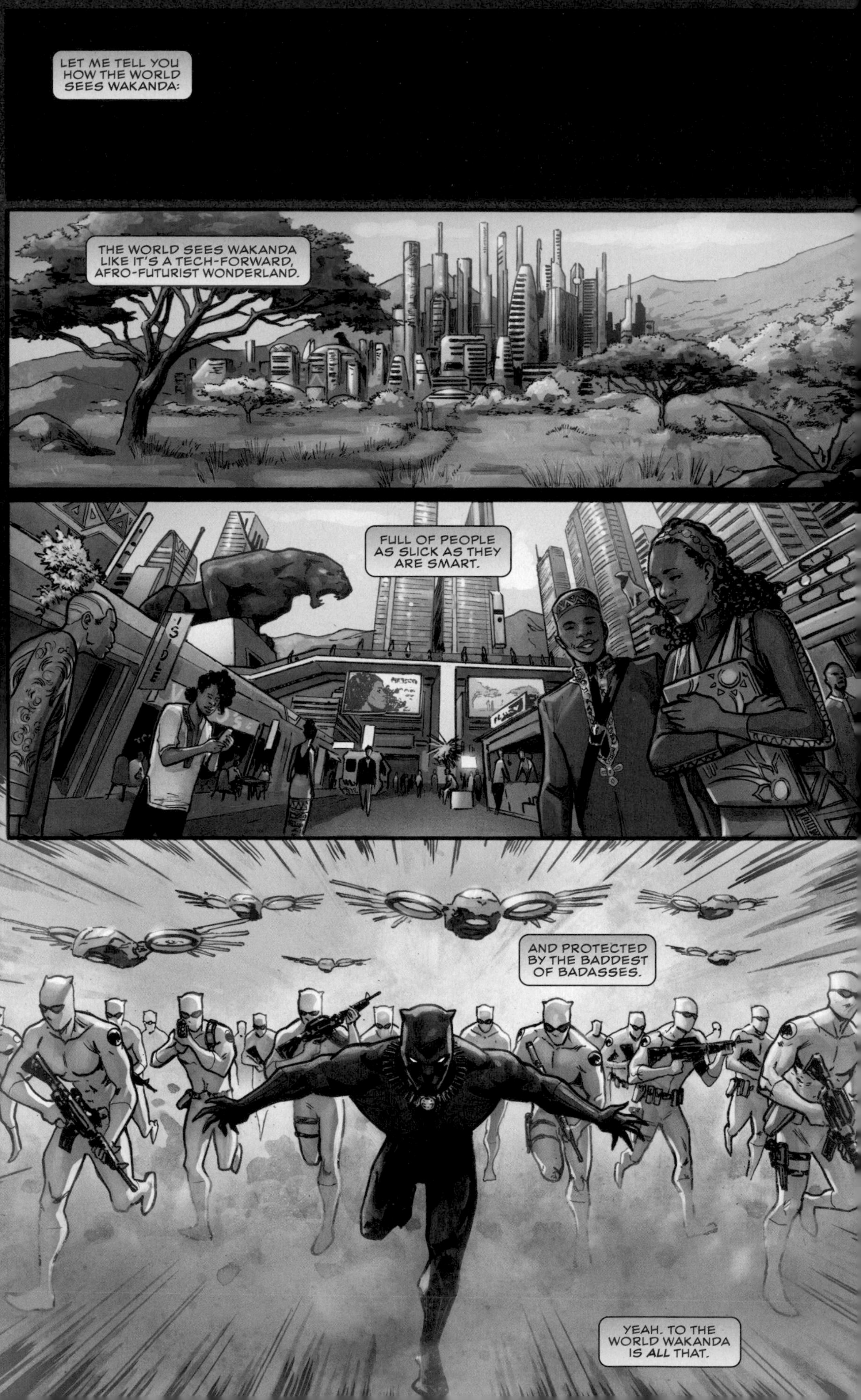
LET ME TELL YOU HOW THE WORLD SEES WAKANDA:
THE WORLD SEES WAKANDA LIKE IT'S A TECH-FORWARD, AFRO-FUTURIST WONDERLAND.
FULL OF PEOPLE AS SLICK AS THEY ARE SMART.
AND PROTECTED BY THE BADDEST OF BADASSES.
YEAH. TO THE WORLD WAKANDA IS *ALL* THAT.

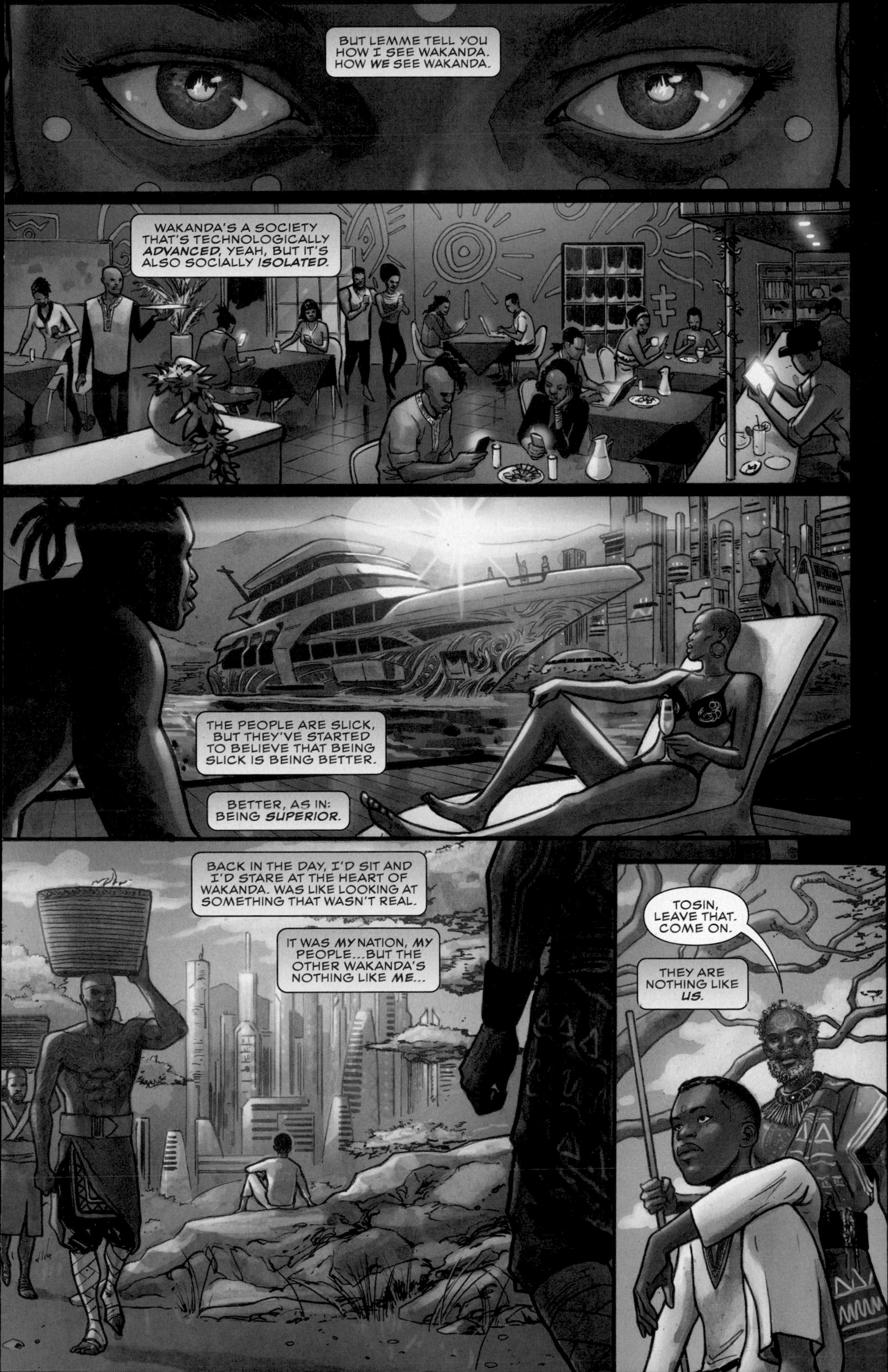
BUT LEMME TELL YOU HOW I SEE WAKANDA. HOW WE SEE WAKANDA.
WAKANDA'S A SOCIETY THAT'S TECHNOLOGICALLY ADVANCED, YEAH, BUT IT'S ALSO SOCIALLY ISOLATED.
THE PEOPLE ARE SLICK, BUT THEY'VE STARTED TO BELIEVE THAT BEING SLICK IS BEING BETTER.
BETTER, AS IN: BEING SUPERIOR.
BACK IN THE DAY, I'D SIT AND I'D STARE AT THE HEART OF WAKANDA. WAS LIKE LOOKING AT SOMETHING THAT WASN'T REAL.
IT WAS MY NATION, MY PEOPLE...BUT THE OTHER WAKANDA'S NOTHING LIKE ME...
TOSIN, LEAVE THAT. COME ON.
THEY ARE NOTHING LIKE US.

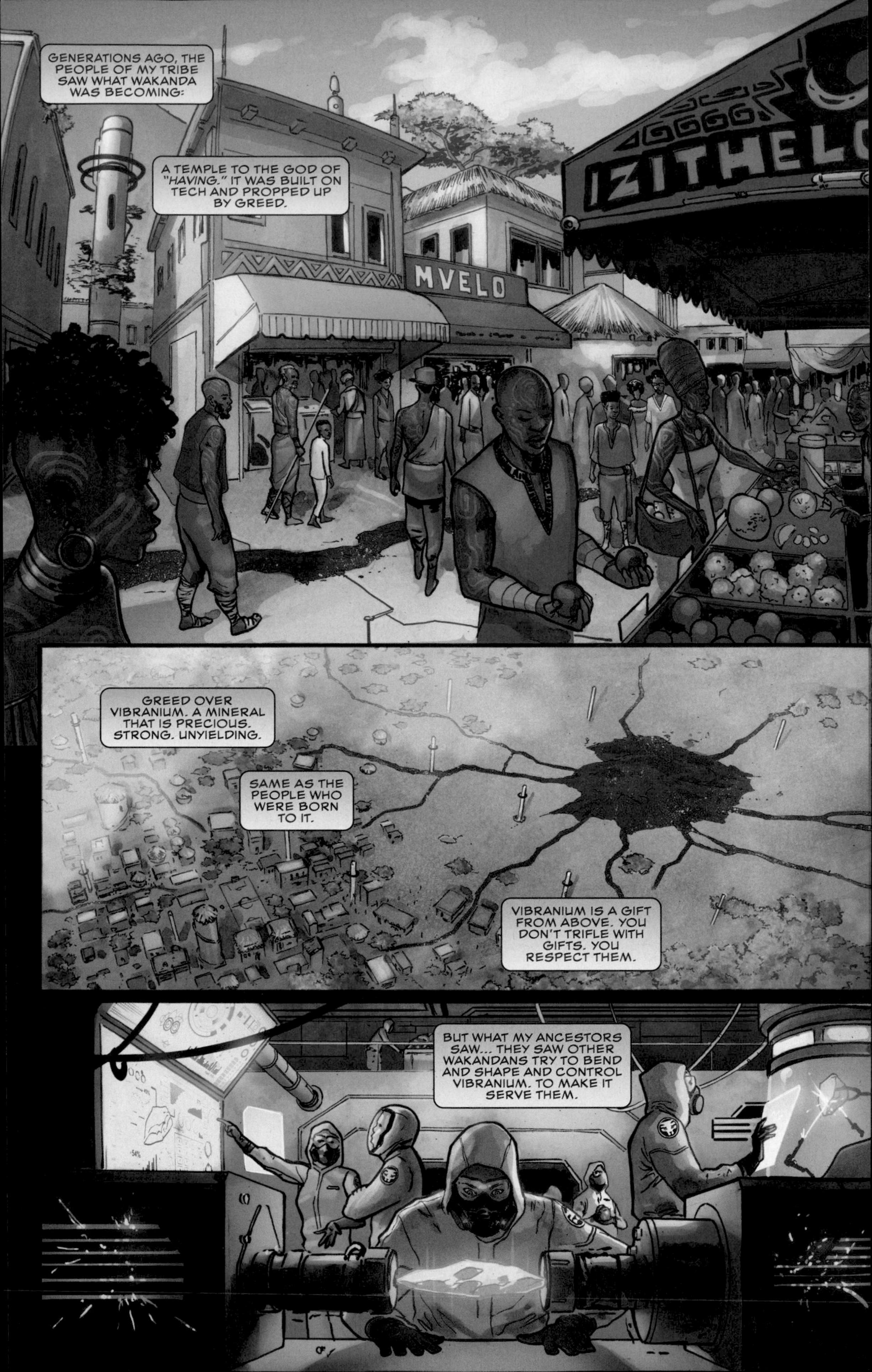
GENERATIONS AGO, THE PEOPLE OF MY TRIBE SAW WHAT WAKANDA WAS BECOMING:
A TEMPLE TO THE GOD OF "HAVING." IT WAS BUILT ON TECH AND PROPPED UP BY GREED.
IZITHEL
MVELO
GREED OVER VIBRANIUM. A MINERAL THAT IS PRECIOUS. STRONG. UNYIELDING.
SAME AS THE PEOPLE WHO WERE BORN TO IT.
VIBRANIUM IS A GIFT FROM ABOVE. YOU DON'T TRIFLE WITH GIFTS. YOU RESPECT THEM.
BUT WHAT MY ANCESTORS SAW... THEY SAW OTHER WAKANDANS TRY TO BEND AND SHAPE AND CONTROL VIBRANIUM. TO MAKE IT SERVE THEM.

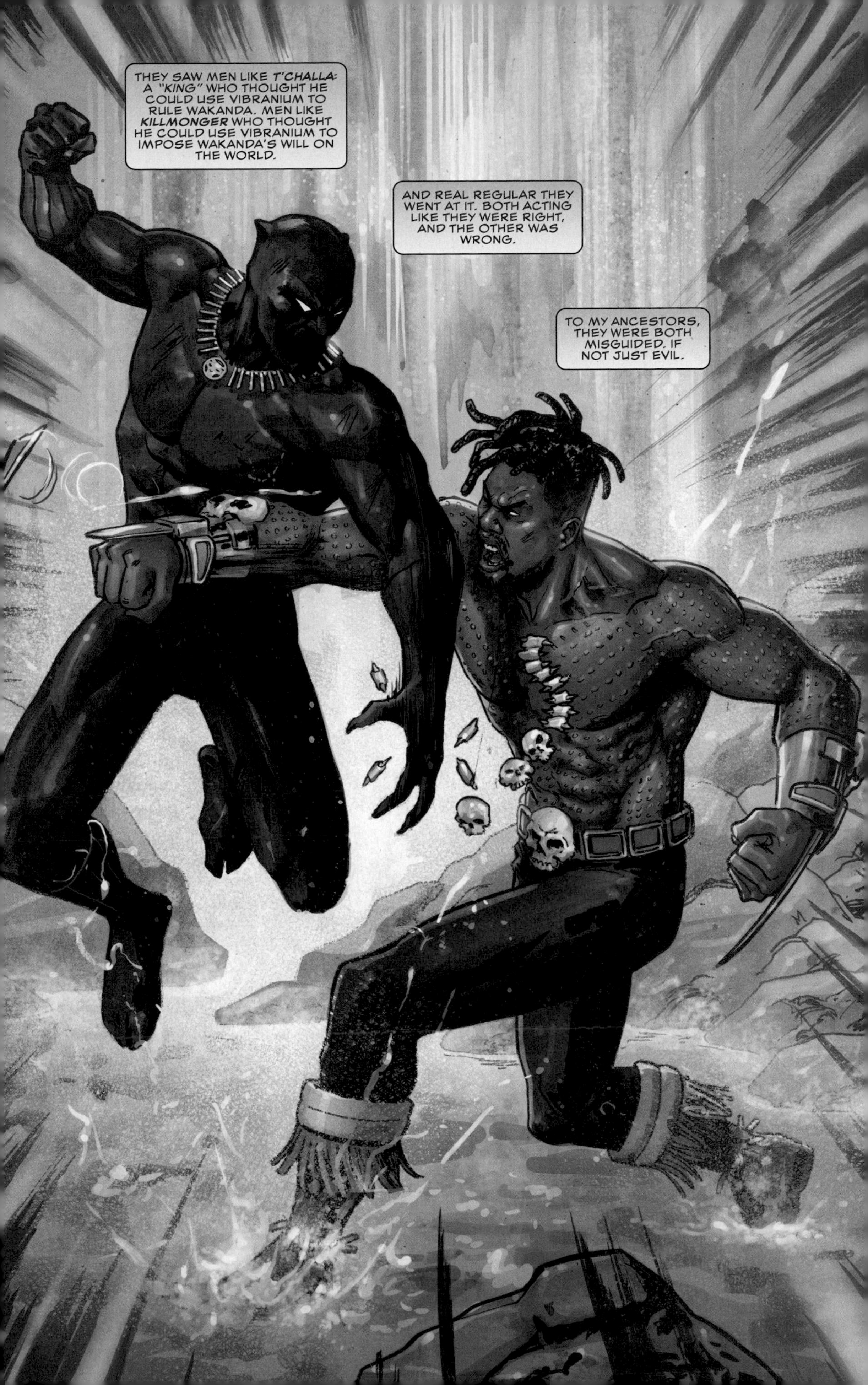
THEY SAW MEN LIKE *T'CHALLA*: A *"KING"* WHO THOUGHT HE COULD USE VIBRANIUM TO RULE WAKANDA. MEN LIKE *KILLMONGER* WHO THOUGHT HE COULD USE VIBRANIUM TO IMPOSE WAKANDA'S WILL ON THE WORLD.
AND REAL REGULAR THEY WENT AT IT. BOTH ACTING LIKE THEY WERE RIGHT, AND THE OTHER WAS WRONG.
TO MY ANCESTORS, THEY WERE BOTH MISGUIDED. IF NOT JUST EVIL.

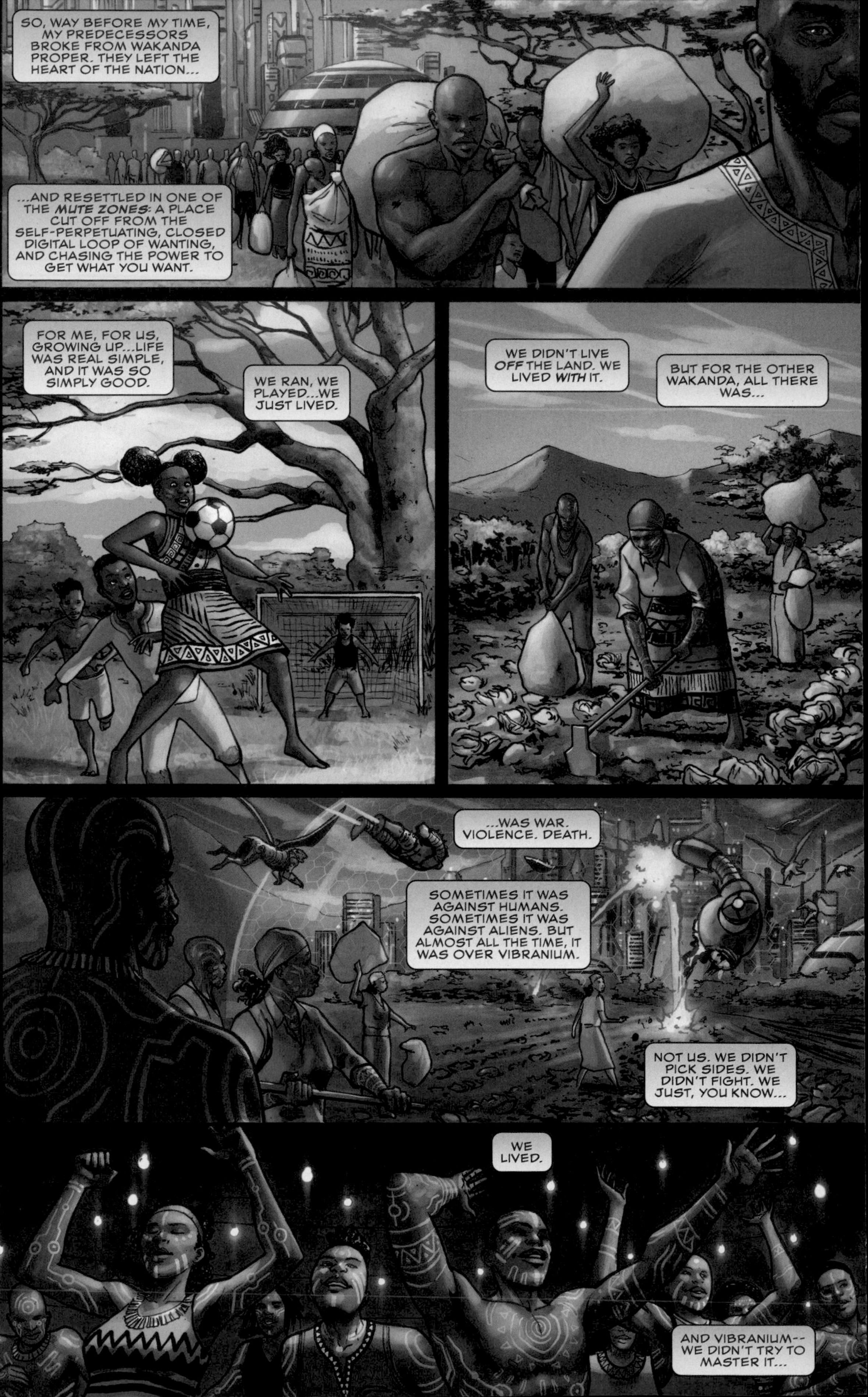
SO, WAY BEFORE MY TIME, MY PREDECESSORS BROKE FROM WAKANDA PROPER. THEY LEFT THE HEART OF THE NATION...
...AND RESETTLED IN ONE OF THE *MUTE ZONES*: A PLACE CUT OFF FROM THE SELF-PERPETUATING, CLOSED DIGITAL LOOP OF WANTING, AND CHASING THE POWER TO GET WHAT YOU WANT.
FOR ME, FOR US, GROWING UP...LIFE WAS REAL SIMPLE, AND IT WAS SO SIMPLY GOOD.
WE RAN, WE PLAYED...WE JUST LIVED.
WE DIDN'T LIVE *OFF* THE LAND. WE LIVED *WITH* IT.
BUT FOR THE OTHER WAKANDA, ALL THERE WAS...
...WAS WAR. VIOLENCE. DEATH.
SOMETIMES IT WAS AGAINST HUMANS. SOMETIMES IT WAS AGAINST ALIENS. BUT ALMOST ALL THE TIME, IT WAS OVER VIBRANIUM.
NOT US. WE DIDN'T PICK SIDES. WE DIDN'T FIGHT. WE JUST, YOU KNOW...
WE LIVED.
AND VIBRANIUM-- WE DIDN'T TRY TO MASTER IT...

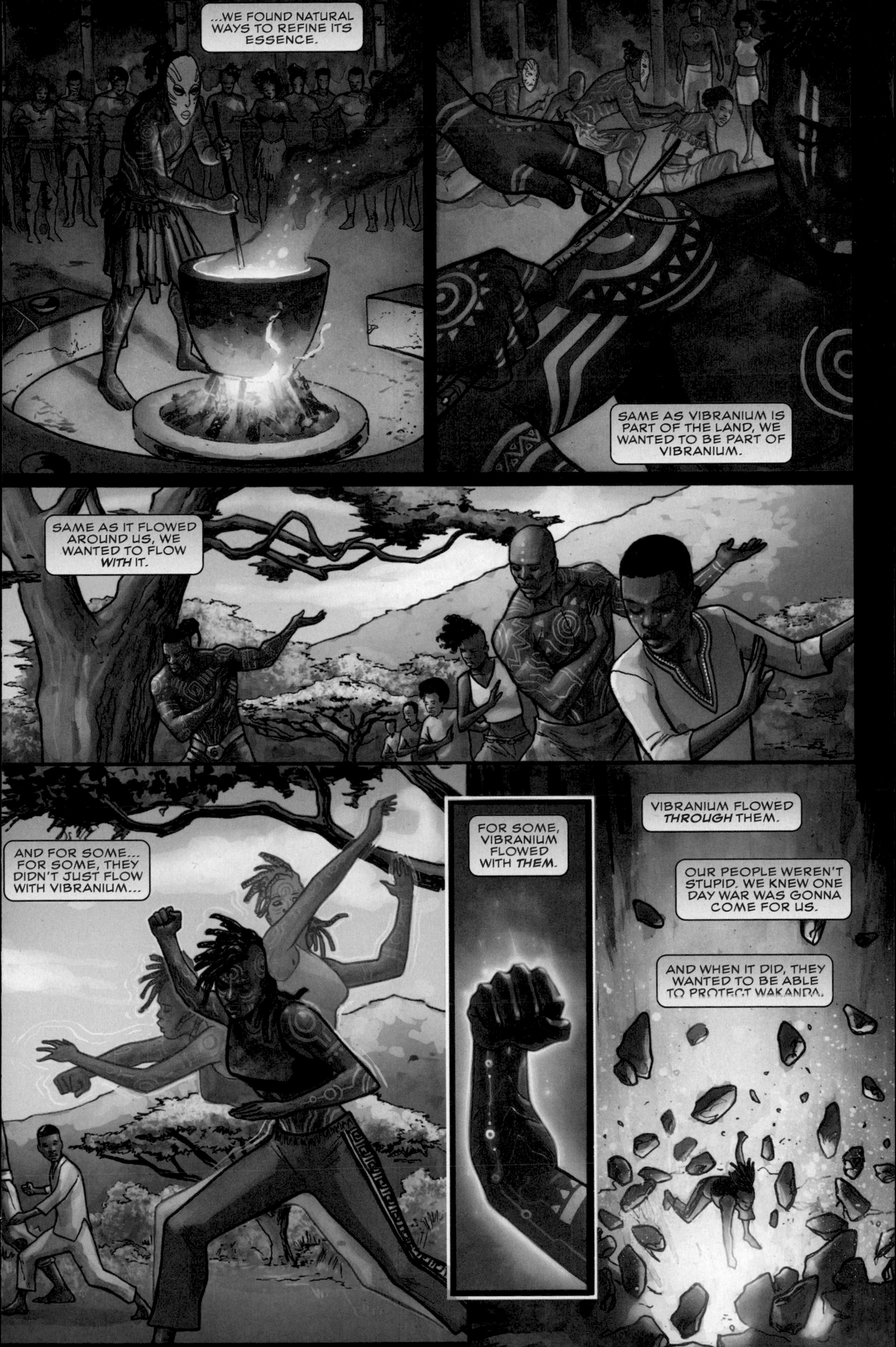
...WE FOUND NATURAL WAYS TO REFINE ITS ESSENCE.
SAME AS VIBRANIUM IS PART OF THE LAND, WE WANTED TO BE PART OF VIBRANIUM.
SAME AS IT FLOWED AROUND US, WE WANTED TO FLOW *WITH* IT.
AND FOR SOME... FOR SOME, THEY DIDN'T JUST FLOW WITH VIBRANIUM...
FOR SOME, VIBRANIUM FLOWED WITH *THEM*.
VIBRANIUM FLOWED *THROUGH* THEM.
OUR PEOPLE WEREN'T STUPID. WE KNEW ONE DAY WAR WAS GONNA COME FOR US.
AND WHEN IT DID, THEY WANTED TO BE ABLE TO PROTECT WAKANDA.

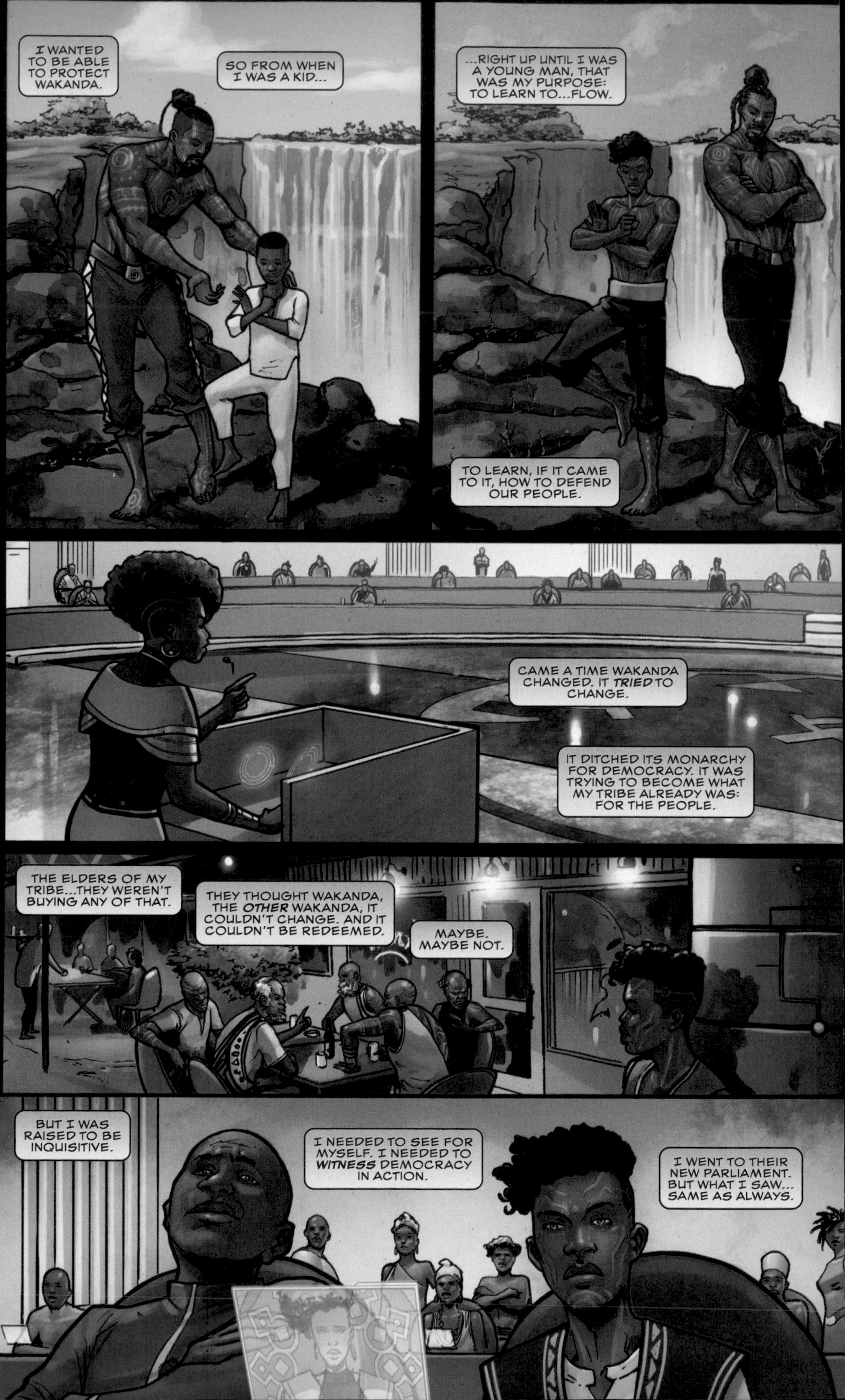
I WANTED TO BE ABLE TO PROTECT WAKANDA.
SO FROM WHEN I WAS A KID...
...RIGHT UP UNTIL I WAS A YOUNG MAN, THAT WAS MY PURPOSE: TO LEARN TO...FLOW.
TO LEARN, IF IT CAME TO IT, HOW TO DEFEND OUR PEOPLE.
CAME A TIME WAKANDA CHANGED. IT *TRIED* TO CHANGE.
IT DITCHED ITS MONARCHY FOR DEMOCRACY. IT WAS TRYING TO BECOME WHAT MY TRIBE ALREADY WAS: FOR THE PEOPLE.
THE ELDERS OF MY TRIBE...THEY WEREN'T BUYING ANY OF THAT.
THEY THOUGHT WAKANDA, THE *OTHER* WAKANDA, IT COULDN'T CHANGE. AND IT COULDN'T BE REDEEMED.
MAYBE. MAYBE NOT.
BUT I WAS RAISED TO BE INQUISITIVE.
I NEEDED TO SEE FOR MYSELF. I NEEDED TO *WITNESS* DEMOCRACY IN ACTION.
I WENT TO THEIR NEW PARLIAMENT. BUT WHAT I SAW... SAME AS ALWAYS.

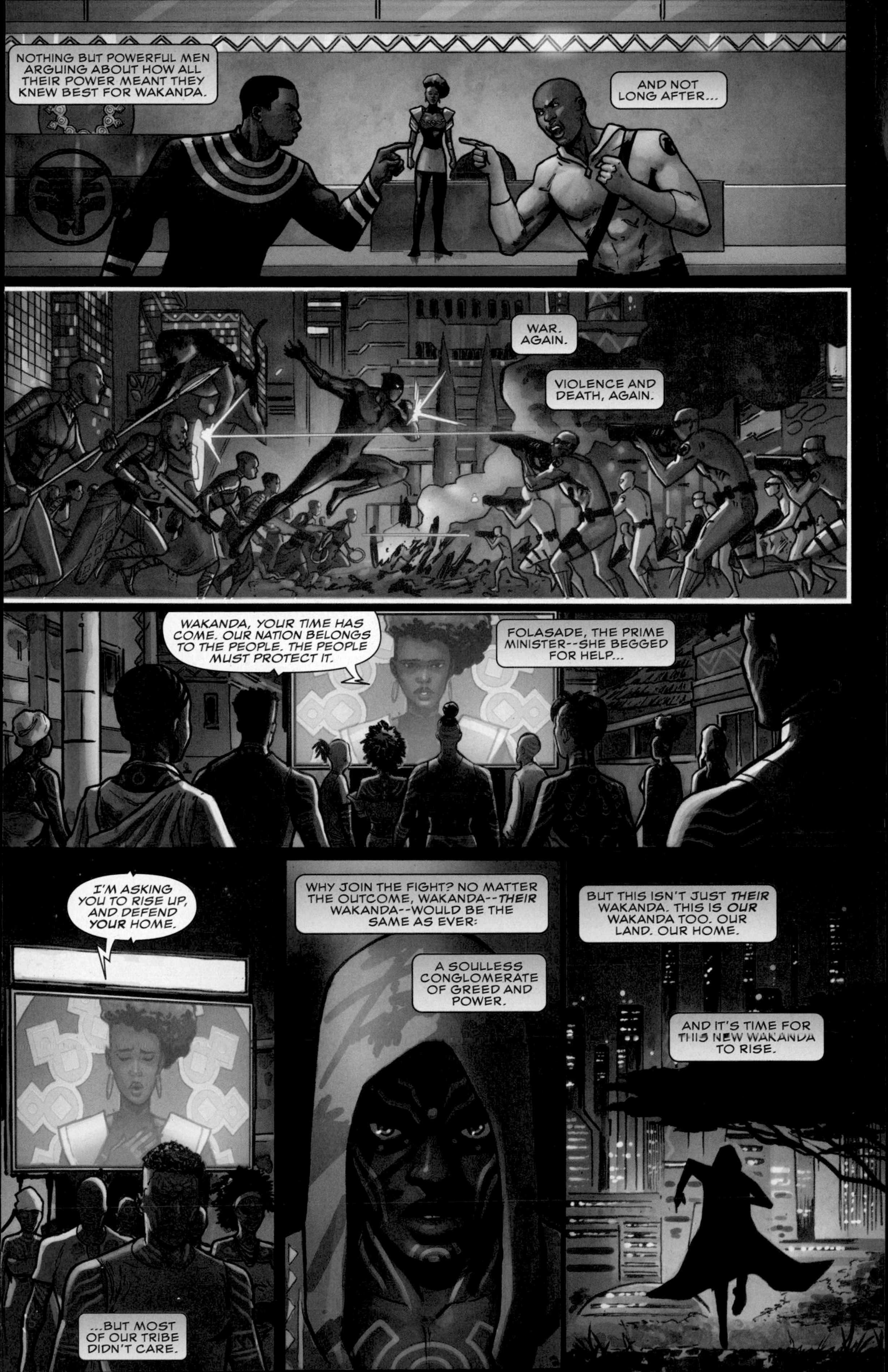
NOTHING BUT POWERFUL MEN ARGUING ABOUT HOW ALL THEIR POWER MEANT THEY KNEW BEST FOR WAKANDA.
AND NOT LONG AFTER...
WAR. AGAIN.
VIOLENCE AND DEATH, AGAIN.
WAKANDA, YOUR TIME HAS COME. OUR NATION BELONGS TO THE PEOPLE. THE PEOPLE MUST PROTECT IT.
FOLASADE, THE PRIME MINISTER--SHE BEGGED FOR HELP...
I'M ASKING YOU TO RISE UP, AND DEFEND YOUR HOME.
...BUT MOST OF OUR TRIBE DIDN'T CARE.
WHY JOIN THE FIGHT? NO MATTER THE OUTCOME, WAKANDA--THEIR WAKANDA--WOULD BE THE SAME AS EVER:
A SOULLESS CONGLOMERATE OF GREED AND POWER.
BUT THIS ISN'T JUST THEIR WAKANDA. THIS IS OUR WAKANDA TOO. OUR LAND. OUR HOME.
AND IT'S TIME FOR THIS NEW WAKANDA TO RISE.

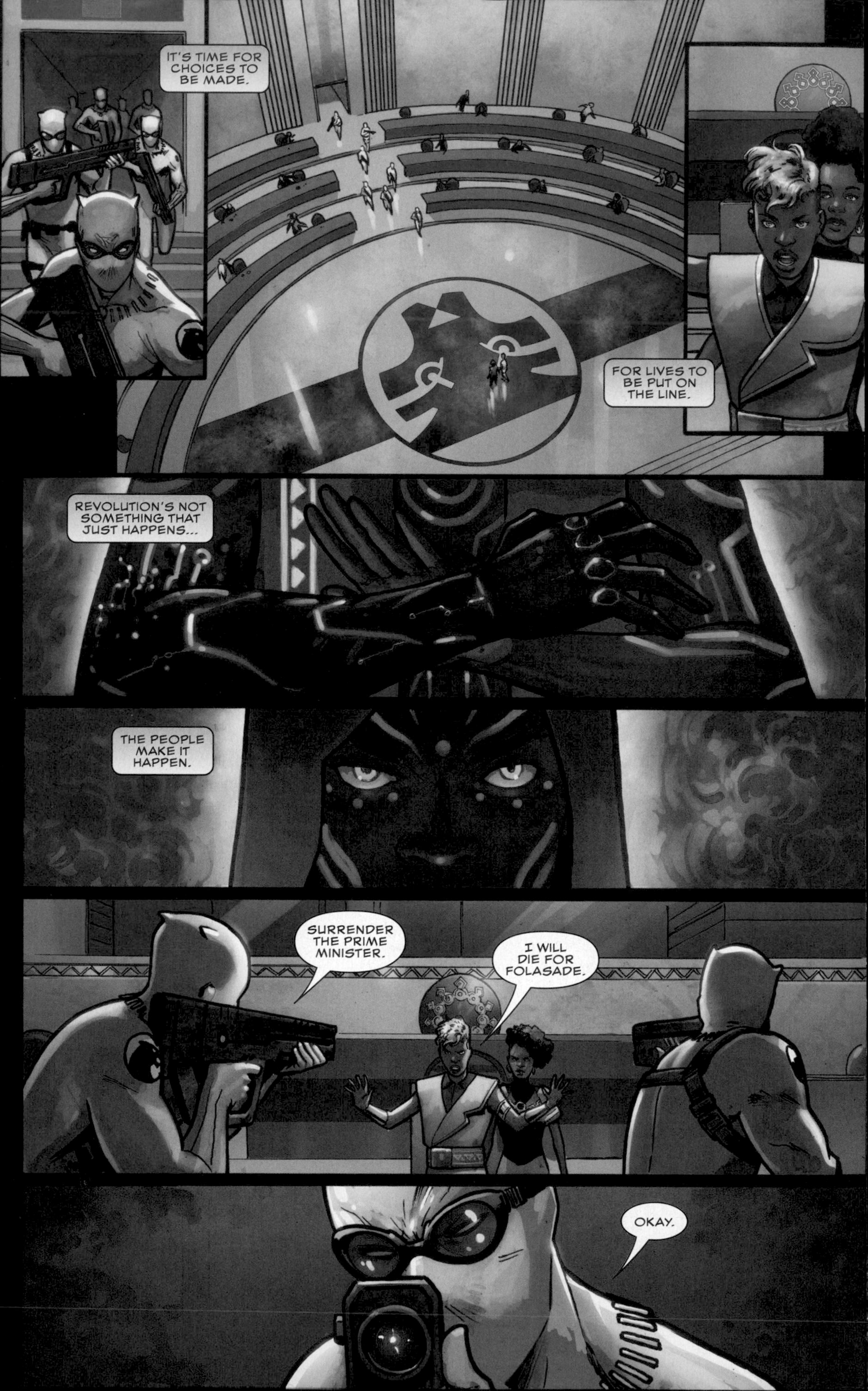
IT'S TIME FOR CHOICES TO BE MADE.
FOR LIVES TO BE PUT ON THE LINE.
REVOLUTION'S NOT SOMETHING THAT JUST HAPPENS...
THE PEOPLE MAKE IT HAPPEN.
SURRENDER THE PRIME MINISTER.
I WILL DIE FOR FOLASADE.
OKAY.

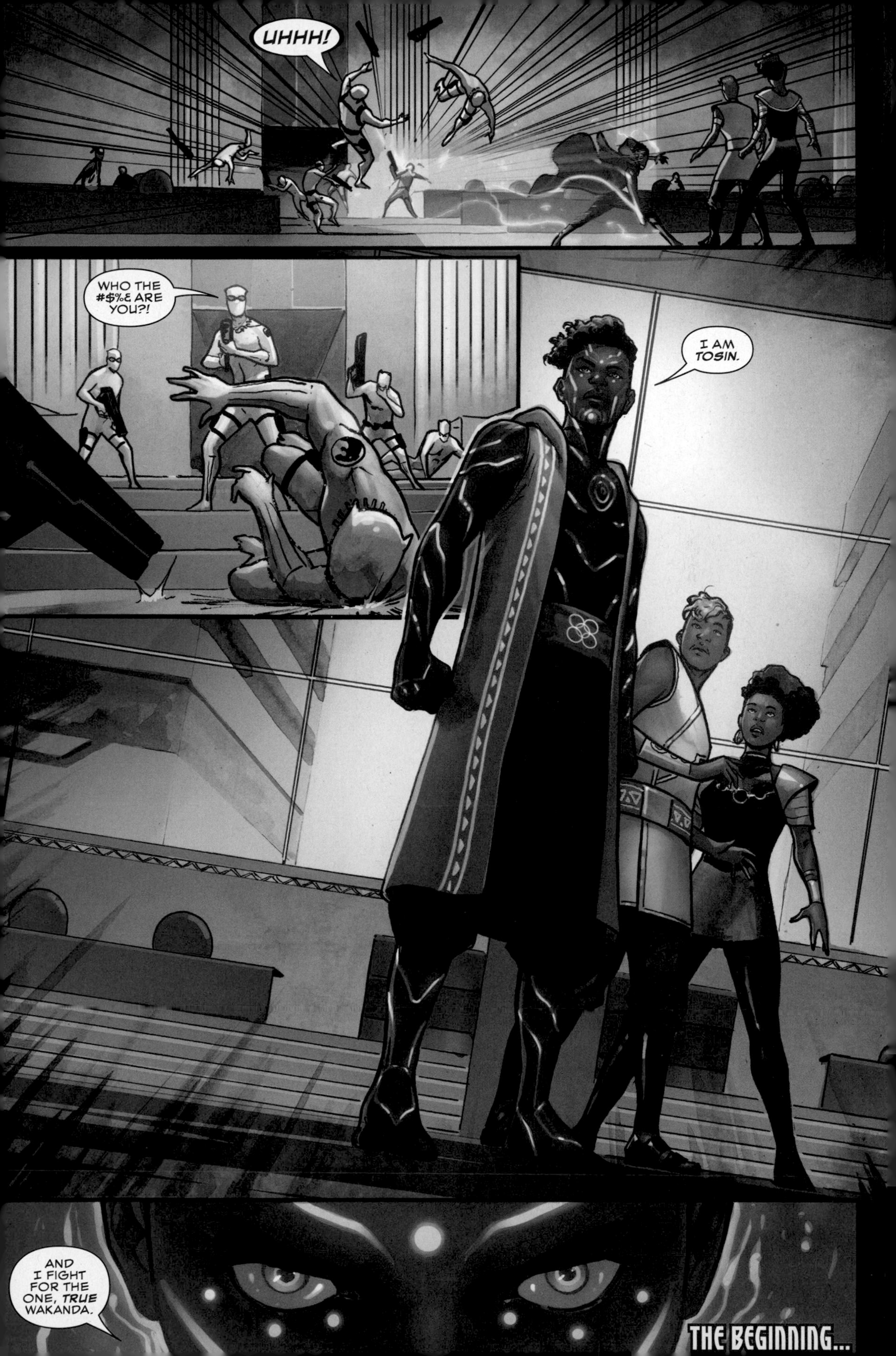
UHHH!
WHO THE #$%& ARE YOU?!
I AM *TOSIN*.
AND I FIGHT FOR THE ONE, *TRUE* WAKANDA.
THE BEGINNING...

4

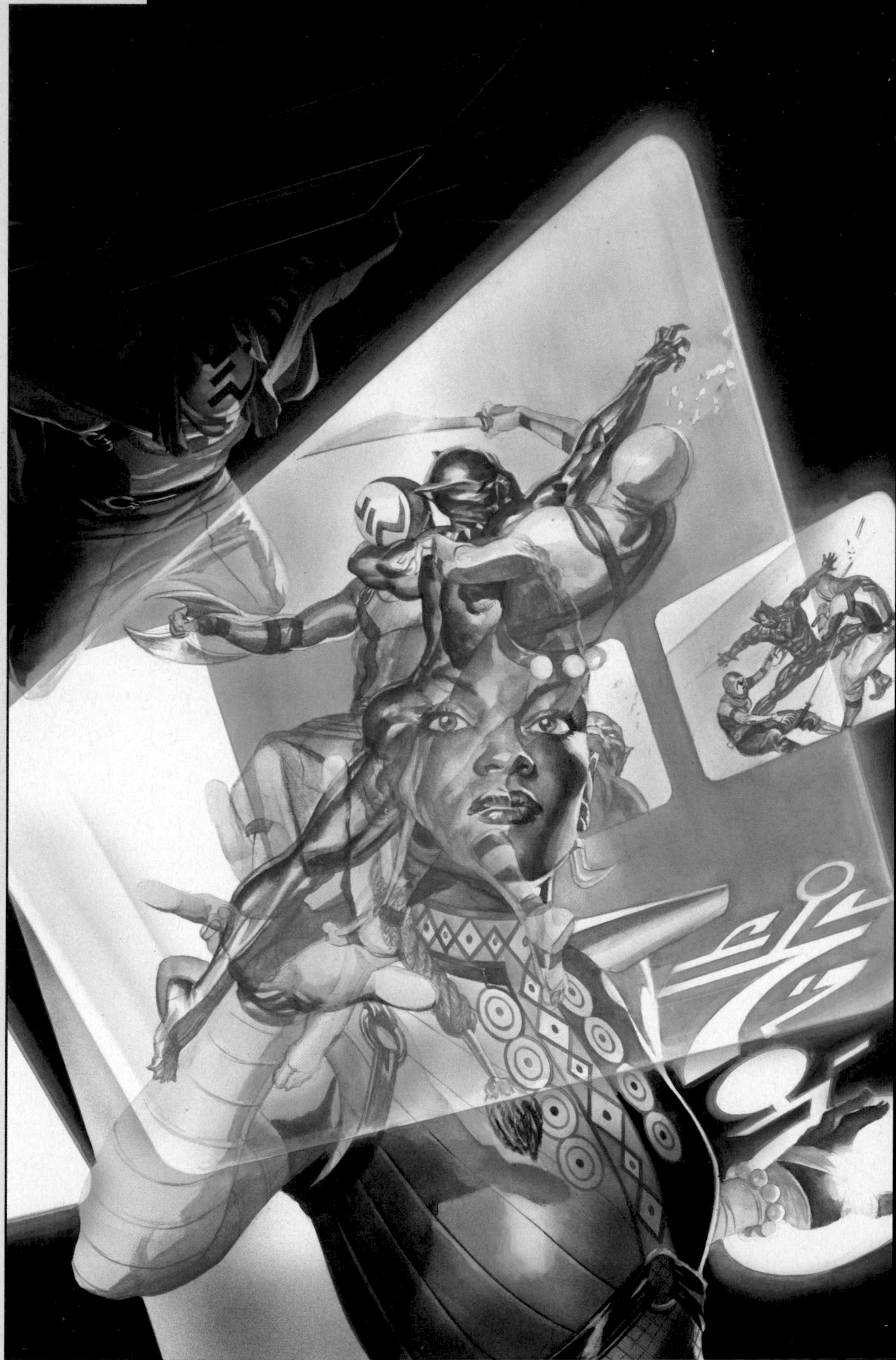

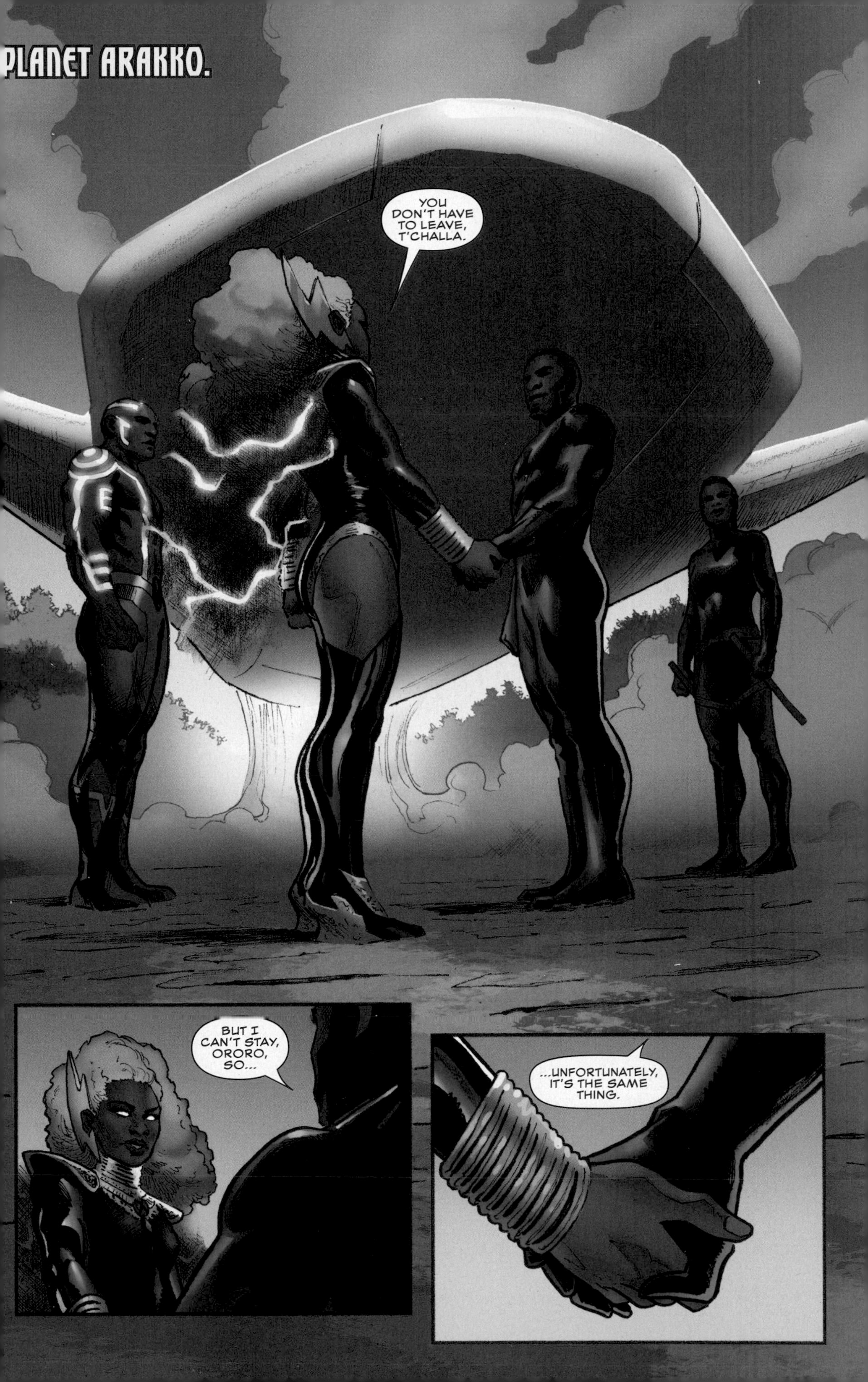
PLANET ARAKKO.
YOU DON'T HAVE TO LEAVE, T'CHALLA.
BUT I CAN'T STAY, ORORO, SO...
...UNFORTUNATELY, IT'S THE SAME THING.

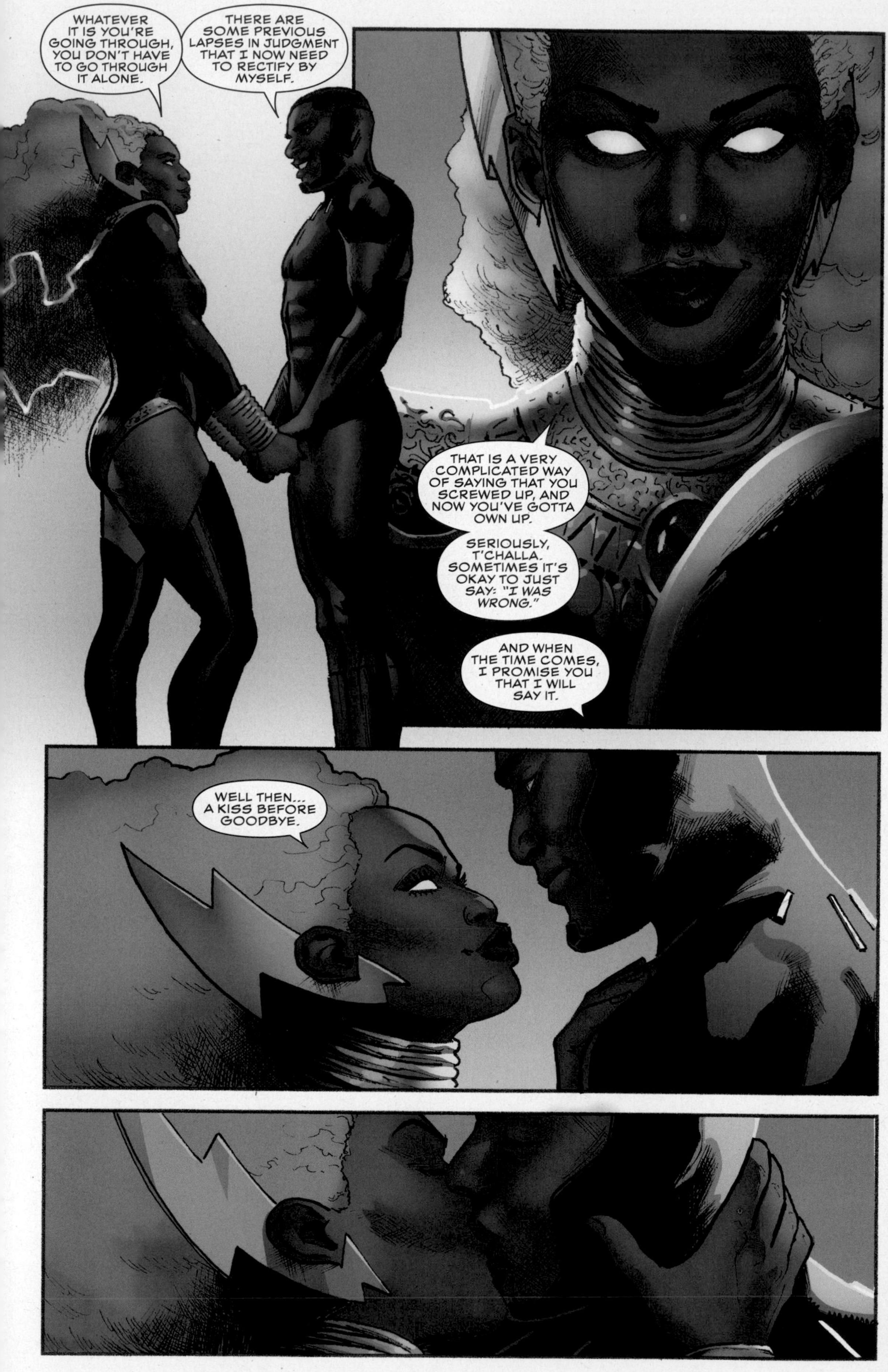
WHATEVER IT IS YOU'RE GOING THROUGH, YOU DON'T HAVE TO GO THROUGH IT ALONE.
THERE ARE SOME PREVIOUS LAPSES IN JUDGMENT THAT I NOW NEED TO RECTIFY BY MYSELF.
THAT IS A VERY COMPLICATED WAY OF SAYING THAT YOU SCREWED UP, AND NOW YOU'VE GOTTA OWN UP.
SERIOUSLY, T'CHALLA. SOMETIMES IT'S OKAY TO JUST SAY: "I WAS WRONG."
AND WHEN THE TIME COMES, I PROMISE YOU THAT I WILL SAY IT.
WELL THEN... A KISS BEFORE GOODBYE.

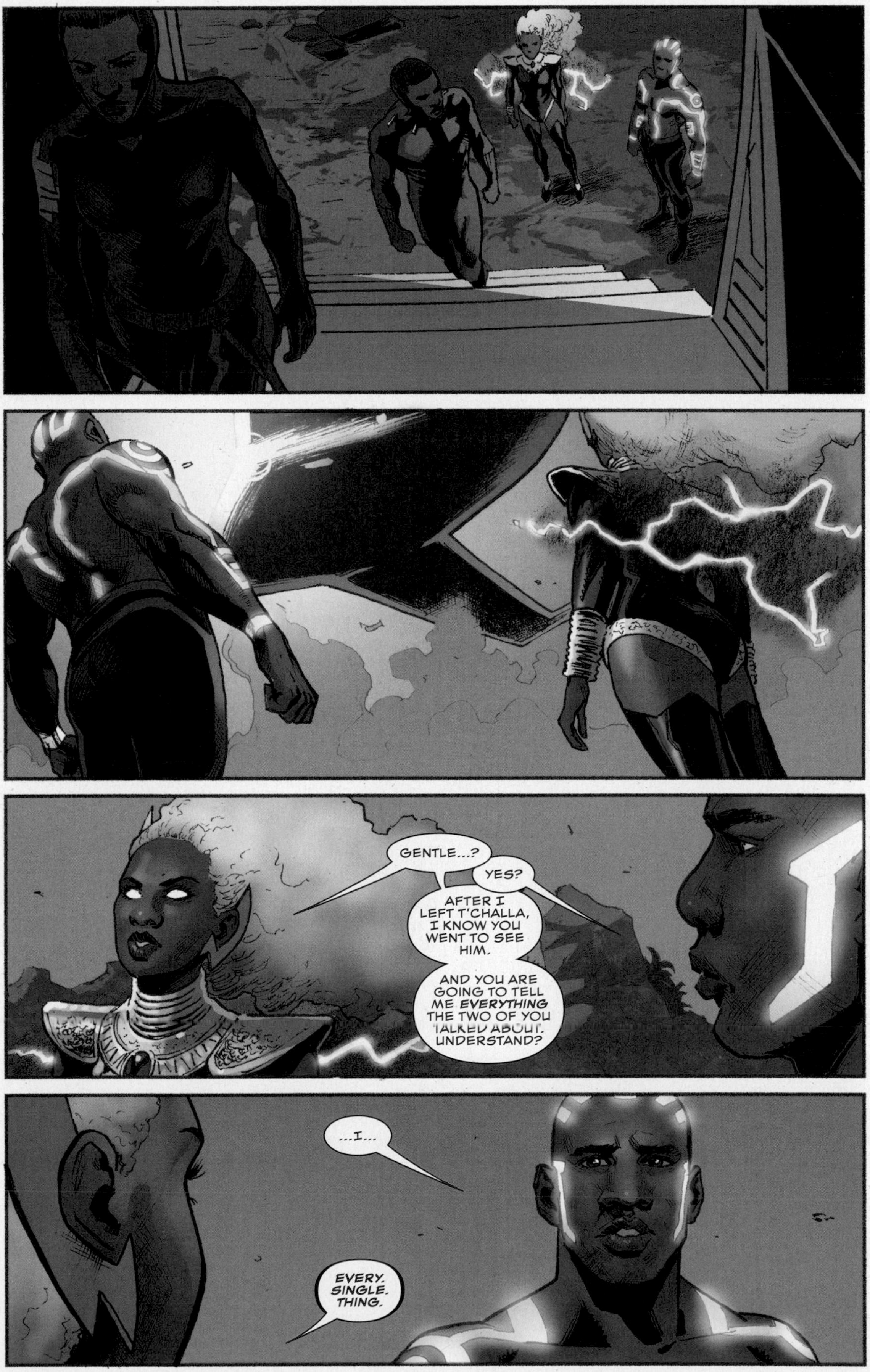
GENTLE...?
YES?
AFTER I LEFT T'CHALLA, I KNOW YOU WENT TO SEE HIM.
AND YOU ARE GOING TO TELL ME EVERYTHING THE TWO OF YOU TALKED ABOUT. UNDERSTAND?
...I...
EVERY. SINGLE. THING.

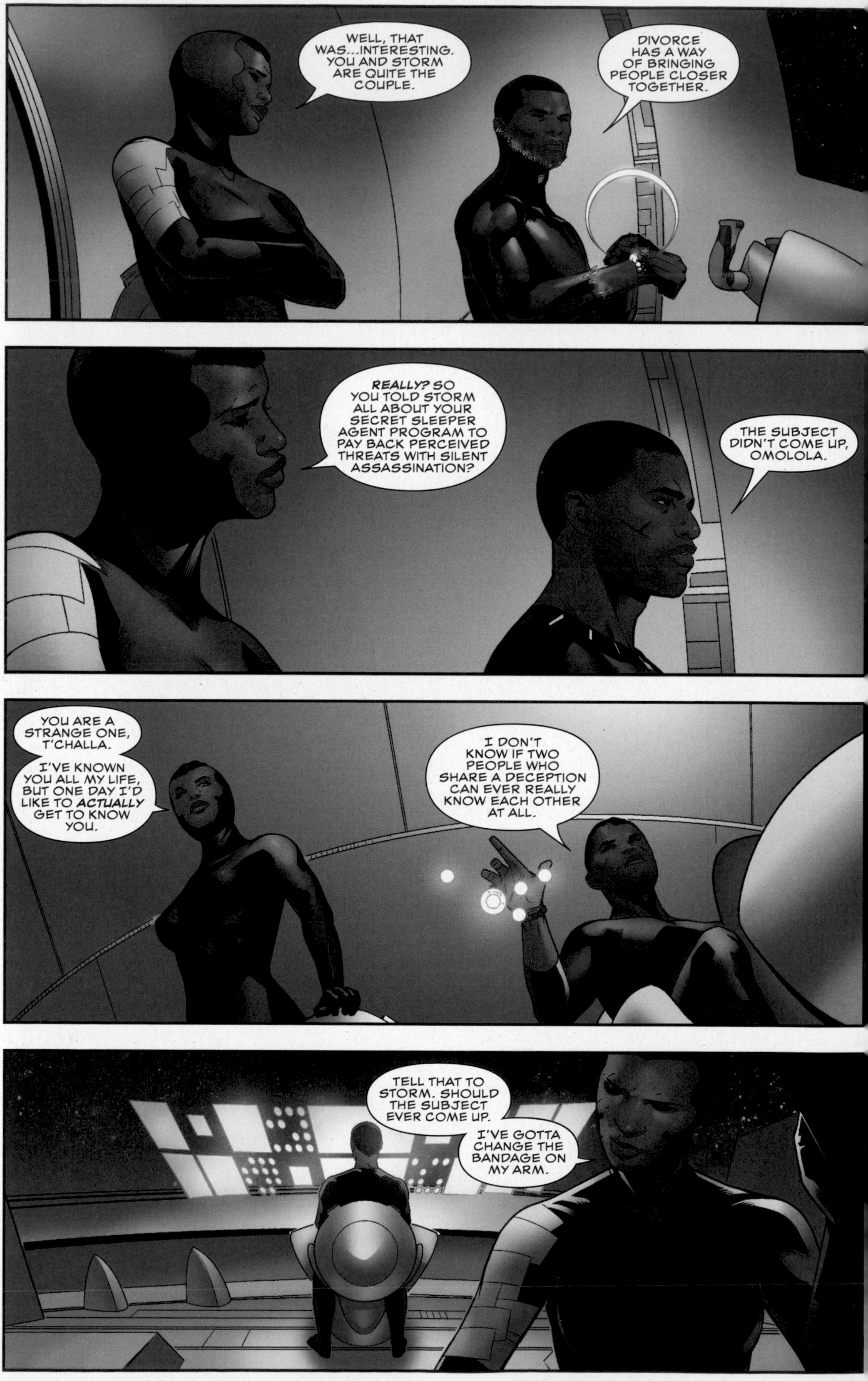

WELL, THAT WAS...INTERESTING. YOU AND STORM ARE QUITE THE COUPLE.
DIVORCE HAS A WAY OF BRINGING PEOPLE CLOSER TOGETHER.
REALLY? SO YOU TOLD STORM ALL ABOUT YOUR SECRET SLEEPER AGENT PROGRAM TO PAY BACK PERCEIVED THREATS WITH SILENT ASSASSINATION?
THE SUBJECT DIDN'T COME UP, OMOLOLA.
YOU ARE A STRANGE ONE, T'CHALLA.
I'VE KNOWN YOU ALL MY LIFE, BUT ONE DAY I'D LIKE TO *ACTUALLY* GET TO KNOW YOU.
I DON'T KNOW IF TWO PEOPLE WHO SHARE A DECEPTION CAN EVER REALLY KNOW EACH OTHER AT ALL.
TELL THAT TO STORM. SHOULD THE SUBJECT EVER COME UP.
I'VE GOTTA CHANGE THE BANDAGE ON MY ARM.

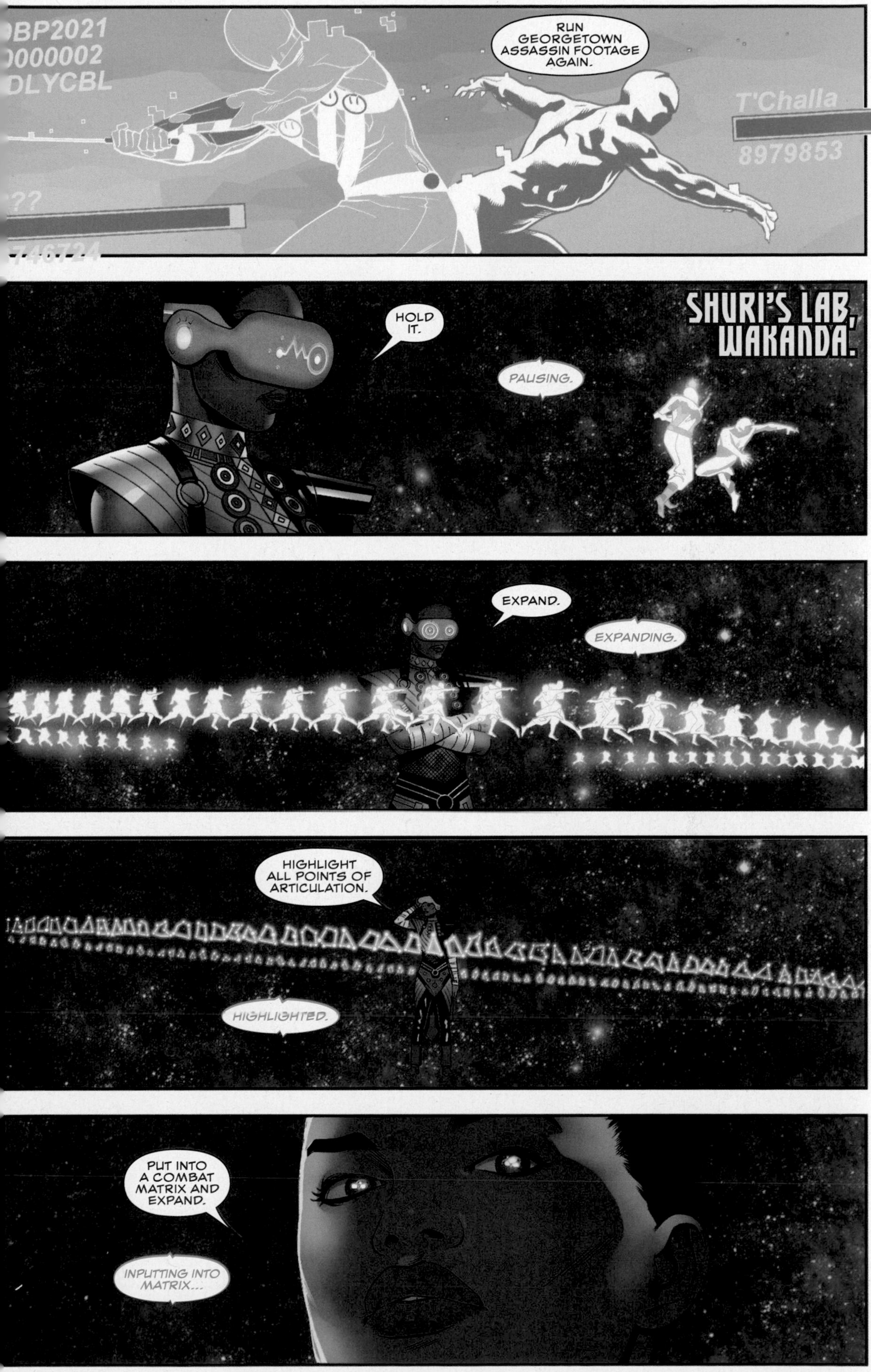

0BP2021
0000002
DLYCBL
T'Challa
8979853
RUN GEORGETOWN ASSASSIN FOOTAGE AGAIN.
SHURI'S LAB, WAKANDA.
HOLD IT.
PAUSING.
EXPAND.
EXPANDING.
HIGHLIGHT ALL POINTS OF ARTICULATION.
HIGHLIGHTED.
PUT INTO A COMBAT MATRIX AND EXPAND.
INPUTTING INTO MATRIX...

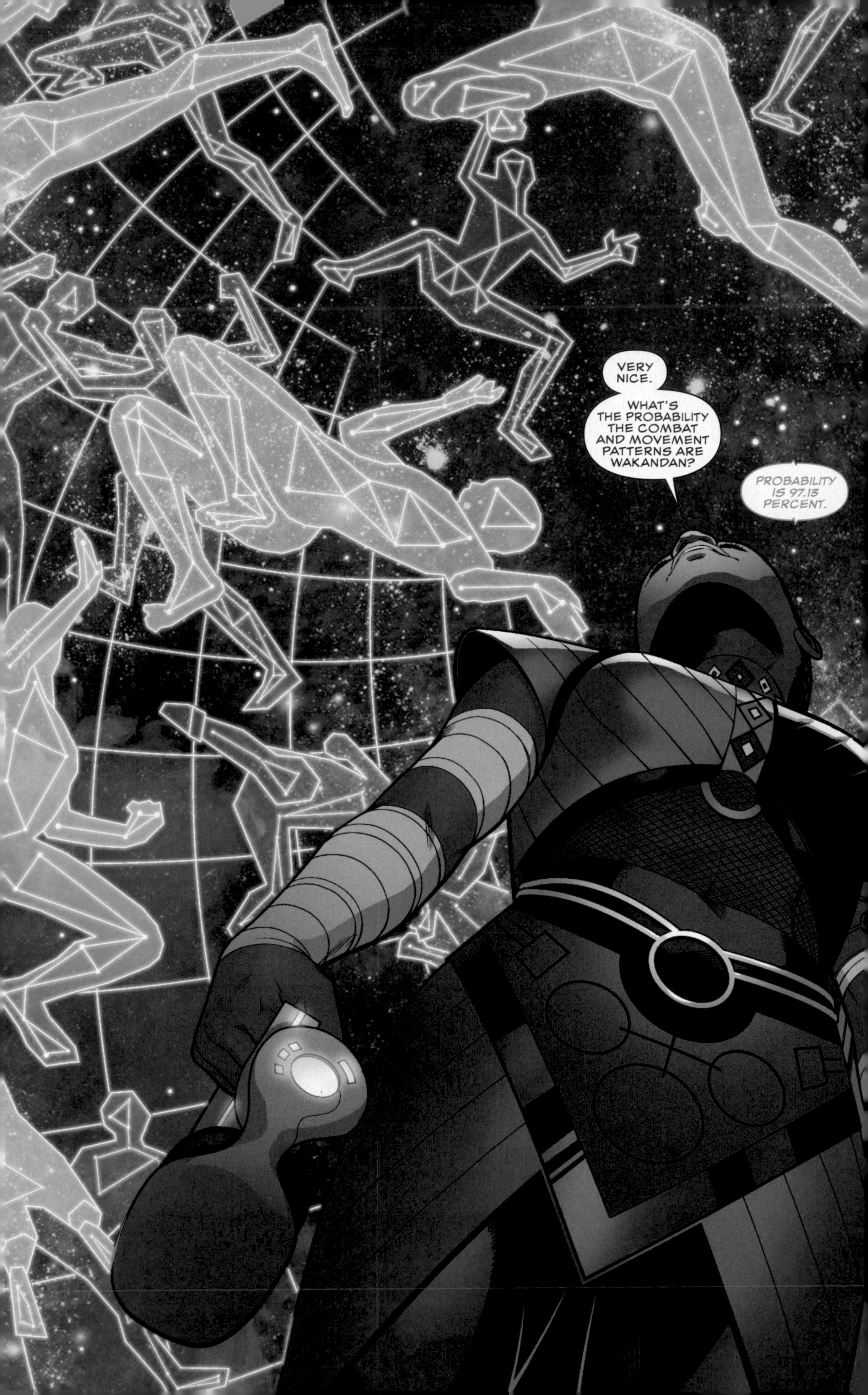
VERY NICE.
WHAT'S THE PROBABILITY THE COMBAT AND MOVEMENT PATTERNS ARE WAKANDAN?
PROBABILITY IS 97.13 PERCENT.

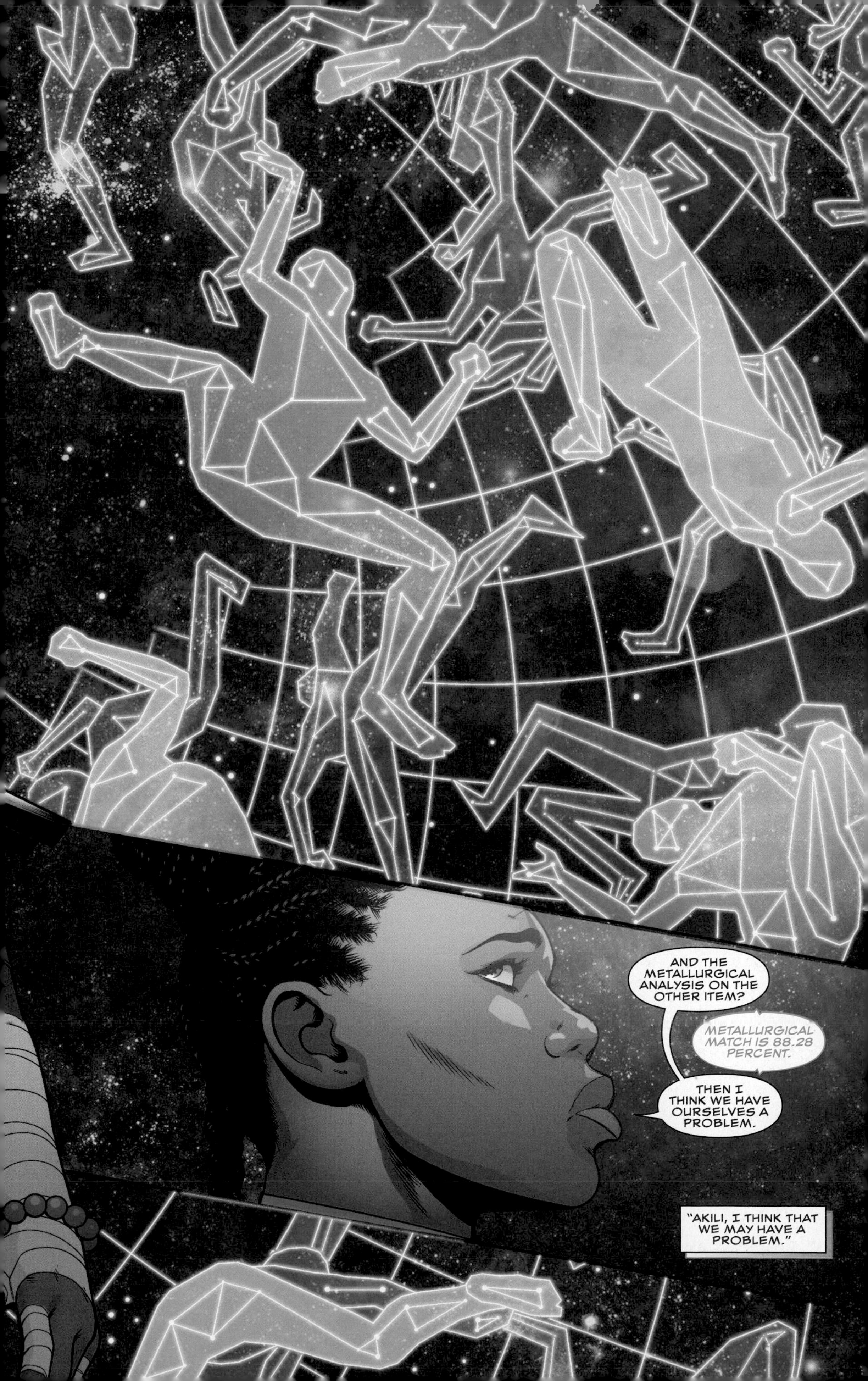
AND THE METALLURGICAL ANALYSIS ON THE OTHER ITEM?
METALLURGICAL MATCH IS 88.28 PERCENT.
THEN I THINK WE HAVE OURSELVES A PROBLEM.
"AKILI, I THINK THAT WE MAY HAVE A PROBLEM."

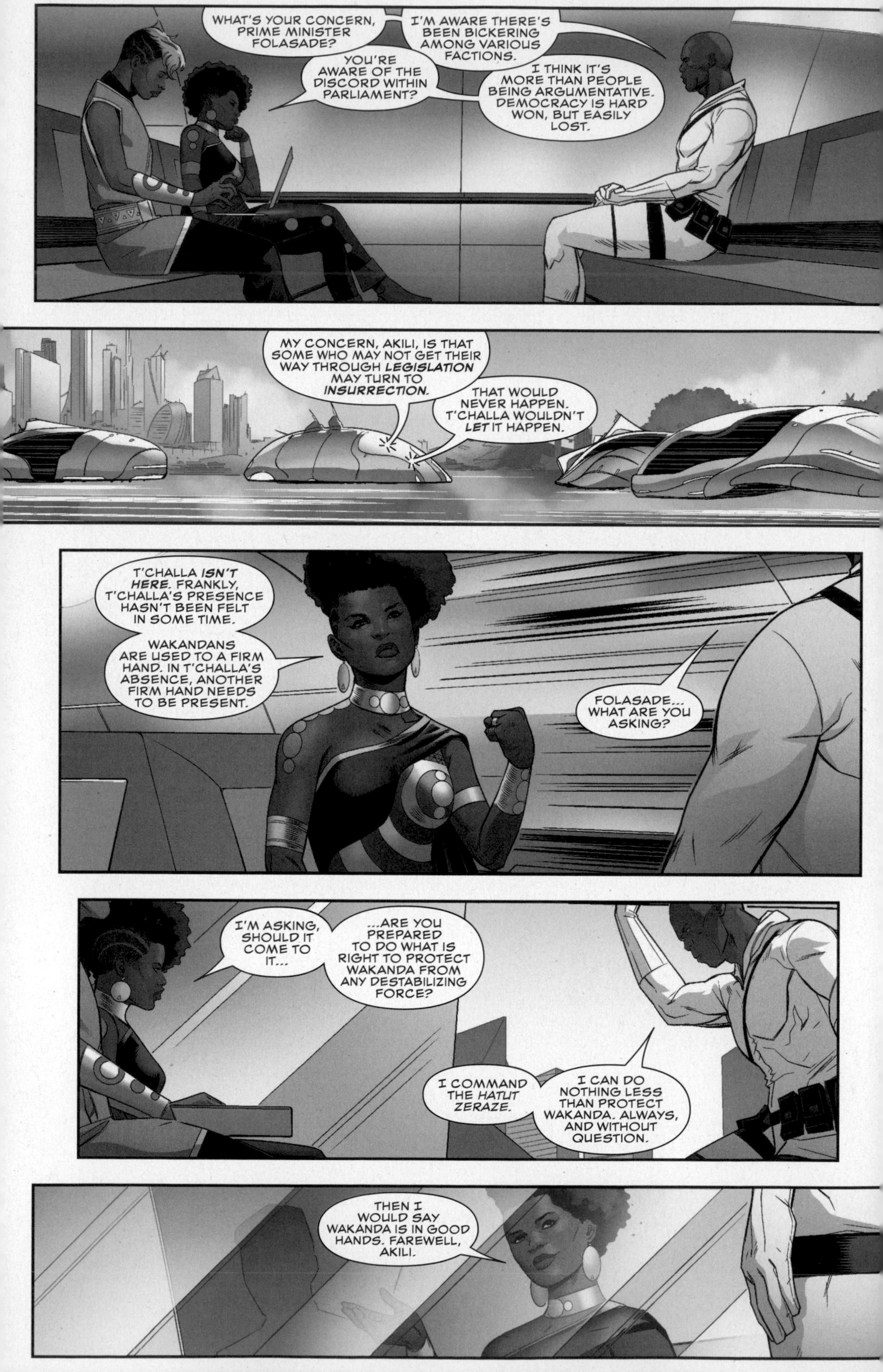
WHAT'S YOUR CONCERN, PRIME MINISTER FOLASADE?
YOU'RE AWARE OF THE DISCORD WITHIN PARLIAMENT?
I'M AWARE THERE'S BEEN BICKERING AMONG VARIOUS FACTIONS.
I THINK IT'S MORE THAN PEOPLE BEING ARGUMENTATIVE. DEMOCRACY IS HARD WON, BUT EASILY LOST.
MY CONCERN, AKILI, IS THAT SOME WHO MAY NOT GET THEIR WAY THROUGH LEGISLATION MAY TURN TO INSURRECTION.
THAT WOULD NEVER HAPPEN. T'CHALLA WOULDN'T LET IT HAPPEN.
T'CHALLA ISN'T HERE. FRANKLY, T'CHALLA'S PRESENCE HASN'T BEEN FELT IN SOME TIME.
WAKANDANS ARE USED TO A FIRM HAND. IN T'CHALLA'S ABSENCE, ANOTHER FIRM HAND NEEDS TO BE PRESENT.
FOLASADE... WHAT ARE YOU ASKING?
I'M ASKING, SHOULD IT COME TO IT...
...ARE YOU PREPARED TO DO WHAT IS RIGHT TO PROTECT WAKANDA FROM ANY DESTABILIZING FORCE?
I COMMAND THE HATUT ZERAZE.
I CAN DO NOTHING LESS THAN PROTECT WAKANDA. ALWAYS, AND WITHOUT QUESTION.
THEN I WOULD SAY WAKANDA IS IN GOOD HANDS. FAREWELL, AKILI.

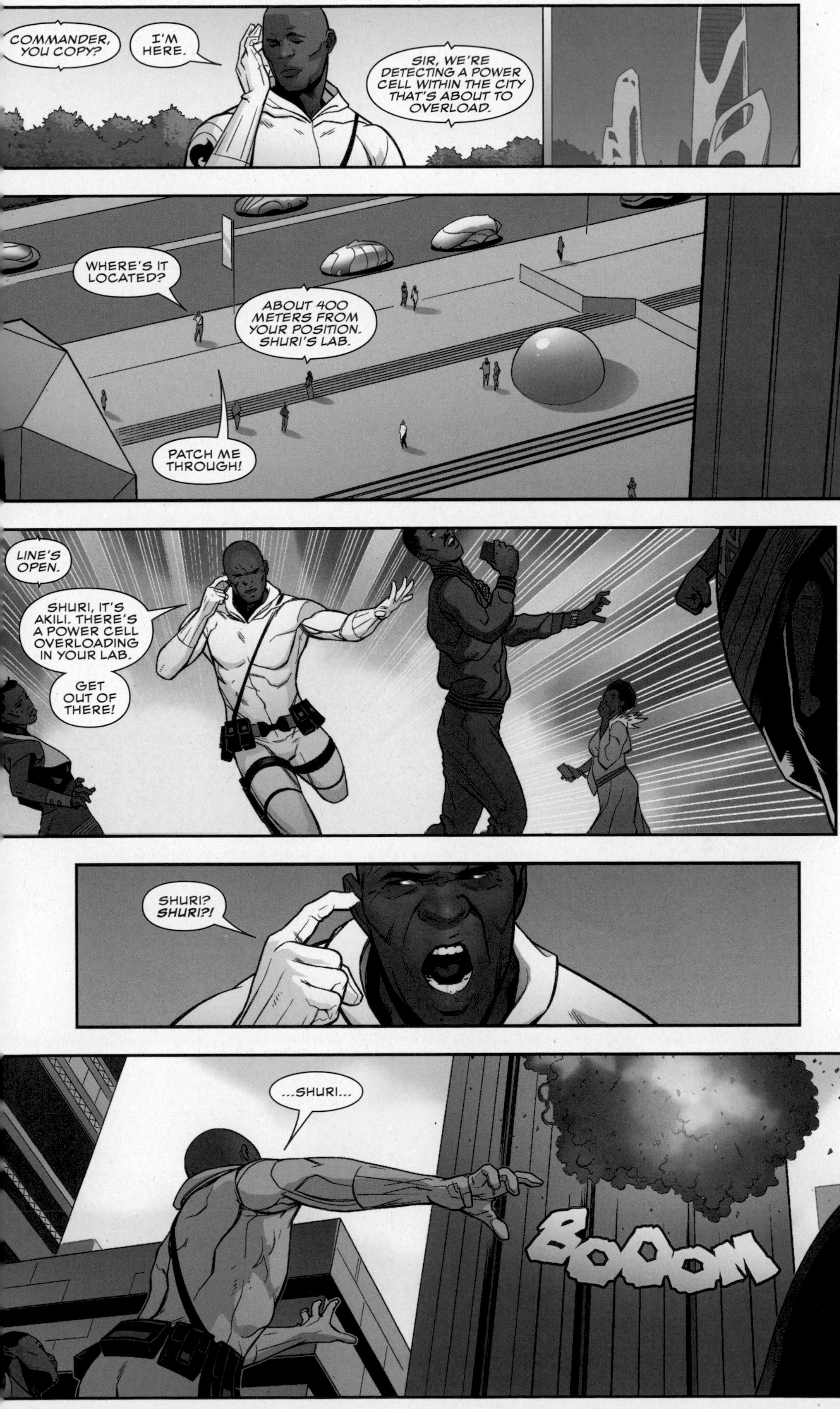
COMMANDER, YOU COPY?
I'M HERE.
SIR, WE'RE DETECTING A POWER CELL WITHIN THE CITY THAT'S ABOUT TO OVERLOAD.
WHERE'S IT LOCATED?
ABOUT 400 METERS FROM YOUR POSITION. SHURI'S LAB.
PATCH ME THROUGH!
LINE'S OPEN.
SHURI, IT'S AKILI. THERE'S A POWER CELL OVERLOADING IN YOUR LAB.
GET OUT OF THERE!
SHURI? SHURI?!
...SHURI...
BOOOM

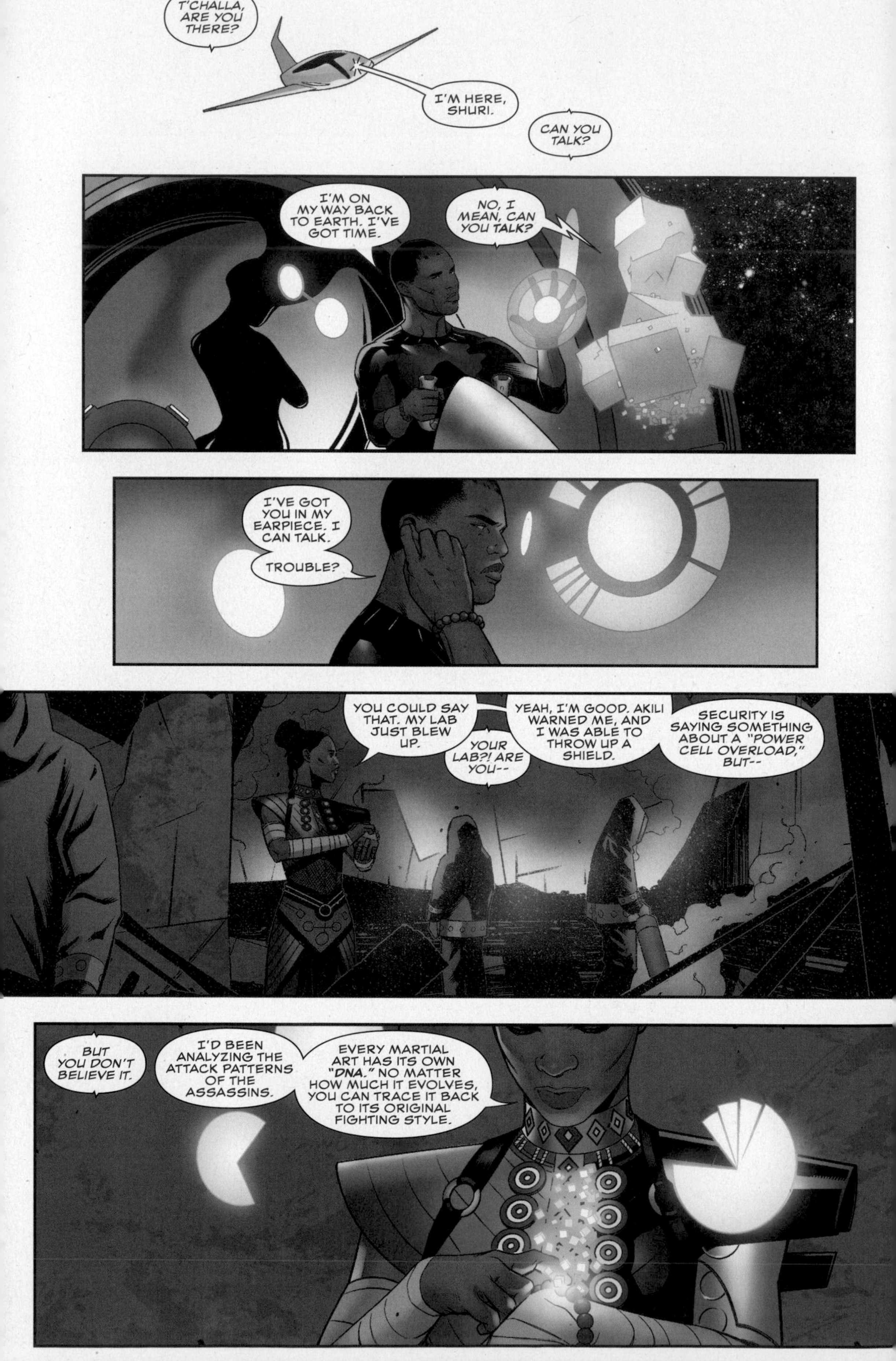
T'CHALLA, ARE YOU THERE?
I'M HERE, SHURI.
CAN YOU TALK?
I'M ON MY WAY BACK TO EARTH. I'VE GOT TIME.
NO, I MEAN, CAN YOU TALK?
I'VE GOT YOU IN MY EARPIECE. I CAN TALK.
TROUBLE?
YOU COULD SAY THAT. MY LAB JUST BLEW UP.
YOUR LAB?! ARE YOU--
YEAH, I'M GOOD. AKILI WARNED ME, AND I WAS ABLE TO THROW UP A SHIELD.
SECURITY IS SAYING SOMETHING ABOUT A "POWER CELL OVERLOAD," BUT--
BUT YOU DON'T BELIEVE IT.
I'D BEEN ANALYZING THE ATTACK PATTERNS OF THE ASSASSINS.
EVERY MARTIAL ART HAS ITS OWN "DNA." NO MATTER HOW MUCH IT EVOLVES, YOU CAN TRACE IT BACK TO ITS ORIGINAL FIGHTING STYLE.

THE STYLE THE ASSASSINS ARE USING...IT'S *WAKANDAN.*

THAT'S NOT ALL. I DID A METALLURGICAL ANALYSIS ON A PIECE OF ONE OF THEIR UNIFORMS--IT'S A SYNTHETIC THAT'S ALMOST A PERFECT MATCH FOR *VIBRANIUM.*

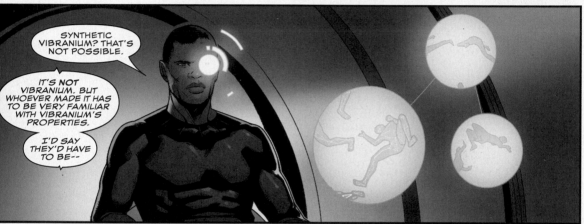

SYNTHETIC VIBRANIUM? THAT'S NOT POSSIBLE.

IT'S NOT VIBRANIUM. BUT WHOEVER MADE IT HAS TO BE VERY FAMILIAR WITH VIBRANIUM'S PROPERTIES.

I'D SAY THEY'D HAVE TO BE--

--WAKANDAN.

T'CHALLA... THERE'S SOMETHING ELSE I NEED TO SHOW YOU.

THERE-- ARE YOU SEEING IT?

YEAH. I AM. AND I WILL DEAL WITH IT.

TALK TO YOU LATER.

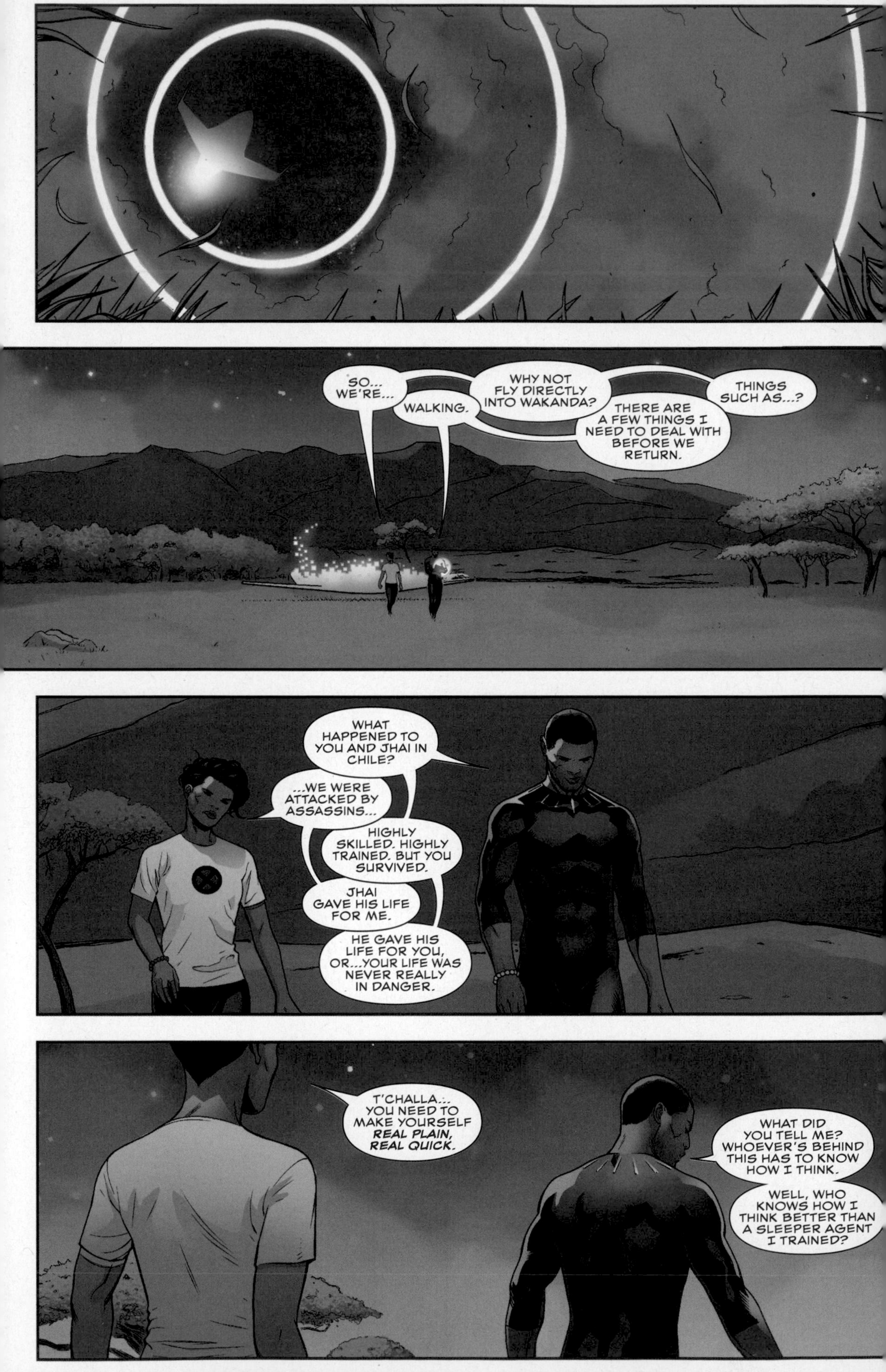
SO... WE'RE...
WALKING.
WHY NOT FLY DIRECTLY INTO WAKANDA?
THERE ARE A FEW THINGS I NEED TO DEAL WITH BEFORE WE RETURN.
THINGS SUCH AS...?
WHAT HAPPENED TO YOU AND JHAI IN CHILE?
...WE WERE ATTACKED BY ASSASSINS...
HIGHLY SKILLED. HIGHLY TRAINED. BUT YOU SURVIVED.
JHAI GAVE HIS LIFE FOR ME.
HE GAVE HIS LIFE FOR YOU, OR...YOUR LIFE WAS NEVER REALLY IN DANGER.
T'CHALLA... YOU NEED TO MAKE YOURSELF *REAL PLAIN, REAL QUICK.*
WHAT DID YOU TELL ME? WHOEVER'S BEHIND THIS HAS TO KNOW HOW I THINK.
WELL, WHO KNOWS HOW I THINK BETTER THAN A SLEEPER AGENT I TRAINED?

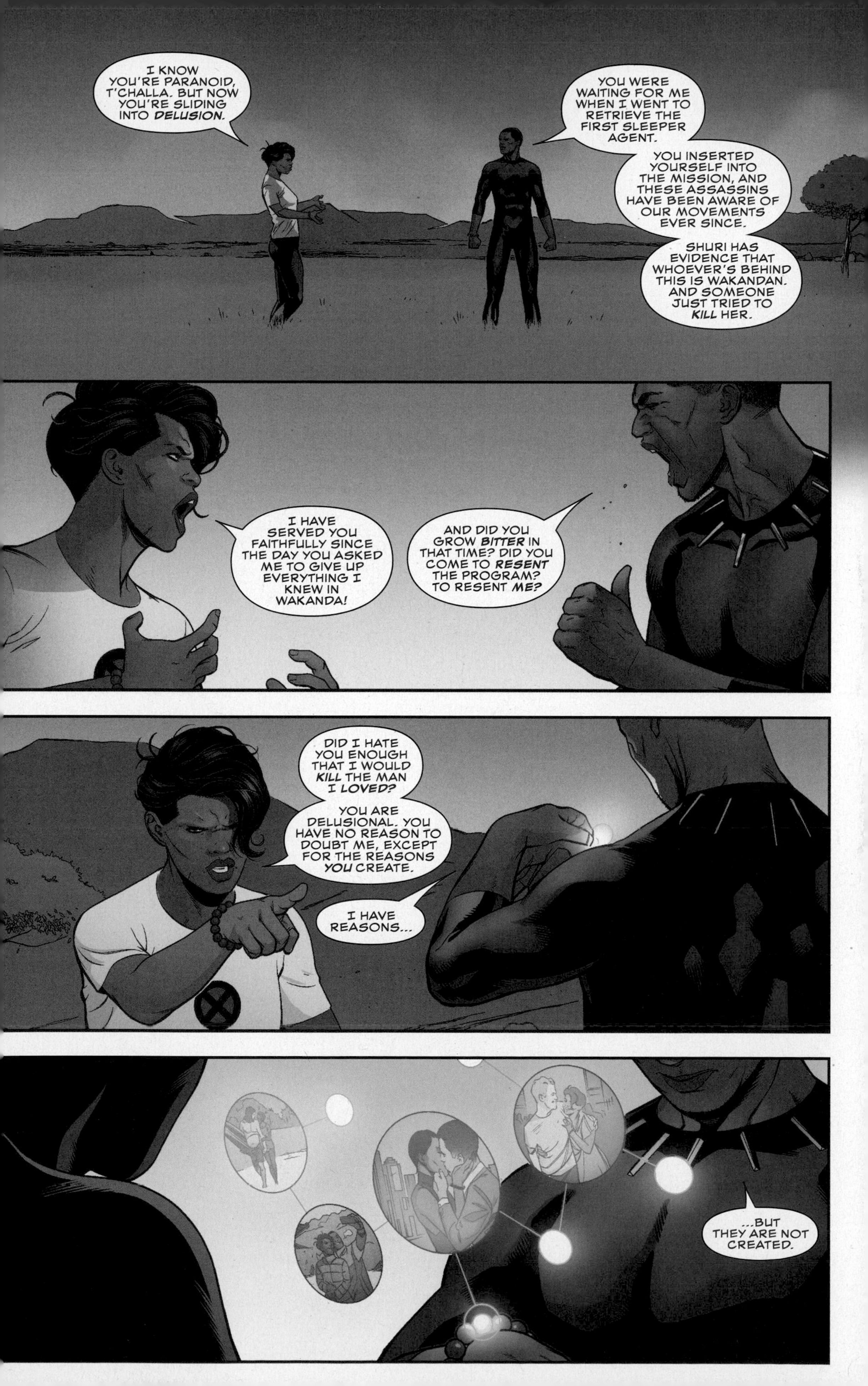
I KNOW YOU'RE PARANOID, T'CHALLA. BUT NOW YOU'RE SLIDING INTO DELUSION.
YOU WERE WAITING FOR ME WHEN I WENT TO RETRIEVE THE FIRST SLEEPER AGENT.
YOU INSERTED YOURSELF INTO THE MISSION, AND THESE ASSASSINS HAVE BEEN AWARE OF OUR MOVEMENTS EVER SINCE.
SHURI HAS EVIDENCE THAT WHOEVER'S BEHIND THIS IS WAKANDAN. AND SOMEONE JUST TRIED TO KILL HER.
I HAVE SERVED YOU FAITHFULLY SINCE THE DAY YOU ASKED ME TO GIVE UP EVERYTHING I KNEW IN WAKANDA!
AND DID YOU GROW BITTER IN THAT TIME? DID YOU COME TO RESENT THE PROGRAM? TO RESENT ME?
DID I HATE YOU ENOUGH THAT I WOULD KILL THE MAN I LOVED?
YOU ARE DELUSIONAL. YOU HAVE NO REASON TO DOUBT ME, EXCEPT FOR THE REASONS YOU CREATE.
I HAVE REASONS...
...BUT THEY ARE NOT CREATED.

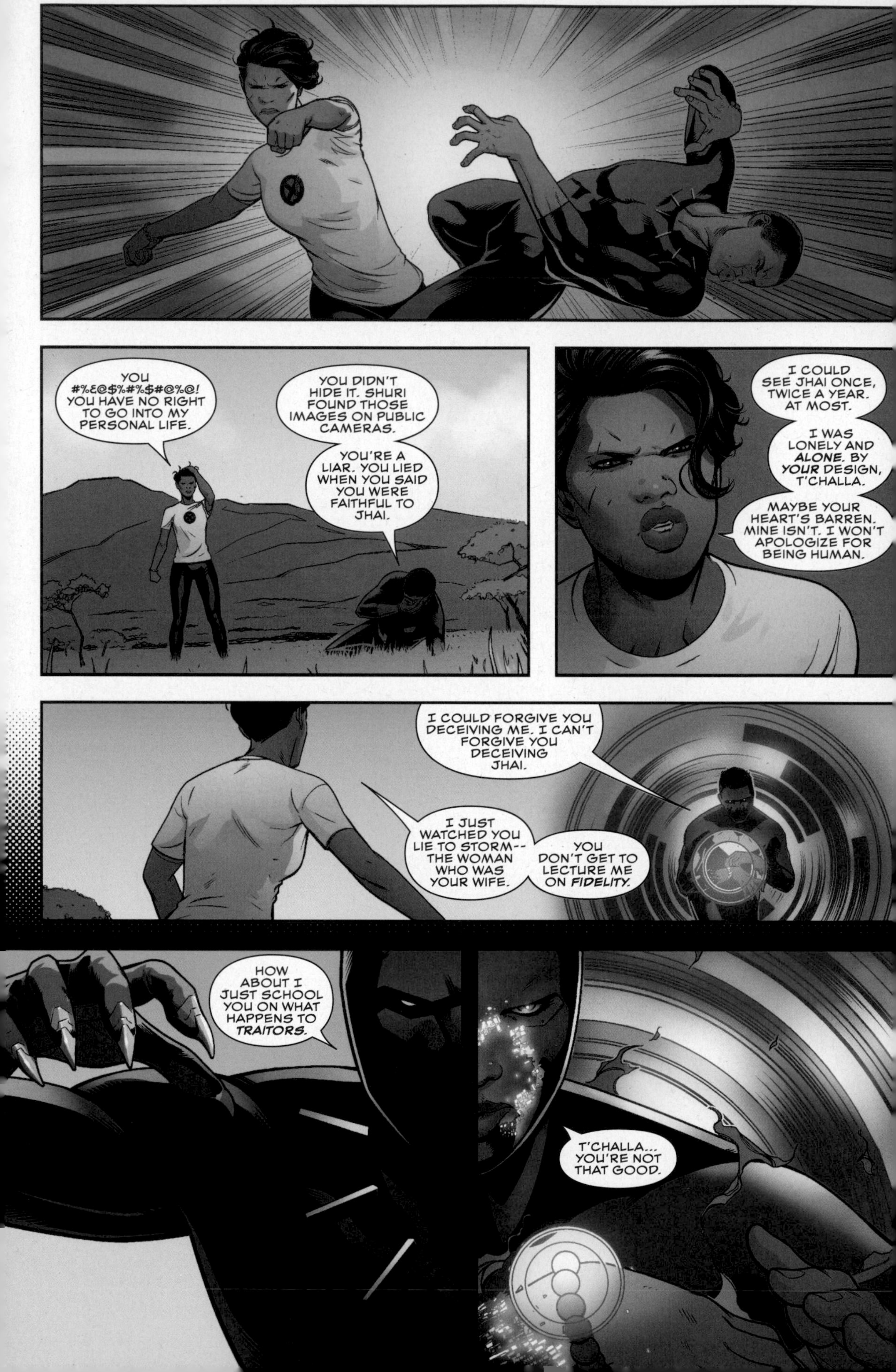
YOU #%£@$%#%$#@%@! YOU HAVE NO RIGHT TO GO INTO MY PERSONAL LIFE.
YOU DIDN'T HIDE IT. SHURI FOUND THOSE IMAGES ON PUBLIC CAMERAS.
YOU'RE A LIAR. YOU LIED WHEN YOU SAID YOU WERE FAITHFUL TO JHAI.
I COULD SEE JHAI ONCE, TWICE A YEAR. AT MOST.
I WAS LONELY AND *ALONE*. BY *YOUR* DESIGN, T'CHALLA.
MAYBE YOUR HEART'S BARREN. MINE ISN'T. I WON'T APOLOGIZE FOR BEING HUMAN.
I COULD FORGIVE YOU DECEIVING ME. I CAN'T FORGIVE YOU DECEIVING JHAI.
I JUST WATCHED YOU LIE TO STORM-- THE WOMAN WHO WAS YOUR WIFE.
YOU DON'T GET TO LECTURE ME ON *FIDELITY*.
HOW ABOUT I JUST SCHOOL YOU ON WHAT HAPPENS TO *TRAITORS*.
T'CHALLA... YOU'RE NOT THAT GOOD.

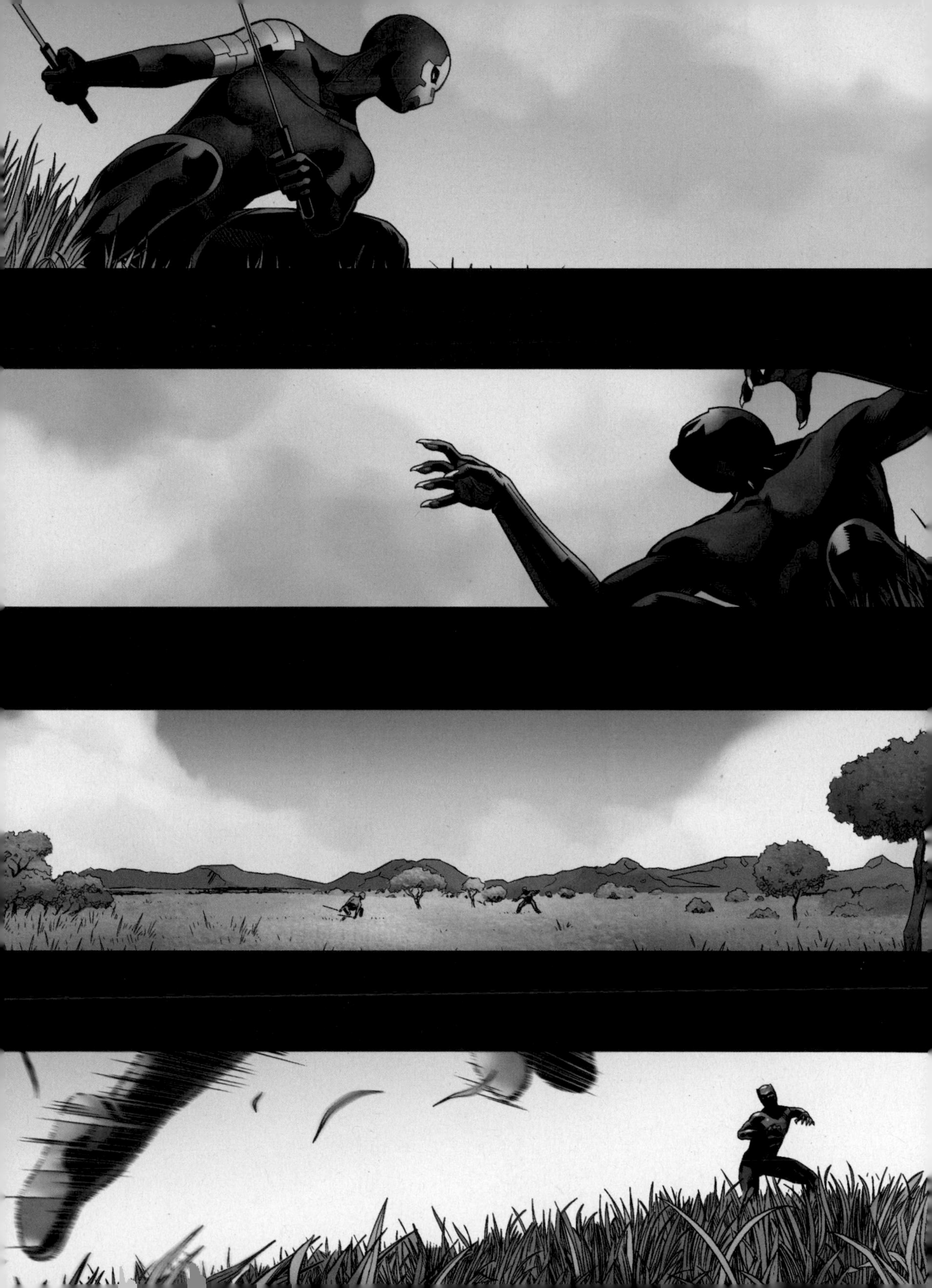

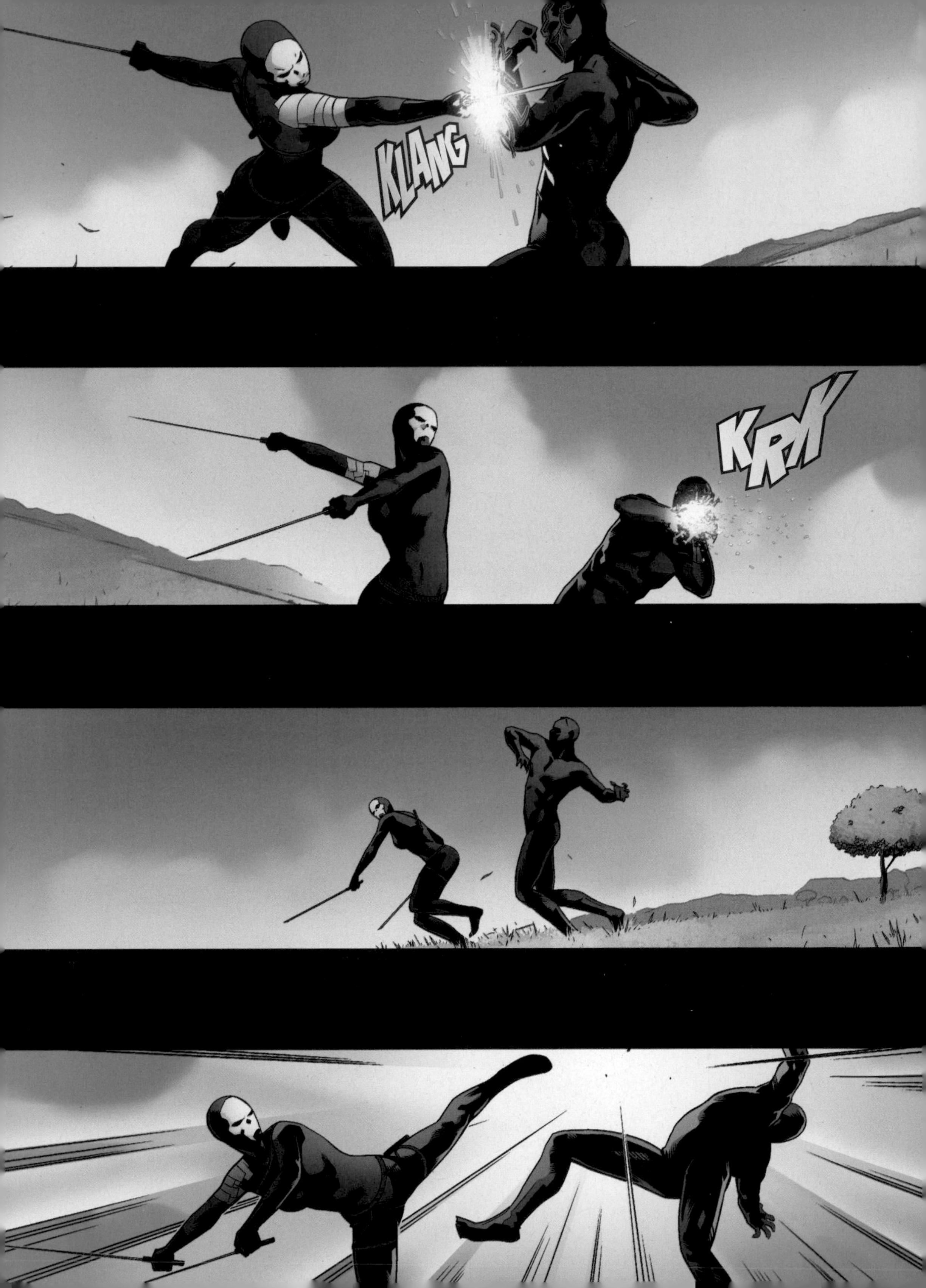
KLANG
KRAK

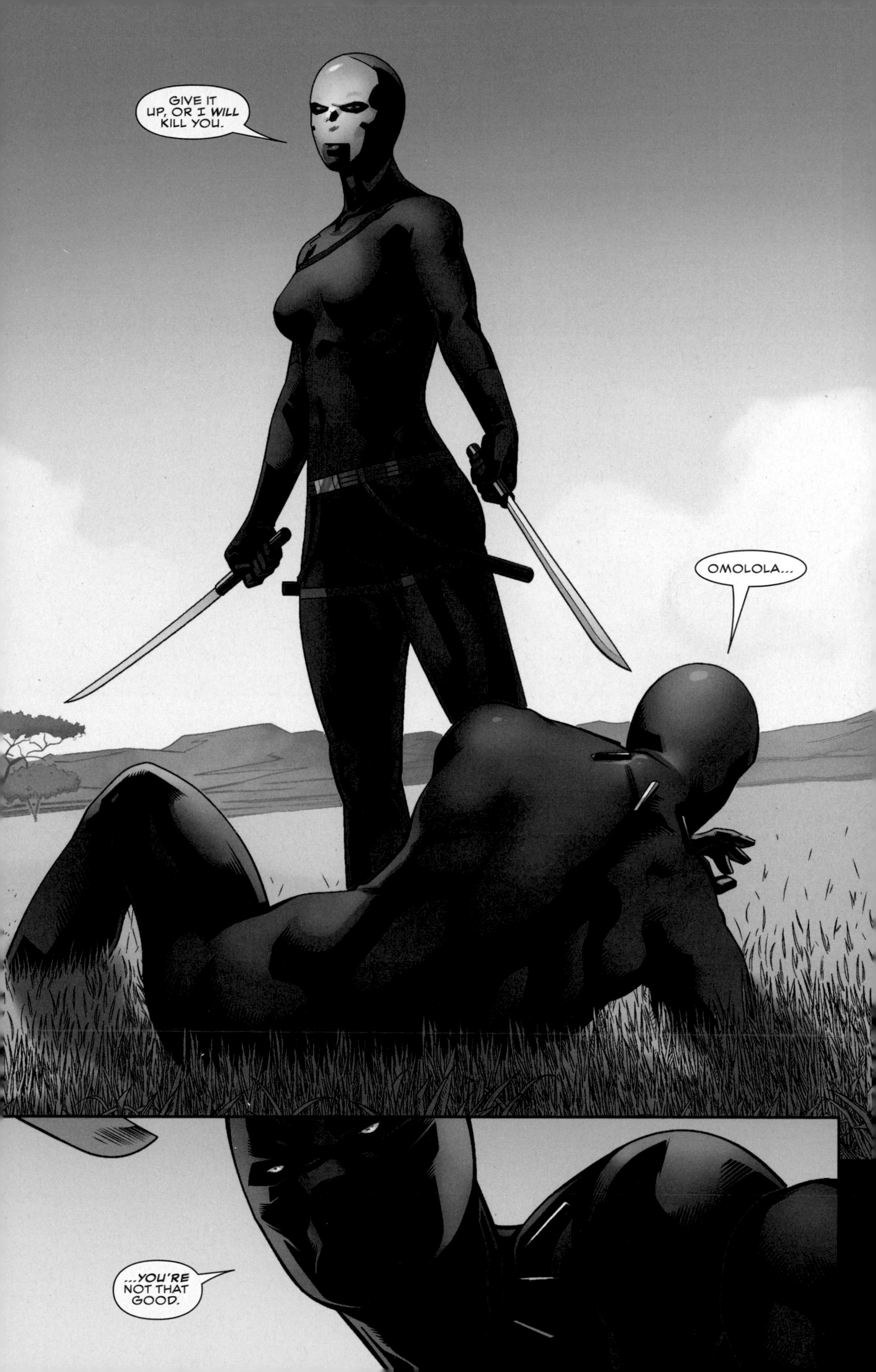
GIVE IT UP, OR I *WILL* KILL YOU.
OMOLOLA...
...*YOU'RE* NOT THAT GOOD.

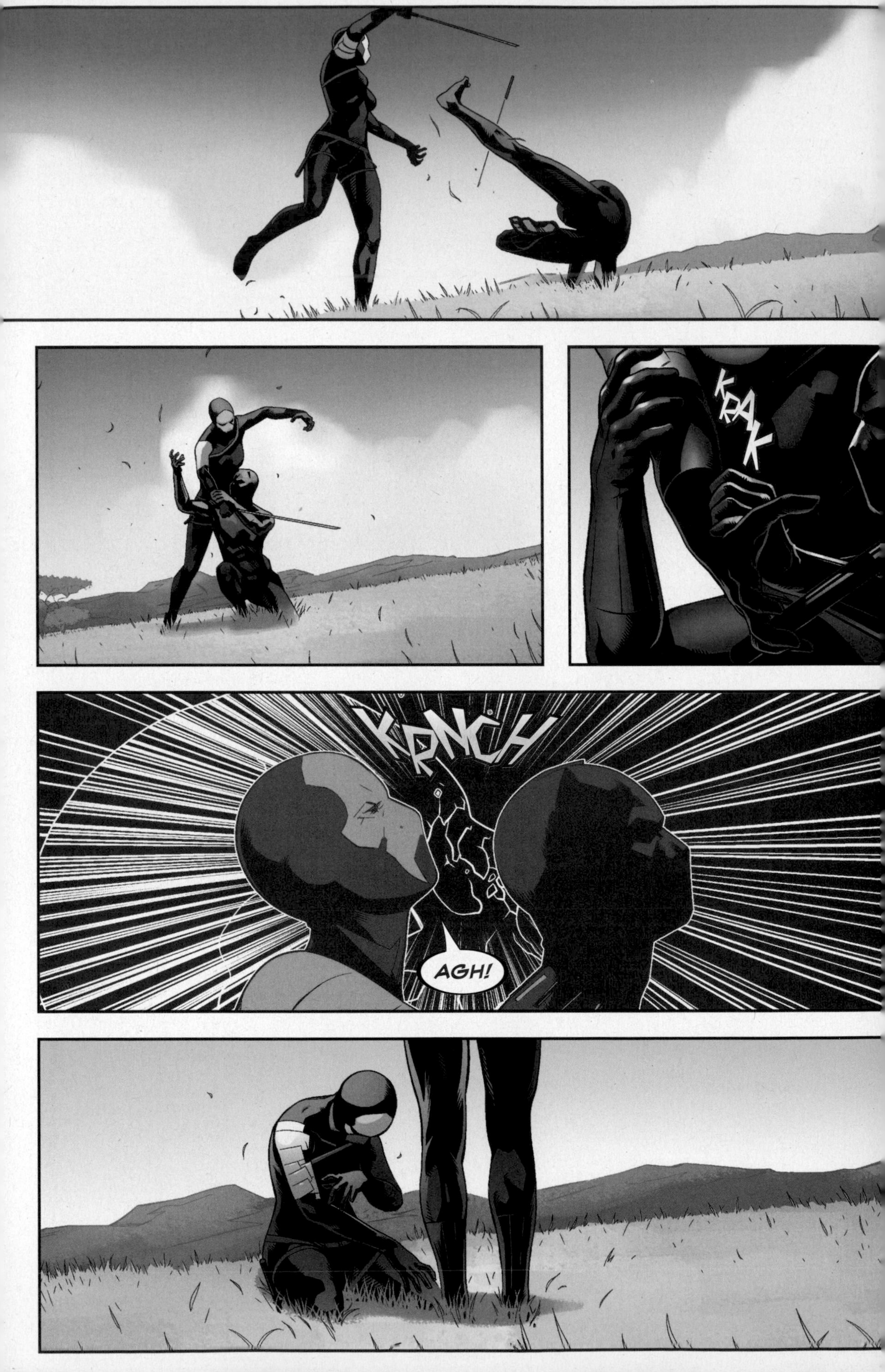
KRAK
KRNCH
AGH!

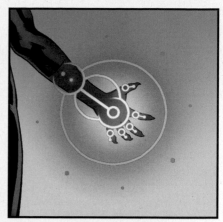

IF YOU WANT TO KILL ME, KILL ME.

BUT BEFORE YOU DO...

...LOOK ME IN THE EYES AND KNOW I AM NOT THE ONE WHO BETRAYED YOU.

NO NEED TO DIRTY YOUR HANDS, BROTHER.

IF SHE TRIES ANYTHING, WE WILL KILL HER.

...."WE..."? WHO THE HELL IS--?

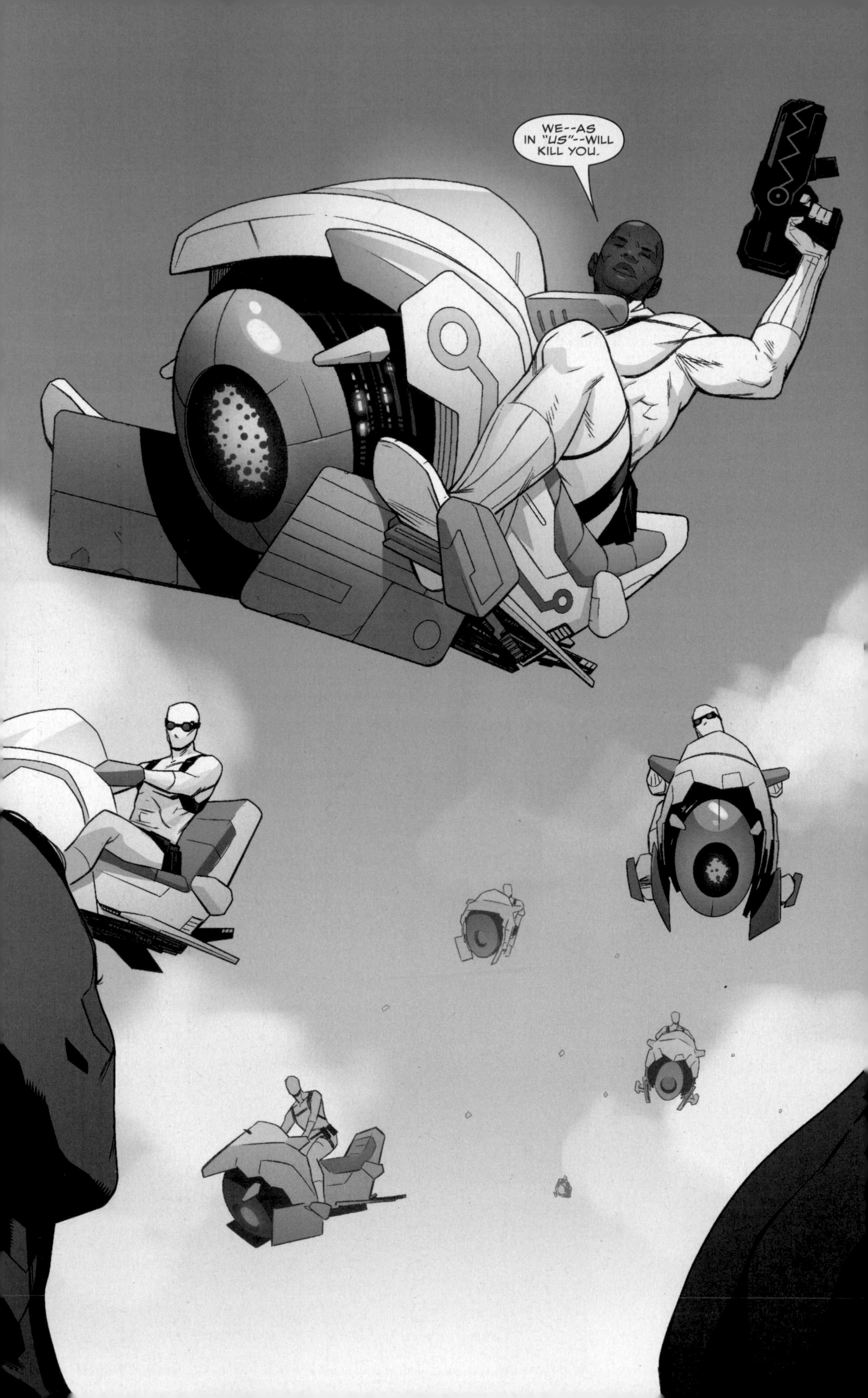
WE--AS IN "US"--WILL KILL YOU.

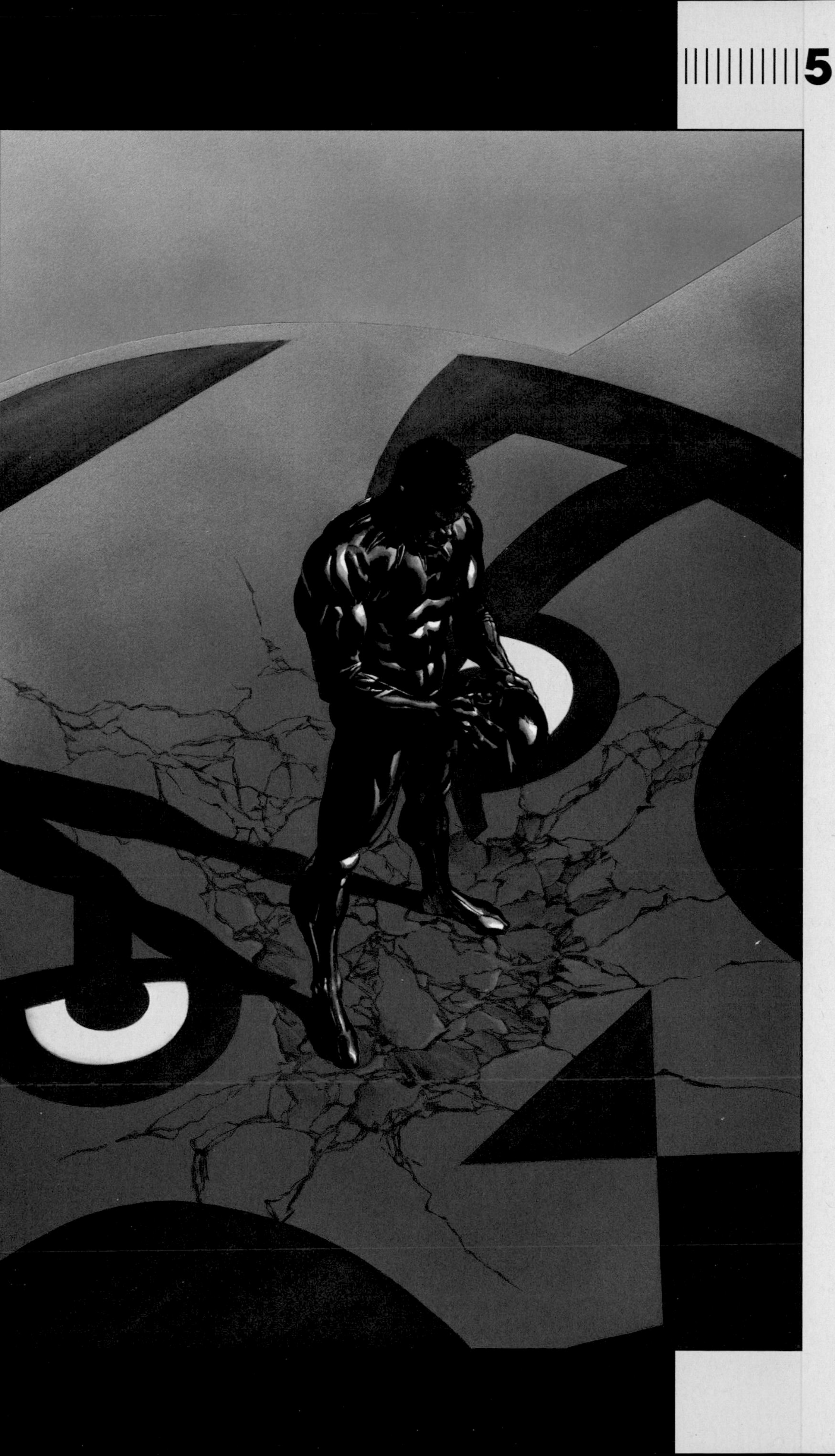

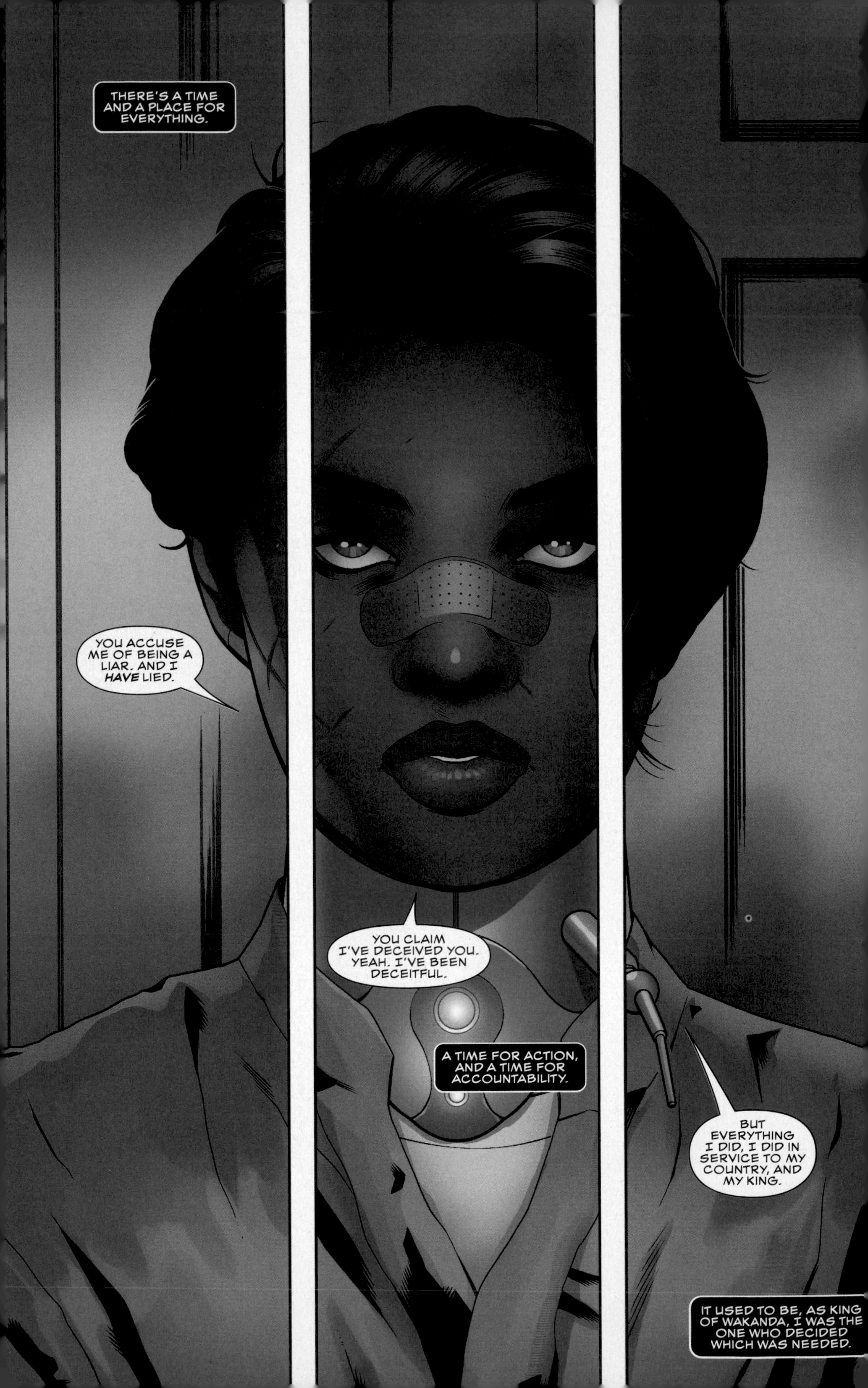
THERE'S A TIME AND A PLACE FOR EVERYTHING.
YOU ACCUSE ME OF BEING A LIAR. AND I *HAVE* LIED.
YOU CLAIM I'VE DECEIVED YOU. YEAH. I'VE BEEN DECEITFUL.
A TIME FOR ACTION, AND A TIME FOR ACCOUNTABILITY.
BUT EVERYTHING I DID, I DID IN SERVICE TO MY COUNTRY, AND MY KING.
IT USED TO BE, AS KING OF WAKANDA, I WAS THE ONE WHO DECIDED WHICH WAS NEEDED.

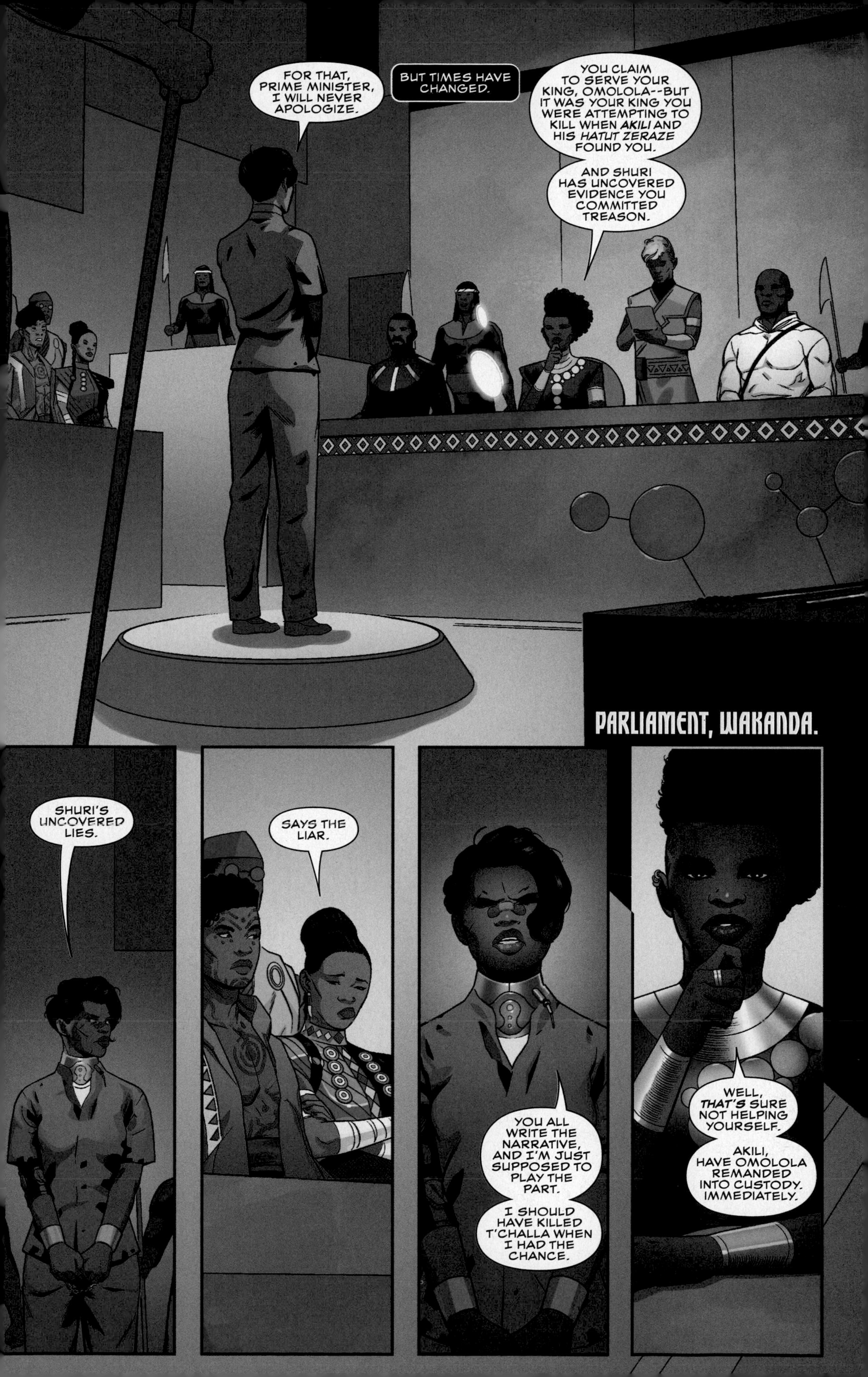
FOR THAT, PRIME MINISTER, I WILL NEVER APOLOGIZE.
BUT TIMES HAVE CHANGED.
YOU CLAIM TO SERVE YOUR KING, OMOLOLA--BUT IT WAS YOUR KING YOU WERE ATTEMPTING TO KILL WHEN AKILI AND HIS HATUT ZERAZE FOUND YOU.
AND SHURI HAS UNCOVERED EVIDENCE YOU COMMITTED TREASON.
PARLIAMENT, WAKANDA.
SHURI'S UNCOVERED LIES.
SAYS THE LIAR.
YOU ALL WRITE THE NARRATIVE, AND I'M JUST SUPPOSED TO PLAY THE PART.
I SHOULD HAVE KILLED T'CHALLA WHEN I HAD THE CHANCE.
WELL, THAT'S SURE NOT HELPING YOURSELF.
AKILI, HAVE OMOLOLA REMANDED INTO CUSTODY. IMMEDIATELY.

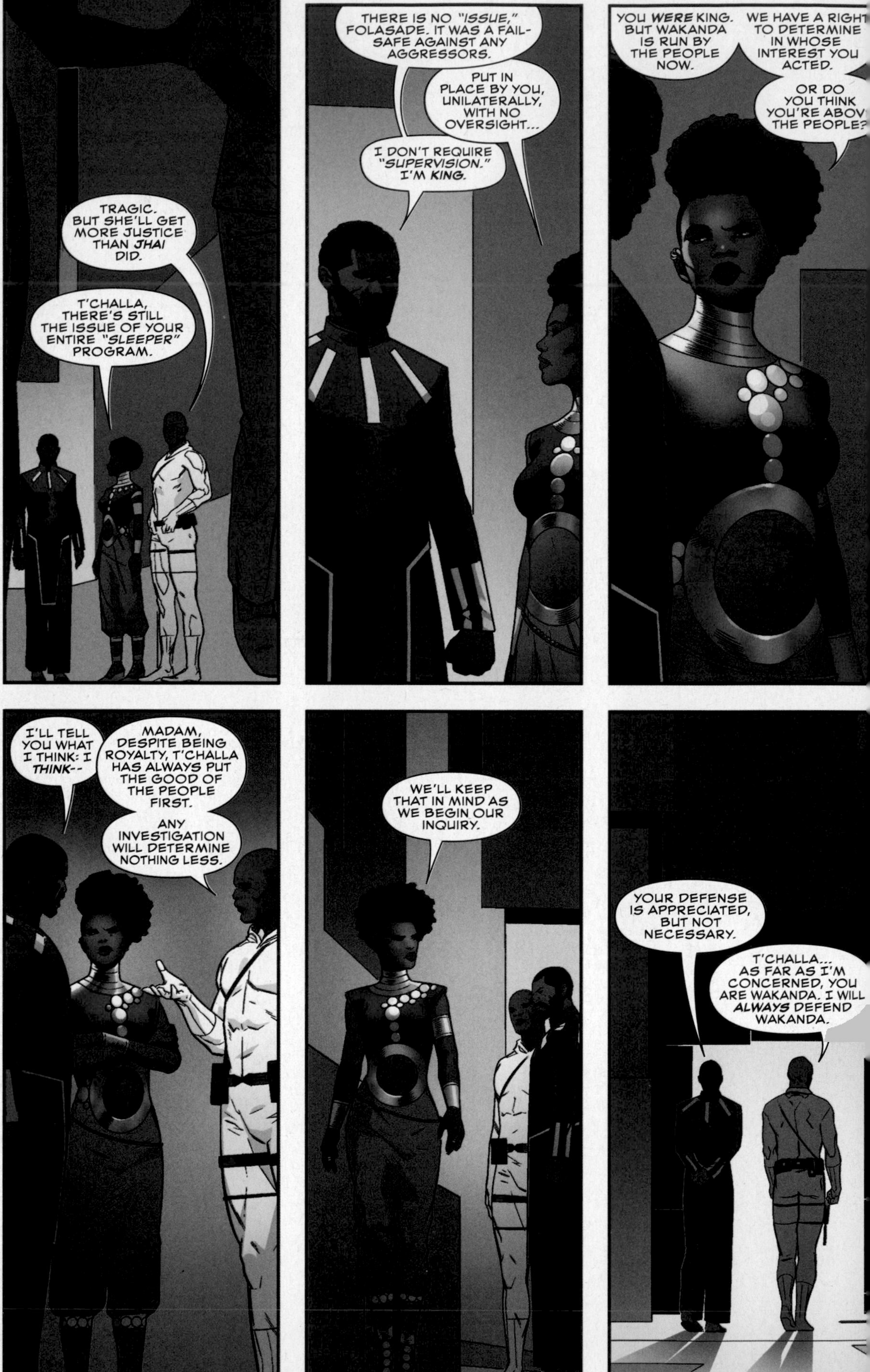
TRAGIC. BUT SHE'LL GET MORE JUSTICE THAN JHAI DID.
T'CHALLA, THERE'S STILL THE ISSUE OF YOUR ENTIRE "SLEEPER" PROGRAM.
THERE IS NO "ISSUE," FOLASADE. IT WAS A FAIL-SAFE AGAINST ANY AGGRESSORS.
PUT IN PLACE BY YOU, UNILATERALLY, WITH NO OVERSIGHT...
I DON'T REQUIRE "SUPERVISION." I'M KING.
YOU WERE KING. BUT WAKANDA IS RUN BY THE PEOPLE NOW.
WE HAVE A RIGHT TO DETERMINE IN WHOSE INTEREST YOU ACTED.
OR DO YOU THINK YOU'RE ABOVE THE PEOPLE?
I'LL TELL YOU WHAT I THINK: I THINK--
MADAM, DESPITE BEING ROYALTY, T'CHALLA HAS ALWAYS PUT THE GOOD OF THE PEOPLE FIRST.
ANY INVESTIGATION WILL DETERMINE NOTHING LESS.
WE'LL KEEP THAT IN MIND AS WE BEGIN OUR INQUIRY.
YOUR DEFENSE IS APPRECIATED, BUT NOT NECESSARY.
T'CHALLA... AS FAR AS I'M CONCERNED, YOU ARE WAKANDA. I WILL ALWAYS DEFEND WAKANDA.

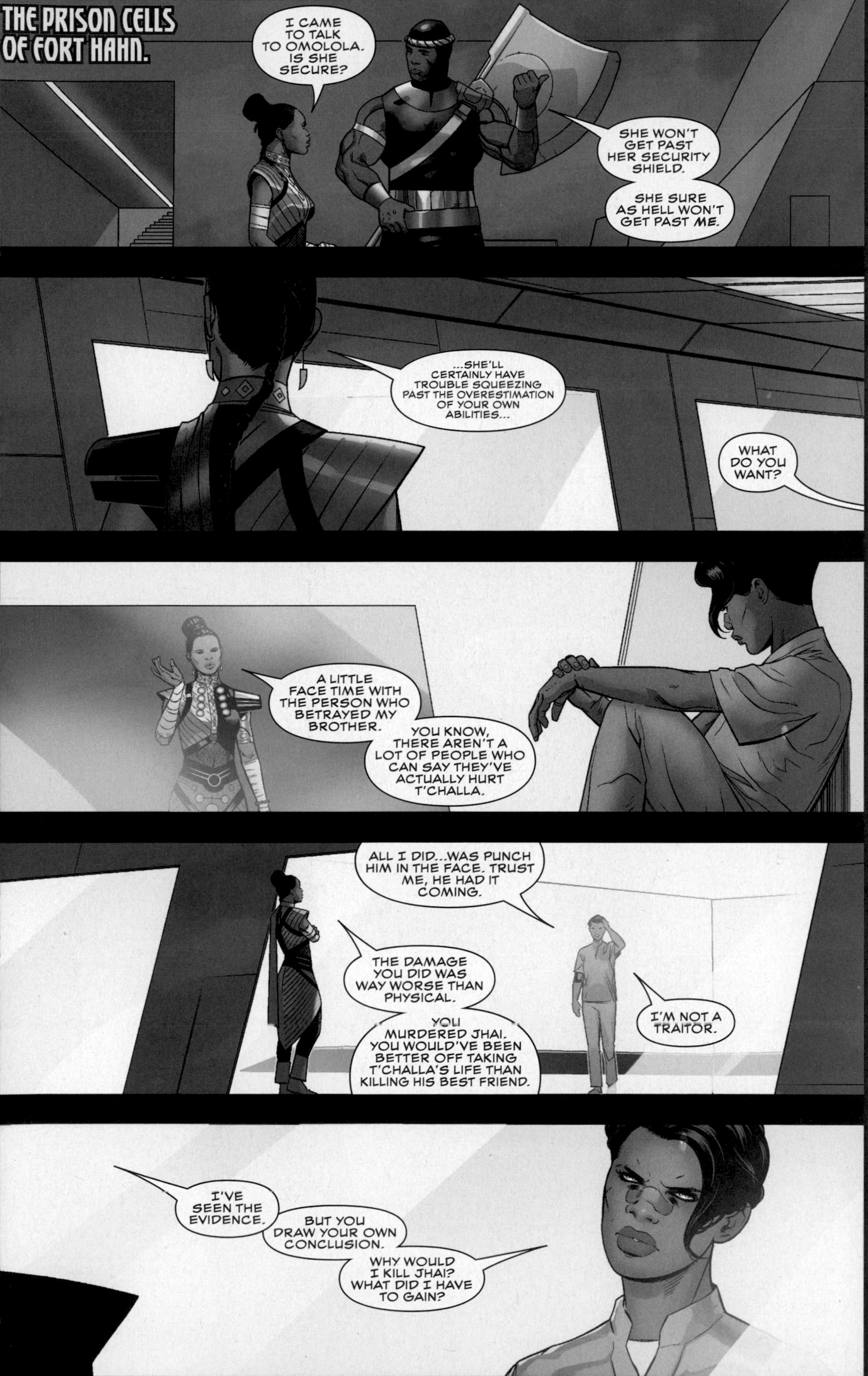
THE PRISON CELLS OF FORT HAHN.
I CAME TO TALK TO OMOLOLA. IS SHE SECURE?
SHE WON'T GET PAST HER SECURITY SHIELD.
SHE SURE AS HELL WON'T GET PAST ME.
...SHE'LL CERTAINLY HAVE TROUBLE SQUEEZING PAST THE OVERESTIMATION OF YOUR OWN ABILITIES...
WHAT DO YOU WANT?
A LITTLE FACE TIME WITH THE PERSON WHO BETRAYED MY BROTHER.
YOU KNOW, THERE AREN'T A LOT OF PEOPLE WHO CAN SAY THEY'VE ACTUALLY HURT T'CHALLA.
ALL I DID...WAS PUNCH HIM IN THE FACE. TRUST ME, HE HAD IT COMING.
THE DAMAGE YOU DID WAS WAY WORSE THAN PHYSICAL.
YOU MURDERED JHAI. YOU WOULD'VE BEEN BETTER OFF TAKING T'CHALLA'S LIFE THAN KILLING HIS BEST FRIEND.
I'M NOT A TRAITOR.
I'VE SEEN THE EVIDENCE.
BUT YOU DRAW YOUR OWN CONCLUSION.
WHY WOULD I KILL JHAI? WHAT DID I HAVE TO GAIN?

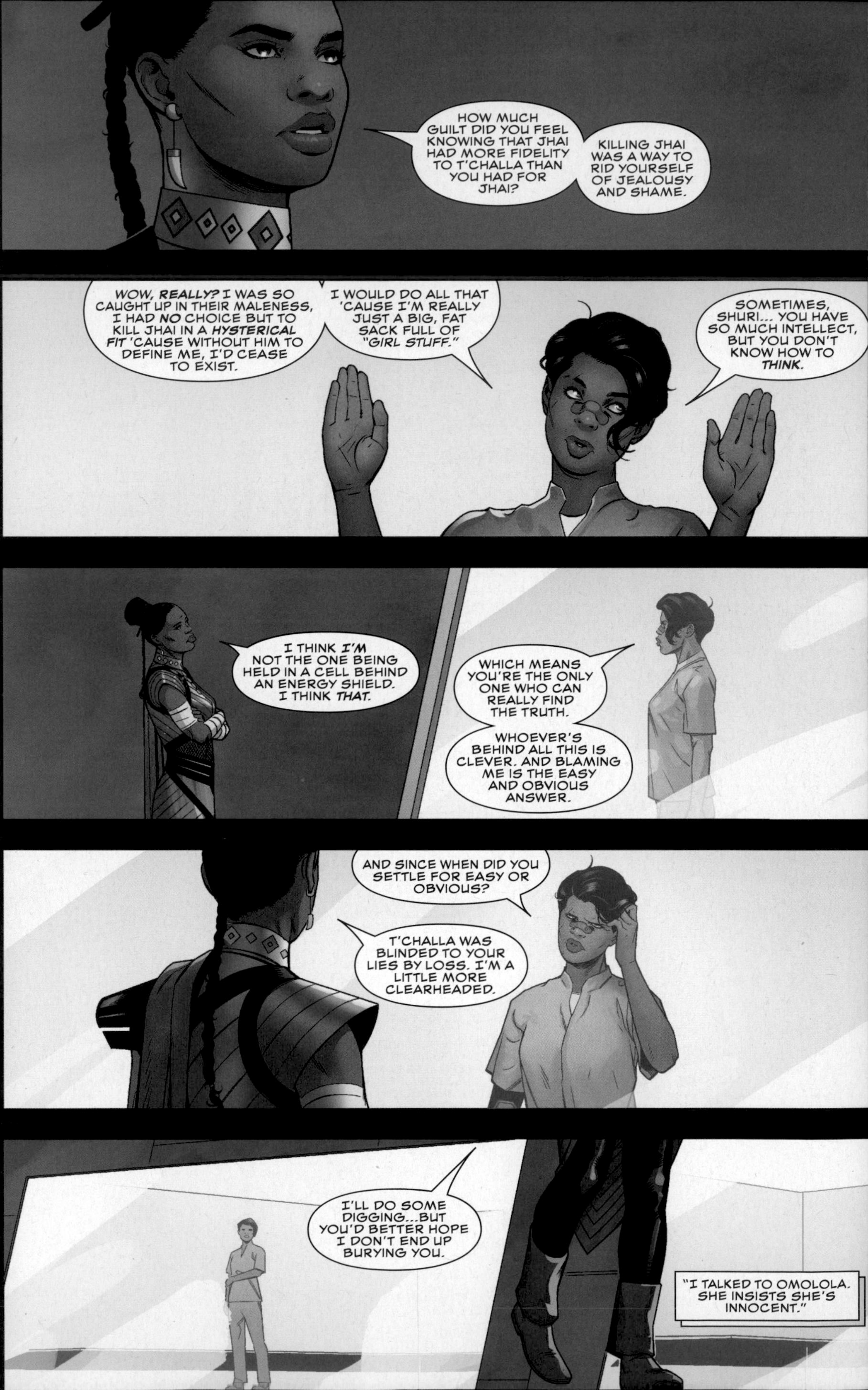
HOW MUCH GUILT DID YOU FEEL KNOWING THAT JHAI HAD MORE FIDELITY TO T'CHALLA THAN YOU HAD FOR JHAI?
KILLING JHAI WAS A WAY TO RID YOURSELF OF JEALOUSY AND SHAME.
WOW, REALLY? I WAS SO CAUGHT UP IN THEIR MALENESS, I HAD NO CHOICE BUT TO KILL JHAI IN A HYSTERICAL FIT 'CAUSE WITHOUT HIM TO DEFINE ME, I'D CEASE TO EXIST.
I WOULD DO ALL THAT 'CAUSE I'M REALLY JUST A BIG, FAT SACK FULL OF "GIRL STUFF."
SOMETIMES, SHURI... YOU HAVE SO MUCH INTELLECT, BUT YOU DON'T KNOW HOW TO THINK.
I THINK I'M NOT THE ONE BEING HELD IN A CELL BEHIND AN ENERGY SHIELD. I THINK THAT.
WHICH MEANS YOU'RE THE ONLY ONE WHO CAN REALLY FIND THE TRUTH.
WHOEVER'S BEHIND ALL THIS IS CLEVER. AND BLAMING ME IS THE EASY AND OBVIOUS ANSWER.
AND SINCE WHEN DID YOU SETTLE FOR EASY OR OBVIOUS?
T'CHALLA WAS BLINDED TO YOUR LIES BY LOSS. I'M A LITTLE MORE CLEARHEADED.
I'LL DO SOME DIGGING...BUT YOU'D BETTER HOPE I DON'T END UP BURYING YOU.
"I TALKED TO OMOLOLA. SHE INSISTS SHE'S INNOCENT."

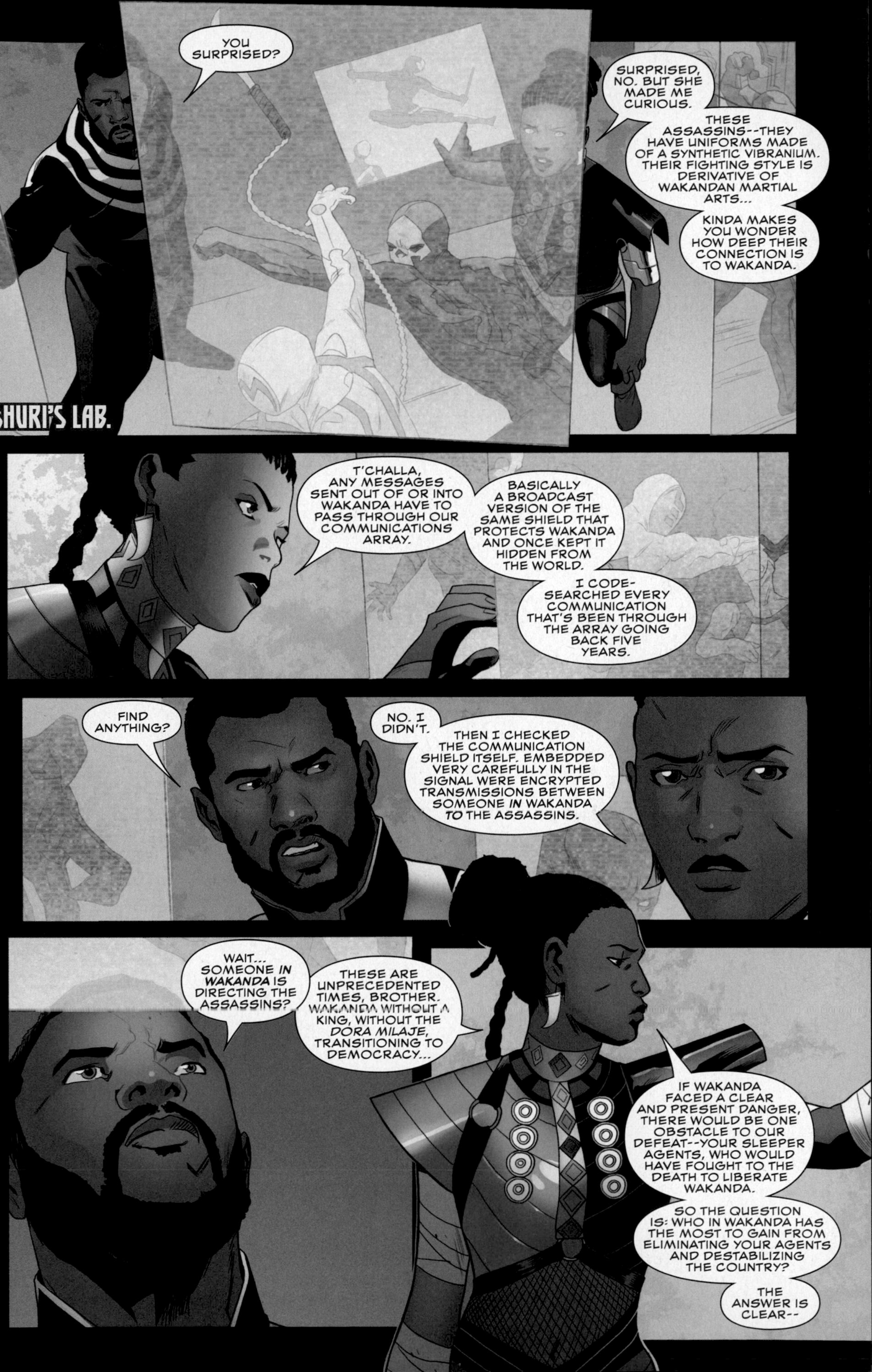
SHURI'S LAB.
YOU SURPRISED?
SURPRISED, NO. BUT SHE MADE ME CURIOUS.
THESE ASSASSINS--THEY HAVE UNIFORMS MADE OF A SYNTHETIC VIBRANIUM. THEIR FIGHTING STYLE IS DERIVATIVE OF WAKANDAN MARTIAL ARTS...
KINDA MAKES YOU WONDER HOW DEEP THEIR CONNECTION IS TO WAKANDA.
T'CHALLA, ANY MESSAGES SENT OUT OF OR INTO WAKANDA HAVE TO PASS THROUGH OUR COMMUNICATIONS ARRAY.
BASICALLY A BROADCAST VERSION OF THE SAME SHIELD THAT PROTECTS WAKANDA AND ONCE KEPT IT HIDDEN FROM THE WORLD.
I CODE-SEARCHED EVERY COMMUNICATION THAT'S BEEN THROUGH THE ARRAY GOING BACK FIVE YEARS.
FIND ANYTHING?
NO. I DIDN'T.
THEN I CHECKED THE COMMUNICATION SHIELD ITSELF. EMBEDDED VERY CAREFULLY IN THE SIGNAL WERE ENCRYPTED TRANSMISSIONS BETWEEN SOMEONE *IN* WAKANDA *TO* THE ASSASSINS.
WAIT... SOMEONE *IN WAKANDA* IS DIRECTING THE ASSASSINS?
THESE ARE UNPRECEDENTED TIMES, BROTHER. WAKANDA WITHOUT A KING, WITHOUT THE *DORA MILAJE*, TRANSITIONING TO DEMOCRACY...
IF WAKANDA FACED A CLEAR AND PRESENT DANGER, THERE WOULD BE ONE OBSTACLE TO OUR DEFEAT--YOUR SLEEPER AGENTS, WHO WOULD HAVE FOUGHT TO THE DEATH TO LIBERATE WAKANDA.
SO THE QUESTION IS: WHO IN WAKANDA HAS THE MOST TO GAIN FROM ELIMINATING YOUR AGENTS AND DESTABILIZING THE COUNTRY?
THE ANSWER IS CLEAR--

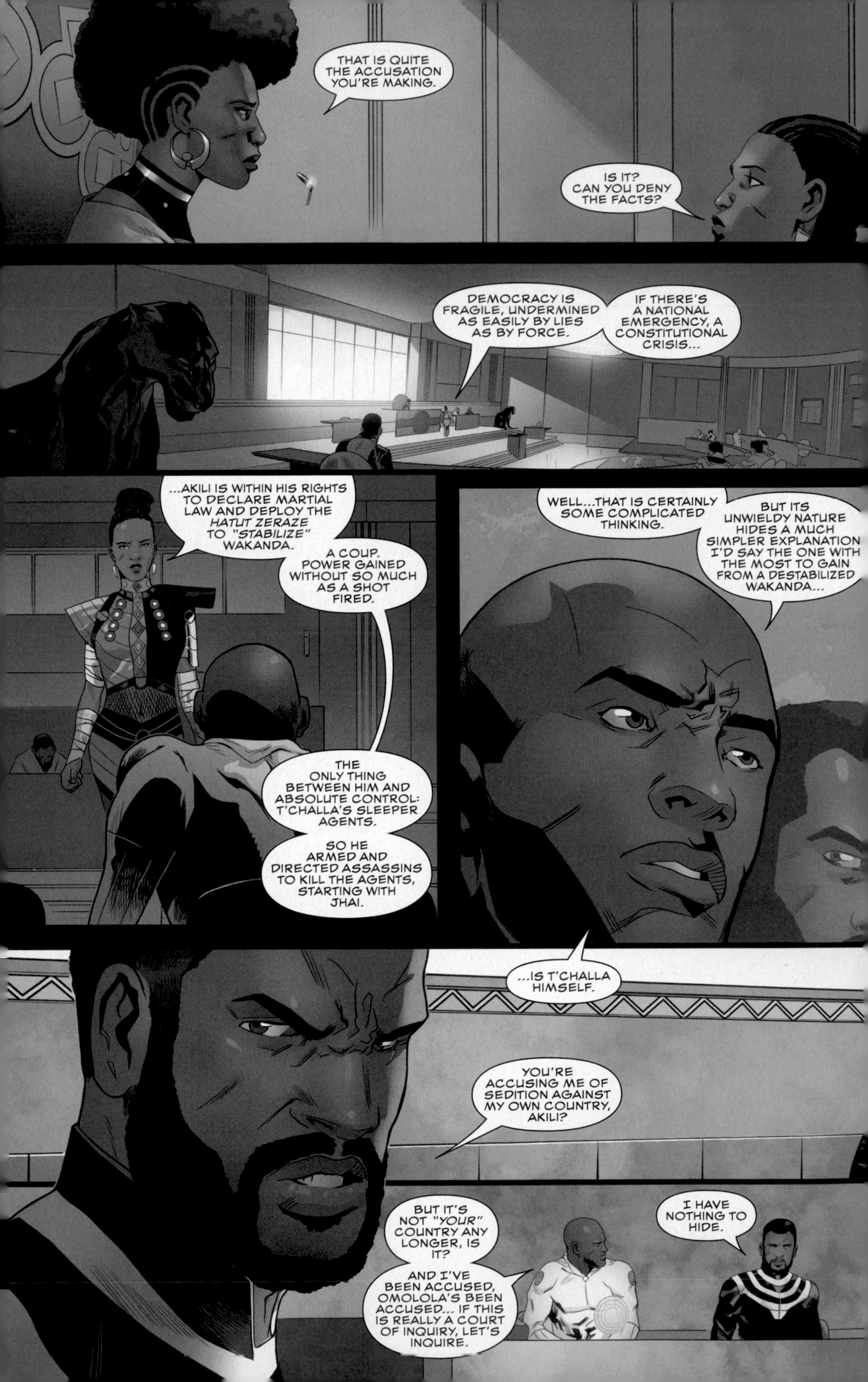
THAT IS QUITE THE ACCUSATION YOU'RE MAKING.
IS IT? CAN YOU DENY THE FACTS?
DEMOCRACY IS FRAGILE, UNDERMINED AS EASILY BY LIES AS BY FORCE.
IF THERE'S A NATIONAL EMERGENCY, A CONSTITUTIONAL CRISIS...
...AKILI IS WITHIN HIS RIGHTS TO DECLARE MARTIAL LAW AND DEPLOY THE *HATUT ZERAZE* TO *"STABILIZE"* WAKANDA.
A COUP. POWER GAINED WITHOUT SO MUCH AS A SHOT FIRED.
THE ONLY THING BETWEEN HIM AND ABSOLUTE CONTROL: T'CHALLA'S SLEEPER AGENTS.
SO HE ARMED AND DIRECTED ASSASSINS TO KILL THE AGENTS, STARTING WITH JHAI.
WELL...THAT IS CERTAINLY SOME COMPLICATED THINKING.
BUT ITS UNWIELDY NATURE HIDES A MUCH SIMPLER EXPLANATION I'D SAY THE ONE WITH THE MOST TO GAIN FROM A DESTABILIZED WAKANDA...
...IS T'CHALLA HIMSELF.
YOU'RE ACCUSING ME OF SEDITION AGAINST MY OWN COUNTRY, AKILI?
BUT IT'S NOT *"YOUR"* COUNTRY ANY LONGER, IS IT?
AND I'VE BEEN ACCUSED, OMOLOLA'S BEEN ACCUSED... IF THIS IS REALLY A COURT OF INQUIRY, LET'S INQUIRE.
I HAVE NOTHING TO HIDE.

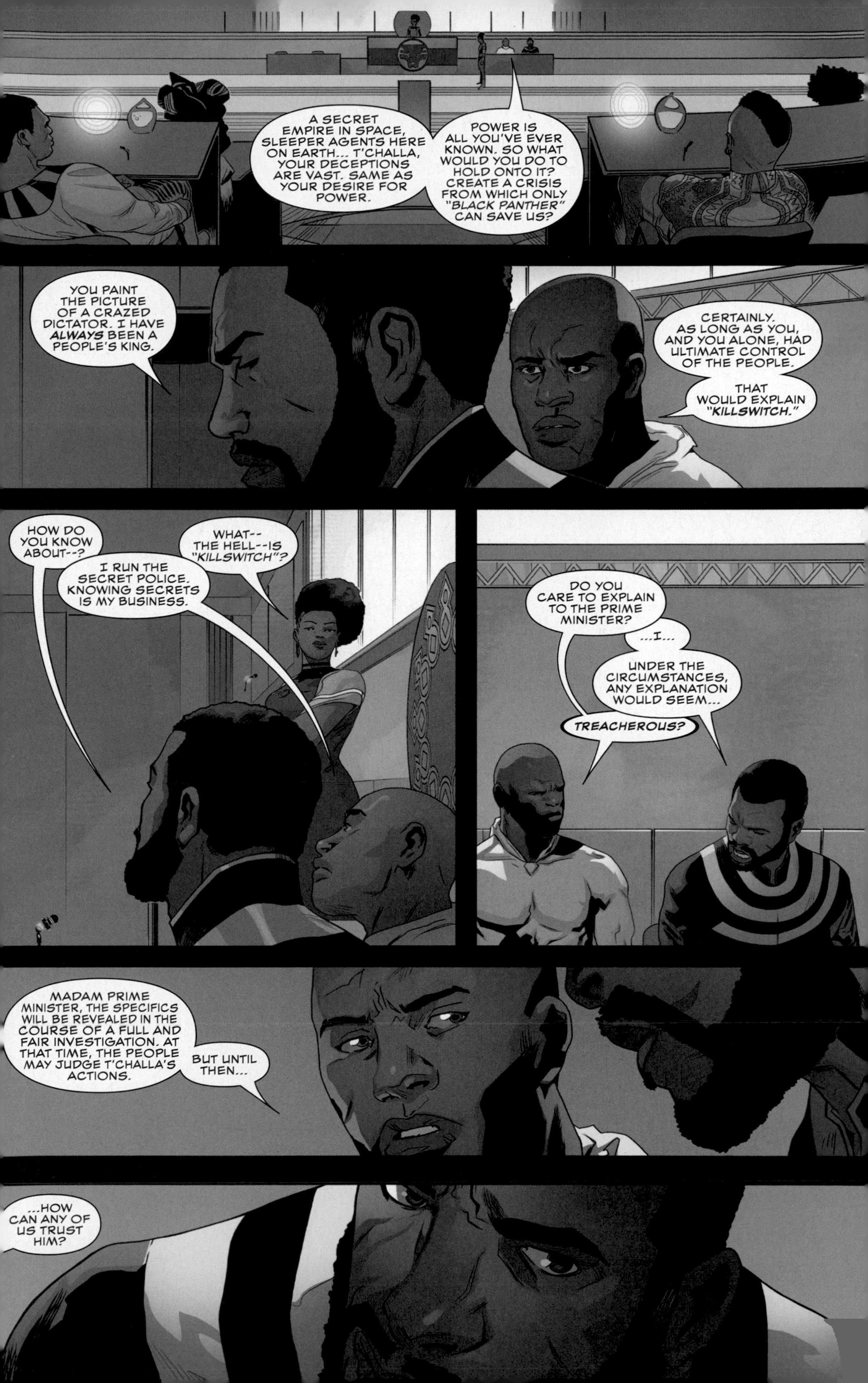
A SECRET EMPIRE IN SPACE, SLEEPER AGENTS HERE ON EARTH... T'CHALLA, YOUR DECEPTIONS ARE VAST. SAME AS YOUR DESIRE FOR POWER.
POWER IS ALL YOU'VE EVER KNOWN. SO WHAT WOULD YOU DO TO HOLD ONTO IT? CREATE A CRISIS FROM WHICH ONLY "BLACK PANTHER" CAN SAVE US?
YOU PAINT THE PICTURE OF A CRAZED DICTATOR. I HAVE ALWAYS BEEN A PEOPLE'S KING.
CERTAINLY. AS LONG AS YOU, AND YOU ALONE, HAD ULTIMATE CONTROL OF THE PEOPLE.
THAT WOULD EXPLAIN "KILLSWITCH."
HOW DO YOU KNOW ABOUT--?
I RUN THE SECRET POLICE. KNOWING SECRETS IS MY BUSINESS.
WHAT-- THE HELL--IS "KILLSWITCH"?
DO YOU CARE TO EXPLAIN TO THE PRIME MINISTER?
...I...
UNDER THE CIRCUMSTANCES, ANY EXPLANATION WOULD SEEM...
TREACHEROUS?
MADAM PRIME MINISTER, THE SPECIFICS WILL BE REVEALED IN THE COURSE OF A FULL AND FAIR INVESTIGATION. AT THAT TIME, THE PEOPLE MAY JUDGE T'CHALLA'S ACTIONS.
BUT UNTIL THEN...
...HOW CAN ANY OF US TRUST HIM?

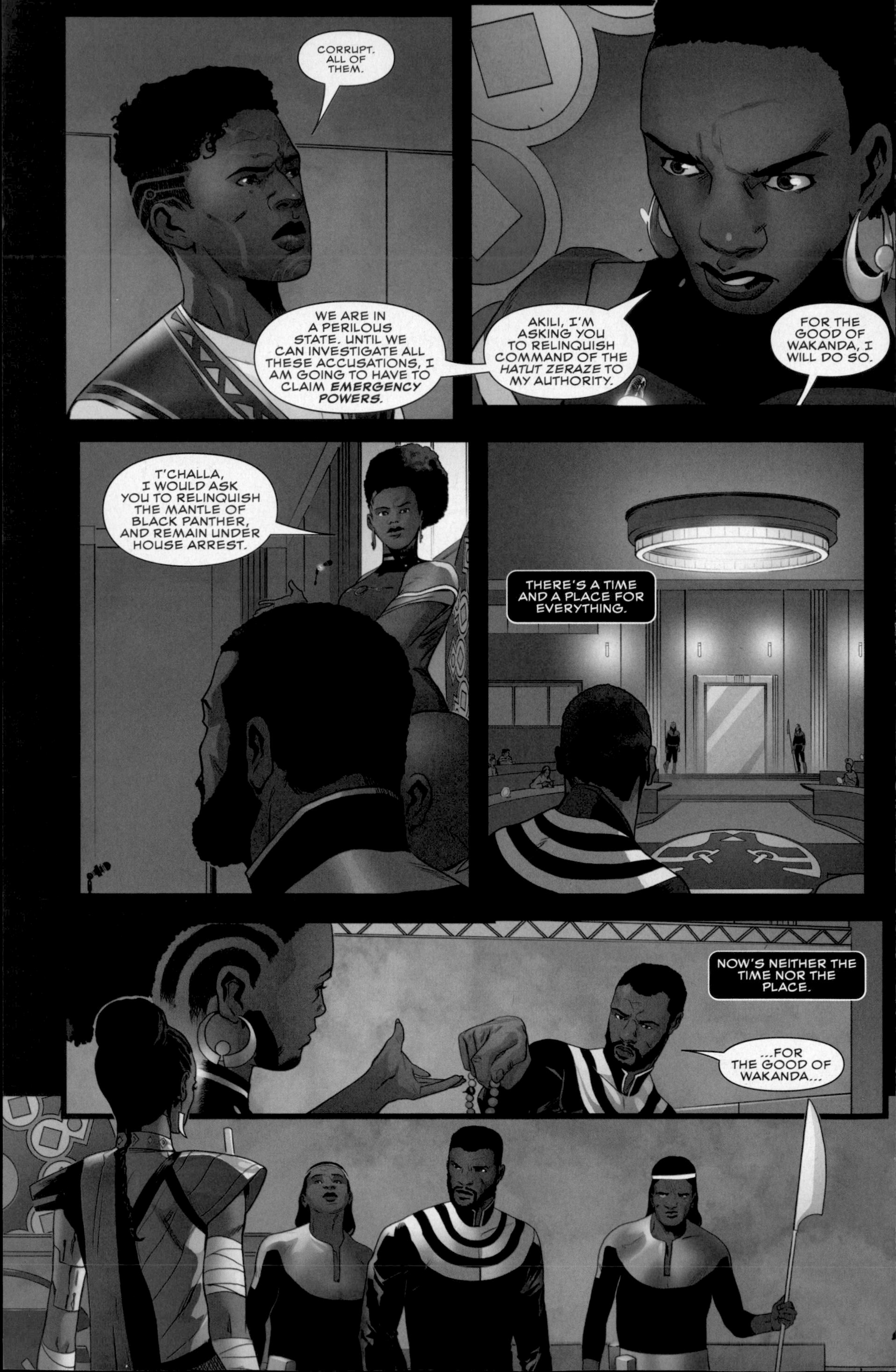

CORRUPT. ALL OF THEM.
WE ARE IN A PERILOUS STATE. UNTIL WE CAN INVESTIGATE ALL THESE ACCUSATIONS, I AM GOING TO HAVE TO CLAIM EMERGENCY POWERS.
AKILI, I'M ASKING YOU TO RELINQUISH COMMAND OF THE HATUT ZERAZE TO MY AUTHORITY.
FOR THE GOOD OF WAKANDA, I WILL DO SO.
T'CHALLA, I WOULD ASK YOU TO RELINQUISH THE MANTLE OF BLACK PANTHER, AND REMAIN UNDER HOUSE ARREST.
THERE'S A TIME AND A PLACE FOR EVERYTHING.
NOW'S NEITHER THE TIME NOR THE PLACE.
...FOR THE GOOD OF WAKANDA...

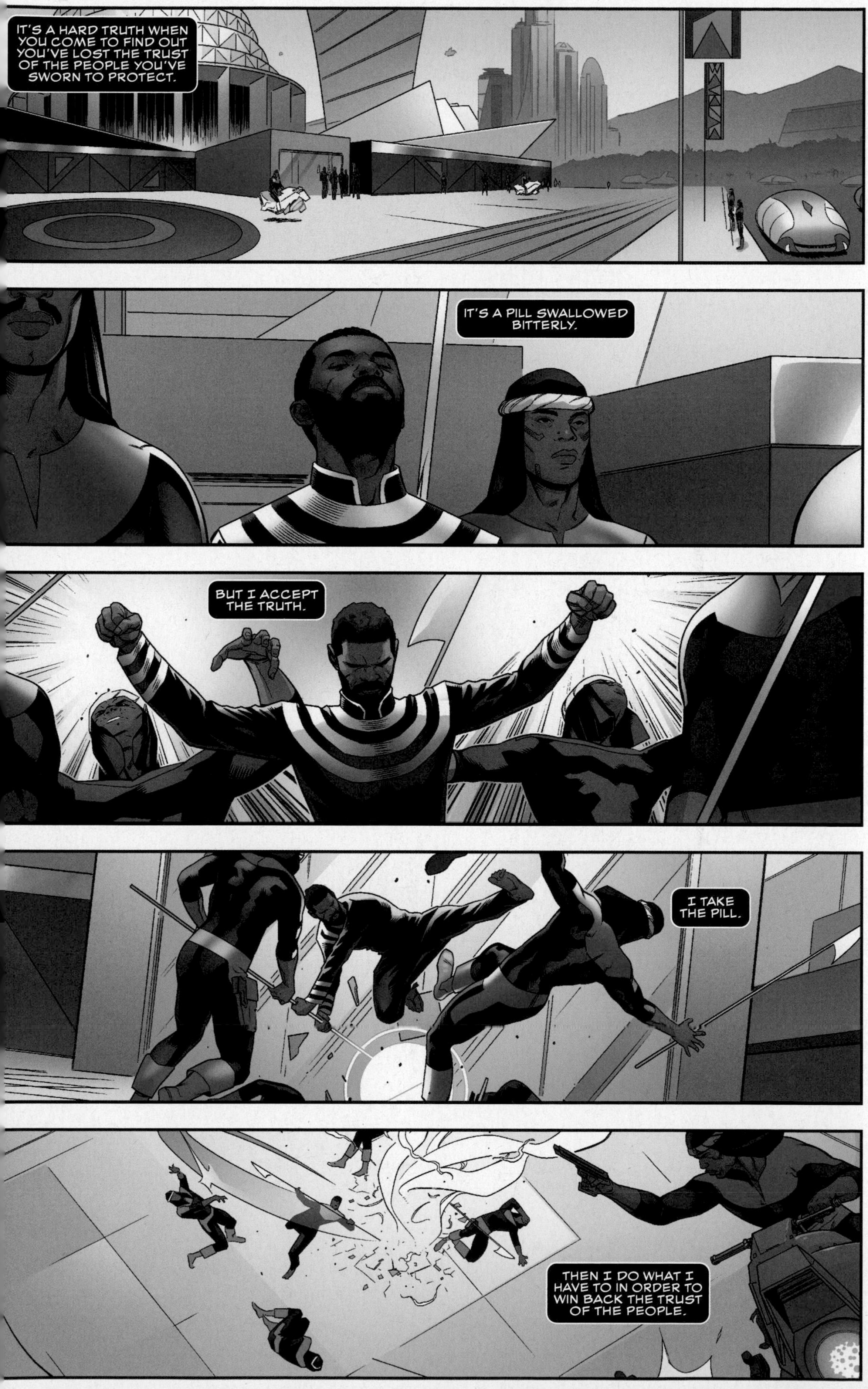
IT'S A HARD TRUTH WHEN YOU COME TO FIND OUT YOU'VE LOST THE TRUST OF THE PEOPLE YOU'VE SWORN TO PROTECT.
IT'S A PILL SWALLOWED BITTERLY.
BUT I ACCEPT THE TRUTH.
I TAKE THE PILL.
THEN I DO WHAT I HAVE TO IN ORDER TO WIN BACK THE TRUST OF THE PEOPLE.

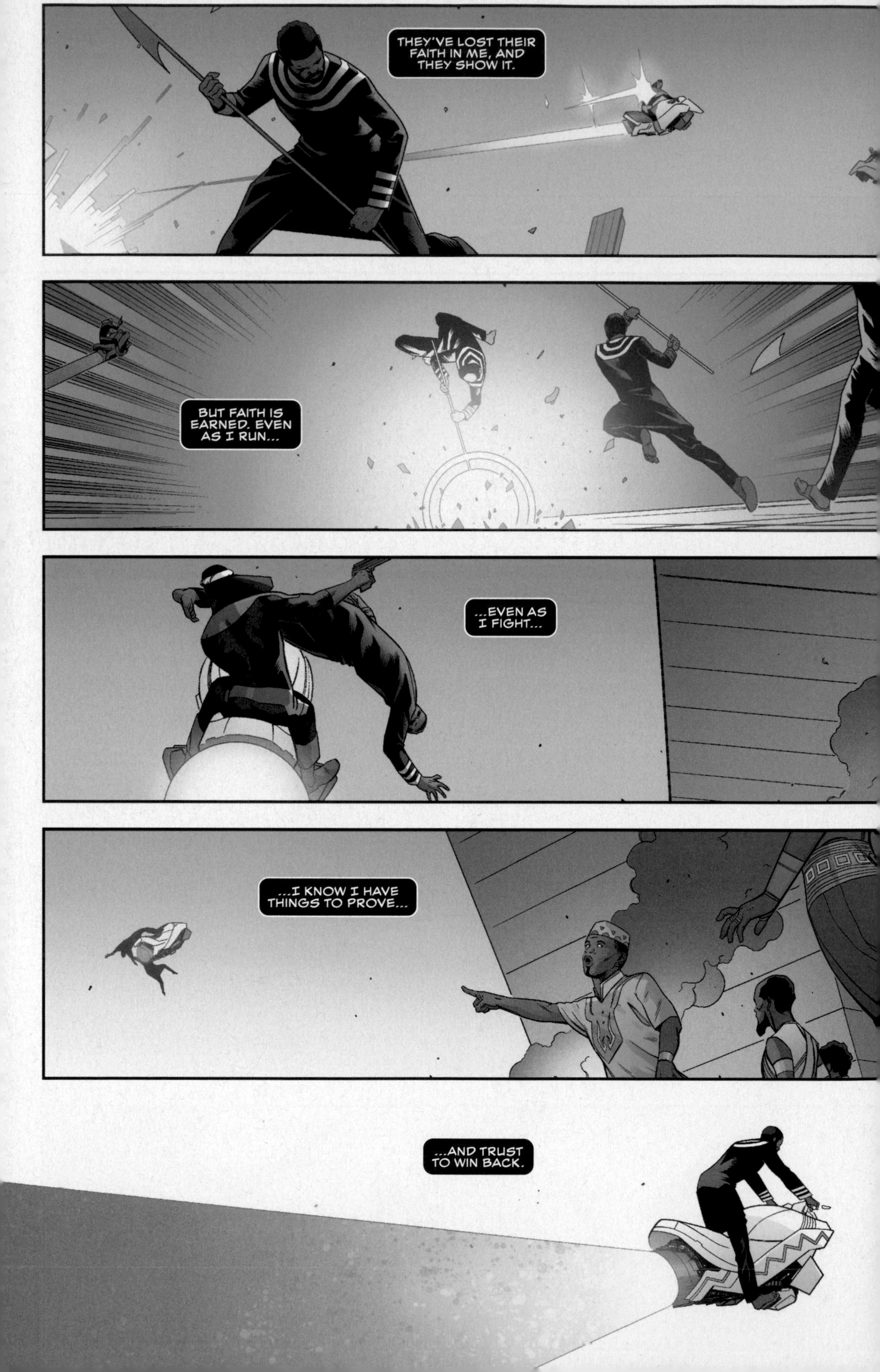
THEY'VE LOST THEIR FAITH IN ME, AND THEY SHOW IT.
BUT FAITH IS EARNED. EVEN AS I RUN...
...EVEN AS I FIGHT...
...I KNOW I HAVE THINGS TO PROVE...
...AND TRUST TO WIN BACK.

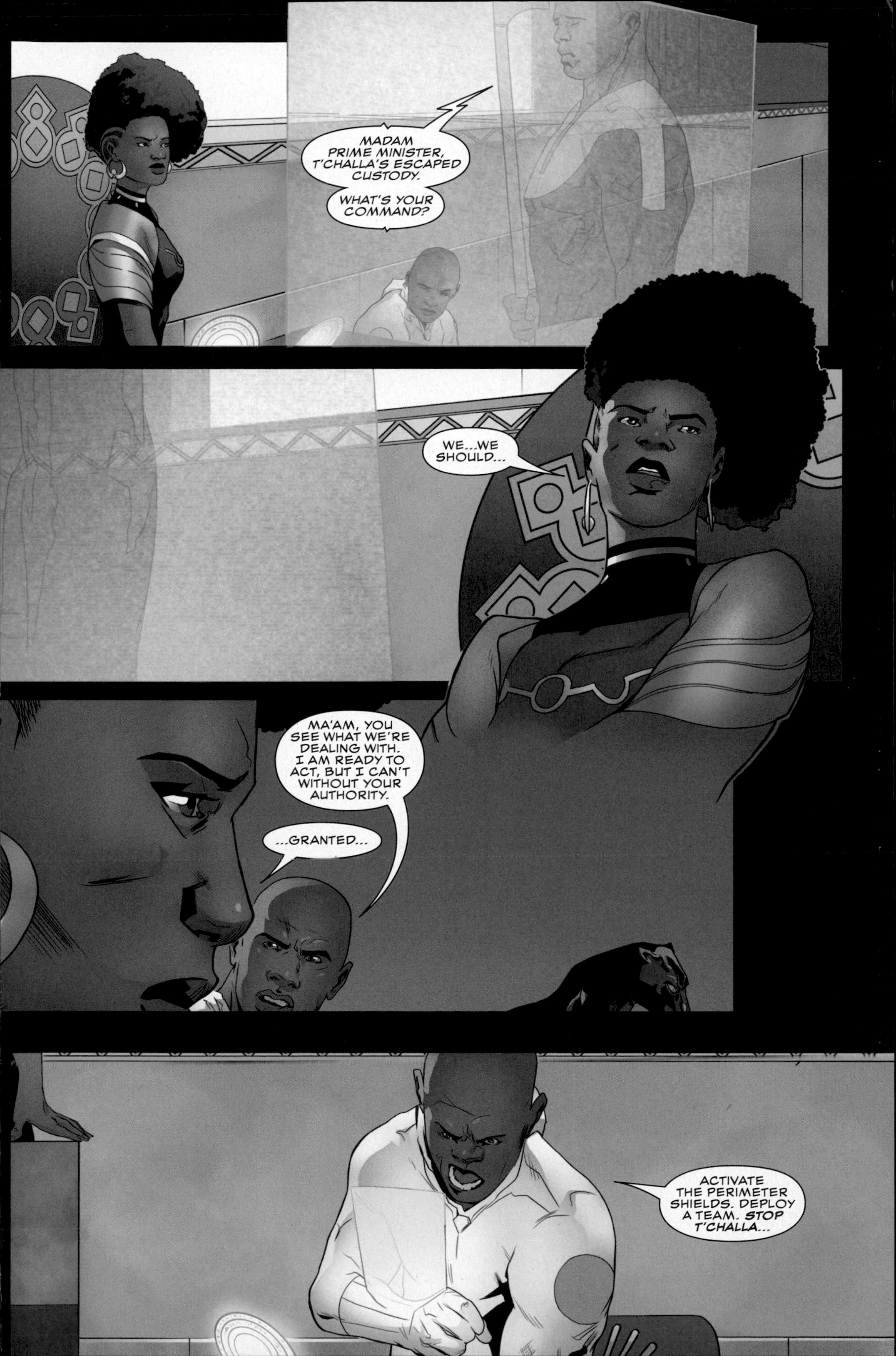
MADAM PRIME MINISTER, T'CHALLA'S ESCAPED CUSTODY.
WHAT'S YOUR COMMAND?
WE...WE SHOULD...
MA'AM, YOU SEE WHAT WE'RE DEALING WITH. I AM READY TO ACT, BUT I CAN'T WITHOUT YOUR AUTHORITY.
...GRANTED...
ACTIVATE THE PERIMETER SHIELDS. DEPLOY A TEAM. STOP T'CHALLA...

"...ANY WAY YOU HAVE TO."

I KNOW AKILI. I KNOW HE WILL HAVE INVERTED THE SHIELD. WHAT WAS MEANT TO KEEP OTHERS *OUT...*

PING

PING

...WILL NOW KEEP ME *IN.* UNLESS...

ZZAP

ZZAP

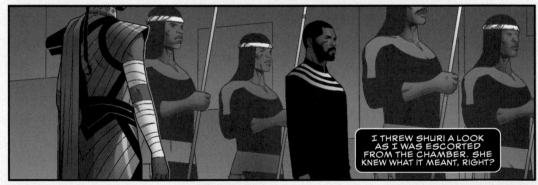

I THREW SHURI A LOOK AS I WAS ESCORTED FROM THE CHAMBER. SHE KNEW WHAT IT MEANT, RIGHT?

ZZAP

BOOM

SHE KNOWS *NOW'S* THE TIME FOR SOME HELP...

...RIGHT...?

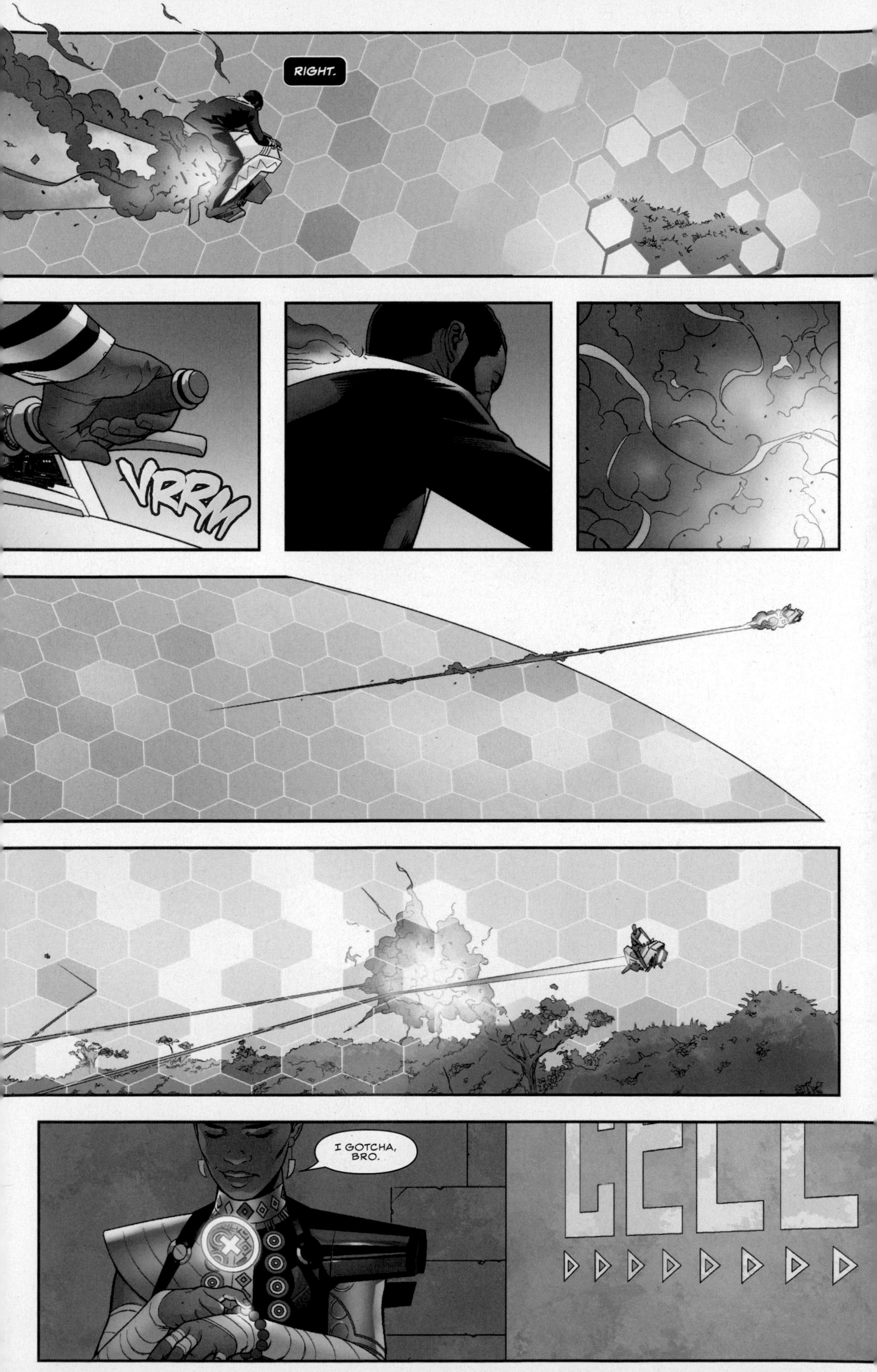
RIGHT.
VRRM
I GOTCHA, BRO.
CELL

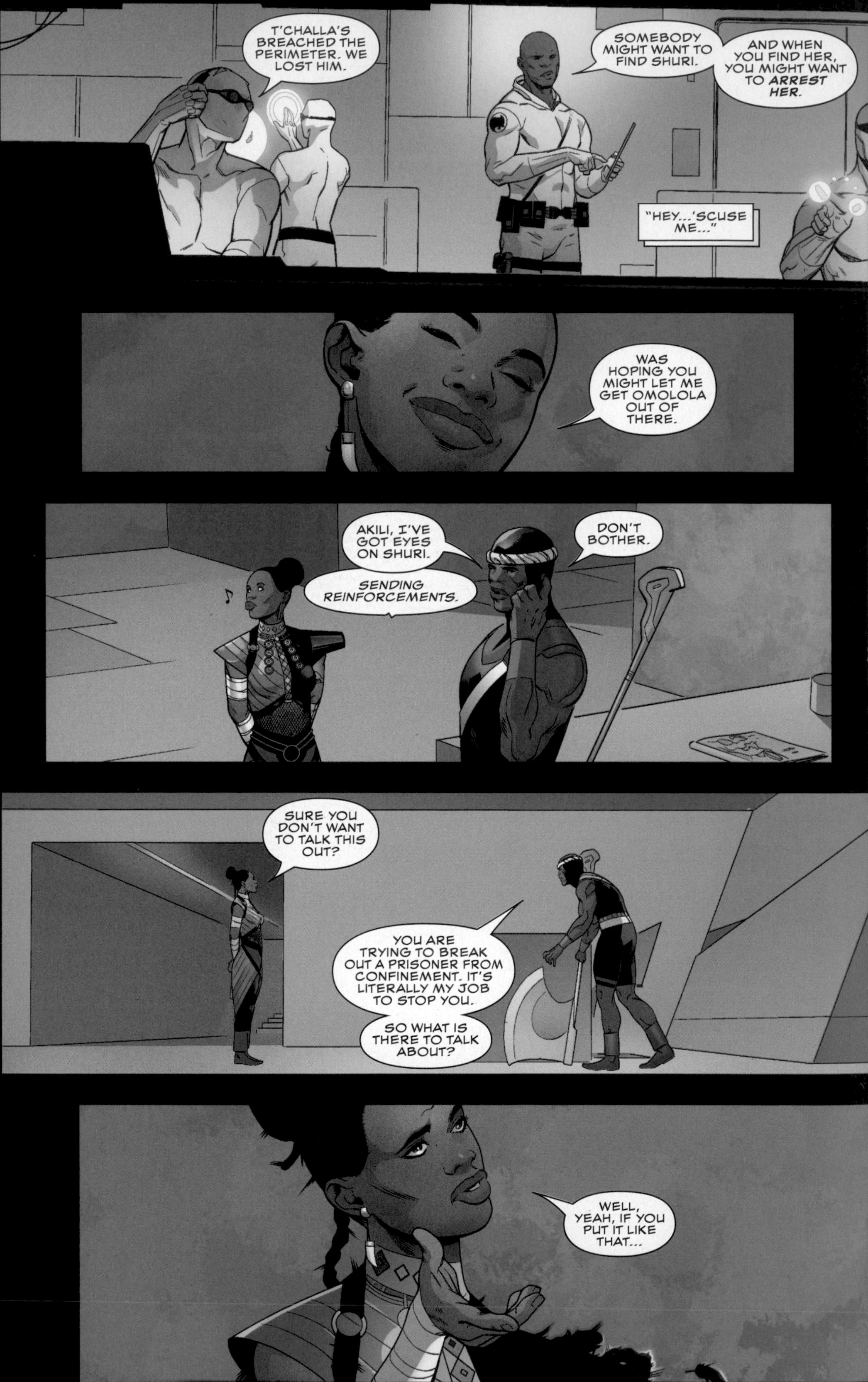
T'CHALLA'S BREACHED THE PERIMETER. WE LOST HIM.
SOMEBODY MIGHT WANT TO FIND SHURI.
AND WHEN YOU FIND HER, YOU MIGHT WANT TO ARREST HER.
"HEY...'SCUSE ME..."
WAS HOPING YOU MIGHT LET ME GET OMOLOLA OUT OF THERE.
AKILI, I'VE GOT EYES ON SHURI.
SENDING REINFORCEMENTS.
DON'T BOTHER.
SURE YOU DON'T WANT TO TALK THIS OUT?
YOU ARE TRYING TO BREAK OUT A PRISONER FROM CONFINEMENT. IT'S LITERALLY MY JOB TO STOP YOU.
SO WHAT IS THERE TO TALK ABOUT?
WELL, YEAH, IF YOU PUT IT LIKE THAT...

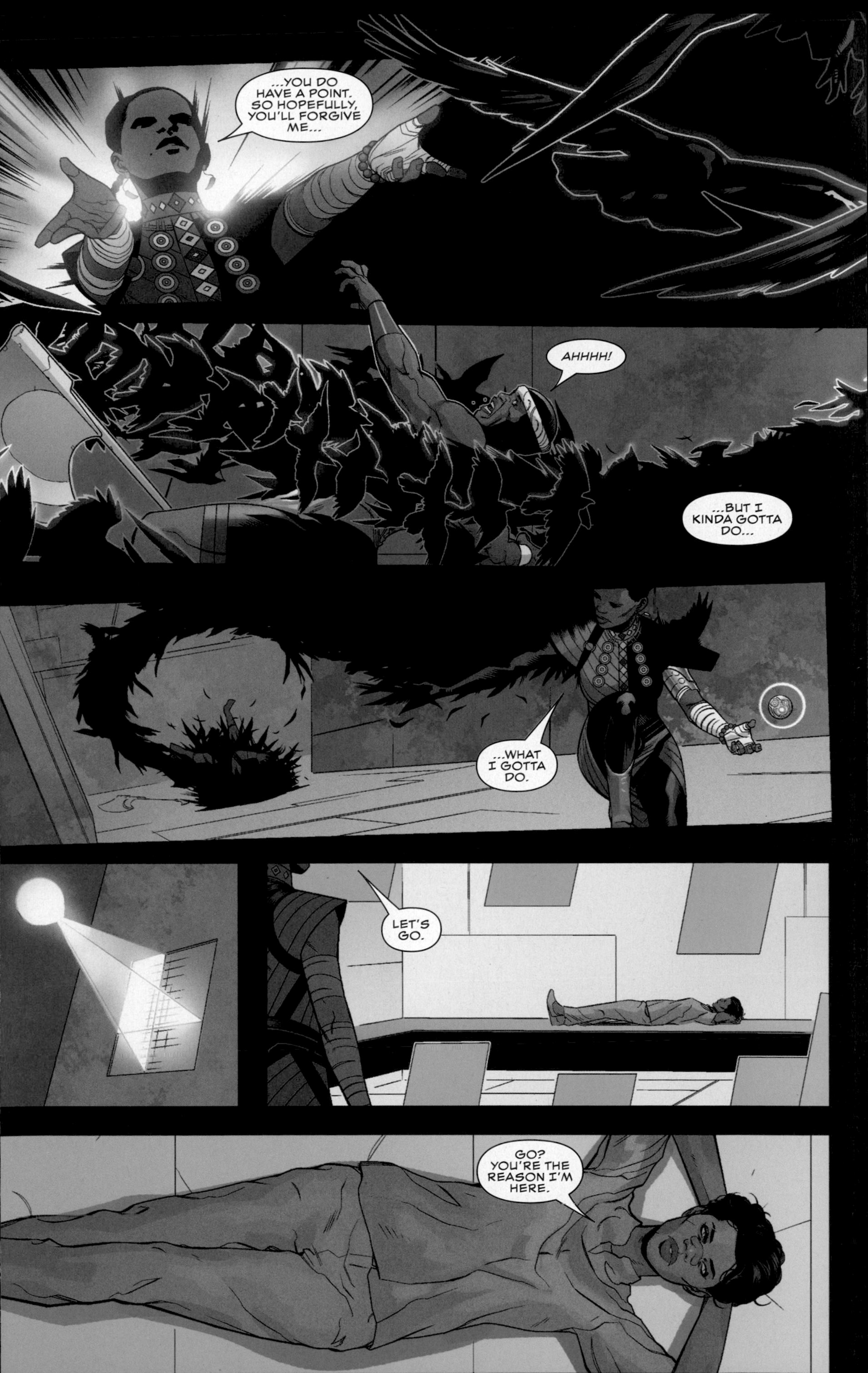
...YOU DO HAVE A POINT. SO HOPEFULLY, YOU'LL FORGIVE ME...
AHHHH!
...BUT I KINDA GOTTA DO...
...WHAT I GOTTA DO.
LET'S GO.
GO? YOU'RE THE REASON I'M HERE.

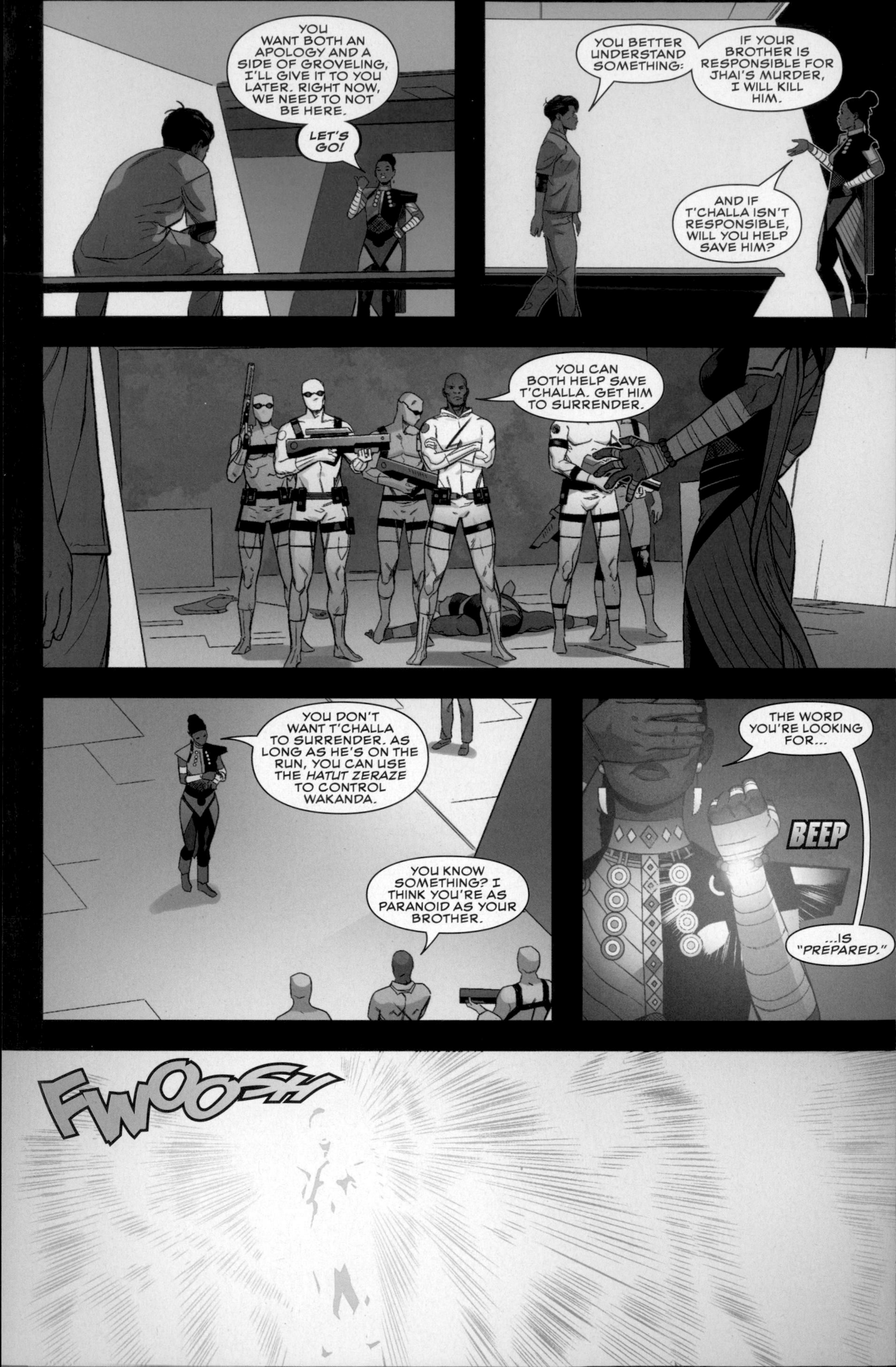
YOU WANT BOTH AN APOLOGY AND A SIDE OF GROVELING, I'LL GIVE IT TO YOU LATER. RIGHT NOW, WE NEED TO NOT BE HERE.
LET'S GO!
YOU BETTER UNDERSTAND SOMETHING:
IF YOUR BROTHER IS RESPONSIBLE FOR JHAI'S MURDER, I WILL KILL HIM.
AND IF T'CHALLA ISN'T RESPONSIBLE, WILL YOU HELP SAVE HIM?
YOU CAN BOTH HELP SAVE T'CHALLA. GET HIM TO SURRENDER.
YOU DON'T WANT T'CHALLA TO SURRENDER. AS LONG AS HE'S ON THE RUN, YOU CAN USE THE *HATUT ZERAZE* TO CONTROL WAKANDA.
YOU KNOW SOMETHING? I THINK YOU'RE AS PARANOID AS YOUR BROTHER.
THE WORD YOU'RE LOOKING FOR...
BEEP
...IS "*PREPARED.*"
FWOOSH

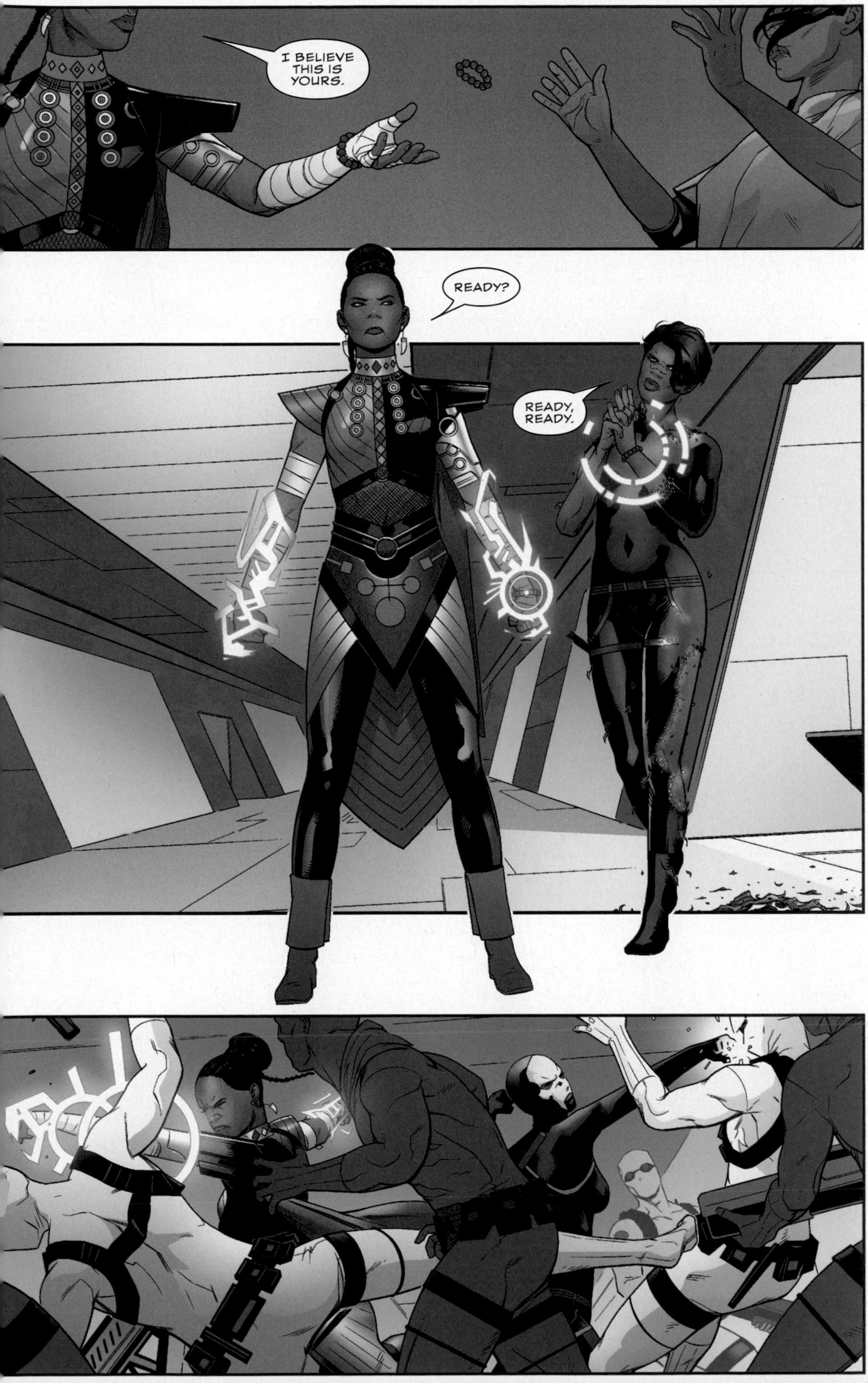
I BELIEVE THIS IS YOURS.
READY?
READY, READY.

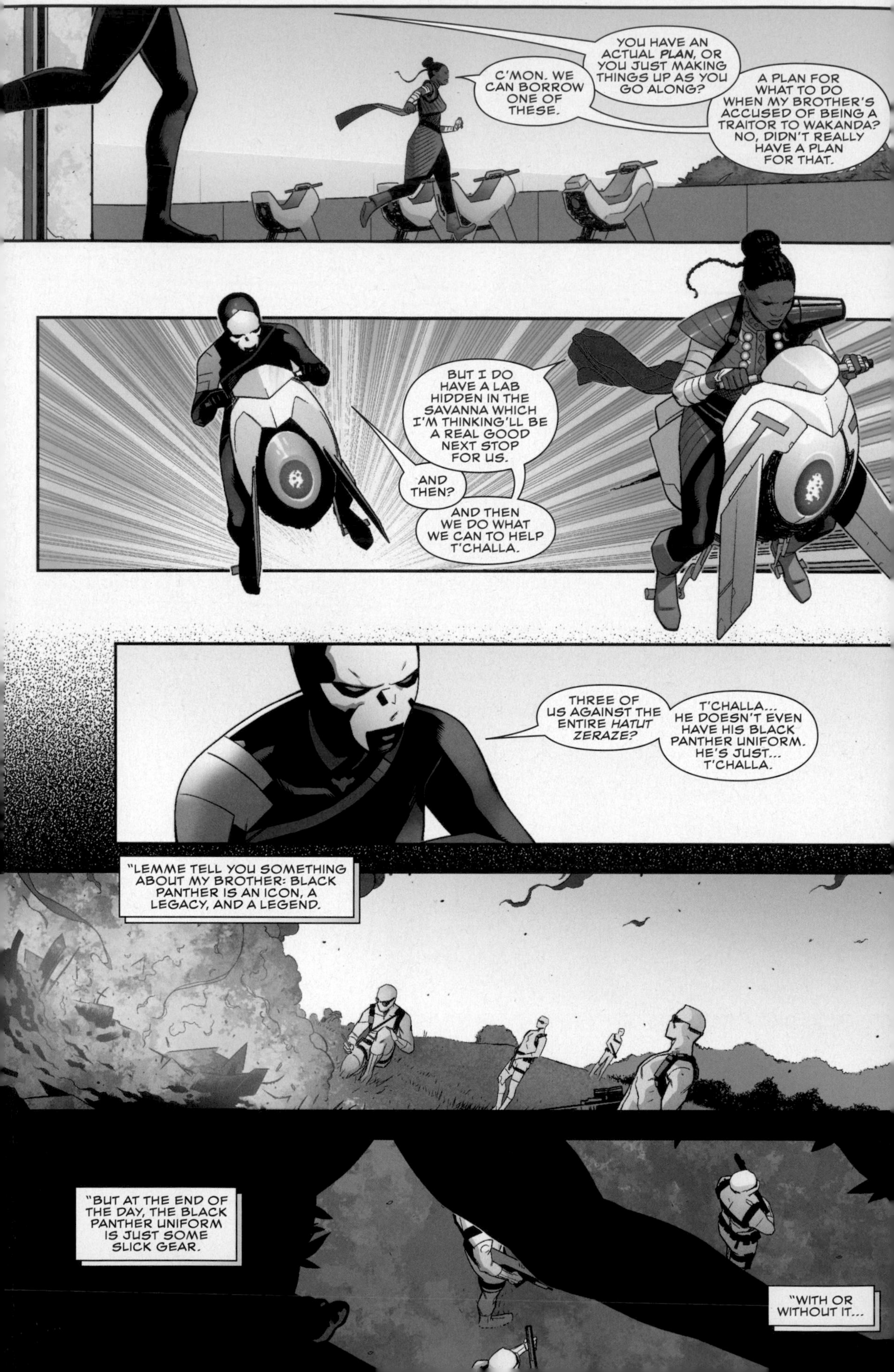

C'MON. WE CAN BORROW ONE OF THESE.
YOU HAVE AN ACTUAL PLAN, OR YOU JUST MAKING THINGS UP AS YOU GO ALONG?
A PLAN FOR WHAT TO DO WHEN MY BROTHER'S ACCUSED OF BEING A TRAITOR TO WAKANDA? NO, DIDN'T REALLY HAVE A PLAN FOR THAT.
BUT I DO HAVE A LAB HIDDEN IN THE SAVANNA WHICH I'M THINKING'LL BE A REAL GOOD NEXT STOP FOR US.
AND THEN?
AND THEN WE DO WHAT WE CAN TO HELP T'CHALLA.
THREE OF US AGAINST THE ENTIRE HATUT ZERAZE?
T'CHALLA... HE DOESN'T EVEN HAVE HIS BLACK PANTHER UNIFORM. HE'S JUST... T'CHALLA.
"LEMME TELL YOU SOMETHING ABOUT MY BROTHER: BLACK PANTHER IS AN ICON, A LEGACY, AND A LEGEND.
"BUT AT THE END OF THE DAY, THE BLACK PANTHER UNIFORM IS JUST SOME SLICK GEAR.
"WITH OR WITHOUT IT...

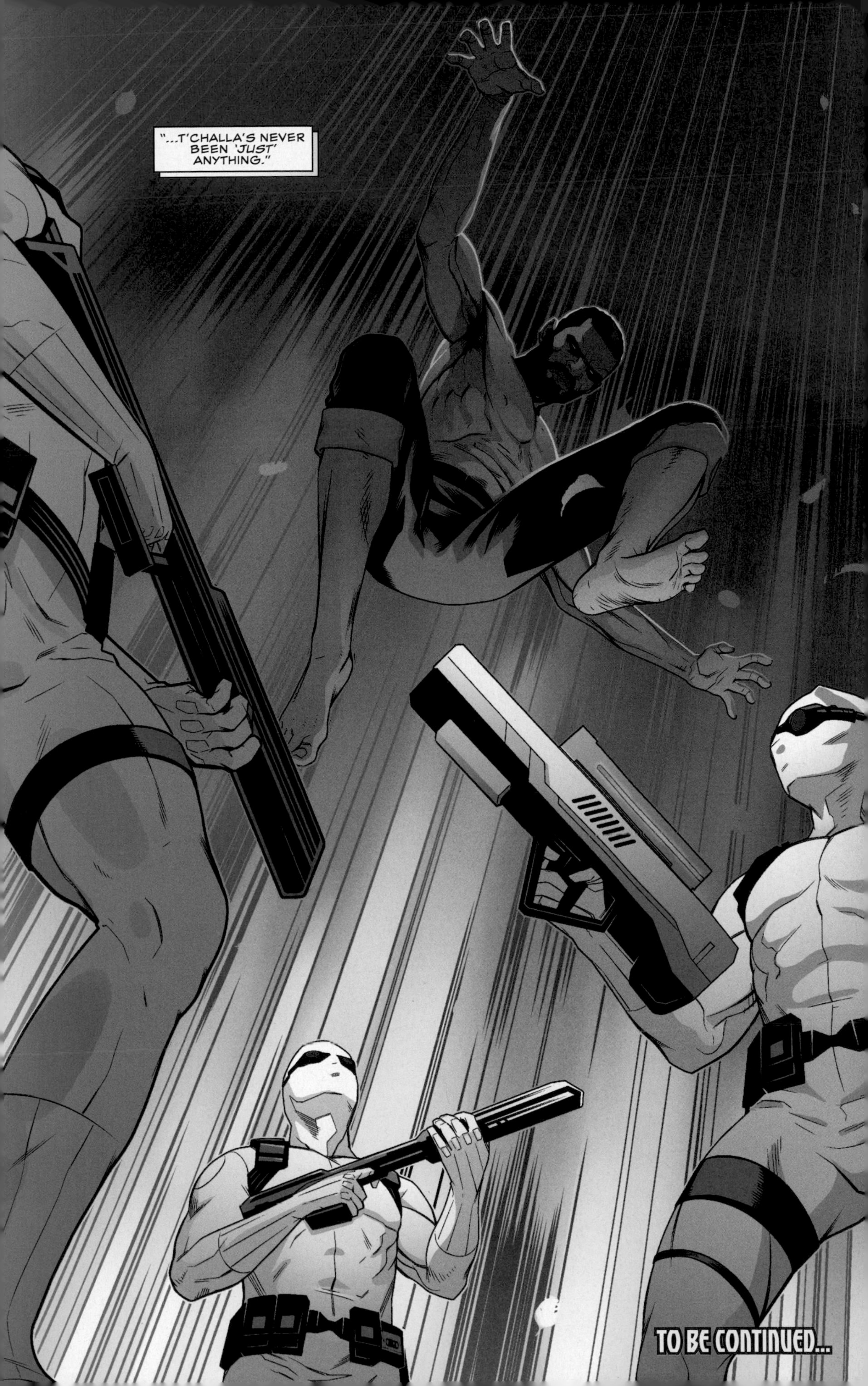
"...T'CHALLA'S NEVER BEEN 'JUST' ANYTHING."
TO BE CONTINUED...

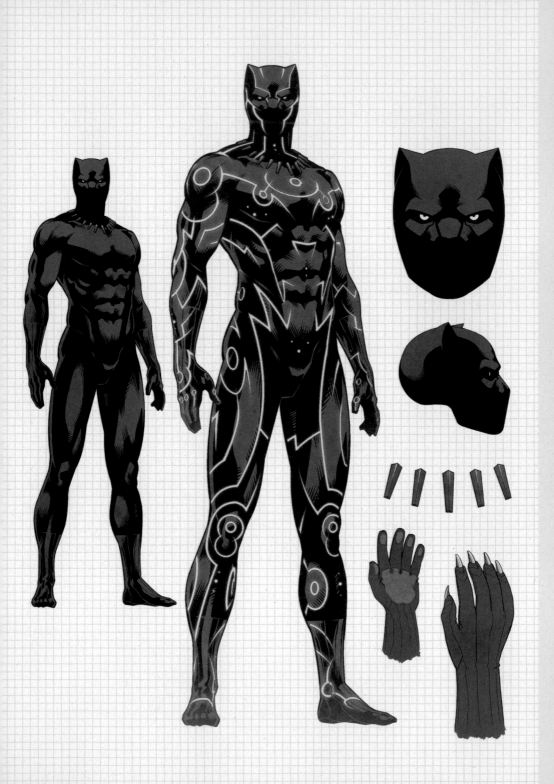

#1 2ᴺᴰ Printing Design Variant ||||||||||||||||||||||||||||||||||||| **JUANN CABAL**

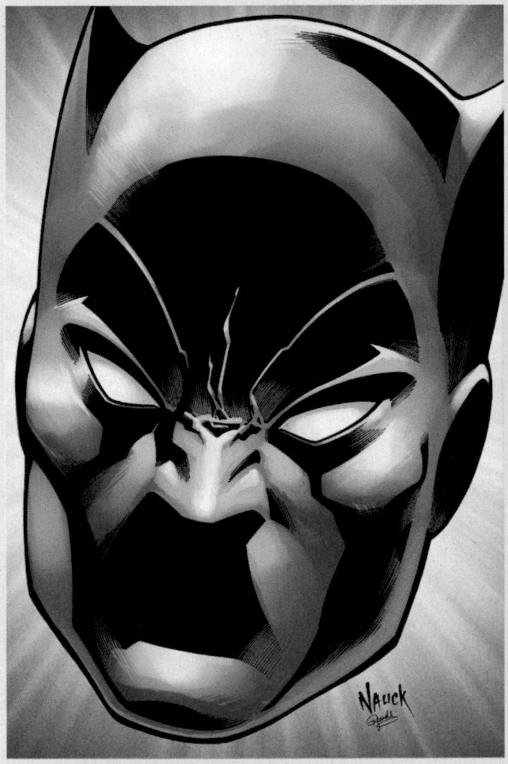

#1 Headshot Variant
TODD NAUCK & **RACHELLE ROSENBERG**

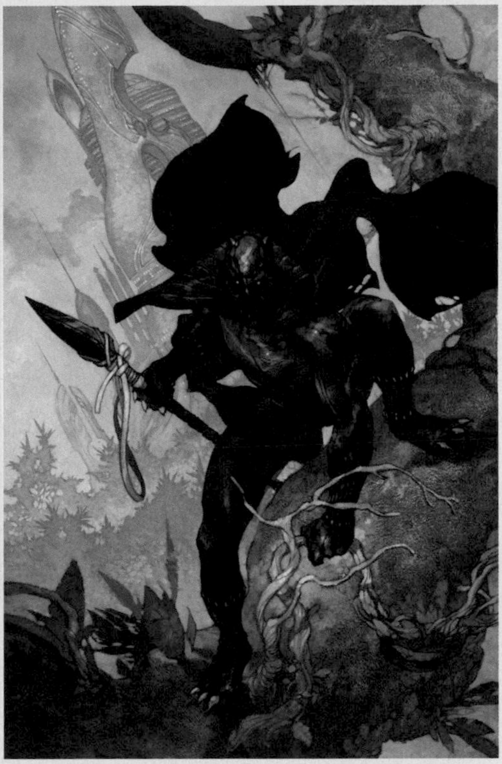

#1 Variant
SIMONE BIANCHI

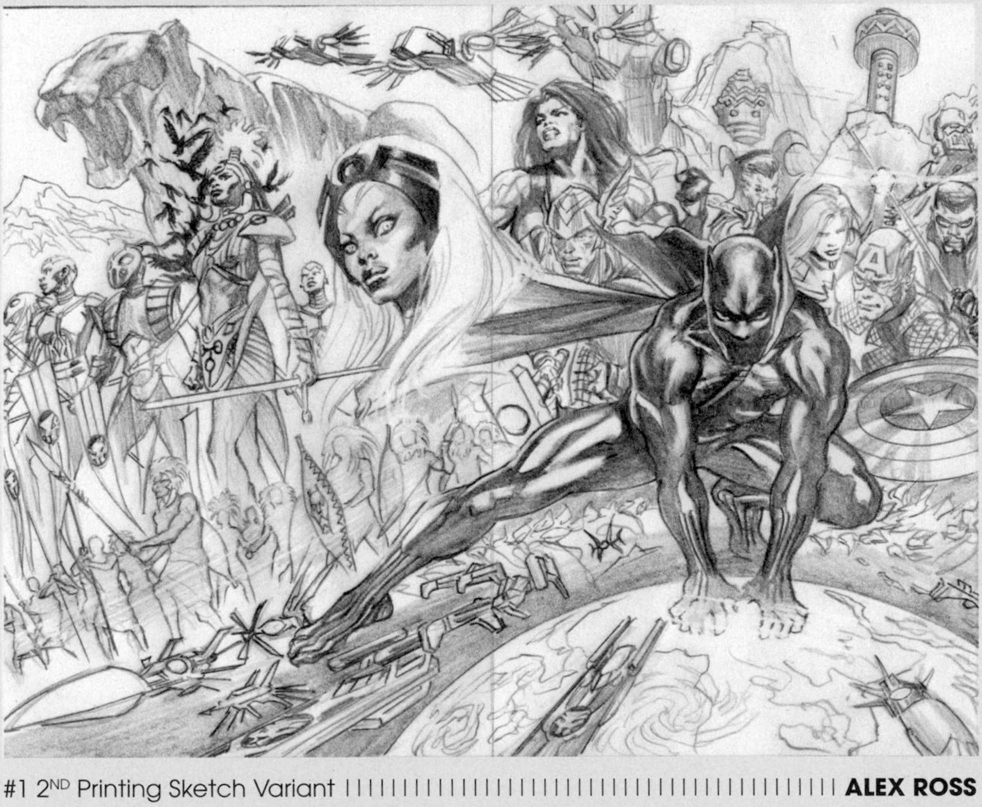

#1 2ND Printing Sketch Variant **ALEX ROSS**

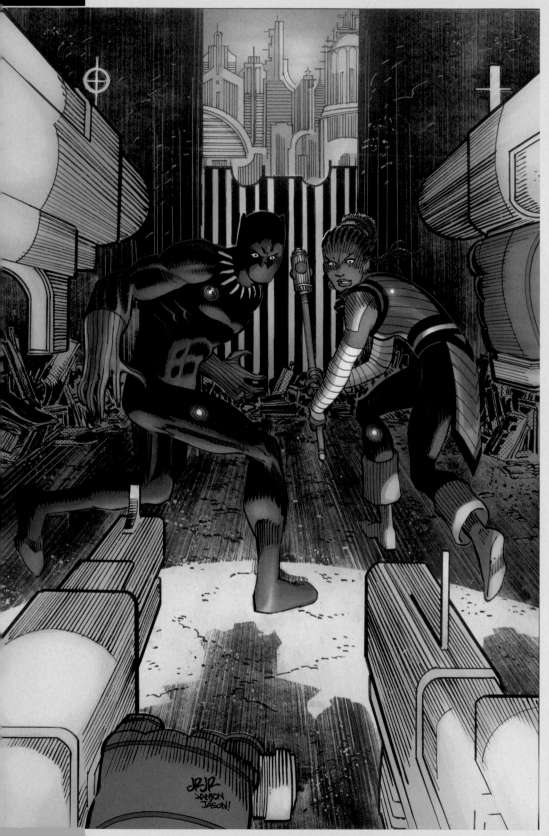

#1 Variant |||||||||||||||| **JOHN ROMITA JR.**, **KLAUS JANSON** & **JASON KEITH**

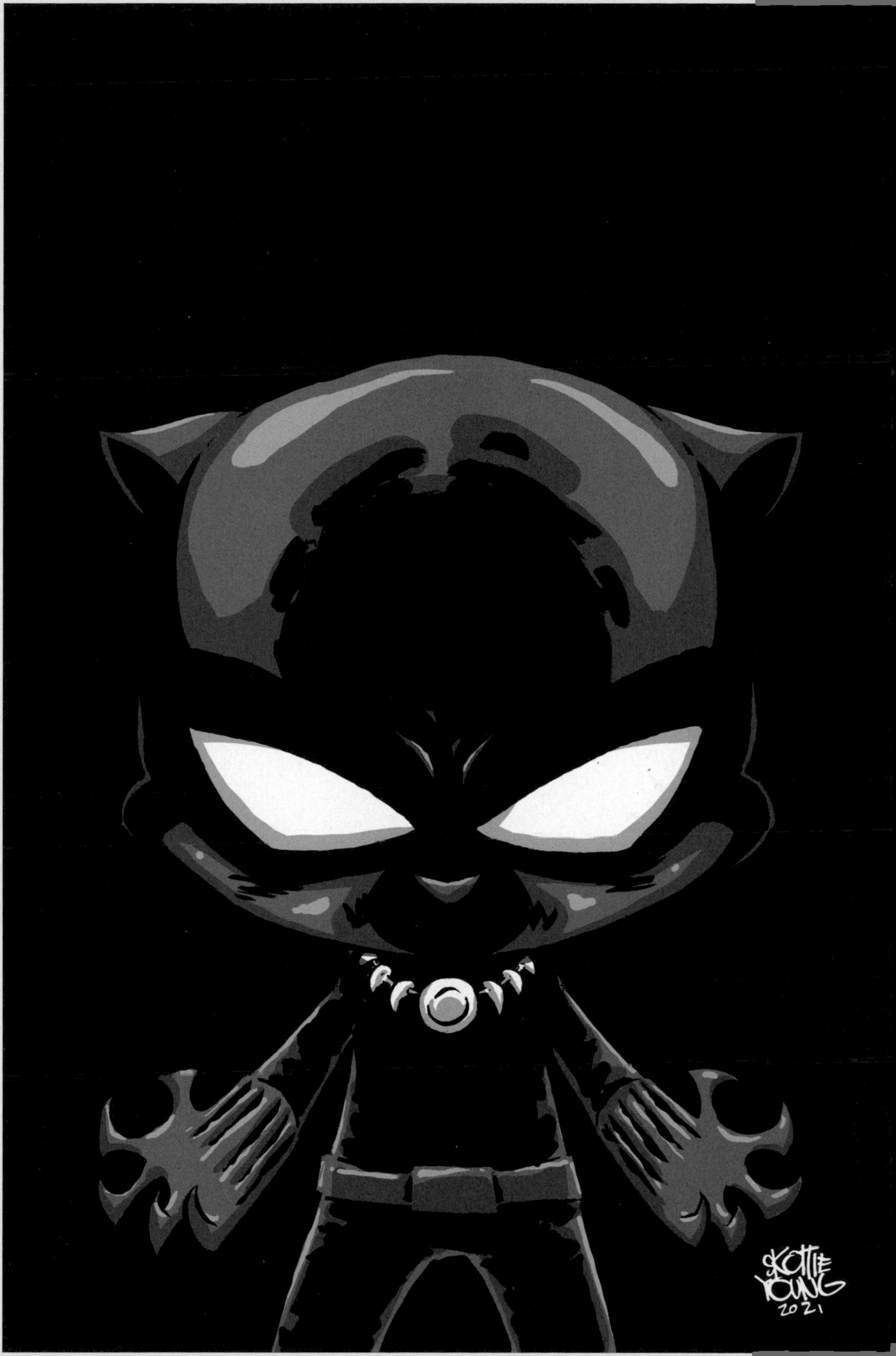
SKOTTIE YOUNG 2021

#1 Variant **SKOTTIE YOUNG**

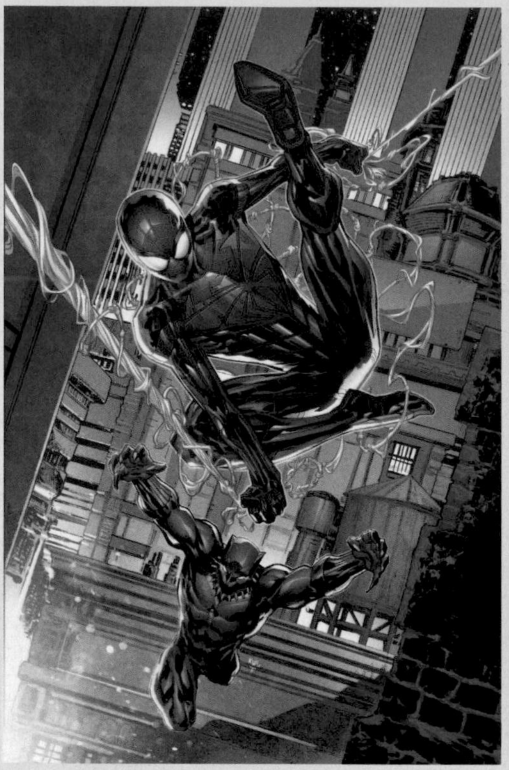

#2 Miles Morales: Spider-Man 10TH Anniversary Variant **KEN LASHLEY** & **JUAN FERNANDEZ**

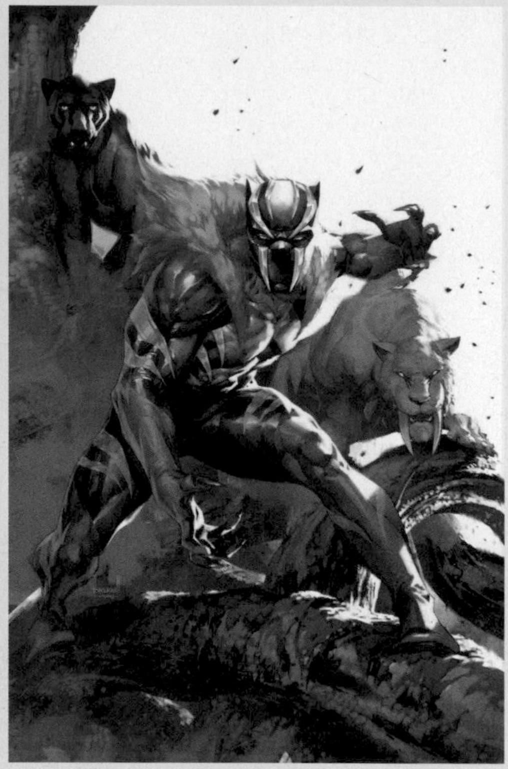

#2 Devil's Reign Variant **KAEL NGU**

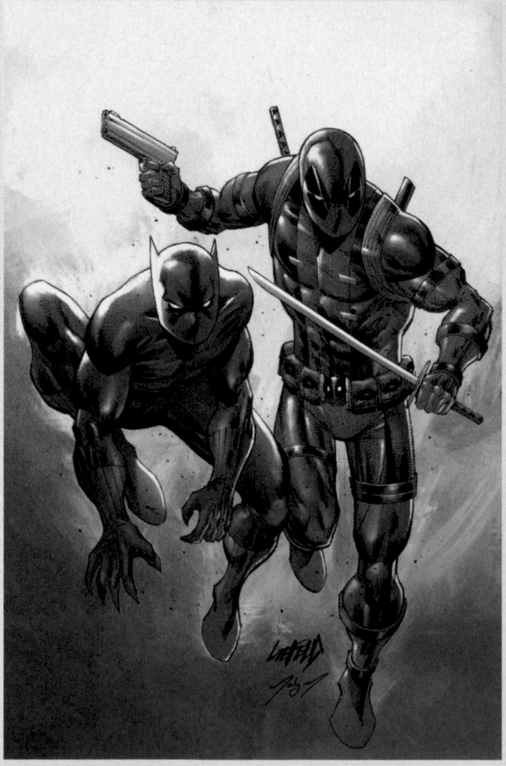

#2 Deadpool 30TH Anniversary Variant **ROB LIEFELD**

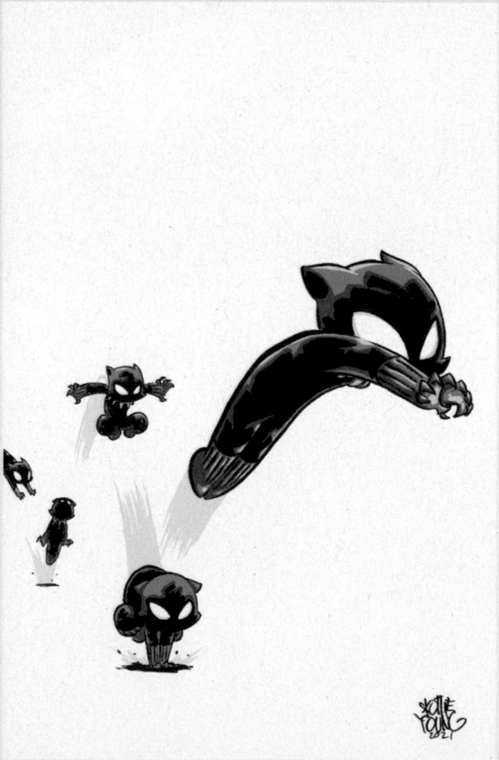

#2 Variant **SKOTTIE YOUNG**

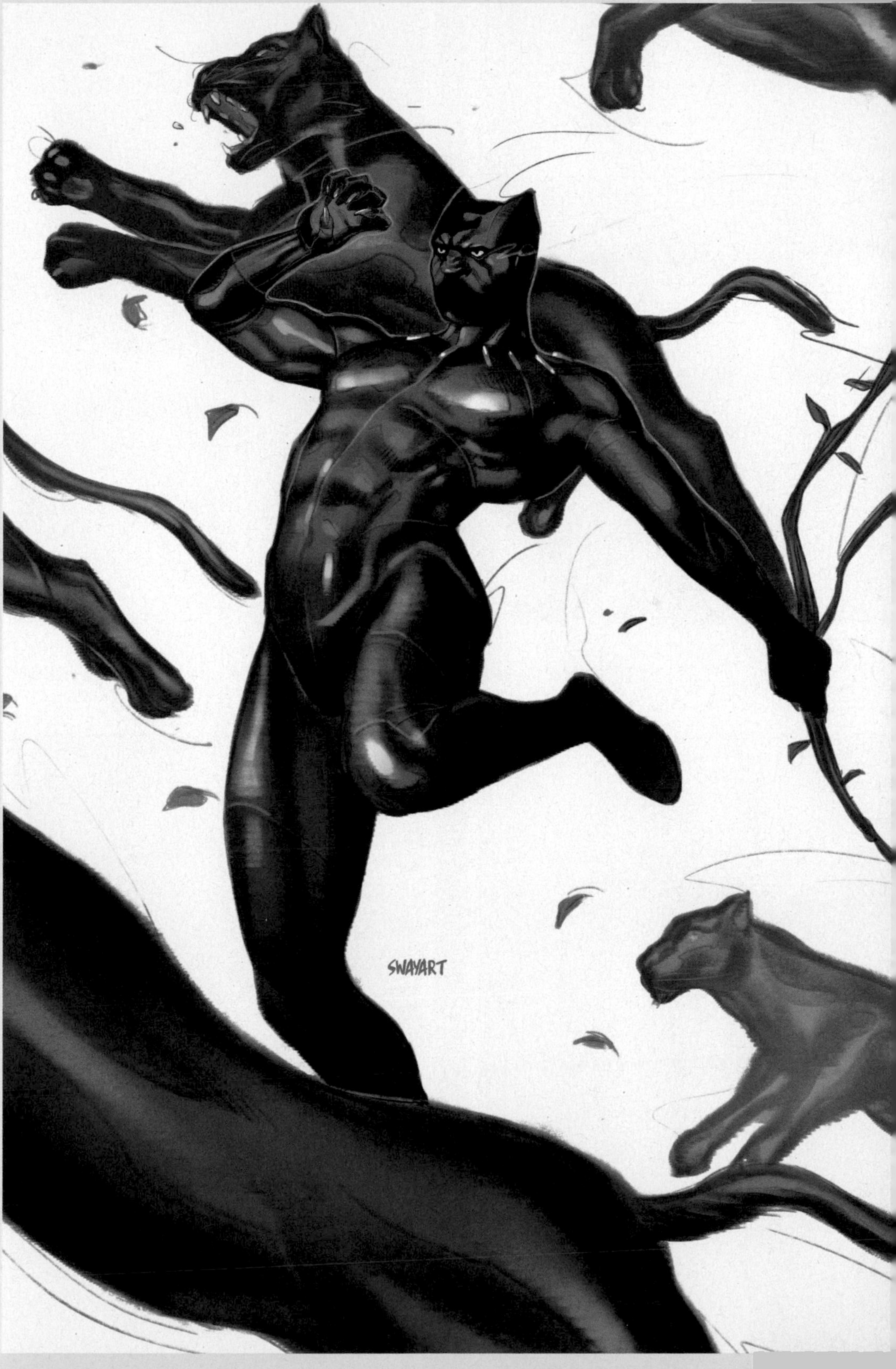
SWAYART

#2 Variant | | | | | | | | | | | | | | | | | | | | | | | | | | | | | | | | | | | | | | | | | | | | | | | **JOSHUA "SWAY" SWABY**

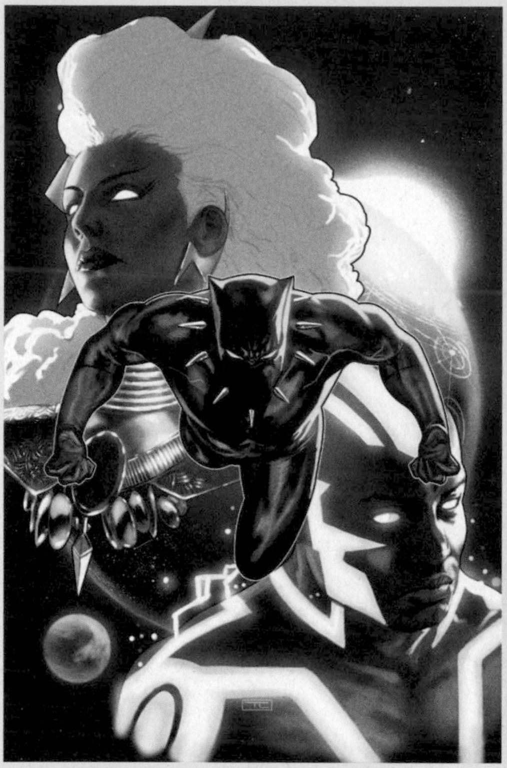

#3 Variant **TAURIN CLARKE**

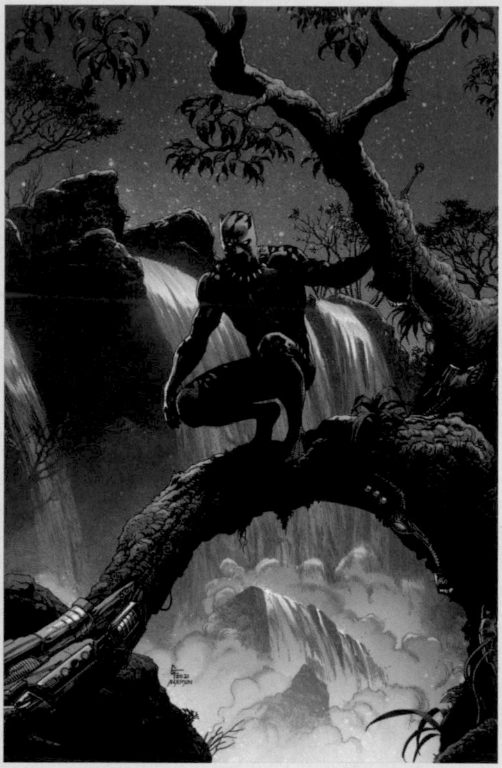

#3 Variant **GARY FRANK** & **BRAD ANDERSON**

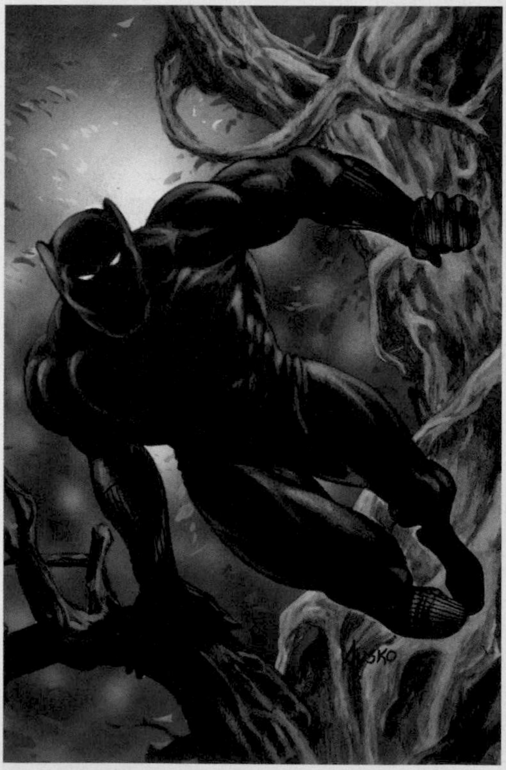

#3 Marvel Masterpieces Variant **JOE JUSKO**

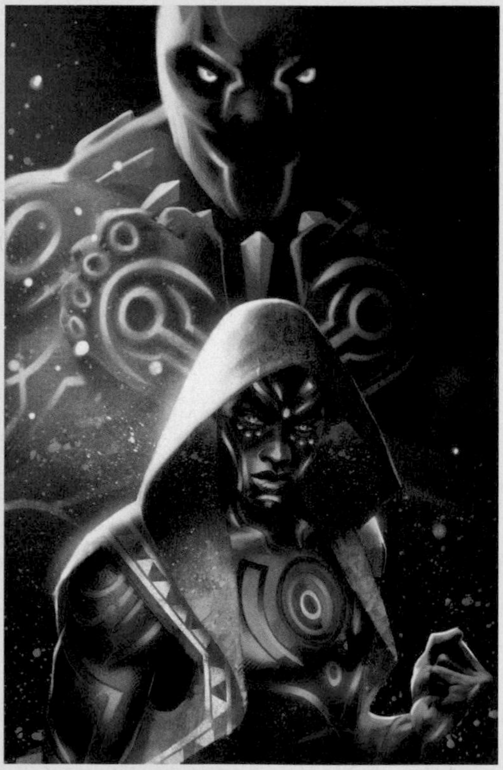

#3 2ND Printing Variant **MATEUS MANHANINI**

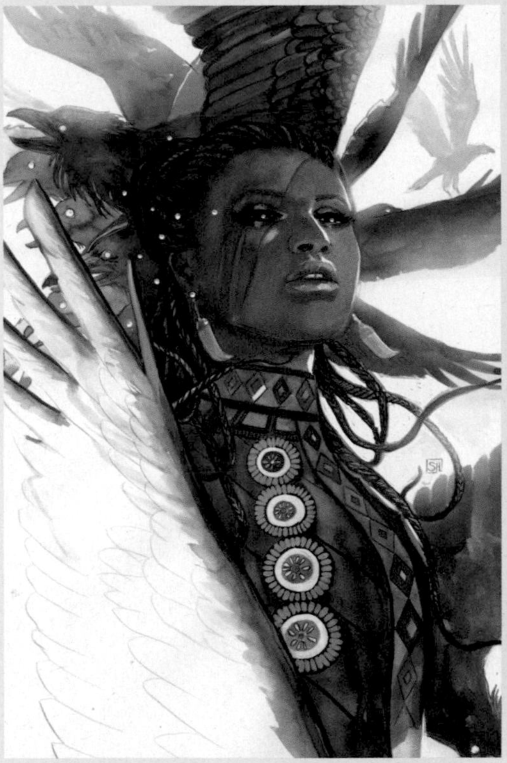

#4 Variant **STEPHANIE HANS**

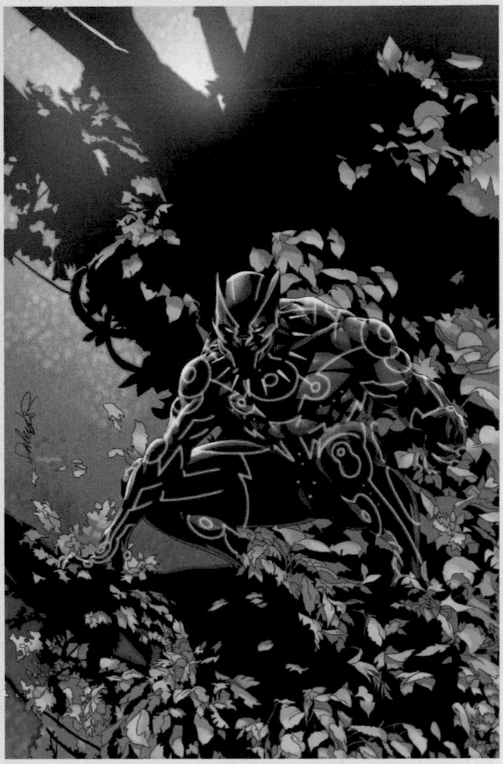

#4 Variant **SALVADOR LARROCA** & **EDGAR DELGADO**

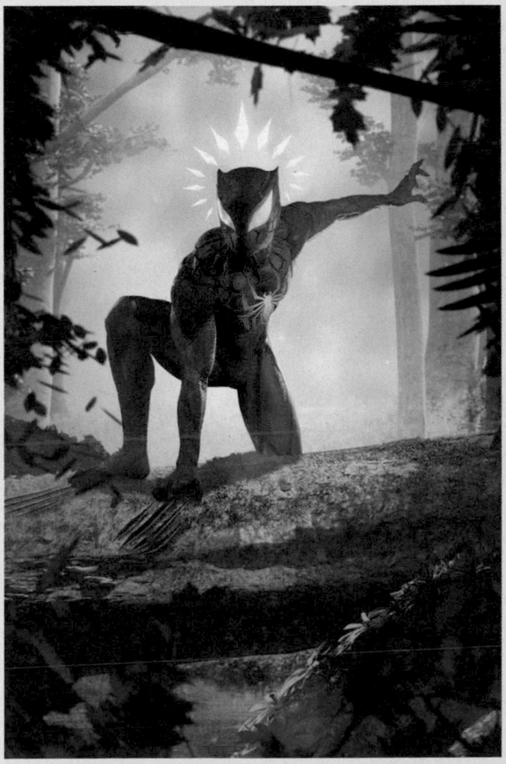

#5 Spider-Man Variant **BOSSLOGIC**

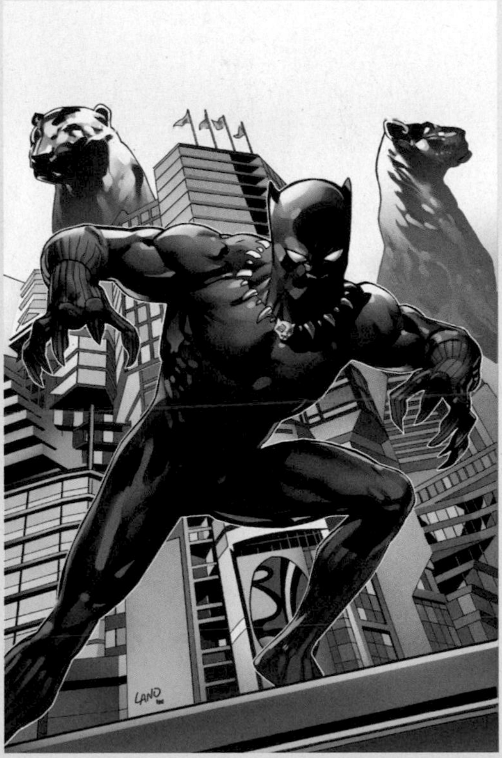

#5 Variant **GREG LAND** & **FRANK D'ARMATA**

ASSASSINS

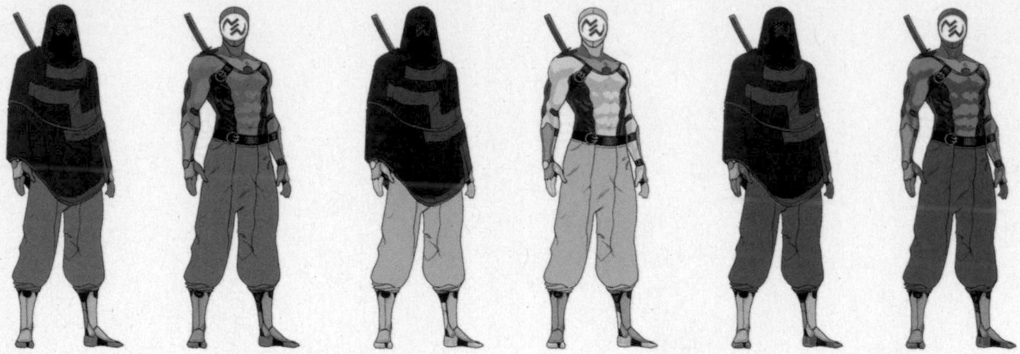

JHAI & OMOLOLA

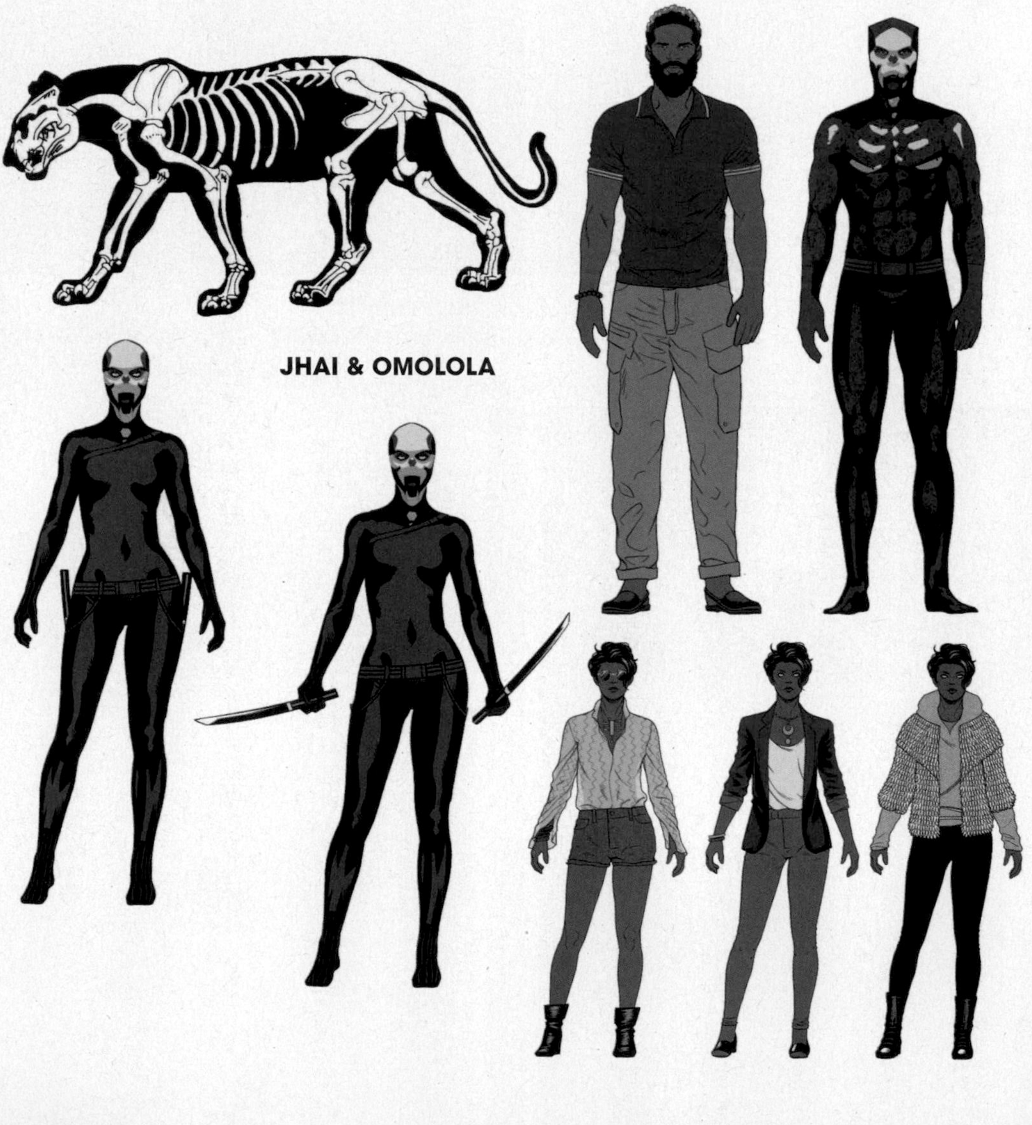

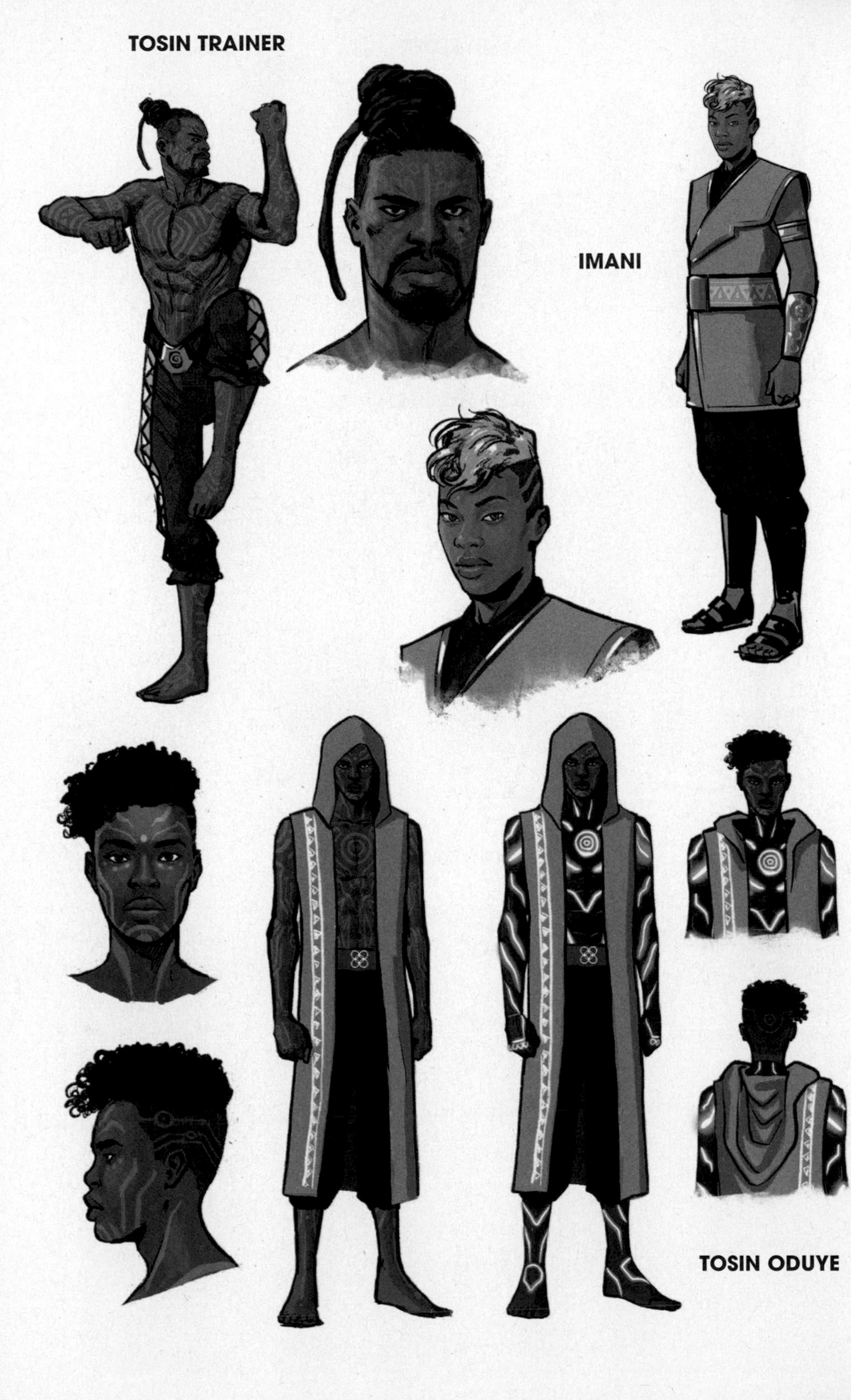
TOSIN TRAINER
IMANI
TOSIN ODUYE

TOSIN ELDER

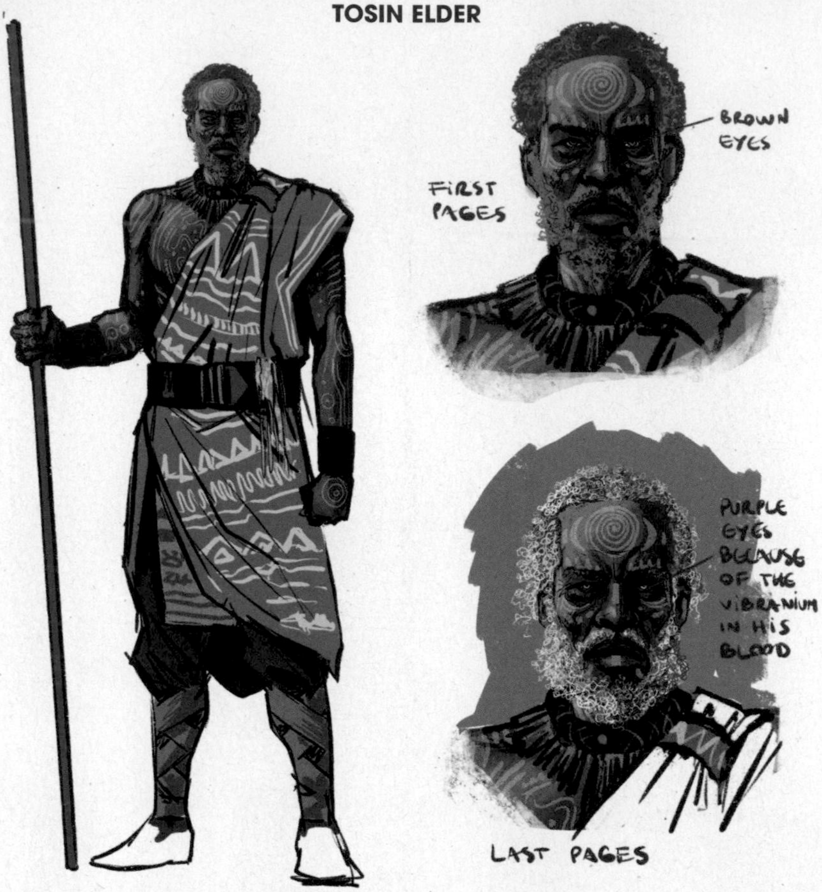
BROWN EYES
FIRST PAGES
PURPLE EYES BECAUSE OF THE VIBRANIUM IN HIS BLOOD
LAST PAGES

TOSIN VILLAGE

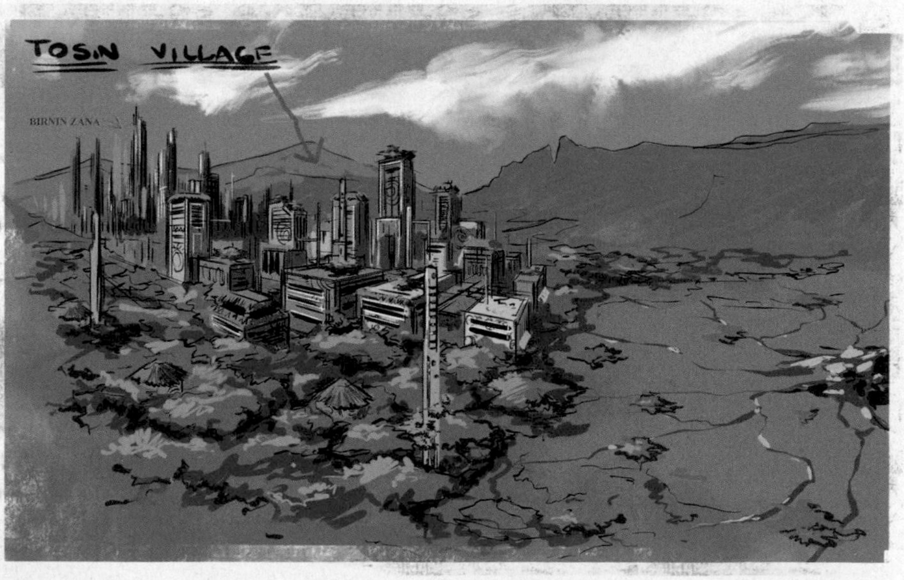
TOSIN VILLAGE
BIRNIN ZANA